THE
LAST
DIVE

A FATHER
AND SON'S
FATAL DESCENT
INTO THE
OCEAN'S
DEPTHS

THE
LAST
DIVE

BERNIE CHOWDHURY

HarperCollins*Publishers*

HarperCollins books may be purchased for educational, business, or sales promotional use. For information please write: Special Markets Department, HarperCollins Publishers Inc., 10 East 53rd Street, New York, NY 10022.

FIRST EDITION

Designed by Elliott Beard

Printed on acid-free paper

Library of Congress Cataloging-in-Publication Data

Chowdhury, Bernie
    The last dive: a father and son's fatal descent into the ocean's
    depths/Bernie Chowdhury.
        p. cm.
    ISBN 0-06-019462-6
    1. Scuba diving—Accidents—Atlantic Coast (U.S.) 2. Shipwrecks—
Atlantic Coast (U.S.) 3. Rouse, Chris. 4. Rouse, Chrissy. 5. Scuba divers—
United States. 6. Fathers and sons—United States. I. Title
GV838.673.A75 C46 2000
363.14—dc21   00-033426

00 01 02 03 04 ❖/RRD 10 9 8 7 6 5 4 3 2 1

For my wife, Diana, and our son, Gil

Also in memory of Chris and Chrissy Rouse and Tony Smith

Part of the proceeds of this book go to the Rouse Memorial Fund to benefit divers worldwide through safety initiatives, research, diving site preservation, and expedition funding.

Contents

Foreword

I FIND MYSELF HAUNTED by the Rouse family and very impressed and touched by the sensitive manner in which Bernie Chowdhury tells their story. *The Last Dive* is a fascinating and mesmerizing read, hard to put down. Like *The Perfect Storm*, it's a deceptively simple tale about very ordinary people placed in extraordinary situations.

As an avid scuba diver, instructor, and wreck diver for more than thirty years, I know the Rouses—not personally, perhaps, but as a type of person who often gets involved with our sport. In fact, all of the divers in this story are familiar to me, although I've actually met only one of them. Since I was among the first divers to get aboard the *U-352* and the first to research the full history of the *U-85*, I can fully understand the lure that the *U-869* must have held for the Rouses. A sunken ship, no matter what type it is, is filled with mystery, but a sunken German U-boat seems to capture our imagination like none other. How and why did it sink? Who and what was aboard it? Why was it even there? Some divers become obsessed with trying to discover the answers, even to the point of risking their lives. They become engaged, often without fully realizing it, in a deadly competition with other divers in a game with rules they may never understand.

Although I retired from serious wreck diving before technical diving
got a foothold in our sport, I, too, suffered a serious bout of decompression sickness. Oddly enough, mine—an "undeserved hit," if there is
such a thing—took place during a placid dive off the island of Guanaja
in Honduras. For years, I had skirted the edges of decompression theory
and occasionally crossed into uncharted theoretical territory and gotten away with it. Then, during an easy, relatively shallow dive, well
within the safety limits of the decompression tables, a bubble chose to
appear in my spinal cord, triggering a desperate series of events that
could have left me paralyzed. Fortunately that did not happen, but
there were consequences, as there always are when the nervous system is
compromised. Despite the fact the damaged connective nerve tissues
have since rerouted themselves, sometimes, especially when I get tired,
the destruction caused by that singular bubble becomes evident to me
in subtle but undeniable ways. Mr. Chowdhury knows what I mean.
Like him, I still dive, though not so deep nor so long.

The Rouses' story is a tragedy not because they died but because they
died so unfulfilled. Even had they ultimately brought back an artifact
that could have precisely identified the U-boat, this prize would not
have satisfied them or brought them the recognition they seemed to
crave so desperately. The Rouses, despite their social and personal
shortcomings, were great men, fully capable of doing great things. Their
fate, however, was to live in a country and an age in which such great-
ness is often shunned, even seen as antisocial. Although I believe they
would have thrived in an era of celebrated exploration, it was their
unfortunate fate to be stuck in the drab present. The only way they
could fulfill their hungry spirit was to become part of a small, select,
adventurous, and potentially deadly society.

The diving community, for all its references to the gentle contem-
plation of the beauty of the undersea world, is actually a very harsh
group. From all those who dare to enter it, we demand near perfec-
tion in skill and form, including the method and style of our dying.
To die while diving is one thing, but to die poorly is to wipe clean all
the tributes and laurels we might have gathered during our diving
careers. All divers know this, and so it is somewhere in our minds on
every dive—the need, if it comes to that, to die cleanly and bravely, if
not wisely. We are a band of brothers and sisters who admire the lost

cave diver who stubbornly clings to life to the end, breathing down his tank to the nubs, but we disdain the diver who panics and dies with a tank still half-filled with gas. Both divers are just as dead, just as foolish, but one is allowed to ascend into our version of Valhalla while the other is sent to diving Purgatory for all eternity.

Readers, even those who are not divers, will love this book. Whether they will fully grasp the character of the Rouses and the other divers that Bernie Chowdhury has so skillfully captured, without knowing firsthand the lure of the depths and the competitiveness of those of us who want to go there, I don't know. All I know for sure is that they, like me, are going to find the Rouse boys often in their minds. I can only hope that they will also appreciate the Rouses for whom they wanted to be, even if they didn't quite make it there.

Bernie Chowdhury has written a book that seems to explore diving and the deep, cruel sea; in reality he has written a book about exploring a place even deeper and far crueler, the human psyche and our often unfulfilled souls. We should thank him for the illumination.

—HOMER HICKAM,
number one *New York Times* bestselling author of *October Sky* and *The Coalwood Way*.
He can be reached at www.homerhickam.com.

1

Deadly Secrets

OCTOBER 12, 1992. NORTH ATLANTIC OCEAN,
approximately 60 miles offshore,
equidistant from the New Jersey and New York coastlines.

THE WIND MOUNTED STEADILY throughout the night as Chris Rouse, cocooned in his sleeping bag, braced himself against the side of his bunk. He felt a bit uneasy, his stomach tossed by the dark waves that slammed against the 60-foot length of the dive charter boat *Seeker*. He was not that far from the New Jersey coast, but he might as well have been in the middle of the Atlantic Ocean. Chris peered out from between his sleeping bag and the bunk. In the dawn's soot-gray light, all he could see through the boat's windows was a blanket of sky and dark-blue waves with white spray blowing off their crests. Somewhere in the distance lay the horizon, but he couldn't tell where; the sea and sky were seamless. He judged the waves to be five feet high, with occasional rollers over eight feet. Not a good day to continue the exploration of the most technically challenging dive site he had faced in more than seven hundred logged dives.

Only yesterday, the thirty-nine-year-old Rouse and his twenty-two-year-old son, Chrissy, had conducted two dives to the unidentified submarine 230 feet below them. The wreck lay in three pieces, like a cigar with its middle torn out and angled between the ends. The middle section included the conning tower, the large tubular structure perpendicular to the vessel's body. The tower, though still intact, had been torn from its mount and thrown aside by whatever unknown force had sunk this submarine, probably back in the Second World War. Underneath the conning tower was the control room, the submarine's brain. Nothing was left of this nerve center but a jumble of jagged, sharp-edged steel plates and debris, the result of some violent explosion. Yesterday, Chrissy Rouse had crawled under and between the steel plates, wriggling his way inside while his father hovered outside the wreck. Somewhere in those razor-edged ruins lay something that would identify this sub, and father and son were determined to find it. Maybe the captain's logbook—it had to be nestled amid the wreckage just inside the opening. Chrissy hadn't found it yesterday, but the Rouses knew they were close. All that stood in their way was time, effort, and eight-foot waves.

The *Seeker* bobbed and tugged at its anchor line, like a trapped animal seeking to break its tether. It had fought the ocean incessantly throughout the night, and its wooden beams and planking let out creaks of protest at the restraint. The passengers and off-duty crew had tried to sleep in their bunks while wedged in such a way as to prevent being thrown to the heaving deck. John Chatterton, a commercial diver, sport-diving instructor, highly respected wreck diver, and one of the *Seeker*'s two captains (required by Coast Guard regulations during an overnight boat charter), burst into the main cabin and threw the light switch. "It's six o'clock," he announced. "If any of you want to do two dives today you need to hit the water early. Weather report's calling for steadily increasing seas, and you can see"—he nodded toward the window—"it's snotty already. If you wanna dive, get in the water fast. We'd like to pull the hook and get out of here soon, before we really get slammed. I'm gonna blow off my personal dive, and I'll just go down to pull the hook."

The blond Chatterton looked as if he'd fit in more readily on a college campus than on a dive boat, with his wire-rim glasses and boyish face. Unlike many hard-bitten sea captains, Chatterton had a receptive mind; he was happy to discuss diving techniques and gear configuration with his customers, even as he remained soft-spoken when talking about his own expertise and accomplishments. Chatterton never made others feel stupid or inadequate. His demeanor, combined with the depth of his experience, lent his advice more weight, and divers sought it out.

Chatterton was on intimate terms with the wreck that Chris and Chrissy Rouse aimed to conquer. The captain was credited with having been the first diver to identify the mysterious object as a submarine. On Labor Day, 1991, Chatterton had headed out on the *Seeker* with a group of divers to check out a potential wreck site that the boat's owner, Captain Bill Nagel, had heard about from a fisherman during one of Nagel's frequent drinking bouts. The captain's alcohol-sodden memory had been accurate. On a follow-up dive, Chatterton had recovered a single dinner plate bearing the German eagle and swastika, with the date 1942 stamped on it. The wreck was a World War II submarine, which the Germans called an *Unterseeboot*—"under-sea boat," shortened to U-boat. The first U-boat was *U-1;* the highest-numbered German vessel to see service was *U-4712.* Because the Germans did not number the U-boats consecutively, 1,152 German U-boats were actually commissioned and put into service during the Second World War. For lack of an official name or number, Chatterton and other divers had dubbed the discovery *U-Who.*

Every year along America's East Coast divers find new wrecks—victims of storm, collision, fire, and war—but the *U-Who* was an unusual find. U.S., German, and British naval archives listed the location of every U-boat that lay on the ocean bottom worldwide, but they had no reference to anything even close to the *U-Who*'s location, a half day's mission from the entrance to New York Harbor. The wreck seemed to have been sunk by an explosion, but if it did not go down in a battle recorded in the archives, how did it end up in such a sorry state? Chatterton's discovery made headlines. His underwater video was aired on television. Why was this U-boat not listed with the other German submarine wrecks? What had its mission been? Could it have been sabotaged while on a secret foray? Had it been carrying spies? Or Nazi party members fleeing the fall of the Thousand-Year

Reich? The search was on. Divers like Chris and Chrissy Rouse were attracted to the wreck—and a mystery.

In September 1991, I had passed up the opportunity to join Bill Nagel and John Chatterton on the trip when they discovered the *U-Who*. I had already been on a few expeditions on Nagel's boat, and one day he told me, "I've got a new site to check out, if you're interested. I'd like to put together a special trip and see if there's anything down there. It's deep, Bernie, and it may just be a hunk of rocks. But you never know. It could be something good." Nagel and Chatterton were extending this invitation only to experienced divers. It was a very unusual opportunity.

The invitation taunted me like buried treasure. Ever since I had learned to scuba-dive in 1984, I had gotten increasingly more involved in wreck diving off the New York and New Jersey coasts. In 1988 I became a diving instructor and taught with a dive shop in Manhattan in the evenings and weekends, in addition to my full-time job working with computer networks as a data communications technician. I loved to teach people about the rich historical heritage of shipwrecks. When I taught the introductory first scuba lesson, I gave a slide show depicting various underwater environments. My students expected to see slides only of the bright, colorful coral reefs of the Caribbean, the main destination most of the divers in the class sought to experience. When I showed historical slides of ships that had gone down off the northeastern coast of the United States, and then slides of the underwater shipwreck environment, most students were shocked that there was anything at all to see off their own, heavily populated coastline.

Cold-water wreck diving had intrigued me ever since my first wreck dives, in 1985, just off the coast of Brooklyn. On good days, at a depth of 50 or 60 feet the visibility was a murky 10 or 15 feet. Completely disintegrated, the wrecks I encountered resembled nothing more than underwater junkyards, the damage done by a combination of forces: the ships' sinking; the Coast Guard's efforts to destroy the sunken ships because they jutted too close to the surface, posing a hazard to navigation; and the ravages of storms that further scattered the wrecks' remains. The murky water obscured the extent of the ruin, yet no matter how far I swam it seemed there was always more to see. Steel beams crossed at odd angles, bent into weird forms through which fish swam and in which reddish-brown lobsters made their homes. The beams themselves were covered by life forms that looked like brown sponges with white-stranded tips waving in the water. Green eels poked their heads out from various crevices and gaped at me. I encountered odd-looking gray fish with big mouths bordered by fat lips, their large eyes following my movements. Brown fish hovered just above the bottom, long white feelers protruding from their undersides to probe the areas around them in search of food. When I approached them, they moved effortlessly away with a slight wag of their tails and thrust of their fins, disappearing into the murky curtain of greenish-brown water. The world I discovered down there was surreal, yet possessed of an immediacy and purity of survival that I could not find on the surface at my full-time job. It was a far more intriguing world down there.

And it got more engaging. With deeper-lying wrecks, farther offshore, there was greater visibility, but as I became more experienced, that was not what really attracted me to the deep. These wrecks were more intact. The better underwater visibility—anywhere from 30 to 100 feet, depending on the ship, the time of year, and the luck of the dive—allowed me to explore far more of a wreck than I could off the Brooklyn coast. On the deep, offshore wrecks, I could actually identify the hulks and their various parts. And there were large lobsters to be caught by hand and put into a mesh "goodie bag," thence to the pot of boiling water that awaited them onshore. Not only that, I could retrieve artifacts from the wrecks: china dishes, glassware, silverware, brass portholes, cage lights, and a host of other collectibles still left unclaimed.

To descend to an undived, virgin wreck was the dream of every enthusiastic wreck diver, and I was no exception. Nagel and Chatterton's invitation to dive a possible new site was something I had eagerly awaited while honing my skills and deepening my appreciation of the sport. Yet the week before the scheduled exploratory trip, I had a difficult choice to make.

Although I was now working full-time as a systems analyst on Wall Street, I had also gotten a contract from a Japanese trading company, Inabata, as a consultant for the development and marketing of a new line of wrist-mounted diving computers. Earlier in the year, I had presented to Japanese representatives a market overview of the diving industry, the trends I saw, and the opportunities these trends promised to open up. The company decided to go ahead with the development of at least one of the three types of computer I proposed. An engineer from Inabata's partner in the venture, Seiko, who was also a certified diver was flying over from Japan to survey both how Americans dived and the various diving environments they regularly explored. I was supposed to take the engineer to several diving locations in the United States during a single week; as an instructor, I could take the engineer as my student on some dives where he would not otherwise be allowed. At first, I did not think that I could get the time off from my Wall Street job, but at the last moment, my manager generously gave me a week off. Now I had the time either to pay a good deal of money to be part of Bill Nagel's exploratory trip to what might possibly be a rock pile, or go on an expense-paid diving trip around the United States with a client. I chose the latter. When I returned from my routine journey with the Japanese diver, I found out that Bill Nagel and John Chatterton had found a U-boat; I had missed the chance to fulfill a dream—a chance that might not arrive again in my lifetime.

In 1992, diving to the depth of the *U-Who* at 230 feet was considered by training agencies to be well beyond what amateur divers should or even could undertake. As a U.S.-based recreational diving instructor, I was limited to teaching people to dive to a maximum depth of 130 feet, and then only briefly—the time limit to stay at 130 feet was ten minutes, including the time it took to descend. Some non-U.S.-based diver-training agencies set the limit for sport-diving depths down to 165 feet. Knowledgeable divers like Chris and Chrissy Rouse and me found those varying limits both arbitrary and unrealistic. The water did not stop abruptly at a depth of 130 feet, or 165 feet, and neither would we.

According to training agencies, the main factor limiting amateur divers was an impaired state of mental functioning much like drunkenness that is brought about by breathing compressed air at depth. The air in a scuba tank is the same air humans breathe on land. Air consists of about 79 percent nitrogen and 21 percent oxygen and includes trace elements such as argon, neon, helium, and hydrogen, as well as pollution, which together make up less than 1 percent of the air. Our bodies use only oxygen for their metabolism and simply expel the nitrogen back into the air during exhalation; because the human body expels nitrogen without making use of it, it is called inert.

Underwater, however, all nitrogen is not expelled during exhalation; when pressure increases, the nitrogen is forced from the lungs into the blood, and from the blood into the tissues, including the brain. This causes a condition known as nitrogen narcosis, and it becomes more pronounced with the increase in pressure, the deeper a diver descends. Nitrogen narcosis mimics alcohol intoxication. And just as with alcohol, different divers have different degrees of susceptibility to nitrogen's effects and may experience varying intensities of narcosis from one day to the next. The exact mechanics of the syndrome are not well understood. One theory is that the nitrogen blocks neurotransmitters and receptors in the brain, resulting in a distortion of electrochemical signals. The level of the disability varies, depending on the physical and emotional state of the diver that day, the water temperature, and the extent of disorientation that can occur with ever-changing underwater visibility. The sense of time itself can grow distorted, and the diver may feel euphoric. Sometimes, a diver may feel sad, but he may also feel paranoia—especially if any problems arise with equipment, marine life, or sense of place. Hand-eye coordination generally deteriorates during the dive. All of these symptoms are usually far more pronounced in cold water than in warm, clear water. Unlike an alcohol buzz, which lasts for a while even after the person stops drinking, nitrogen narcosis is thought to leave no comparable negative residual effect, and all the diver who is unduly affected has to do is ascend to a shallower depth, and his wits will return immediately. Afterward, a diver who has experienced nitrogen narcosis may not be able to accurately remember details of a dive.

"The Martini Law" is a rule of thumb for estimating the danger of nitrogen narcosis. As is sometimes the case with laws, there are different definitions of it. One standard is that every 33 feet you dive is like drinking a martini on an empty stomach. Another version states that every 50 feet is like having a martini. Still another version claims that the Martini Law comes into play only after 100 feet of depth. This last version does not, however, take into account that a diver is influenced by nitrogen as soon as pressure is increased, just as he is influenced by alcohol as it is consumed. And the effects of nitrogen narcosis, like those of alcohol, are at first usually extremely subtle, even imperceptible, but then mount exponentially with ever-greater depth. By the time a diver reaches 130 feet, the effects may be so pronounced that he or she cannot function properly; problem-solving ability is seriously compromised, and the diver may lose a sense of place and the ability to accurately assess the danger of an alien environment requiring a life-support system. Divers sometimes hallucinate and hear voices calling them to go deeper. They may completely forget that they have a very limited quantity of breathing gas in their scuba tanks, and use up their gas capacity, and drown. For our purposes, we will consider the Martini Law to be that every 50 feet of depth is equivalent to one martini drunk on an empty stomach.

Diving to the *U-Who*—a depth of 230 feet—while breathing compressed air, as the Rouses would be doing, would be like functioning under the influence of four and a half martinis.

Sport divers like me and the Rouses who dived beyond 130 feet were often considered cowboys, taking unnecessary risks, especially as we used compressed air and not one of the special breathing gases, called mixed gas, that in 1992 were just starting to become—expensively—available to sport divers. For the vast majority of the world's amateur divers, descending to 130 or 165 feet was as deep as they needed to go, and each year millions of divers safely stayed, and continue today to stay, within the limits recommended by recreational diving-training agencies. But there was a big difference between the desires and abilities of these recreational divers and those of sport divers like the Rouses, just as there is a big difference between the desires and abilities of casual rock climbers and those of the mountaineers who scale Mount Everest, or at least make the attempt.

Perhaps it was for the best that I missed the dives that led to the discovery of the *U-Who*. As my wife always tells me, "Everything has a reason."

Nagel quickly planned a second trip to the mysterious wreck, and the spots were limited to those from the previous trip. Steve Feldman had dived the wreck on the first trip to the site. After his first dive of the second trip, he remarked to another diver, "My regulator sure feels hard to breathe from on the bottom. It's like sucking pea soup through a straw." On his next dive, Feldman apparently passed out from his exertions in a strong current, and he drowned. Divers could not recover his body, which drifted along the sea bottom for many months until commercial fishermen caught it in their trawler nets among the seafood catch destined for New York City restaurant tables. After Feldman's death, many divers saw the *U-Who* mission as even more challenging and appealing. Many wreck divers are like big-game hunters: The more difficult and dangerous the trophy, the more status you gain when you bag it. Diving 230 feet into cold, clouded water and burrowing into the notoriously cramped quarters of a U-boat to bring out an identifying piece of the wreck—that would be like planting your flag on Everest.

From the day he first dived the wreck, Chatterton made a gentleman's agreement with expedition members that they would be the only people invited to dive the *U-Who,* unless one of them dropped out of a future expedition and left a spot open. All agreed. Feldman's death prompted several divers on the expedition either to give up the sport entirely or to scale back their efforts and conduct only shallow, less dangerous dives. This left several spots available for divers on upcoming *U-Who* expeditions. One of those spots was filled by Richie Kohler, an experienced deep-wreck diver who had developed a reputation for being fearless underwater. Chatterton invited Chris and Chrissy Rouse to fill the other two spots.

Chris Rouse found Chatterton's invitation hard to believe, even though most divers who knew the Rouses would agree that they had earned their spots over several years of intense activity that had proved they were both competent and also well liked by others in the small community of hard-core divers. Chris remarked to a friend, "Can you believe that we got invited to be part of this expedition with all these great divers? I mean, us, the Rouses. We're just nobodies from nowhere. But we got invited. I just can't get over it!" Chris, a tough, driven diver, would grin like a boy when he talked about Chatterton's implicit acknowledgment of his and his son's skills and expertise.

The Rouses' expertise included the ability to rescue other divers. Both Chris and Chrissy had come to other divers' assistance, saving them from drowning. One diver was a friend who got disoriented in a cave and swam in the wrong direction through the winding maze of tunnels looking for a way out. Chris and Chrissy both methodically searched the cave in the area where their friend was likely to be. They found him before he ran out of air and led him to safety. One month before their *U-Who* expedition, Chrissy Rouse was diving alone on a shipwreck in 170 feet of water when a diver Chrissy did not personally know signaled frantically to him. In spite of the danger that a panicked diver poses to a would-be rescuer, Chrissy swam to the other man without hesitation. Chrissy saw that the diver was kneeling in the sand and his tanks' pressure gauge indicated that he had very little breathing air remaining. Chrissy provided the other diver with air, made the ascent with him, and stayed with him until they were both safely back on the dive boat. The Rouses saw it as their duty to help a diver in need, whether or not they knew the person.

After Chatterton invited the Rouses on the *U-Who* expedition, they excitedly declared that they were going to find something to identify the wreck and evidence of why it sank. Chrissy went a step further than his father. "I'm going to solve the U-boat mystery and do lots of other stuff," he confided to me. "I think I'm destined to be the next Sheck Exley." Chrissy was making a tall statement, comparing himself to the Michael Jordan of diving. Sheck Exley held almost every conceivable record in cave diving, including deepest cave dive and longest cave penetration, and was widely regarded as the world's best at that perilous sport. Chrissy, very much his father's son—handsome, enthusiastic, and even cocky, but very good at what he did—figured he would be even better than Exley because he would be an expert at diving both ocean wrecks and the world's networks of treacherous flooded caves. Chrissy figured that solving the *U-Who* mystery would be the next of many notches in his diving belt.

Aboard the *Seeker,* at the sound of Chatterton's voice Chris Rouse sprang out of his bunk, glad to get out of the bucking bed. He went over to his son and prodded him insistently several times with his hand. "C'mon, get up, ya lazy bum. We got a dive to do."

Chrissy let out an exasperated groan. "Ohhh, I can't get out of bed now."

Unperturbed by his son's intransigence, Chris spotted Barb Lander, the only woman on board, still lying in her bunk. "Hey, Barb, I've been waiting almost eight hours to pick on you. You awake yet? The sink's full of dirty dishes. I can see you've been neglecting your woman's work." Barb, a nurse by profession, was an experienced wreck diver familiar with the very macho, male wreck-diving scene. She rolled over and gave a grinning Chris the finger.

Chris laughed. "Hey, Barb, ya gotta do something about your hair, 'cause ya got a serious case of the uglies this morning."

Barb decided to set aside Chris Rouse's barbs. She had learned early that her fellow diver teased, prodded, and needled everybody—especially his son, who gave as good as he got. Chris's banter prompted the others to get up. All of them—Steve Gatto, Tom Packer, Richie Kohler, Steve McDougall, and John Yurga—were veteran wreck divers. It didn't take much pondering of the sea conditions for them to decide that it was pretty damn dark for diving. Although they all had done their share of night diving, they knew that this kind of roiling daytime darkness, combined with rough seas, made diving dangerous and unpleasant. Chatterton had given everyone a last dive time of one-thirty that afternoon, because of worsening weather conditions, and this meant that some haste would be required if anyone wanted to accomplish two dives that day. Gatto and Packer, who always dived as a team, decided to hurry and get one dive in. They went about getting their dive suits on.

Chrissy Rouse emerged from his bunk, shook his head, and ran his hands through his brown, shoulder-length hair, pulling out the tangles accumulated through a night of being tossed about in his bunk. He moved carefully, dreamily, around the carpeted cabin, his usual swagger replaced by cautious steps among the clothing and grocery bags littering the heaving floor. The odor of twelve divers, their dirty, sweaty clothes, and various foods left in the sink reminded him of the frat-style house in Pennsylvania he had shared with diving buddies when he could afford his own digs. Lately, he had been living at home with his father and his mother, Sue, thanks to a couple of minor but costly car accidents. When he could, he would escape to his friends' house with his girlfriend, Julia.

Chrissy had met Julia Bissinger while she was taking diving lessons and he was assisting the instructor during the pool training sessions. Chrissy and Julia casually flirted with each other; Julia liked Chrissy's playful, innocent manner, and she relished his attentions. Chrissy was not coming on to her in some sort of macho fashion; he was just

enjoying the attention of the attractive dive student. During their conversations, they had made it no secret that they were both involved in
other serious relationships. Yet their flirtatious gazes made their attraction no secret.

When the class ended, Chrissy and Julia went their separate ways. A
year after they had first met, Julia ran into Chrissy again at the dive
shop. Both of them had ended their serious relationships, and were now
left with the confused and painful emotions that are the inevitable
aftermath of youthful romantic disappointment. Tentatively, they took
a chance with each other, and started dating very casually. Without
quite realizing it, they treated each other with the tenderness, gentle
touch, and soothing words of a compassionate caregiver treating a seriously wounded patient.

Though it was now only six months into their relationship, they
were both so relaxed with each other they felt as if they had been
together far longer. Still, they were going slowly, each of them feeling
vulnerable, cautious. Neither wanted to spoil their enjoyment by pressing for a more committed relationship, though neither really wanted to
date anyone else. Julia was only twenty-three, Chrissy a year younger.
Time was on their side.

Chrissy squinted out the *Seeker*'s main cabin windows. "Yeah, sure is
a shitty day out here. Who started the boat rocking anyway?" Then he
asked no one in particular, "What's for breakfast?"

His father grimaced at him. "Hah! The lord of the manor has
awakened and wants to be served! Why are you standing up? Don't
you want breakfast in bed?" He turned to Barb. "I want some eggs.
Hey, Barb, rustle us up some eggs, will ya? Make yourself useful."

Chrissy added, matter-of-factly, "I don't want eggs. Barb, hold the
eggs. Make us some toast instead."

Barb Lander, like the Rouses, was a paying customer on the boat; she
was under no obligation to make anything for anyone. But that was lost
on Chris and Chrissy, who continued arguing with each other about
what they should eat for breakfast. Lander shook her head. The Rouses
were at it again. Listening to them bickering reminded her of her son
fighting with a playmate, only these two were grown men.

As Chatterton's cool warning reverberated aboard the *Seeker* that

October morning, most of the divers had already decided conditions were bad enough already; they wouldn't risk diving at all today. Chatterton's words only confirmed their decision. Yesterday the wind had been less strong, the waves only three feet high, but even then the current had been forceful, making divers work hard to propel their 150 pounds of diving gear through the water and then back up the *Seeker*'s ladder at the stern of the boat after the dive. This morning, looking at the roiling surface, Chris Rouse felt in his muscles the effects of yesterday's effort. But he was a strong man, and he scoffed at diving friends who trained for the sport and suggested he do the same. "An exercise program? Yeah, right," he would snort. "Try doing my job for one day and then going diving the next. That's plenty enough exercise program for me." His excavating business in eastern Pennsylvania demanded frequent manual labor from him; where his heavy machinery couldn't do the job, Chris Rouse would dig with pickax and shovel. Besides, he figured, it wasn't really the diving that was strenuous; the equipment weighed nothing at all underwater. Moving within the ocean was as close as you could come to weightlessness on earth. No, the hard part of this sport was carrying the equipment to and from the boat and the truck. That, and climbing out of the water in full regalia. In rough seas, like today, a diver had to make sure he had enough energy left to make it back up a ladder that was tossing like a rodeo bull. Chris knew he could do it.

On deck, the wind whipping around them, Chris looked over at his son, who was frowning at the ocean. "Dad, I'm not going to dive today," Chrissy said.

His son wasn't going to dive! That meant Chris would be left without a partner. They always dived together. "What? You pussy! *I'm* gonna dive. What's the matter with you?"

Chrissy swallowed. "I don't think it's a good idea," he retorted. "Let's just forget it."

"What, so a big, strong kid like you is afraid?"

"I'm not afraid, just smarter than you," Chrissy shot back.

Chris grinned. "Hah! That's a good one: My *load* is smarter than me. I taught you everything you know. I carry you through the dives."

Chrissy's face reddened in anger. "You couldn't even keep up with me if I didn't swim real slow!"

Chris kicked at a diver-propulsion vehicle, commonly referred to as a scooter. "Yeah, right, that's why I was smart enough to learn how to fix scooters, which you don't seem to mind using. Hey, smart one: When are you ever gonna learn how to fix those things anyway?"

That remark hit Chrissy hard. He knew he lacked the natural mechanical abilities of his father. "I'd rather let you play with the toys while I go play with the girls. I don't need to marry the first one that comes along."

Chris had gotten married while he was still a senior in high school, after his girlfriend, Sue, had gotten pregnant—with Chrissy. He glared at his son. "If you hadn't gotten my good looks, you'd have shit—and girls wouldn't come near you."

Back and forth they went, hurling insults and digging at each other, while the other divers laughed occasionally at the exchange, which seemed to some of them like watching a modern version of Abbott and Costello. Chris gave a final murderous jab. "Fine, don't dive. You were always a loser and out here you're just another wanna-be diver."

Chrissy looked at the waves, and then back at his father's feet. He relented. "Okay, fine. Let's do it."

A grin flickered on Chris's face. "Nah, you're right. I was only kidding."

This was too much for Chrissy. His father had baited him. He laced into his father. "Oh, yeah, right, call *me* a pussy and a wanna-be diver 'cause *I* don't wanna dive, then pussy out yourself when you talk me into going! *You're* a weenie. You're just pretending to be a diver. If ya hadn't gotten lucky with Mom, you'd be nowhere. You're a pussy and a chicken."

Check and checkmate. With Chrissy questioning his father's motivation, diving ability, and—most important—his manhood, Chris Rouse could not back out of the dive. Questionable conditions or not, both men would have to dive, if only to prove that they could, that they were *real* divers.

Chatterton went about his business as the two Rouses argued. He had seen them do this so often that it was as ordinary as wind. After all, the Rouses were widely known as the Bicker Brothers, or Bickers for short. Though Chris and Chrissy Rouse were father and son—their identical builds and facial features left no doubt about that—they were only seventeen years apart, and they acted less like parent and child than siblings strutting on the high school parking lot. Chatterton always wondered how much of their jousting was real and how much was just for show. Each of them personified the diver as cowboy, all rugged swagger—was their bickering part of the mask? Many divers were amused by the Rouses and looked on their bickering as a polished comedy routine that kept them at the center of attention. Others thought the bickering got old fast. That October morning, Chatterton worried once again that their thrust and parry was a signal of conflict that could get them into serious trouble underwater.

Two hours went by as the waves and wind thickened, Gatto and Packer dived, and the Rouses bickered—arguing over what they should eat for breakfast, whether Chrissy should shave, and how long a dive they should conduct. By the time Gatto and Packer returned from their dive, the waves were six to eight feet high. "The waves toss ya around like a milkshake," Gatto remarked simply. "It's pretty bad out there." Chris pondered this news for a moment and then went back to putting his dive suit on.

In full gear, the Rouses looked as if they were about to explore another planet. Chris and Chrissy were outfitted in drysuits made of watertight rubber, underneath which were outfits resembling ski suits, insulating them from the 42-degree water. Chris had attached several battery-powered lights to his plastic helmet. Their masks made them seem like otherworldly insects. Strapped to their arms was an array of gauges and knives. The two large scuba tanks each carried on his back would allow—at best—a one-hour stay on the wreck. Two other tanks, attached to their harnesses at two points and dangling under their arms, would allow their safe return. With no way to communicate with the surface, and no oral communication possible between them, they could make contact only with simple hand or light signals, or by writing brief messages with the small lead pencil attached by a thin rubber hose to a plastic slate mounted on each man's forearm. If they bickered on the ocean bottom, they would be limited to gestures and single words.

I spoke with the Rouses two weeks before their *U-Who* expedition. I knew they wanted to venture inside the wreck to recover the captain's logbook. As a fellow cave diver who used the techniques learned in Florida's caves and applied them to wreck diving, I would often talk with the Rouses and occasionally dive with them. We were all men who shared a passion for underwater exploration, and like aficionados of golf or cars, we discussed everything from our equipment to our dive adventures, our ambitions, and dive-scene gossip. Usual stuff for those consumed by their passion for the sport.

Chris told me they planned to dive the wreck using compressed air as their main breathing gas. I thought of the four-and-a-half-martini buzz they would experience while exploring the wreck, and I was alarmed. As a diving instructor, I knew Chris and his son were taking a big chance. But being an effective teacher means letting divers come to the obvious conclusions themselves, so I asked, "Why aren't you diving mix?"—"mix" being a breathing mixture that includes expensive helium gas, which lessens the narcotic, "martini" effect of breathing air at depth.

"Well, I can't afford mix right now. Business has been real slow."

Chris and I both knew the financial difference between using air and using a helium-based gas was a few hundred dollars. I could hear the shrug in his voice and was shocked. "If you can't afford helium to make the dive safer, why risk the dive—why not leave it for later?"

"Oh, Chrissy and I have been much deeper than two-thirty on air. We can handle it," replied Chris dismissively.

"Have you done any dives on U-boats other than that one trip we made to the *U-853*?" This was a U-boat that had been sunk off Rhode Island, several hundred miles east of New York City, in the waning days of World War II.

"Well, I dived the *U-Who* a few weeks ago," Chris explained. "Besides, going inside a wreck isn't really any different than going inside a cave. And Bernie, you know how good I am at that." When I didn't respond, he added, "Plus, Chrissy will be going in and I'll just wait outside as a safety diver."

No mix and minimal experience inside U-boats—I was more than uneasy about what my friends were up to. I knew firsthand how treacherous U-boats can be. I had repeatedly dived three off the East Coast, and had entered the cramped interiors on many dives. The U-boats I had dived all lay in much shallower waters than the *U-Who*—

the deepest one I'd explored was the *U-853*, which rested in usually murky, cold, northeast water at a depth of 130 feet, whereas the others were in warm, clear, tropical water off North Carolina; these wrecks provided challenging but reasonably controlled environments for divers to build experience. I shuddered, thinking of the one dive that the Rouses had done on the *U-853*, as part of a trip we had taken the year before. On that trip, one experienced dive member had severed a breathing hose on the sharp metal inside the wreck, which caused massive, loud torrents of air to be released, reducing the already low visibility to practically nil as silt and rust were knocked loose. He exited the wreck and Chrissy Rouse shut off the gas supply to the leaking hose, preventing the diver from losing all his gas.

I tried one last question. "Hey, Chris, why don't you wait on this dive, build up your U-boat experience on the shallower wrecks like the *U-853*, wait until you can afford the helium, and then try for the *U-Who*'s logbook? It's a hairy dive you're planning."

"Nah, we'll be okay."

As Barb Lander helped Chris finish gearing up, he looked at her and said, "I hope I don't regret making this dive."

"Don't dive, Chris—bag it," Barb replied.

"Junior's diving. I've got to go with him."

"Let Junior dive alone."

"No, I've got to go with him" came the surprisingly somber reply.

Tom Packer and Steve Gatto finished getting out of their diving equipment. They looked at the Rouses gearing up and could not believe that others would want to dive in these conditions. Gatto turned to Packer and quietly remarked, "These guys are nuts. They don't know what they're in for!" Packer agreed, "Yeah, they sure are nuts. But they're good guys, and good divers. And they add a lot of color to the trip! Steve, we should include these two in all our expeditions." Gatto simply nodded.

While Barb was helping Chris with the last pieces of equipment, Chrissy lifted himself to his feet. Bearing four scuba tanks, he lumbered in his swim fins across the heaving deck to the entry point. As the boat rolled, he fell, crushing a piece of somebody else's equipment with his knees. Gatto and Packer helped him up, and again he shuffled toward the boat's side. Before he could make it, he fell again, this time rolling over so that his back-mounted double tanks were pinned against the deck and his feet were waving in the air. He resembled a helpless, upside-down turtle. Some of the other divers swallowed their laughter and helped Chrissy to his feet. He managed to roll over the boat's side and into the ocean without falling on the deck a third time.

Chris Rouse followed his son into the water with a loud splash. As Chatterton, Barb Lander, and the other divers watched, father and son disappeared below the turbulent water.

2

Prevent Your Death!

SPRING 1988.
A modest, middle-class home in Coopersburg, eastern Pennsylvania.
Twelve men and women are seated around a dinner table, their plates
mostly emptied of food.

D IVING IS CRAZY. You're going to kill yourself doing it."
When Chris Rouse was first introduced to diving in 1988 at a
dinner party with a group of sport pilots, he told his friend Ken Reinhart that plunging into the watery depths was stupid. Flying—now
that was a sport for a man.

Reinhart had taught Chris to fly at the Famous Ugly Aeroplane
Company headquartered at Quakertown Airport in Pennsylvania, back
in 1981. Chris had been a very conservative student, preferring not to fly
in anything but tranquil weather. During his training for an instrument
rating—where the pilot learns to fly the plane relying solely on instruments, as he would have to in bad weather or at night—Chris would
have to fly in unpredictable, often nasty conditions, and that unnerved
him. In a small, private plane, he felt completely at the mercy of the

winds and turbulent weather, his stomach rising and dropping, his torso thrown from side to side as if on an amusement park ride. For some people, giving up some control is exhilarating, but for Chris it was frightening.

Still, Chris liked the no-frills functionality of the Cessna he was learning to fly. Although its flimsy fiberglass panels made it look less sturdy than a riding lawnmower, a plane like that seemed like something a man could master. As a child, he was constantly tinkering and liked to take things apart to see how they worked, and as a teenager, he rebuilt a 1955 Chevy so that it ran perfectly. Not one for appearances, he never bothered to paint the car beyond giving it a coat of gray primer. The raw simplicity and logic of the airplane appealed to Chris immensely, just as the Chevy had.

Ken Reinhart, Chris's flight instructor, coached his student on the nuances of flight and watched as Chris slowly grasped the flying arts. One day, while they were flying, Reinhart instructed Chris to land. When Chris brought the plane to a halt on the tarmac, Reinhart climbed out and said, "Congratulations. You're ready for your first solo flight. Take it up." Reinhart closed the door behind a stunned Chris, who didn't have time to reply. Chris now had to rely solely on his own skills. The riding mower of an airplane suddenly felt much bigger. But Chris knew he could do it; both his plane and his confidence soared.

After several solo flights, Chris was ready for the final phase of training. Just before his check flight, the pilot's equivalent of the driver's road test, Chris made the fairly common mistake of walking directly into the high wing of the Cessna. In spite of the bloody dimple pattern the wing created on his forehead, he took the examination flight—holding a handkerchief to his head—and passed, getting a basic pilot's certificate. Soon, Chris and his wife, Sue, began flying together for fun, with Sue acting as the navigator. At first the couple would take short, local trips to sightsee from the air. As Chris accumulated more flying experience and felt increasingly comfortable without an instructor present, they both developed confidence in Chris's flying ability and in their ability to work together as pilot and navigator. It was time for a much longer excursion. Chris's first flight instructor, Pete Miller, lent them his plane and his credit cards in case of an emergency, and sent the pair off to Florida with the words "A crash is as good as a sale!" In the air or on the ground, Chris inspired close friendship, generosity, and black humor.

Now, after some years of flying, Chris was growing curious about going deep. Only a few days after he made his dinner party remark about the dangers of diving, Chris and Sue went over to Ken Reinhart's house to look over his diving equipment. Chris was already familiar with compressed gas cylinders through his excavating business; he used them when he had to do welding. The single-hose regulator that delivered breathing gas to the diver seemed uncomplicated, and the various gauges for depth, dive time, and gas remaining in the cylinder were as logical to Chris as a car manifold, and less complicated than the flight panel of a Cessna. Chris and Sue went straight to Underwater World, a dive shop in Horsham, Pennsylvania, where he signed up for a class. Chris enrolled his eighteen-year-old son, Chrissy, in the class too, without asking him first. The sport-flying group was planning a family trip to the Bahamas that would combine flying with diving. For Chris, learning how to dive meant he could be better buddies with his fellow sport pilots. Just as important, diving was something he and his family could do together.

Sue had to defer training, because she was studying business in evening college classes. But she had enjoyed flying with her husband and was now intrigued, on his behalf, with diving. Evening classes were practical because the college was conveniently close to home and the studies would enable her to get a better-paying job.

At home, Chris excitedly told his son about the diving course they would be taking—another of the many activities father and son could do together. Chris had always enjoyed spending as much time as possible with Chrissy. The two would listen to music together, and their tastes ranged from classics like Beethoven to popular music like Frank Sinatra. Father and son would spend hours singing to the music, animatedly belting out the songs as if they were on stage. They also devoured science-fiction and action movies voraciously. Their favorite television show was *Dr. Who*, a British sixties sci-fi series, a forerunner of *Star Trek*, about a doctor who invents a time-space machine. Chris and Chrissy were both fascinated by the worlds Dr. Who managed to explore, and the strange, often hostile beings he encountered in his adventures. Father and son eventually attended *Dr. Who* conventions together; unlike many of the attendees, they did not dress up as one of the numerous characters that appeared in the series.

Chris well knew how important it was for Chrissy to have a strong bond with his father and a sense of belonging. When Chrissy was eight years old, he had been diagnosed as hyperactive, with what today is called attention deficit disorder. In 1978 there were no medications to treat Chrissy's hyperactivity. Although Chrissy was not stupid or backward, schoolteachers felt that his inability to concentrate on reading for extended periods was holding him back. The school recommended to Chris and Sue that their son be put in a few special classes each day to help him focus on reading and other learning skills. Although Chrissy took most of his classes with the other children, the special sessions made him the target of cruel teasing and jokes. Chrissy would come home from school and tearfully tell his mother that he felt like an outsider, that the special classes made it hard to fit in with his regular classmates. After one year, Chris and Sue did not see any big improvements in Chrissy's education, and they were distressed that their son was enduring so much emotional pain from his classmates' abuse. They came to the decision to take Chrissy out of the special classes. "We want Chrissy to be treated just like everyone else," Sue firmly told school authorities, over their protests. "Put him back in all of the regular classes."

Chrissy's school performance and his grades were not outstanding, but they were not bad, either. Throughout his schooling, he was an average student and his parents were relieved as Chrissy gradually worked his way back into his classmates' good graces, and the teasing eventually stopped.

Now eighteen, Chrissy, however close he was to his father, hated the idea of learning diving with him. This reaction had nothing to do with the sport and everything to do with his relationship with his father and his attitude toward himself. Old enough to vote, join the military, or go off to college if he wanted to, the Rouses' only child was having trouble finding his own niche. Although Chrissy liked the many activities he did with his father, there were some things that he needed to do on his own. The night they were supposed to go to their first class, the two men argued. His dad could go on his own—Chrissy had better things to do, like hanging out with his best friend and picking up girls. He didn't need his father for that.

Chris went alone. He loved it. His enthusiasm about the class and the possibility it offered of enabling him to explore the alien underwater environment inspired Sue to talk Chrissy into reconsidering. Intrigued by the sport if not by his father's participation alongside him, Chrissy joined his father. Maybe this diving thing was worth it, Dad or no Dad.

Their instructor, Denny McLaughlin, saw that both Rouses were at ease in the water and would quickly master diving basics. It was clear they both aimed to be top dog among the many students, both in the water and the classroom. An experienced instructor, McLaughlin took care to evaluate not only the Rouses' diving skills, but their interactions and demeanor. He noticed how the smallest provocation would have the Rouses verbally dueling. During the start of one pool training session, Chris remarked to his son, "Hey, you've got your tank strapped on wrong. The valve's off-center."

Perplexed, Chrissy frowned and rolled his eyes. "No, I don't. You're just looking at it off-center." His father was always a perfectionist, and that caused friction with Chrissy's "close is good enough" mind-set.

"What do you mean I'm looking at it off-center? That's ridiculous. The opening of the valve is supposed to be pointed right at the back of your head, and it's not!"

"Oh, yeah? How can you tell?"

"Well, it's obvious. Your hoses are not coming off the tank connection properly." Chris went at the gear. "You're just not doing it right. God, how could I have raised such a numbskull?"

Chrissy shrugged him off. "It's inherited."

Minutes later, after some of the underwater swimming exercises, Chrissy rose to the surface, pulled off his mask, and spat out, "Gee, I know it must be tough being an old geezer and all, but do you think you can swim like you want to go somewhere?"

McLaughlin watched as, for a second, the elder Rouse let his face betray hurt. "Well, I guess for an old geezer I did *all right,* 'cause I had no problem keeping up with you. But I did have half a mind to swim ahead of you 'cause you just looked so *spastic.*"

"Sure, sure. I had to keep moving out of your way." Chrissy swam to the edge of the pool as McLaughlin took a deep breath and decided not to intervene. "Hey, see those big things on your feet? They're called fins. Denny told us they were for swimming. You should try using 'em instead of flailing around with your arms."

"I did *not* use my arms!"

"Did too."

"Did not."

"Yep. You hit me three times with your arms. I counted."

McLaughlin thought for a minute that the two men would go at each other physically, acting out a rivalry more befitting brothers than father and son. Their constant banter and bickering made it seem that they were on the verge of killing each other, but McLaughlin came to realize it was all part of the way they interacted. Maybe they would spur each other to be better divers. And they were an asset to the class: They were helpful with the other students, assisting them with minor equipment adjustments and encouraging them whenever they felt doubts about their abilities after the pool sessions.

During the ten-week class, the students got to know one another very well, and they would gather after class at a local diner to socialize. Both Chris and Chrissy wanted to include Sue, their wife and mother, and when they came home after the first meeting at the diner, they encouraged her to join them. "But I don't know anyone. I'll feel a bit silly crashing your class get-togethers," said Sue.

Both men chimed in at once, "No, everybody's so nice. We want you to meet them. They'll all make you feel like one of the family."

Sue knew how much her husband enjoyed meeting people. She had been amazed when he had gone to her five-year high school class reunion. Her former classmates had changed so drastically—just as she felt she had—that she felt a bit awkward, and had trouble initiating conversations. Having gained some weight since high school, and with her life so drastically different from what she had imagined it would be, Sue was self-conscious at the reunion. Chris, on the other hand, went up to everyone he could, cheerfully and unabashedly introducing himself, shaking hands and smiling like a politician on the campaign trail. He would always find something of common interest to talk about and his relaxed manner, constant smile, and plentiful jokes made other people warm up and feel good. When the event was over, Sue had to drag him away.

At home, Sue told Chris how awkward she felt at the reunion. Chris hugged his wife and told her, "You're so strong and full of encouragement all the time. You know, I could never live without you. If you ever died, I know I wouldn't be able to go on without you. But I know if I die, you'll be able to pick up and you'll be dating other guys. Then you'll find a nice guy and get married again."

She got strength from her husband's cheerfulness, and was grateful for his obvious love for her in spite of the pounds she had put on during their marriage. Whenever she brought up the extra weight in their private conversations, he smoothly, lovingly cast aside her self-doubts and recriminations. "We're perfect for each other. Nobody else would be right for me. We fit together like puzzle pieces. You're my Puz," Chris would say as he snuggled up to his wife.

Chris appreciated how trustworthy his wife was and relished their partnership; he would never think of doing anything without talking to her about it first, and trying to include her. She was always supportive of him, no matter what plans he came up with, or how their fortunes turned, and she always encouraged him to follow his dreams: "Chris, you only live once. Whatever you want to do, go for it, and make the best of it," she would remark to him, reiterating what she believed and what he wanted to hear. Sue was Chris's anchor, keeping him rooted, yet letting him flow with his current in whatever direction he wanted to go.

Sue joined Chris and Chrissy at the diner after her evening class let out. She was thankful for a break from her studies—and from having to cook. The other members immediately welcomed her. "We couldn't wait to meet you! We wanted to see the superwoman that could put up with the dynamic duo!" one of them declared. At one point, over pie and coffee, someone asked, "Sue, how do you do it? These two never stop, never slow down. How do you possibly keep up with them?"

Sue laughed. "I get people like your instructor to baby-sit occasionally so I can get a break." Chris and Chrissy could only grin sheepishly.

After ten weeks the classroom and pool sessions were over, and McLaughlin held his final training at Dutch Springs, a local rock quarry that had suddenly flooded years before and taken on a new life as a swimming hole, and a testing site for divers. The quarry's owners had installed underwater platforms rising several feet off the bottom so that students could demonstrate their skills without having to wallow in the fine silt that covered the floor of the quarry. The Pennsylvania water was cold, and in spite of the platforms, the sheer number of diving students from many different schools caused turbidity. Silt stirred as the masses walked in and out of the water, or when they swam along the bottom to examine some of the many boats that had been sunk here purposely for their amusement.

On dry land, before and after each dive, McLaughlin had to overhear both Rouses keep up a steady stream of bickering. "Hey, Chrissy, where did you put the spare parts box?" Chris called out at one point.

"Me? You were supposed to bring it."

McLaughlin saw Chris's eyes flash. "Don't *start* with that again! Every time I ask you to bring something you forget it and then try and blame *me*."

Chrissy threw his fins to the ground. "No. Definitely not. You didn't ask me to bring anything other than what I brought. Don't try and blame me for something *you* forgot!"

"Yeah, right, just like the tools I asked you to bring to the job last week. Remember? It took you two fucking hours to go and get the tools, and *I* had to work late to make up for it."

"Yeah, I remember. That *was* my fault, and I said I was sorry. Ya don't need to keep bringing it up. You *always* do that. Besides, I told you I would have worked late to make up for it. This time, I did *not* forget anything!"

Chris set his jaw. "All right, all right. Let's try and forget it. How about getting me a sandwich from the cooler? I *know* we managed to bring *that* with us!"

"Why do I have to get everything for you? What am I—your fucking gofer?"

Chris let out a long sigh. "Man, you can't even get me a sandwich without whining? After all I've done for you?"

The other diving students were long familiar with the Rouses' ritual of mutual abuse and tried to ignore it. They knew that underwater the Rouses' breathing regulators kept them from snapping at each other—somewhat. They still used hand gestures. But with only one dive left in the final two days of training, McLaughlin had had enough. "Okay, that's it," he said, getting up to insert himself between the two men.

"If you two can't get through this dive without arguing, you'll have to wait until next week for another shot at your certification."

The prospect meant failure. *That* was unacceptable. Both Rouses bit their lips and sank into sullenness. They voluntarily separated themselves and prepared for the dive, contenting themselves with nasty glances at each other. They went through the dive without incident, passed the course, and received their diving certification cards.

After finishing her evening college course, Sue joined a woman friend from the flying group to take diving lessons. The woman had already signed up for classes given by a different shop from the one Chris and Chrissy had used for their training, but Sue did not think it would make a difference. Besides, it was nice to have as a diving partner someone she already knew. Instead of the intense, ten-week course that Chris and Chrissy had undergone, Sue found herself in an abbreviated one-weekend class. On Sunday evening, she arrived home with the news that she'd be going on her checkout dives the next weekend. "I can't believe the instructor said I'm ready for the checkout dives," she told Chris and Chrissy. "I don't feel comfortable at all. It was such a short class. I didn't get anywhere near the training you two had."

Without hesitating, Chrissy said, "Don't worry, Mom, there's nothing to it. Dad and I will go with you if you want."

Chris agreed right away. "That's the spirit, Junior. Sue, we'll be right there with you. No sweat."

Sue liked the idea that her two guys would rally round her. When she donned her equipment to get in the water with her class at the quarry, Chris and Chrissy looked on from a distance. As she would find out later, husband and son did not like what they were seeing. "I don't like this instructor," Chrissy said to his father. "Can't he see that Mom's not really comfortable? He should be giving her more pool training instead of dragging her out here before she's ready." Chris turned to his son and said, "Junior, we gotta keep an eye on Sue. I really wish she would have done the training with us, and with Denny."

Chrissy agreed. "Yeah, Mom's not real comfortable with this. I'm gonna be ready to get in the water fast in case she needs help."

"Good idea. Why don't we just slip into the water and hang around without making it look too obvious?"

"I don't care about not making it look obvious."

"Let's just be cool, and not piss off the instructor. We want Mom to get her card, and after that she'll be diving with us," said father to son.

During the checkouts, Chris and Chrissy swam with Sue and the class on their underwater tour. The quarry was cold and the visibility bad, with silt particles suspended in the water, turning it an unappealing brown. At one point, the instructor turned to Chris and wrote on his slate, "Which way to shore?"

Chris couldn't believe it. Here was an instructor who was lost, and was asking a newly certified diver for directions. Chris pointed into the brown haze, indicating which way back. When the instructor turned away, Chris looked at his son, pointed to the instructor, rolled his eyes, and shook his head. Chrissy nodded in agreement.

With the support of Chris and Chrissy, Sue persevered and completed her certification dives, which was more than some of the other students accomplished. Two divers had joined the class specifically for the checkouts, one a firefighter, the other a former Special Forces soldier. Both men gave up after the first day of dives; the cold, murky water made them uncomfortable and put them off diving. Chris and Chrissy would ensure that Sue could follow through; no matter how they bitched at each other, the Rouses always stuck together. At least when the task at hand demanded it, they were a team, no matter how murky and perilous the water.

All three of the Rouses were now certified divers and headed each weekend to Dutch Springs quarry, with every descent leaving Chris and Chrissy more relaxed and adventurous in the water, eager to explore every silty corner of the immense quarry. Sue didn't feel so adventurous and contented herself with diving with Ken Reinhart, Chris's former flight instructor and a close friend. Although he wasn't a diving instructor, Reinhart had enough experience teaching people how to fly planes to know Sue required someone at her side until she became completely comfortable underwater. He patiently coached Sue on the finer points of diving.

From Ken, Chris and Chrissy found out how much additional instruction Sue needed. They insisted that their former diving instructor, Denny McLaughlin, dive with Sue, check out her techniques, and coach her. Impressed with Chris and Chrissy's concern for Sue's well-being and comfort, McLaughlin agreed and refused to accept money from the Rouses for any extra instruction. It was compensation enough to see a family so enthusiastic and conscientious about diving.

At the quarry, all three Rouses were soon diving each weekend on their own, picnicking together in the fields between dives, helping the harried instructors get their numerous students in and out of the water, attending to occasional equipment problems, and reassuring those whose nerves faltered. They embraced the sport with fresh and infectious enthusiasm.

It had taken both enthusiasm and grit for Sue and Chris to win their prosperity and ensure the success of their relationship. They had started out with challenges of their own making: Sue became pregnant while Chris was still in high school. They were both so young when they started dating—Chris was sixteen and Sue was seventeen—that neither of them thought they wanted children. Sue didn't think she would even marry until she was thirty or forty years old. She was very studious, liked foreign languages and political science, and wanted to pursue a career, maybe as an interpreter, or something to do with international business. Now, eighteen years old and pregnant, Sue had some difficult choices to make.

Her father had stepped back, telling her to make her own choice. Sue and Chris knew they were in love, and both were excited about having a baby. They agreed they should get married. Although she had been an outstanding student, and had earned a state scholarship to the University of Pittsburgh, motherhood forced Sue to put aside her plans to go away to college. At first the newlyweds lived at Chris's parents' house, and the new husband and father worked up to three jobs at a time. Chris was peacock-proud when both his wife and newborn son attended his high school graduation.

Chris's hard work paid off quickly. That fall, the couple rented some property, bought a mobile trailer home, and moved out of Chris's parents' house. But only one month later Sue was hospitalized and diagnosed with kidney stones, which required surgery. In their effort to save money so that they could move out and be on their own, the couple had decided not to purchase medical insurance. They were

young and healthy, they thought, so the insurance seemed unnecessary. Now, they had to pay all of Sue's medical bills out of their own
pocket. When Sue was released after the surgery and a ten-day hospital stay, the couple faced several thousand dollars of medical bills. And
the convalescent young mother could not lift anything, including the
seven-month-old Chrissy. All this meant they had to move back in
with Chris's parents so that Sue could recover from the operation, and
also have help caring for Chrissy. It was a hard blow for the newlyweds,
but they were both determined to make their marriage work.

Chris found a job at a car dealership doing mechanical work, which
allowed him to quit his other jobs. With Chris and his parents helping
her out Sue recovered from her surgery, and after a month the couple
and their infant were able to move back to their mobile home, their
hard-won second independence a family Christmas present. Sue's medical bills still hung over the family's head, and she got a part-time job as
a waitress at a local restaurant; both sets of grandparents took turns
caring for Chrissy while Chris and Sue worked.

After a year and a half Chris was growing frustrated at his job.
"These guys give me all the crap work, all the stuff they don't want to
do, all the stuff that pays the least amount of money," he would complain to Sue. "I mean, how many oil changes can I do in a day, or a
week or a month? It's like that's all they've given me. I can do better
stuff than that!"

"You've got to say something, Chris. They're going to keep walking all over you unless you speak up!"

As much as Sue encouraged her husband to be more forceful and
aggressive so that he would be given more challenging and better-
paying car repair jobs, Chris kept quiet at work, slowly seething
because he was not being given an opportunity to do different kinds
of work for which he was qualified. Sue worried when his job so upset
Chris that he started getting frequent stomachaches and would be so
sick that he could not go to work.

Another six months passed. Then one day he came home to tell his
twenty-one-year-old wife he had quit his job. Sue was shocked, but
she decided to support his impetuous choice. She saw that her husband was too easygoing and wasn't good at asserting himself and

insisting he be given better-paying work. He deserved to be happy, after all, and surely he'd provide for the family somehow.

Chris sold his motorcycle and bought a front-loader tractor that could dig trenches and lift large amounts of just about anything. He started an excavating business, clearing land for roadways and driveways, and digging drainage ditches and holes for pools and septic tanks. He liked his job and knew that he was good at it. He was happy—and he remained undaunted by his parents' protests that he should get a *real* job, which Chris took to mean a job in which someone else would get to boss him around. Anybody else's doubts about him only made him more determined to generate enough work to pay for the machinery he needed, put food on the table, and provide a home for his wife and son.

Chris bought a small dump truck so that he could haul materials to and from work sites, which expanded the scope of jobs he could accomplish. Word quickly spread throughout Pennsylvania's Bucks County about the affable, hardworking young man, and soon Chris Rouse found plenty of work through word-of-mouth referrals. His customers liked his honesty, his efficient bids, and his resourcefulness. Chris's parents, notwithstanding their initial protests over their son's choice of work, cosigned a loan application that enabled Chris to buy the larger machinery he needed to expand his business.

Things were going well for the Rouse family, and Chris enjoyed his son immensely. The boy was so energetic, and as soon as he could, he talked incessantly, even carrying on conversations with himself when others weren't nearby. Everywhere Chrissy went people were struck by the cute, engaging, and curious little boy.

When Chrissy was three years old, the family went to the zoo. That night, just when they were trying to fall asleep, Chris and Sue heard Chrissy calling to them from his crib in the next bedroom. "Mo-o-om? Da-a-ad?" Chrissy asked. Both parents responded with a concerned "Yes, Chrissy. What's wrong?"

"Let's talk."

"What do you want to talk about?"

"Let's talk about the zoo."

"Let's talk about the zoo" became the family's catchphrase from then on when they wanted to initiate an emotionally warm discussion, make up after an argument, or apologize.

With a stream of work contracts, Chris was now making a comfortable living. He and Sue started talking about buying some land, rather than renting property as they now did. "Chris, we're only in our twenties, and we have no real assets, just this mobile home. What bank is going to lend us the money?" Sue asked.

"Well, we'll just have to look for some other way to finance it. Maybe a finance company, or even somebody who's selling their property and who'll finance it for us."

Chris and Sue were fortunate and found a seller willing to finance the sale of his remote, eight-acre wooded property. Chris would have plenty of room for his heavy machinery and even a separate workshop. Sue liked the property because it was very much like the rural area where she grew up. And both of them would be close enough to their parents to maintain their family ties, yet far enough away to feel that they were now on their own. They moved their trailer home to the property.

Bolstered by the property loan and the perceived confidence that a stranger had placed in him, Chris decided to make a bid for a huge excavation job, a site that had to be leveled before a vast home center and hardware supply complex could be built. In an ingenious scheme, Chris proposed that his only compensation come in the form of dirt and rock produced by leveling and excavating the hilly terrain. As he saw it, the raw material he removed would be worth a small fortune as landfill. Chris won the bid, then went out and bought a bulldozer to add to his growing fleet of construction vehicles.

Chris earned enough money from the home center job to pay off all the loans on his heavy machinery and still put money in the bank. The local home center and hardware supply company newsletter featured an article titled "The Man Who Moved a Mountain." On the first page, Chris was pictured sitting atop his bulldozer, almost dwarfed by the rocky mountain he would excavate next. His reputation spread. Chris had gambled and won.

It had taken them thirteen years, but now Chris and Sue had a respectable bank account, a thriving business, and a son who was just starting his teenage years. Chris wanted to indulge himself by buying a private plane. Sue forbade it. "I've never said no to you before,

Chris," she told him, "but I want a house. You're *not* buying that plane until we have a house. I'm tired of being trailer trash."

"Okay, well, I guess we're gonna have to build a house then," Chris said promptly. "You and Chrissy will have to help too. I can't do this alone!"

"Of course we'll help. Nobody's saying you've got to do it alone. We've always done everything together, Chris."

Not only had Chris and Sue done everything together, but Chris also made sure to include Chrissy in his and Sue's activities—and even in his excavation business—as much as possible. Chris confided to Sue that he was looking forward to working alongside Chrissy; he thought Chrissy would eventually take over the business. "If Chrissy wants to, he'll have a business and won't have to experience a boss holding him back, or breathing over his shoulder, like I did," Chris told Sue. Chrissy loved working with his father, and especially driving the bulldozer, which he learned to do when he was twelve. And he greatly admired his father's seemingly effortless ability to fix anything and everything, especially the heavy machinery that Chrissy liked so much to ride.

In 1983, the Rouses began building a home on their wooded property. In order to afford the house, Chris bartered work with other contractors in the area for things he could not do himself, like installing plumbing, or electrical wiring. As if erecting his own house while running a burgeoning excavation business was not enough of a challenge, Chris made a deal with his friend Ken Reinhart. "You've wanted a house for a while. Come on, we'll build our houses together. I'll help you with yours, you'll help me with mine." It was too generous an offer for Ken to refuse. Over the next few years, as the two men built their houses together, the friendship between them deepened.

Chrissy was thirteen years old when his father dug the foundation; he helped with the construction, as did Sue. Though it was sometimes frustrating for the Rouses to work on their house after long hours spent earning a living at their jobs, and on weekends, when they should have had free time to relax and enjoy life, the experience strengthened the family, and as their house took shape, their confidence in each other and in their ability to work hard together developed a solid foundation. It was as if the Reinhart and the Rouse families were pioneers in the Old West, building their homesteads together.

It took the family two years to build their new home. Once their house was completed, Chris bought that private plane. On a day when Ken had a flying class to teach and couldn't accompany him to inspect a Cessna advertised for sale, Chris went anyway—and bought it on the spot. By the time Ken got back from his class, Chris was a proud airplane owner. His friend's abrupt decision surprised Ken, who had thought Chris was only exploring options, not that he was ready to lay down money. Ken now perceived a new side of Chris: Here was a man who could spend two years building a house and thirteen years constructing a business, and who could also make a snap decision to spend fifty thousand dollars in ten minutes.

Happily ensconced in their home, the owners of an airplane, and all certified divers, in 1988 the Rouses indulged in a warm-water vacation; they went to Bonaire, a small Caribbean island in the Netherlands Antilles, off Venezuela, renowned for its diving. The water was comfortable, clear, and swimming with life. Long before environmental tourism became trendy, Bonaire's government had seen the merits of creating a national underwater park, where corals remained undisturbed and fishing was not allowed. Divers flocked to the pristine underwater environment.

Most divers saw a warm-water diving trip as a chance to kick back, enjoy two easy dives a day, and spend time sunning on the beach with friends while knocking back a few tropical drinks. The Rouses just dived. In five days, Chris conducted twenty-two dives, accompanied mostly by Sue and Chrissy. After returning from Bonaire, they were back at the quarry the very next weekend. But not for long. An article about the Ginnie Springs dive shop and campground in north-central Florida caught Chris's attention. Ginnie was the site of the Devil's Cave System. He set off in a private plane with Ken Reinhart and another pilot to check it out.

The three men drove through the flat, Florida farmland, the odor of cows and horses hanging in the air, to the sprawling Ginnie Springs property. As they approached it Chris Rouse was immediately intrigued by a large billboard depicting a slim young girl with flowing, curly blond hair sitting on a riverbank with one leg in the water. It was like a picture in a fairy-tale book. Her skin looked silky and lightly tanned. Only her angled leg and arm provided her a little modesty. She regarded a deep-red cardinal sitting on a branch. Ginnie, the water nymph, the sign seemed to imply, was an innocent and benign creature.

Chris, Ken, and their pilot friend turned at the billboard and soon the paved road gave way to a sandy trail. A one-story building sat at the far left corner of the field, marking the start of the Ginnie Springs campground. The structure—well proportioned, spacious, and constructed out of wood that allowed it to fit perfectly with its surroundings—pleased the builder in Chris. The dive shop's walls and several racks were filled with neatly laid-out noncorrosive brass clips, for clipping equipment to the dive harness, as well as an assortment of various-size diving hoses, buckles, harnesses, lights, and other equipment. Chris was awed. He had never seen a place like this. The dive shops back home were not as large or as well equipped, nor did they have the unusual types of diving gear displayed at Ginnie. As he wandered through the building, he noted a classroom, a general store, a merchandise shop offering colorful beach towels, T-shirts with various Ginnie Springs and cave-diving logos and artwork, an equipment repair shop, offices, and a rental facility. For the first time, Chris was witnessing a community created by and for divers. It was a place made just for him.

As Chris and Ken paid their entrance fees and signed in for diving, showing their certification cards, each man was given a form that required his signature; it was a statement that he had been warned of the dangers of diving here. Because they were only open-water divers, in the Devil's Cave System they were prohibited from carrying underwater lights: Without lights they would not be tempted to go beyond the cavern zone in which sunlight makes the way to the surface clearly visible. If they did use lights they would be subject to immediate expulsion. They could carry lights at Ginnie Springs cavern itself, because a heavy metal grate had been installed at the entrance to the tunnel system and they would not be able to physically enter the area where they could no longer see light.

Outside the dive shop, Chris found myriad winding, sandy trails leading from the main path through the campground; along the trails smaller camping areas had been cleared, but each one had numerous trees to provide both shade and privacy. His family would love to camp here. He and his friends continued walking to the Santa Fe River, whose lazy, winding course acts as the natural border along one side of the property. Turtles sunned themselves on the branches of trees that had fallen into the river. The river's murky water was joined by the steady outflow of gin-clear water from the spring systems, which added to the river's volume to provide a smooth, steady flow for the enjoyment of people in canoes or floating on tire inner tubes. At Ginnie Springs, fish darted about, clearly visible in the translucent waters. Chris was captivated. He'd never seen anything like it; the canoes looked as though they were floating on air rather than water. Bonaire, though its water was reasonably clear, was nothing like this. What would it be like to dive in transparent water? He couldn't wait to find out.

That afternoon, Chris and Ken made their first dive in Ginnie Springs. They descended into the mouth of the spring, through a narrow gap between the sand and the rock. Just beyond lay a large underwater room. With the small underwater lights they were allowed to carry into this cavern, their eyes adjusted to the dim light and they could see that the water's constant flow had molded the rocks into eerie shapes. Some rocks looked like animals, some like the face of a screaming person. The entire landscape was like a scene on a science-fiction planet.

As they descended to 55 feet, they came across a solid metal grate, which had been installed many years earlier to block the entrance to the main tunnel system. When Chris swam near the grate, the force of the tunnel water rammed him in the chest. Surprised and a little indignant, he pulled himself close to the bars. He felt like a prisoner, unable to reach the freedom of the mysterious cave beyond him. The water blew his short hair straight back and the water rushing against his face made his skin tingle. It was refreshing—almost like a cool breeze on a hot day. And when he let go of the grate, he was blown backward like an autumn leaf.

When they surfaced, Chris was exhilarated. He insisted the men move on to dive at the Devil's Cave System—another spring on the property, but one that had no grate over the cave tunnel. When they arrived, the large yellow warning sign on the riverbank opposite the entrance steps caused Ken some alarm. He read the sign carefully: WARNING! CAVE DIVING REQUIRES SPECIAL TRAINING AND

EQUIPMENT. DIVERS CAN AND HAVE DIED HERE. Rules for safe cave diving were posted, and Ken, the veteran flight instructor, paid heed.

Many divers are not as cautious as Reinhart. The urge to "boldly go where no man has gone before" is so compelling a human drive it often defies the instinct for self-preservation. Many a bravado-besotted diver will still enter the Devil's Cave System even when his lack of skills, training, and equipment ensures his death.

Florida's limestone caves are not simple caverns or short tunnels in the earth where a person can go inside, turn around, and get out. They are labyrinths formed when rainwater carrying weak acids seeps through and eats away the porous stone, then descends to harder rock areas that finally prevent further downward movement. Always seeking the path of least resistance, the water rushes horizontally in twisting, turning underground rivers stretching for miles beneath the surface landscape. Eventually, the earth disgorges the water at various spring systems, where it bursts forth into swimming spots and feeds the state's rivers. In other parts of the world, water creates cave systems that snake through lava fields, or through cracks and bedding planes of various rocks that are far harder than limestone. Ironically, some of the largest subterranean lakes and cave systems have been found in Africa, a continent that also contains vast expanses of desert. The complete extent of the world's cave systems is still a mystery, but they seem to act as our water planet's arteries, filtering water of impurities and returning it to the surface, where it nourishes animals, plants, and humans.

A diver is like a cat, curious to see what is inside a partially opened box. Just as curiosity can kill a cat, so too can curiosity kill the untrained cave explorer. Some are lucky: Like Christopher Columbus the diver without cave training may stumble forward for at least several cave dives, not knowing what danger he's really courting, before disaster overtakes him. It was Vasco da Gama, not Columbus, who—applying Prince Henry the Navigator's principles and using the maps of previous successful explorers—found the prized sea route to India. The savvy cave diver will also rely on the experience, and the paths, of others who have gone before him. Where Columbus blindly stumbled forward and got lucky in finding a mass of land, da Gama used discipline and methodology to systematically reach his destination.

So will the cave diver who wants to live to tell his grandchildren he explored the Devil's Cave System.

When Chris and Ken dived into the Devil's Cave System that day, they saw a sign very similar to the one that stands there now. Inside the system, at the point where natural light casts its last, faint glow, is a stark black-on-white warning. The sign depicts the Grim Reaper, complete with sickle, and a group of skeletons in dive gear lying at his feet. In large, bold, black letters are these words:

STOP
PREVENT YOUR DEATH!
GO NO FURTHER.

FACT: More than 300 divers, including open water scuba instructors, have died in caves just like this one.

FACT: You needed training to dive. You need *cave training* and *cave equipment* to *cave dive*.

FACT: Without cave training and cave equipment, divers can die here.

FACT: It CAN happen to YOU!

THERE'S NOTHING IN THIS CAVE WORTH DYING FOR!
DO NOT GO BEYOND THIS POINT.

One two-buddy team, untrained in cave diving, ignored the sign and ventured into the Devil's Cave System with two masks, one tank, and one set of swim fins between them. One diver "piggy-backed" on the other diver, breathing from an extra regulator attached to the one tank. They swam into the cave just to see it, driven by their curiosity. But they got lost and couldn't get back out. Had they been trained for cave diving, they would have known to pay out the special white nylon guideline from the reel that cave divers carry for just this purpose. They would have been able to follow the white nylon to the exit, as if following a thread out of a maze. Both divers were found dead, wedged inside a small passage. Around their corpses were signs of terror: They had kicked frantically and left marks in the silt on the cave floor and their fingernails had clawed at the cave ceiling as they breathed their last breaths, trying to dig themselves out through tons of rock.

In the Florida caves, the deadly facts of the foolhardy are fiercer than fiction. Another untrained diver who went in alone, without a guideline, got hopelessly lost and used his knife to carve a last message into his single tank of air: I GOT LOST. I'M SORRY. MOM I LOVE YOU.

Some untrained divers do go into the caves with guidelines, thinking that a guideline is all you need. One pair went to a cave dive shop to purchase a guideline reel—but trained cave divers carry not one but several on every dive. The store owner wanted to see proof of their cave-diving training, and when the two could not produce it, he refused to sell them any cave diving–related equipment at all. Undeterred, the pair went to a local sporting goods store and bought a reel of clear, monofilament fishing line. Their bodies were found inside a cave system, hopelessly entangled in the strong, clear line. Their arms were tightly pinned against their bodies, their breathing regulators dangling away from their anguished faces and gaping mouths.

The reports of deaths like these in Ginnie Springs spurred an even more gruesome rumor. A story circulated involving a team of three untrained divers, at least one of whom ran out of air in the black tunnels. In their struggle for survival, the divers supposedly began stabbing one another with their dive knives, just to secure a few more breaths from the others' tanks. All three died inside the cave. The horror of an underwater knife fight while in the throes of suffocating panic is too much to fathom, even for the hard-core cave diver. Fortunately, the tale is untrue. The truth behind the story is that three brothers went into the Devil's Cave System, got lost, and died—a fate gruesome enough even without the knives. Apparently, a nondiver had seen the bodies being brought out of the water and noticed rips in the dead divers' suits. That was enough to set his imagination in motion. The nondiver never bothered to find out why the suits were torn. The rips were the result of getting the divers' death-bloated bodies out of the cave's confines.

As Chris looked past the underwater warning sign in the Devil's Cave System, he saw a vast tunnel that disappeared into the darkness. It was all he could do to prevent himself from swimming forward to try to see what lay beyond. He was rapt. When he surfaced with Ken,

Chris insisted they immediately take a cavern-diving course. The first step in learning to cave-dive is a cavern-diving course. (Technically a cave is an underground area beyond the reach of sunlight where there is no direct ascent to the surface.)

Ken as well as Chris was awed by the underwater landscape he had just seen. But the warning signs weighed heavily on his mind.

"C'mon," Chris prodded him. "Let's take at least the first course. It'll make us better divers. Think of what we'll learn!" Reluctantly, Ken agreed.

One of the two instructors teaching the cavern-diving course was Steve Berman, a quiet man who, once he entered the caverns, seemed to be transformed into a water creature, moving smoothly, effortlessly, and then hanging weightless and motionless in the water as he monitored his students. The water was so clear that it looked to Chris as though Steve was hovering in air like a genie.

In the two-day cavern-diving course Chris and Ken learned the basics of wearing their equipment in such a way that they had extras of everything they needed to keep themselves alive inside rock caverns, where they could not immediately return to the surface if something went wrong underwater. Caverns and caves were officially termed "overhead environments," and the extra equipment required, including a complete extra air supply and spare lights, was called *redundancy*. All of the lessons Chris and Ken learned about human underwater activity had come at the price of dead divers. Cave diving had led to disproportionately more deaths than open-water diving, where a diver experiencing a problem can ascend directly to the surface and its life-sustaining air.

The histories of cavern and cave diving were intertwined, yet the two had been clearly differentiated for diving and training purposes only after a 1973 study of cave-diving fatalities by the famed Sheck Exley, who had previously written two extensive cave-diving manuals.

Exley, a native of north-central Florida, had taken up cave diving in 1966, when he was only sixteen years old. Back then, there were no rules for safe cave diving—it was far too new a sport. Divers developed their own rules as they went along. As more and more divers died in Florida's caves, both individual landowners and the state started closing cave entrances, using explosives to do so. By 1970, Exley knew that if the cave closings continued, there would soon be no cave diving in Florida. Motivated to save his sport as well as lives, Exley decided to explore what could be done to make cave diving safer. Although he had already survived more cave dives than anyone else, he knew that he and others could ensure their own and others' long-term survival only with education and discipline. Exley analyzed the fatalities and found trends. From this study came what is known as the "rules of accident analysis," which he published as a booklet called *Basic Cave Diving: A Blueprint for Survival.* The manual sets forth ten representative accidents and the rules learned from each one. Exley's catechism became the basis for all future cave training, including the first step, the cavern-diving course, which Chris Rouse and Ken Reinhart took. In a cavern-diving course, participants are limited to the area in which sunlight can still be seen, a maximum depth of 130 feet, and a linear penetration—the horizontal distance from the cavern's rock entrance—of 70 feet.

The most important rule Exley came up with was this: Always carry a guideline that will lead you back to open water. This rule might seem obvious to most people in light of the number of divers who had become disoriented inside caves, hadn't been able to find their way out, and had drowned. Unfortunately, the dictum had not previously proved self-evident in practice: Too many people had died who probably would have survived if they had used a guideline. Exley's succinctly graphic presentation of how to avoid becoming a dead and bloated diving victim led to the establishment of a training regimen and code of conduct for cave diving with an effectiveness never previously achieved. The number of deaths from cavern and cave diving dropped dramatically.

Another key concept that Exley emphasized was redundancy—always having an extra of everything you need underwater. With a single tank, the tank valve onto which the breathing hoses are attached contains a dual outlet, so that if something goes wrong with the first one, the diver can use the other. Cave divers using double tanks connected with a manifold bar have to use the type of bar that contains dual outlets, a device invented by a cave diver. Each outlet has affixed to it a *first stage,* a mechanical device that ratchets down the high-pressure air of the scuba tank to an intermediate pressure.

The breathing hose comes off the first stage and leads to a *regulator*, a simple mechanical device that further reduces gas pressure and provides breathing gas to the diver at the surrounding depth pressure. If any one of the links in the chain—the first stage, the breathing hose, or the regulator—fails, the diver can switch to a second regulator, which is attached to the other outlet. The diver's second regulator, which has a hose at least five feet long, is known as an octopus. This regulator is used to give a buddy breathing gas in the event he runs out or has catastrophic equipment failure.

Underwater diving lights should also be redundant, Exley maintained. Not only cave divers but also cavern divers now always carry at least two. Although the cavern-diving certification allows divers to descend only as far as the last point where they can see sunlight, having battery-powered lights has advantages for cavern divers, letting them behold the cavern's details; monitor gauges showing depth, dive time, and remaining gas; and signal a dive buddy.

Exley also emphasized that every dive team, including cavern divers, should also use a guideline reel, so that divers can find their way out of the cavern in the event of a "silt-out"—a situation where particles of sand, mud, or clay hang suspended in the water, erasing visibility. In this case, the divers gently take hold of the guideline and follow it out. Each diver also should carry a backup reel for use in case he or she loses contact with the primary guideline and has to search for it. Exley and his disciples also emphasized special swimming techniques that allow divers to go safely into an area without stirring up silt.

After Chris and Ken completed the cavern-diving course, they flew on to Key West for a few days of diving on coral reefs. Though exotic, Key West was far from Chris's mind, and all he could talk about was how exciting the cavern diving at Ginnie Springs had been. "Ken, we've got to go back and take the cave-diving course," he told his friend. "The training will make us much better divers. And we'll get to see what's beyond the warning sign." Although Ken had enjoyed diving into the bright limestone caverns, warning flags rose in his mind—especially about venturing from the sunlit caverns to probe the murk of the caves. "Chris," he said, "this cave-diving thing is dangerous. Didn't you read all those warning signs?"

"Yeah, but that was for people who don't have training and the right equipment."

"Even with that, don't you think there's just too much that can go wrong?"

"If you have good training, and you practice, you learn to deal with everything. If you didn't, everybody who ever went into a cave would be dead." Chris leaned forward intently in a chair on the veranda of their hotel, as if convincing Ken would grant him permission to do what he wanted.

"Chris, cave diving is like pulling a tiger's tail." Ken took a quick drink of his juice. "You can get away with it for so long, but sooner or later the tiger is going to turn around and take a swipe at you."

Chris sat back, looking as if his friend had just said he wouldn't lend him a twenty. "Ken, I'm going to go back and take the training, with or without you."

In March 1989 Chris was again at Ginnie Springs. Ken did not go. He considered cave diving too dangerous; when he dived, he wanted the assurance of knowing that if something went wrong he could shoot straight up to the surface. But Chris had just enough of a taste of cave-diving training that he felt he had to give Chrissy the experience. Father and son could now experience in real life a world as strange and exciting as any they had seen in the *Dr. Who* sci-fi television show they both loved so much. Chris repeated the cavern-diving training with Chrissy, to let his son catch up. Then they both went on to the cave-diving course.

The two-day "Introduction to Cave Diving" course trained both father and son to venture well beyond the cavern zone. They were allowed to carry powerful underwater lights that illuminated the vast tunnel complex of the Devil's Cave System like a galactic movie set. The tunnel's limestone walls were covered with a mixture of white and black patches. When they came to a bend in a wall, the light from the diver in back would cause a distorted silhouette of the diver in front to be thrown on the harlequin pattern, like when a child makes finger shadow figures on a movie screen. Nature had taken tens of thousands of years to create these tunnels; a diver's shadow would play on the walls for the geological equivalent of an eye blink.

Their instructor was Marc Eyring, a man whose history and demeanor embody the word "extreme." This rugged man had been a sergeant on the "A" Team in the Green Berets, briefly served in Vietnam, and then worked for NASA as an electrical engineering supervisor on the space shuttle. Although he did not have an electrical engineering degree, his exceptional drive and intelligence had gotten him into the space program. After the shuttle *Challenger* blew up, NASA fell into disarray, and future projects were either seriously delayed or canceled. Frustrated, Eyring left to become a cave-diving instructor at Ginnie Springs.

Marc Eyring was a perfectionist; he realized that what he drilled into his students was nothing less than the means of survival, the same skills and sense that had been pounded into him during his Green Beret training. His intense focus and self-imposed demanding teaching schedule would frequently lead him to go all day without eating. A student in a cave-diving class has to dive only twice a day, but Eyring, running two or more classes simultaneously, often made four or more cave dives within sixteen hours. When his students emerged into daylight, he would critique the performance of each individual, as well as that of each dive team. In his view, the divers were soldiers storming enemy barricades while wearing hundred-pound packs, which in a way they were.

Like Denny McLaughlin before him, Eyring recognized the Rouses' natural talent as divers. Normally, after passing the introductory course, divers have to get some experience under their belts before advancing to the next level. But the Rouses' skills and eagerness prompted Eyring to let the father-son team continue directly into the grueling four-day "full cave" course. There was no guarantee of passing any of the cave courses: An instructor had to be absolutely confident that a student possessed not only diving competence but also the right attitude and level of maturity necessary for safe cave diving. An instructor was free to fail a student for demonstrating unsportsmanlike conduct or arrogance, taking technical shortcuts, or exhibiting lack of awe at the prospect of diving the dangerous caves. This training was far more focused than anything the Rouses had previously undergone, and that was part of its appeal. Passing into the ranks of the "full cave" certified diver was an accomplishment few divers even aspired to. It would set them apart.

Usually, before students were allowed to continue their cave-diving training beyond the introductory level, they were encouraged to get a year or so of experience at the basic cave level to perfect certain skills: The guideline could be tricky to use, and care had to be taken to lay it securely on the way in; the reel could jam, and the diver had to be able to manage wrapping the line manually around the reel, often while contending with a fast current. Divers had to learn how to use their legs—which of several kicks to use in different circumstances—and when it was more efficient to use their hands and arms to gently tug themselves along, a technique known as the pull-'n'-glide. They also had to get used to wearing two full-size tanks, necessary to provide enough breathing gas for penetrations deep into cave systems—and a reserve in case of emergency.

Eyring noted that the Rouses performed as a team from the onset of their training. He'd found that this kind of teamwork was unusual among people who came to diving knowing each other from the regular world. He had witnessed a tendency for even experienced divers to react as individuals and abandon their partners in the hostile cave environment to press ahead alone out of curiosity and in the grip of an adrenaline surge. The phenomenon was common enough so that he knew students did not do it deliberately; it was the nature of the stronger partner to want to move forward, to excel. For this reason, he usually broke up husband-and-wife teams, or other partnerships where one member was clearly superior in skills to the other. Physically, the nineteen-year-old Chrissy had the benefit of youth and was stronger than his father. But Eyring saw that Chris demonstrated a maturity that came only with age: "Chrissy was the limiting factor," he would say later. "Chris was stronger, both—I would say—in character and mentally. He took action to deal with problems, although Chrissy, being younger, was more physically fit. They each had strengths and limitations."

Chris and Chrissy had enjoyed their cave diving so much that when they got home they both begged Sue to give it a try so that the family could all go cave diving together. Father and son were eager to camp at Ginnie Springs because it provided convenient access to the diving sites and they would not have to waste valuable underwater time traveling back and forth the long distance between the nearest motel and the water. Neither of them knew anything about camping. Sure, Chris and Chrissy had both camped there before, but they had come with a group that included experienced campers who set everything up. Sue was reluctant at first—she remembered how uneasy she had felt after her initial diving training and did not want to go through that experience again—but her two men kept insisting that she would love it. "Okay, okay, I'll go," Sue said, relenting. "But I can tell you now, I don't think I'm going to like it."

As soon as they arrived, Chris and Chrissy were both eager to go diving right away, before they had set up camp. "Oh, no, you don't!" Sue chided. "We've got to put up the tent. No diving until the tent's up." She knew that once the diving started, she would have a difficult if not impossible time getting her husband and son focused on domestic chores. Chris and Chrissy grumbled, but they both knew that when Mom put her foot down she meant it.

"There." Chris pointed to the first campsite he saw. "That looks like a great spot!" Chrissy agreed. The men unhooked the equipment-laden trailer they had towed behind their compact family car from Pennsylvania and unloaded the tent, which they hastily erected. Throwing their sleeping bags into the tent without much attention to where they landed, Chris and Chrissy declared that they could now all go diving.

When the family surfaced after their dive into the cavern at Ginnie Springs, they were met by a blinding downpour. "Oh, no! We left the tent open," Chris shouted. Still clad in their rubber diving suits, the family jumped into the car, with Sue driving. Not only was it hard to see anything through the rain, but she was completely unfamiliar with the maze of roads that led through the campground. Sue drove around aimlessly until they finally glimpsed their tent, which they had unwisely set up on low ground. The rain had caused a small flash flood, and a river now ran right through their tent's opening flap. All three sleeping bags resembled submerged sponges. Sue's open suitcase looked like a portable washtub filled with clothes.

The Rouses grappled the tent and their belongings from the swirling water. "Well, we'll have to do a better job of it this time," Chris remarked as he surveyed the area for a more appropriate spot to erect the tent.

"We're still going to camp here?" Sue asked, dumbfounded. A motel sounded like a good idea right about now.

Chris looked at her with surprise. "Of course we're going to camp here. That's why we came here. To camp."

"And to dive," Chrissy quickly added.

Sue knew how much her two men could react like little boys, and if a soaking tent and drenched sleeping bags were not spurring them toward a motel, nothing short of a major family argument would. She was too exhausted for that. "All right," she said. "Let's get all the stuff and go dry it out." The family headed with their wet things to the campground's shower and rest-room facilities, where Sue began using a blow-dryer to get everything as dry as possible. Overwhelmed by the long drive followed immediately by the dive, Sue wanted to lie down and rest, not spend hours blow-drying her sleeping bag. She complained about the selection of the campsite, the weather, the wet things, and anything else she could think of.

"Stop whining, Mom," Chrissy pleaded. "It's not *that* bad." He quickly added, "Let's talk about the zoo."

Chris walked over to his wife and hugged her. "Yeah, Puz. Let's talk about the zoo."

Sue woke up the next morning to still-damp clothes. But she took the two-day cavern course and then the "Introduction to Cave Diving" class. To her surprise, she found the caves fascinating, just as Chris and Chrissy had said she would.

After their initial waterlogged foray into the world of camping, the Rouses were determined to get it right on subsequent trips. A pickup truck had replaced their compact car for these excursions. Over several camping trips during the next year, the Rouses developed their camp compound so that it looked like a campsite on an expedition in deepest Africa. They used all manner of blue plastic tarps to help shelter themselves and their equipment from rain and sand. They now used a trailered, pop-up camper instead of the old canvas tent. The camper was situated in the middle of a clearing, complete with a five-foot canopy that led to their picnic table. Two additional tents— including their original old-fashioned canvas model—were erected on either side of their camper and housed their equipment, which

included multiple pieces of backup gear for each of them, in case anything should not perform flawlessly. The extra tents also served as
convenient places for one of them to retreat to, like Achilles, when the
bickering became too much. Around the perimeter of their campsite
they had roped together their five-foot-high green oxygen-supply
cylinders, making a green stockade. Anyone who knew the Rouses
could figure out quickly whether they were in residence at Ginnie
Springs by looking for their distinctive encampment.

Every chance they got, the whole Rouse family went to Ginnie
Springs. Word spread about them among the hard-core cave-diving
community. And Chris and Chrissy soon got to know those hard-core
divers. The Canadian diver John Reekie spent winters in Florida. He
ran his own roofing business in a suburb of Toronto, where he made
sure to work as much as he could when weather permitted. Once the
snow set in, Reekie loaded his truck with diving and camping equipment and headed to Ginnie Springs, sometimes taking a break to go
as far as the Florida Keys for some wreck diving. He dived every day
from his arrival in mid-November to his departure in April.

During one of the Rouses' trips to Ginnie Springs, they were
camped near Reekie, who was alone. Spotting the Buddha-bellied
Reekie, Chris and Sue Rouse invited him over to their campsite. As
Reekie strolled over, he noticed the large, boxy, old-fashioned brown
canvas tent and the diving equipment spread about on blue plastic
tarps. Reekie thought to himself that these must be the "tarp people"
he remembered hearing about; this was the lighthearted way Ginnie
Springs personnel referred to the family with the old-fashioned
equipment and an artfully arranged array of tarps.

Chris grinned from ear to ear and stretched out his hand to John.
"Hi. I'm Chris Rouse. This is my load, Junior, and my wife, Sue.
Wanna join us for dinner? Come on, sit down and make yourself at
home." Reekie immediately felt a tinge of liking toward this gregarious person, but by nature he was skeptical, leery of making friends
with anyone. Reekie had found out the hard way that though people
could be friendly enough on land, inside an underwater cave system
their true character traits would surface. The Canadian didn't want
to be disappointed, didn't want to waste his time with another would-be
diver. Sure, he'd talk to the Rouses, but he'd reserve judgment until he

had administered his own special test. If they passed that, then he'd feel a lot more friendly.

Reekie had the reputation in the cave-diving community of being not just a serious diver, but "extreme." His diving philosophy was quite simple: You didn't end the dive for anything but a serious emergency, or until you had breathed one third of your gas supply. The Rule of Thirds—another piece of the Exley catechism—called for a diver to expend no more than one third of his breathing gas on the way into the cave, and then turn around. This would leave one third for the return, with the remaining third reserved in case of emergency.

Reekie's absolutist philosophy of not ending a dive except in case of a full-scale emergency was in sharp contrast to the approach that was officially propounded in cave-diving classes. When Marc Eyring taught the Rouses cave diving, he stressed, "Remember, any diver can turn the dive at any time, for any reason." The signal to turn the dive was a sharp thumbs-up. This would be acknowledged by the other diver or divers, and the team would turn around and head out of the cave. Eyring underscored the importance of this rule. "When the thumbs-up is given, I don't want to see any hesitation. The dive's over. Period. Acknowledge the thumbs-up with your own thumbs-up and then head out. If you want to know why the diver is turning the dive, have a discussion when you're all safely out of the cave."

John Reekie demanded that when you went on a cave dive with him, you had better not waste his time and turn the dive before you breathed every last ounce of your first third of your gas supply. Chris Rouse reveled in that philosophy. He would soon learn that Reekie was respected, feared, or viewed as a maniac, depending on the quarter. During one of Reekie's cave dives, for example, a diver's main dive light went out, he went to his backup, and with the thumbs-up signaled Reekie to end the dive. Reekie swam over to the diver, looked at him, and grabbed the diver's pressure gauge to see how much gas he had left. With a grunt, he threw the gauge back at the diver and continued on into the cave. As Reekie figured it, the diver had not reached the end of the first third of his gas supply, and he still had two working dive lights left. When asked about it, Reekie responds with a "What are you, stupid?" expression and says, "Yeah, sure, cave-diving rules say ya gotta *start* the dive with at least three lights, but they don't say how many ya gotta *end* the dive with. One stinkin' light failin' is no reason to call the dive." Steve Berman, who dived often with Reekie, says with a slight grin, "Yep, Reekie's a wild man. Ya better be *real* serious about divin' if you're gonna dive with him." Berman's nod and widened eyes reinforce the message.

Reekie tested Chris Rouse during their first dive together, in the Devil's Cave System. As he often would in these situations, the large Canadian would "disappear" during the dive, usually hovering above his dive partner, sometimes in a recessed area of the cave. Then he would wait. And observe. If his partner noticed Reekie was missing, and—more important—if he initiated a search for the lost diver, the "wild man" knew that his new dive partner was a person who had awareness, skill, and the fortitude not to abandon someone in a cave. Over the years, Reekie had observed how many dive partners never noticed he was missing, and simply left the cave without him. He knew not to conduct serious dives with that person. During the unannounced test, Chris Rouse noticed right away that Reekie was missing, and he initiated a search for the lost buddy. Seeing this, Reekie descended with a slow, smooth grace and presented himself to Chris, making an O with his meaty index finger and his thumb in the universal diver's "OK" signal. Chris acknowledged by returning the signal, then indicated the way out by making a child's "gun" gesture, the index finger pointing forward and the thumb up. Reekie returned the directional signal, and knew he had found a competent diver he could trust underwater.

The friendship between Chris Rouse and John Reekie strengthened as the two went on cave-diving excursions together, sometimes driving for hours from Ginnie Springs to reach another cave system. Reekie and Rouse developed a mutual respect for each other, and each loved to tell stories about the other. Although they were about the same age, they were an unlikely duo from a physical standpoint. Where Chris was a trim, reasonably fit five feet ten, Reekie's most prominent feature was his expansive belly, held amidships on a six-foot frame. When he walked into a restaurant that offered an "unlimited buffet," managers who knew him would sweat as they imagined profits being absorbed in an endless stream as Reekie's belly expanded. Chris loved to tell how Reekie ate so much at one restaurant that the manager came over and apologetically cut off the food supply. Reekie, of course, was indignant: "Doesn't your sign say 'Unlimited Buffet'? Man, I'm not done yet." The restaurant manager refunded half of the buffet fee and asked Reekie to leave.

Despite their physical differences, both John Reekie and Chris Rouse shared an insatiable diving appetite. Chris would say, "Man, Reekie's nuts in the water. When ya dive with him, you better be prepared to do really long dives, because he doesn't want to turn around till he absolutely has to."

Reekie preferred to dive with Chris Rouse alone, without Chrissy and Sue. He had noticed that Chrissy placed a priority on conducting two cave dives a day, no matter how long or short those dives were. Reekie preferred to conduct one long cave dive, instead of two shorter ones. When Chris accompanied Chrissy, the father felt obligated to go on every dive with his son, but when he was with Reekie, one long dive, lasting up to six hours, satisfied him. Reekie also noticed that strange things happened when all three of the Rouses—or even any two of the Rouses—dived together. Although all three were good, smooth divers, their equipment—and even Reekie's equipment—always seemed to break down during the dive. Reekie knew that the Rouses were meticulous about keeping their equipment in shape, so he knew that the gear failures did not result from neglect. After a dive with the Rouses, Reekie would shake his head and say to the three of them, "I've never had equipment fail on me as much as I have when I dive with you! You guys have a black cloud over your heads."

Chris Rouse was awed at Reekie's ability, and after one dive he told Sue, "I don't know how he does it, but he gets himself into places I can't even get in. You'd figure that fat bastard would get stuck in a tight area like a cork in a bottle, but no. Underwater, he's like Gumby. He just pours himself through the openings." Chris also remarked that the chain-smoking Reekie had excellent gas consumption; his lungs expended air with surprising efficiency. This was important in cave diving, because the distance you could go into the cave was determined in great part by how efficiently you breathed. If a diver developed a reputation for being a "Hoover"—consuming gas at too great a rate because of poor breathing or propulsion technique, anxiety, poor fitness level, or perhaps genetic predisposition—he or she would not be invited to dive with the best divers, or have the opportunity to do the top dives, because the diver's safe gas supply would run out too soon. Divers like that brought a team back to the surface prematurely and curtailed everyone's fun.

The Rouses had passed the test. They had taken to the cave training, to Eyring, to Berman, to Reekie, and to the entire group of cave divers who hung out around Ginnie Springs like surfers at Malibu. The other divers liked the Rouses' energy and enthusiasm for the sport. Sure, they bickered and teased and taunted each other, but among this eclectic group who seemed to live for nothing more than to penetrate ever farther into the earth's mysterious water-filled tunnels and map the winding passageways, the father-and-son grappling seemed natural.

3

Pretzel Logic

THE ROUSE ENCAMPMENT was always only a few steps away from the three mobile homes that Ginnie Springs management provided to any of its staff who wanted to live there for free. Their only housing-related expense was the phone bill. The trailers were hidden by bushes and a row of trees that lined the sandy road in front of the dive shop. The commute for Ginnie Springs staff was a few steps across the road.

The staff's trailers were the headquarters for the off-hours parties and diving discussion groups that formed casually as divers wandered in and out. The interior of Steve Berman's trailer was dark, and he always left the blinds and old curtains closed to discourage unwanted or curious visitors. The walls were covered with cave maps and posters. Diving gear in various stages of assembly was strewn everywhere: Heavier equipment such as scuba tanks and diver-propulsion vehicles rested on the floor, while more delicate items, like dive lights and diving computers, occupied both the kitchen table and the coffee table in the living room. A few empty beer bottles and abandoned bottle caps lay among them. Every available electrical outlet had something plugged into it, whether a household appliance or a battery charger for the diver-propulsion vehicles or lights. A musky, damp smell filled the air, and sand particles lodged themselves in the abused living-room carpet and on the linoleum floors throughout the rest of the trailer home. The heavy buildup of dust and mold around the sinks and bathtub in the kitchen and bathrooms suggested that they hadn't been cleaned since the invention of the cotton gin. The linoleum floor around the perimeter of the bathroom was lifting. A stack of diving magazines rested on the toilet tank.

Steve Berman lived in the trailer that had once been Marc Eyring's before Marc had gone off to pursue a doctoral degree. First the degree was to be in chemistry, then it was physics, then engineering: Marc changed his goal so often, none of us could be sure in what area of science he would finally get his doctorate, yet we were all confident that he would achieve some advanced degree, even if he had to invent a new field of science that encompassed all of his intellectual interests. Marc would still come around on occasion and teach a class, so he had left his huge television, two VCRs, and the high-quality stereo in the living room, where the devices formed a solid wall of electronics and the control panel for a lot of high-voltage partying.

From an appearance standpoint, not much had changed since the days in 1988 when the trailer had been Marc Eyring's official home. The only thing that was noticeably different was the lack of pornography videos that Marc liked to have running in the background—with the sound off so as not to be too distracting. When Marc was in residence, both men and women would wander in and out of the trailer, glance at the television screen while on their way to the refrigerator for a beer, and usually make a remark like "What? This tape again? Hey, Marc, when are you going to get some new tapes?" Others might remember the tape fondly and ask if they had missed a particular scene. During the course of the night's discussions about the finer points of cave diving, the tapes would still be running. When I stayed at Marc's trailer as a guest I thought it odd for him to be playing the porn tapes constantly, but I took the "when in Rome" philosophy and did not say anything.

Sometimes, the background porn tapes would get to be too much and someone would turn on the second VCR, which would start playing a cave-diving tape. Slowly, sexual frustration would give way to an urge that felt just as primal and powerful: cave diving.

In December 1990, I was staying at Berman's when the Rouses stopped in. Chrissy, Steve, Sue, and I drank beer, while Chris, who said he had never been much of a drinker, contented himself with juice. I was meeting the family for the first time, and I was struck by their energy, enthusiasm, and gregariousness. We were kindred spirits, and within minutes it felt like we had known one another for a long time. I was also impressed by how much father and son looked alike, as if I were seeing the Rouse men in a fun-house mirror that took age into account. Both men's slim, athletic frames seemed wired for electricity, as if ready to plunge into whatever action presented itself. Chris's faded blue jeans were slightly worn at the knees and had collected dust and dirt smudges to go with the permanent oil stains that blotched the front of the legs. His T-shirt depicted the devil smiling as he looked on at a cave diver entering the cave system named after him. The words GINNIE SPRINGS, FLORIDA ran along the bottom of the picture. Like his jeans, Chris's T-shirt displayed obvious signs of wear and few signs of washing. His face was unshaven, with a dark, thick growth that looked almost a week old, in spite of rumors that Chris had battled with his facial hair only two days prior. His brown hair was unkempt, and just long enough to resemble a mop placed on his head. His hands were worn, with oil and dirt worked deeply under his skin and nails. Even his face showed streaks of oil, which I gathered was from recently working on some piece of automotive or even diving equipment. Chris's appearance lent the distinct impression that he had just walked in off a construction job.

Chrissy was dressed in similar fashion. His youth combined with his tattered blue jeans, worn sneakers, wrinkled T-shirt, and brown, straight, shoulder-length hair to make him look as if he'd fit in more readily with a rock group partying in their dressing room after a performance than with a group of cave divers almost twice his age. Sue was relaxed, and seemed content to observe our interactions while enjoying her beer. An earth mother surrounded by the fiery spirits of her men, she was jolly but appeared tired from the combined exertions of diving that day and having to contend with Chris and Chrissy's bickering, which I was witnessing for the first time and was mightily impressed by.

Steve Berman preferred to play only cave-diving tapes, and with this in the background, Steve, the Rouses, and I relaxed and discussed plans for diving together in several local cave systems.

When people talk about cave diving in Florida, it doesn't take long for the name Sheck Exley to come up. The north-central Floridian who learned to dive in 1966, at the age of sixteen, became fascinated by the water-filled caves dotting the countryside. Soon he was spending every available spare moment cave diving. When Exley started cave diving, the world record for a linear cave penetration was 1,000 feet, set by the U.S. diver John Harper in 1962, in Hornsby Spring, Florida. It was a remarkable accomplishment, considering that the average cave penetration was only 200 linear feet. Exley became so proficient at the sport that he set numerous new cave-diving records, including the record for linear penetration. In December 1990, he extended that record to 10,939 feet, diving in Florida's Cathedral Canyon. Exley was strong, had great stamina, and tolerated the narcotic effects of air at depth very well. Other divers experimented with different breathing gases to ease their narcosis, but not Exley. He could be seen breathing air and swimming past them at depths down to 360 feet—over seven martinis!

During the 1960s and 1970s, sport divers gradually reached depth barriers in their explorations as a result of the Martini Law, and they sought breathing-gas alternatives to compressed air. Compressed air was easy to get, inexpensive, and widely used, but its riskiness increased as divers pushed their explorations ever deeper, thus intensifying nitrogen narcosis. Unfortunately, many tragic lessons about the hazards of compressed air and other aspects of deep-water diving had been learned in the context of military or commercial diving operations, and were kept secret from the public. Sport divers were left with no alternative but to arrive at deep-water secrets without the benefit of elaborate research facilities available to the military and commercial diving establishments—without detailed knowledge of what had gone before, and why. As sport divers experimented with mixed-gas diving in the 1960s and 1970s, Exley watched unfolding events with justified skepticism.

Divers had to beware not only of the narcotic effects of nitrogen, but of the toxic effects of oxygen. As pressure increases, oxygen becomes toxic. The toxicity causes seizures that inevitably result in drowning as the diver convulses and his breathing regulator drops from his mouth at depth. In the 1960s, it was generally held that divers could descend to about 300 feet breathing compressed air before the oxygen in the air became toxic. Some divers, like Exley, could go deeper, whereas others encountered the toxicity at shallower depths. Various navies around the world had experimented and found that a diver might be subject to oxygen toxicity at different depths on different days. It was unpredictable. Recommended diving limits with compressed air have steadily been revised to shallower depths, and some people today advocate a limit on compressed-air diving of 150 feet—three martinis. Deep diving with compressed air is a time bomb, with either nitrogen narcosis or oxygen toxicity waiting to claim even the best diver.

The oxygen toxicity problem first reared its head publicly in the 1960s. At this time, American cave divers first started experimenting with helium in their breathing gas to lessen the martini effect of nitrogen in compressed air at depth. In order for the body to expel the helium at a safe rate on the ascent to the surface, divers concocted gases that had very high concentrations of oxygen: They would even breathe pure oxygen starting as deep as 60 feet. When several divers died of convulsions during their ascent, Exley grew even more convinced that mixed-gas sport diving remained too dangerous for him to risk it. Clearly, oxygen presented its own risks to divers.

As if the problems of nitrogen narcosis and oxygen toxicity were not enough to deal with, divers also noted that when they breathed helium mixtures they felt incredibly cold and they worried about the possibility of life-threatening hypothermia. Helium is an excellent conductor of heat, and sport divers concluded they were losing heat both during breathing and through the skin, which was surrounded by a thin layer of water between the body and the rubber wetsuit—called that because it allows water to enter. Most divers used wetsuits in the relatively warm water of Florida's caves, and heat loss was not a problem when they were breathing normal compressed air. To overcome their perceived heat loss when they breathed helium gases, sport divers wore a drysuit, which was watertight and used as insulation a combination of underwear resembling a ski suit and a gas, usually air. Even with a drysuit, though, divers breathing helium mixtures noticed that they felt cold. The culprit was at first thought to be the insulating gas itself. Divers would inflate their drysuits when they were already underwater, and if they were breathing a helium mixture, they used this gas to inflate their drysuits. Instead of insulating, it felt as if the helium mix had the opposite effect because of helium's high heat conductivity. The solution was to pump a different gas—compressed air or even argon, a heavy gas that is an excellent insulator—into the drysuit, but this meant adding yet another compressed-gas bottle to the diver's equipment load.

With all of the complications entailed in breathing mixed gases, Exley kept on diving using only compressed air. But then, in 1981, the German diver Jochen Hasenmayer, using mixed gas, succeeded in diving down to 476 feet in a French cave, shattering Exley's cave-diving depth record by over 100 feet.

Ever competitive and willing to revise his own beliefs, Exley decided that the path to greater depths could now be safely negotiated using mixed gases. Hasenmayer had obviously worked out the various complications of mixed-gas diving. Exley wrote to Hasenmayer, and the two became friends, sharing information and even diving together. In 1983 Hasenmayer managed a mixed-gas cave dive to 656 feet; it would take Exley until 1987 to best his friend's efforts. By 1989, Exley had again set the world deep-scuba-diving record when he descended to 867 feet inside Mante, a cave in Mexico that plummeted downward at a slight angle to depths unknown. Many who knew him well observed that Exley seemed obsessed with holding the deep-cave-diving record, and with beating Hasenmayer in their friendly rivalry.

The Rouses had taken the mixed-gas diving course with Exley two months before I met them at Steve Berman's. At the time I myself was preparing to take Exley's course. Whenever I hung out at Fort Rouse, they bubbled with excitement about the experience of learning from and diving with the master. The Rouses had been impressed with

Exley, Chrissy especially so: "The guy's amazing in the water, and he's in such great shape," he said to me when we discussed cave divers at camp. "He swims so *fast* all the time! Like a human torpedo. Man, it was an effort to keep up with him."

During the class, the Rouses had learned both the theories and the practical aspects of mixed-gas diving, including how to calculate ideal gas mixtures for a given depth, and how a gas should be mixed. Trimix, for example, contained three gases, typically oxygen, helium, and nitrogen. In order to brew trimix, the diver needed only to put the correct amount of helium into an empty scuba tank, and then top it off with air, which naturally contained the two other required gases, oxygen and nitrogen. For the gas called nitrox, an oxygen-nitrogen mixture, the diver only needed to put in a given amount of pure oxygen in an empty scuba tank, and then top it off with air.

Exley emphasized hands-on experience. In addition to the classroom lectures, students learned how to mix their own gases. Chris remarked to me later, "It was weird to see that Sheck doesn't believe in checking the mix with an analyzer. He says that if all the gauges you're using are good, and your mathematical formula is right, then the mix will come out right." I too was surprised to hear this, because I knew that divers who were doing mixed-gas diving held it as gospel that after mixing a gas, you should analyze the oxygen content. Exley, who had a degree in mathematics and taught the subject in a Florida high school when he wasn't diving, was confident of his formulas.

Chrissy was impressed as much by Sheck's aquatic style of living as he was with the man himself: "It's cool. Imagine living in a double-wide trailer with dive gear all over the place and a cave in your backyard!" Exley lived in Live Oak, and there was an entrance to Cathedral Canyon cave behind his house. Chrissy added, "He's even got a hot-water hose set up." The hose piped hot water down as far as 20 feet into the spring, where the diver had to rest so as not to surface too quickly.

Sue, overhearing the conversation from inside the camper, yelled out, "Hey, Chrissy, tell Bernie how you two dummies didn't listen to Sheck and how you wish you had. Go on, tell him!" Chrissy's face sank into chagrin for a moment. "Oh, okay, Mom," he mumbled. "Sheck told us not to wear drysuits when we went into Cathedral cave, but Dad and I did, figuring we'd be cold if we didn't. Mom took his advice. We didn't know about the hot-water hose until the end of the dive, and Sheck and Mom were taking turns putting the hose down their wetsuits to warm themselves up. Dad and I did get a little cold in our drysuits because we didn't have heavy underwear on, and of course we couldn't use the hose in our suits." I heard Sue laughing from the camper.

All divers have to contend with other problems besides cold, narcosis, and toxicity. The greatest and most enduring problem divers face— one still not fully understood—is decompression sickness. Decompression sickness is caused by the body's inability during an ascent to remove all of the biologically inert gas—nitrogen, in the case of divers breathing compressed air—that it absorbs while breathing underwater. On the ascent, the excess inert gas emerges from the tissues to be expelled during exhalations. If the body cannot eliminate the gas fast enough through breathing, the gas forms bubbles in the bloodstream, which press on nerve endings and can block the flow of blood; this stops oxygen from getting to parts of the body and causes injury to those areas. It is extremely painful; the common term for decompression sickness, the bends, refers to the contortions of victims in agony as a result of pain in the joints and muscles.

If a diver comes up slowly from a dive and stops at different depths for various lengths of time, the body has the chance to eliminate the excess gas before bubbles form. Severe cases of the bends can cause the victim to experience numbness in certain parts of the body, or even to lose bodily functions such as eyesight, hearing, clear speech, bladder or bowel control, sexual function, and even life itself. Getting bent is no laughing matter. Although methods of treating decompression sickness have been around for some time, an understanding of exactly what happens to the body during treatment is still elusive.

From the time that human beings first began to penetrate deep waters, many observers felt that depth quests would lead to nothing but tragedy and that sport divers would never be able to handle extremely deep dives. Sadly, Jochen Hasenmayer fell victim to an operational problem while diving in the 200-foot depth range in a European lake; he could not stop his diving suit from inflating with insulating gas, making him look like a lethally buoyant balloon with arms, legs, and a small head. He shot uncontrollably upward and broke the surface like a cartoon-character missile. Hasenmayer was rushed to the hospital in severe pain, crippled by decompression sickness. Medical treatment in a recompression chamber—a small tubular machine typically no longer than a car, in which the diver is put under increased pressure, simulating diving depth, and slowly brought back to surface pressure—failed to alleviate his paralysis, though it may well have saved his life. He will spend the rest of his days in a wheelchair.

Long before the arrival of sport diving, human beings have been stirred by curiosity and driven by economics to explore what lies beneath the surface of the waters of the seas, rivers, flooded quarries, and caves, and to retrieve what we have lost beneath the water. Not being able to see under the waves led the human imagination to conjure all sorts of beasts lying in wait to trick, or even devour, those who entered a seemingly forbidden realm. But there have always been people who ventured into the deep despite the superstitions. Depending on your philosophy, they were either brave, foolish, or insane.

For those who have never been underwater before, "deep" is definitely a relative term. Already within just 20 or 30 feet of the surface can be found another world, now familiar to us via television and still images, as well as elaborate private and public aquariums. But all of this was completely unknown until fairly recently. Ventures into the deep were once as impossible or exotic as a trip to the Moon. And, as with going to the Moon, we had many obstacles to overcome before we could make the journey. Our mentally induced terror was perhaps the least of these obstacles.

Without technology, people don't do very well breathing underwater, but even with the crudest devices, we have always striven to overcome this physical barrier. An Assyrian relief from 900 B.C. shows a man swimming underwater, breathing from a hand-carried bladder, not unlike those used for wine. In the fourth century B.C., Aristotle described a simple diving bell that allowed divers to descend to the bottom, swim about, come back to the bell for more air, and continue their underwater activities. All manner of diving dress and helmets were used through the ages, with varying degrees of success. Salvaging sunken ships for their cargo, cannons, or treasure provided economic incentive. If simple curiosity did not help us overcome our initial fears and superstition of the water, greed did.

The first truly successful diving apparatus was invented by the Englishman John Lethbridge in 1715. He described his device in an article published in *Gentleman's Magazine* in 1749. It consisted of a tubular structure made of wood and resembling an elongated wine barrel, sealed with resin, and reinforced with iron rings. The tube was laid flat, and a man would climb into it through the head end, and lie facedown. In this position he could peer through a tiny porthole. He would put his arms through two short sleeves made of leather that protruded from the body of the cask, so he could perform actions with his arms free. The head end would then be sealed, and the tube lowered so the diver remained flat, facedown. Air was not supplied. Once the diver was sealed in, he breathed only the air he had. Down he went. He would work on the sea bottom with his leather-enclosed arms and signal the surface by means of a rope when he wanted to be hauled to the surface for fresh air. On the surface, two plugs would be removed; a bellows would be inserted into one hole and fresh air pumped in, and the stale air evacuated through the second hole. As might be imagined, dive times under such circumstances were limited: Lethbridge declared that he went to depths of 60 feet for up to thirty-four minutes with this contraption. He also reported that he went to depths of 70 feet and, with British understatement, that this was achieved with much greater difficulty. At the time the article was published, Lethbridge himself had been diving for three years with his device.

The limited time that Lethbridge could spend on the bottom was a blessing in disguise—had he stayed longer he would have encountered the difficulties of decompression. Although it seemed unlikely, that blessing was revealed as a by-product of new inventions that made possible a flourishing industry of the industrial revolution: bridge and tunnel building.

In 1841, the French mining engineer M. Triger developed the first working caisson, a watertight chamber that enabled men to work in compressed-air environments underwater to build bridge foundations, tunnels, and other underwater structures. A hollow steel tube was floated to the area by barges and placed upright so that it rested on the bottom, but its top protruded from the water's surface. A ladder inside the tube allowed workers, known as sandhogs, to commute back and forth between the surface and the caisson on the riverbed, where they worked. The caisson didn't have a "floor," but air, pumped from the surface by a compressor, exerted a greater pressure on the water than the water on the air and prevented flooding. Compressor failure would mean that water entered as the sandhogs breathed the air that held back the seawater. The sandhogs dug into the river's bottom, removing loose sediment and passing it up to the surface to be disposed of. As the caisson sank deeper, extensions were added at the top. When the sandhogs could no longer dig loose sediment but had hit a solid stratum, the caisson was filled with concrete to form the base of a bridge tower.

After the initial success of this radical new work method, the caisson was widely employed, for example on the Brooklyn Bridge construction. But it was noted that strange things happened to the sandhogs. As they ascended after their work shift, many experienced pain, paralysis, and even death. Thousands of workers were afflicted with the malady they called caisson disease. Coal miners had also been known to have these symptoms. Even though they weren't surrounded by water, coal miners and sandhogs worked in a high-air-pressure environment. Now, not only coal miners but also sandhogs were ending up bent, crippled, and dead. Caisson and mine work was of course extremely hazardous, but at the time, caisson disease was viewed as just another consequence of industrialized work, and was deemed inevitable. As fast as workers were disabled or killed, others filled their place in this relatively high-paying type of unskilled manual labor. For his brilliant invention of the caisson, Triger received the prestigious engineering award the Prix de Méchanique, in 1852.

Prior to the time that Triger's caissons were gaining widespread popularity with construction companies, commercial diving entered a new era. In England, Charles Deane had patented a breathing device conceived to aid in firefighting. In 1823, he and his brother, John, modified the device and turned it into a diving suit supplied with compressed air by a surface bellows. This suit allowed divers more time on the bottom than the Lethbridge contraption, yet the Deane brothers realized the need for an even stronger suit with a better gas supply: Lucrative ship salvage contracts awaited them if they could reach deeper depths for longer bottom times. They drew up specifications for a copper helmet that could be supplied with compressed air from a surface-based piston-type air pump. The German entrepreneur Augustus Siebe started manufacturing the Deanes' hard hat in England in 1827.

Dive times were greatly extended with the surface-supplied hard hat—but not without a price. When divers surfaced, they sometimes noticed lack of function in their arms or legs or pain in their joints. In extreme cases, they were in such pain that they cried out and curled into a fetal position. It was this symptom that led divers to call the malady "the bends" and say that the bent diver had "taken a hit." It debilitated divers, crippled them, and even killed them. No one knew why. Perhaps the sea was a forbidden realm after all. Some cultures believed that the divers' malady was caused by a spell put on them when they intruded upon mermaids, or by some other evil. Some divers who suffered the bends and thereafter on land were cripples who had difficulty moving their legs and hands were amazed that when they went underwater they could function like young men again. They thought the sea had cast a spell and would not let them go.

Yet diving deaths did not always come in the form of the bends. The earliest air compressors were hand-powered and required one or two men to crank a large wheel to keep air supplied to the diver in his waterproof canvas suit. If the men got tired of pumping, or the compressor failed for some other reason while the diver was deep, the water pressure literally squeezed the diver's body. In extreme cases, if he was deep enough, the diver's body would be squeezed up into his helmet. When the diver was hauled to the surface, topside personnel found a bloody blob of mush in the helmet, and sometimes in the air hose. They were horrified. In an attempt to prevent suit squeeze, and to contain the overcompressed remains, a one-way valve was invented and inserted into the air hose, just above the helmet. With the new valve installed, a compressor failure now meant that the diver would not be squeezed to death but would drown as he breathed in his remaining air and water entered his suit.

Diving was expanding rapidly, and in 1870 the Siebe-Gorman

Company was founded in England to manufacture diving suits and helmets to meet the needs of the growing industry. Siebe's company is still in business and the "hard-hat" suits it makes are still in use; the distinctive Siebe-Gorman helmet is a universally recognized diver symbol.

As more men applied highly developed mechanical skills in the lucrative field of commercial diving, more divers got bent. The British Royal Navy also noted a high incidence of the bends among its divers. Some solution to preserve the investment in diver training and experience was required. In 1906 the British Admiralty hired the services of a Scottish physiologist, John Scott Haldane, to solve the bends mystery. Haldane first reviewed data gathered on sandhogs who built the Brooklyn Bridge, which was constructed from 1869 to 1883. He also conducted experiments in a recompression chamber.

Haldane knew that sandhogs, coal miners, and divers all breathed compressed air, which has the same composition as air on land at sea level. Nitrogen in the air would enter the lungs during inhalation and then be carried into the bloodstream and from there would be forced into the tissues. This nitrogen was more than the body was used to holding. As early as 1878, the French scientist Paul Bert determined that the bends was caused by excess nitrogen released from tissues and blood as pressure on the body was eased. Bert discovered that the nitrogen formed bubbles in the bloodstream that gathered around the joints, cut off the flow of blood, and pressed on nerve endings. On the basis of Bert's findings and other data at his disposal, Haldane experimented on goats; he put them under pressure, and simulated various depths for different lengths of time. Haldane observed that when a goat has pressure-induced joint pain, it kneels, the goat's equivalent of a bent diver's urge toward the fetal position.

At sea level, the weight of air on the body, or pressure, is one atmosphere. Because water is heavier than air, the weight of the seawater pressing on a body at a depth of just 33 feet is equivalent to an atmosphere of pressure. In the water, the weight of the air needs to be added to the weight of water, so that a depth of 33 feet is two atmospheres absolute ("absolute" means combining the weights of the air and water), 66 feet is three atmospheres absolute, and so on. Haldane experimented by placing goats first at 33 feet of depth pressure, for various periods of time, then at 66 feet of depth pressure, and then at 99 feet of depth pressure. He noticed that he could bring the goats from 33 feet directly to sea-level pressure without any ill effect, but when he brought them straight up from 66 or 99 feet, they were clearly in pain. He then tried easing the pressure on the goats one atmosphere at a time, leaving them at the lesser pressure for various times before easing the pressure again. This method worked. It allowed more time for the body to eliminate nitrogen during exhalations, and prevented excess bubbles from developing. By various adjustments to the pressure-depth profile, the times exposed to those pressures, and the time taken to ease the pressure, he could bring the goats to sea-level atmosphere without their experiencing pain. Or dying.

Before he could test humans, Haldane had to create standardized charts that could be used by those responsible for hauling the divers back up. The charts had to be easily read and interpreted, especially since they would be used on boats, in uncertain sea conditions. He came up with a set of three charts, known as diving tables, that correlated depth, time at depth, and time taken to surface. The charts also took into account excess nitrogen that remained in the body from a previous dive. In such cases, on a subsequent dive, the diver was allowed to spend less time at depth. If a diver exceeded time at depth, Haldane included depths and times for stops to be made so that his body could release excess nitrogen before he was brought to the surface. This process is known as stage decompression.

Haldane presented his research and charts to the Admiralty, which conducted tests using human subjects. Divers achieved record depths of 210 feet without getting bent. It was miraculous. Deeper depths could not be attempted because the maximum limit of technology had been reached: Three compressors, each hand-powered by six men, were attached to the diver's suit and supplied him with the required air. So strenuous was the effort required of the men cranking the pumps that they had to be relieved by another crew every five minutes, lest the diver suffocate. Haldane's dive tables were published in 1907 and were soon adopted by all of the world's navies and commercial diving companies.

Divers learn and relearn the history of decompression theory at every level of diving instruction, and progressing to advanced open-water diving was no exception for the Rouses. All three Rouses had taken the

"Advanced Open Water" diving course in Horsham, Pennsylvania, in the spring of 1989 with Bob Burns, who had been teaching for several years and was also a dive-boat captain certified by the Coast Guard. Burns was one of the owners of the diving charter boat *Dina Dee*, based in Brielle on the New Jersey shore and specializing in excursions to the many offshore shipwrecks. Although Chris and Chrissy were already fully cave-certified when they took the class with Burns, the instructor was impressed with their attitude of thorough engagement. The Rouses did not act like know-it-alls, even though they had a far greater degree of knowledge than most open-water divers, including most instructors. They absorbed Burns's lessons and then went home to read at length about the subjects touched on in class. During the following lesson, they would add significantly to the class discussions, relating what they had found in their readings. Burns, delighted to have such enthusiastic students, would later ask Chris and Chrissy to come in and give lectures to his students about the techniques, challenges, and risks of cave diving, which they were happy to do.

One of the things the Rouses learned in their readings was that decompression is more an art than a science, and is still one of diving's great mysteries. Even if the diver does everything correctly and follows the tables, he can still get bent. Many factors influence the diver and his probability of getting bent, including fatigue, hydration, physical condition, and underwater exertion level. In the first class any diver takes, he learns the basics of decompression theory and how to use the dive tables. Many divers have difficulty grasping the concept of the dive tables, intimidated by the grid of letters and numbers. When the Rouses took Burns's course, Sue was still confused about the proper use of the dive tables. Her one-weekend basic class had left her feeling lost when it came to using these critical tools, so Chris and Chrissy tutored her at home between sessions of Burns's advanced class.

"Come on, Mom, Dad and I will show you how the tables work. They're easy," Chrissy urged her.

Sue frowned. "Oh, I don't know. It seems so complicated, with all these numbers everywhere."

Chris chimed in. "You gotta be kidding. You were such a whiz in school. Hey, if I can do it, you should be able to manage it in your sleep."

"Yeah, but I was good in languages and stuff like that. Math was never something I liked."

Sue appreciated the support from her two men, who pulled out various books and entertained her with the story of one of diving's great mysteries and how it came to be at least partially solved. Sue got the hang of using the dive tables with the patient coaching of her husband and her son.

As divers ventured deeper using the decompression tables worked out by Haldane, they noted a new problem: the debilitating narcotic effects of nitrogen in the air they breathed at depth. Some people experimented with different gas mixtures. Since nitrogen is a biologically inert gas—the body does nothing with it—it was reasoned that hydrogen, neon, or helium could be used in its place. These lighter-than-nitrogen gases would allow divers to descend far deeper before they encountered narcotic effects. However, different decompression schedules had to be used that would take into account the lighter weights of these other gases and their faster absorption and elimination from the body.

In 1945, the Swedish engineer Arne Zetterstrom dived to 500 feet using hydrogen to replace nitrogen in his breathing mix. He died on the ascent, when inexperienced surface tenders misunderstood his instructions and raised him prematurely 130 feet above his planned decompression stop. Later, the British Royal Navy diver George Wookey successfully descended to 600 feet, a record that held until the Swiss mathematician Hannes Keller—after consulting his countryman, the renowned professor and medical doctor Albert Bühlmann—dove to 730 feet using helium gas mixtures, and then in 1962 to 1,000 feet. But the 1,000-foot dive was marred by tragedy: Owing to operational problems, a news reporter who went on the dive with Keller died, as did a support diver, although Keller himself was unscathed. These high-profile diving experiments served to fix in naysayers' minds the fickle dangers of the deep. Surely, sport divers would not be able to succeed in these deep dives where professionals had failed?

With all of the dangers associated with deep diving, and with economic incentive to overcome those dangers, some professionals sought another way to explore the deep. They reasoned that narcosis, toxicity, and the bends could all be avoided if a diver was encased in a protective suit that would maintain his body at surface pressure no matter what the surrounding pressure. Such a hard suit would also have the advantage of allowing the diver to ascend directly to the surface when his work was done. John Lethbridge's 1715 diving device was a crude type of hard suit, though it exposed the diver's arms to pressure. The first truly successful suit was made by the German firm Neufeldt & Kuhnke in 1917. It resembled a science-fiction robot. The German Navy tested the suit to a depth of 530 feet in 1924, and in 1930 the suit was used in 400 feet of water to recover over one million dollars in gold bullion from the British ocean liner *Egypt*. During the Second World War, the German Navy employed a number of N & K suits, which were appropriated by the Allies after the conflict ended.

Nineteen twenty-two was a busy year for armored-suit inventors in the United States. Victor Campos patented a suit reportedly tested to 600 feet, and Joseph Peress patented the first spherical-type joint, which utilized a fluid to transfer pressure and made it easier for the diver to move his arms and legs. Peress built his first suit three years later, but it was not successful. His second attempt, in 1930, resulted in a suit that could take divers as deep as 447 feet; it was later successfully tested by the British Royal Navy. Peress's suit was modified in 1969 by a British company, whose several versions over the years culminated in the JIM suit, named after the diver who tested it, Jim Jarrett. In 1976 it was used in a dive to 905 feet under the ice in the Canadian High Arctic during an oil exploration expedition.

Spectacular as these diving feats were, armored suits still had depth limitations, just as submarines do. Ventures too deep would result in the suit's being crushed—along with the diver inside—like an eggshell caught in the teeth of a tightening vise. For most sport divers, the cost of an armored suit and its attendant topside support requirements put it financially out of reach. Even if a sport diver could afford an armored suit, the devices were too cumbersome, and their umbilical cables connected to the surface made them impractical for significant exploration into underwater caves. Shipwreck exploration could be done with hard suits, but excursions into an intact wreck's interior could be accomplished only by cutting away exterior metal or using explosives to make a massive hole in the wreck's hull.

In spite of significant advances in hard-suit design, most divers—commercial, military, and sport—had to content themselves with using traditional diving suits that left them relatively naked against the mental and physical challenges of the deep.

One of those divers was Glenn Butler, an American who started his commercial diving career in 1968, at the age of seventeen. He made a somewhat untraditional entrance into the world of professional diving. His father had been a diver when in the U.S. Army and worked to clear shallow waters of submerged mines in the immediate aftermath of the Second World War. When he returned to civilian life, the elder Butler started a marine salvage company. His fascination with the sea was passed on to his son, who first scuba-dived when he was seven. When he was fifteen, Glenn Butler became a certified diver, and he went on to teach classes and lead dive trips for the next three years. He loved the water and knew that his life's work would somehow involve the sea. Butler's father tried to help his son get commercial dive training and took him to the navy yard in Washington, D.C. Glenn took one look at the equipment the navy divers were using, turned to his father, and said, "Dad, these guys are ten years behind. I want to be on the cutting edge of diving. There's got to be a better place for me."

There was. In the late sixties, the place young Glenn Butler knew was at the cutting edge of diving was a commercial diving and research company called Ocean Systems, which was owned by Union Carbide. Only seventeen years old, the six-foot-three-inch Butler used his personal contacts in the New York City diving community to wangle himself an interview at the Tarrytown, New York, research facility. When Butler arrived for his interview, down the steps of the concrete building bounded Dr. Bill Hamilton, a man with long brown hair that flowed well past his shoulders, wearing overalls and an emblem of a large, bright pink pig on his chest. Hamilton did not look at all like the fighter pilot and astronaut candidate he had once been.

Hamilton and his boss, Dr. Heinz Schreiner, headed the diving equivalent of the Edison Laboratories and Bell Labs combined. Glenn Butler was happy to get his foot in the door; he labored as an intern, without pay, for six months before he was asked, "Would you like to work as an experimental diver?"

Being a diver in the research facility was unlike being a diver anywhere else. For one thing, divers at the research facility went into deep-water pressure, but did not get wet. Butler's official title was "inside investigator," which meant that he worked inside a recompression chamber as a human guinea pig. While Hamilton and others manipulated the controls from the safety of the outside, they sent Butler to various simulated depth pressures to test new breathing gases, decompression tables, decompression theories, and the limits of human physiology. Butler and other "inside investigators" would frequently get bent when they were brought back to surface pressure. Without leaving the chamber, they would immediately be repressurized and then brought back to lower surface pressure more slowly, while Hamilton and the other researchers noted the results and modified their theories and decompression tables. During one chamber dive, Butler was sent down to 1,000 feet in eleven minutes. He wasn't on the edge of diving—he had been plunged into its abyss. Somehow, he survived intact.

One of the offshoots of Ocean Systems' research was the implementation of a standard for fire safety in hyperbaric (increased pressure) chambers. Improper materials used in conjunction with pure oxygen under high pressure would result in explosions and fire. These lessons were applicable outside of the diving world, though it took the launch pad fire of Apollo 1 in 1967 and the fiery deaths of the astronauts Roger Chaffee, Gus Grissom, and Edward White to stun the world and bring the connection between diving research and space exploration into focus. Though Butler, Hamilton, Schreiner, and the others at Ocean Systems would not go into space anytime soon, they did help make space exploration safer in the aftermath of the Apollo 1 tragedy, by helping NASA to develop materials safety selection criteria for use in the space program.

With the influx of big money for oil exploration research in the 1980s, Butler moved on to become one of commercial diving's elite, a saturation diving supervisor and diver. He directed operations and also worked under constant depth pressure, sometimes for weeks at a time, at great depths to ensure longer working times than could be achieved by having the diver decompress after each work shift. Pressure surrounding such divers is maintained at all times, which means that they have to decompress only once, at the end of the entire job.

Their bodies become saturated with inert gas because they do not decompress after each shift. Butler worked anywhere in the world he was needed: Africa, Europe's North Sea, both sides of the North Atlantic, and the Pacific. When Butler wasn't actually in the water, working at depths sometimes exceeding 700 feet, he was confined to a cylindrical diving bell, a pressurized habitat whose floor contained a hatch that allowed him to enter and exit. Each day, the habitat was lowered from the dive platform and Butler would exit when the habitat landed on the ocean floor. After eight hours of installing or inspecting pipelines or wellheads, Butler would wearily walk along the ocean floor, kicking up clouds of sand and mud as he went—resembling Pigpen, the cartoon character in *Peanuts* perennially surrounded by dust—and crawl back into the refuge of his stark, constantly moist, prisonlike home. It would then be hauled back to the surface while the pressure he had been working at was maintained. No prison on earth has ever been more remote: Butler could not leave his pressurized world for the freedom beyond the habitat's tiny viewing port, for to do so would have meant excruciating death from the bends. His body was not the only thing saturated: His bank account swelled with bonus money. In exchange for risking his life around the clock, a saturation diver receives extra compensation, just as a soldier gets combat pay.

Unlike a soldier, a diver in saturation is slowly being killed by pressure, the unseen enemy. The pressure gnaws away at his body, and after several years of regular work a saturation diver's X rays may show evidence of bone necrosis: blank spaces within the normally solid hip and knee bone structure. Modern medicine has made replacement of these worn bones possible, and sometimes a saturation diver requires a hip or a knee replacement.

Though the job was hazardous, Butler enjoyed it, in spite of the pain brought about by the occasional bout of the bends, which he estimates he suffered at least seventeen times. Butler was like a prizefighter determined to battle his foe to the end. Yet much remained unknown about the physiological risks of repeated decompression sickness.

When I saw Butler at a dive club meeting in 1992, I mistakenly thought he was drunk when I heard his slurred speech and the difficulty he had putting sentences together. I was reminded of my childhood hero Muhammad Ali, whom I met when he was already punch-drunk. During this period, in the early nineties, Butler's memory problems and punch-drunk syndrome of slurred speech were pronounced, and medical doctors were powerless to control them. I wondered whether there was any positive correlation between Butler's numerous bouts with the bends and his slurred speech. Butler told me that a CT scan of his brain had revealed four dormant lesions from diving that his doctors were unable to control. "My speech is all messed up because of an aneurysm—you know, a bleed in the brain," Butler informed me. "It might have been caused by one of my diving lesions, but doctors think it was caused by hypertension."

Butler made steady progress and recovered normal speech and memory by 1995, as his doctors said he would. Incredibly, by the year 2000 all but one of the lesions had healed themselves, and his aneurysm- or pressure-induced slurred speech syndrome had subsided. According to Butler, his doctors' evaluation is that he is "as good as new and not especially prone to bleeds, as long as I keep normal blood pressure." He is still in the diving industry as a consultant, specialty equipment manufacturer, and operator of a major hyperbaric medical facility. At forty-nine, Butler still maintains an intense, almost childlike fascination with diving.

In 1990, the use of anything other than air for sport dives was considered radical and dangerous. There were no official classes offered for the sport diver interested in using helium breathing mixtures. The public thinks of diving into caves and shipwrecks as dangerous for good reason. Only recently, since the 1950s, has diving even become a sport. Although the invention of scuba (an acronym for self-contained underwater breathing apparatus) is credited to the Frenchmen Jacques Cousteau and Émile Gagnan, in 1942, others before them had come up with similar devices. The difference was that Cousteau and Gagnan took two pieces of equipment that had existed for quite some time—the compressed gas cylinder and the demand valve, which opens when the diver inhales, allowing him to breathe on demand—and put them together in a system that would provide air to a diver whenever he breathed in. It was a novel approach. The beauty of the Cousteau-Gagnan apparatus lay in its simplicity. After the Second World War, Cousteau continued with his diving research, raised funds, and eventually produced his famous undersea television show, *The Undersea World of Jacques Cousteau,* and wrote many books. One of the ways Cousteau made money was by selling his scuba apparatus, the Aqualung, to sportsmen.

Scuba diving first became a sport when military divers returned to civilian life and wished to explore the underwater realms off their coasts for fun. Self-contained diving equipment was available in limited quantities to civilians, who needed only money to indulge their fascination with life under the waves. No formal training was required.

Most of those who engaged in the earliest days of sport diving were men, and they believed that you had to be a tremendous swimmer in order to safely scuba-dive. There were occasional exceptions in this world of men, such as the beautiful Austrian Lotte Hass, who worked with her husband, Hans, to photograph, film, and write about the underwater realm. Cousteau's marketing was more effective than the Hasses' in the United States, which led to Cousteau's becoming an internationally recognized icon through his television shows, while the Hasses' fame was limited mostly to Europe, where their films were aired.

Both Cousteau's and the Hasses' efforts led to publicity for the possibilities of underwater exploration as a sport. Civilians who were curious about diving could learn from former military divers, who continued to emphasize strong swimming as a prerequisite and weeded out students not possessing superb skills and stamina. This philosophy became the basis for civilian sport-diving training programs founded in the mid-fifties, whose participants had to endure calisthenics such as push-ups and jogging on the beach as a complement to undergoing diving instruction. And no wonder. Early diving equipment required strong lungs to inhale and exhale through the regulator and its large corrugated double hose that provided air. There was no way to tell how much air remained in the tank, other than a safety device that allowed a reserve to be made available to the diver when he had difficulty breathing. He then pulled a long rod on the side of the tank, which depressed a switch on the tank's valve and released the reserve. Of course, if the switch had accidentally been bumped during the dive, the reserve would already have been inadvertently breathed, and the diver would find himself out of gas on the bottom. He would then have to make a controlled ascent, swimming toward the surface slower than his exhaled bubbles, and swim back to shore or the dive boat while breathing from a snorkel. So being a very good swimmer did help you survive.

As the Rouses' diving obsession grew, their collection of diving-related books, magazines, and videotapes proliferated. Their study of the sport led to a level of sophistication that eluded the vast majority of the general public and even many divers. During one of my visits to their house, they asked if I had seen Cousteau's television cave-diving program: "Oh, you've got to see it. It's so funny!" Chris Rouse said, with Sue and Chrissy chiming in, in agreement. As we watched the program, they pointed out the many technical errors made during the Cousteau team's dive with Dr. George Benjamin in the Bahamian Blue Holes, limestone cave systems accessed via holes in the ocean floor. Dr. Benjamin had made cave diving safer by inventing a piece of diving equipment that allowed the cave diver to have redundancy among the critical life-support breathing hoses, or to come to the rescue of a fellow cave diver who needed gas. Although Dr. Benjamin was nothing less than a hero to hard-core cave divers, he lived in obscurity outside that eclectic community.

As the videotaped program played, the Rouses each took turns imitating Cousteau's distinct nasal French accent, while pointing out the errors. "We took special, extra-large tanks for this dive," Cousteau announced, which made Sue laugh. "Yeah, right. Look at those eighties. God, hasn't he heard of one-oh-four's?" "Eighties" are the standard-size scuba tanks the Cousteau team was using, as opposed to the heavy, extra-large tanks resembling small bombs used by serious cave divers.

Chris continued excitedly, "Listen to this bit: 'We had to use special underwater magnesium torches to light our way. The liquid smoke filled the cave and reduced our visibility.' Ha!" Chris turned to me. "Haven't they heard of high-intensity battery-powered cave-diving lights?"

When one of the Cousteau team threw the spent flare aside, we all went into hysterics. The team was violating the most basic principles of cave conservation at every turn. We had all been drilled with the mantra of cave explorers: "Take nothing but pictures, leave nothing but bubbles." The Cousteau team polluted the cave unnecessarily with their flares, when underwater diving lights would have served them far better, and they threw their trash away in the cave with complete disregard for the environment. That this icon of underwater environmental protection should be doing so in front of an international audience was too much for us. Not only that, but their breathing tanks were woefully inadequate for the dive, with insufficient reserve gas for an emergency, and they did not use the equipment invented by Dr. Benjamin himself—which had become standard in the cave-diving community and which would have made this dive much safer.

Chrissy shook his head. "Man, this is a 'smoke and mirrors' show. We should be out there getting paid to show real cave diving, not this bullshit." All of us were saddened that Dr. Benjamin had succumbed to what we perceived as pressure exerted on him to use improper equipment and techniques for the sake of dramatizing cave diving. Though we were all grateful for the invention of scuba and the environmental awareness promoted by the Cousteau Society, our respect for Cousteau's expertise and authority slipped markedly.

Cousteau's cave-diving show illustrated for us the importance of being humble. Although he and Gagnan had invented scuba, he could have been open to advances made by others after him, most notably Dr. Benjamin, whose invention had made diving safer. Cousteau had chosen to go with diving equipment and techniques familiar to him, instead of learning new approaches. For me, the philosophy of a diver like Marc Eyring contrasted sharply with what Cousteau was up to. A highly experienced cave diver, Eyring always maintained that he was a "rookie." Eyring liked to say, "When you think ya know it all, when you're not ready to be open to new ways of doing things, you're in trouble. This is too unforgiving an environment. I'm always learning, 'cause if I don't, I know I'll be dead soon." Eyring had the philosophy of the true explorer.

Some cave dives require hours of decompression, which means waiting in the water and doing nothing for long periods of time while the body eliminates the excess inert gas. The wait can be excruciatingly boring. Steve Berman frequently endured the long decompressions when he taught cave-diving classes, and also after his pleasure dives.

Some divers pass decompression by reading books or magazines underwater, or even playing chess on magnetic boards. Berman read voraciously in his regular life on the surface, and he wanted something else to occupy his mind during decompression, called deco. Music. That would pass the time far more enjoyably. Berman started working on an underwater system to house his Walkman. Protecting the cassette tape unit from water damage proved easy when he used a round canister that usually housed the battery for an underwater light. The headphone proved to be much more problematic—it was the weak link for the unit that Berman dubbed the Diveman. Steve would cover the small, delicate headphones with plastic wrap, or dip them in heated rubber, which worked for a few dives but then developed holes, allowing water into the headphones, which traveled through the wires and into the tape unit, ruining it.

Frustrated after replacing several flooded Walkman units, Berman mentioned the problem to Reekie, the rotund Canadian. The solution was to find headphones that were made for underwater use. During a trade show, Reekie came upon underwater metal detection equipment that used large, durable, waterproof headphones. Reekie approached the manufacturer: "I'd be interested in placing an order for a quantity of your headphones if you can make them in stereo," he said. The manufacturer thought the request odd, but found no reason to pass up a sale, and agreed to modify the headphones. When Reekie and Berman applied the specialty headphones to Berman's Diveman, the flooding problems were eliminated and the sound was nicely stereophonic.

Berman now enjoyed listening to the surreal music of Pink Floyd's *Dark Side of the Moon* while he decompressed in the crystal-clear water above the entrance to the Ginnie Springs Devil's Cave System. He would frequently do solo dives at midnight, relishing the tranquillity of his own private world. While decompressing, he rested lazily on a tree log that had fallen into the water. He was often illuminated only by the Moon, whose light beams rippled through his exhalation bubbles, which rose like rapidly expanding flying saucers, exploding when they hit the surface. The rippling light cast eerie shadows on the rock entrance below Berman, making fish, crabs, and crayfish seem to dance in a strobe light, appearing, disappearing, and reappearing in an instant.

Berman gave a Diveman to the Rouses as a present, and they took their new toy into the water with the anticipation of children. Chrissy preferred rock music to Berman's more mellow selection, and when he was on deco he could be seen shaking and bobbing his head with the rhythm, and making drum-playing motions with both arms, as if he were in a concert. When Pearl Jam released their album *Ten*, Chrissy found a new favorite song, appropriately called "Even Flow," which he grooved to underwater, in his car, at home—everywhere. In contrast to his son, Chris Rouse preferred to rest quietly, introspectively, after a dive, allowing the time to pass with the steady, predictable flow of the spring's current.

Because it is predictable, the cave-diving environment is in many ways easier to dive than the open ocean. In the open ocean, there are currents and varying weather conditions for a diver to deal with. Although the Rouses had been diving on shipwrecks off the New Jersey coast, most often off the dive boat captained by their advanced diving instructor, Bob Burns, they stayed within the recreational dive table limit of 130 feet for ten minutes, to avoid the necessity of decompressing. When they did exceed the dive table time limits, they had to decompress. In the ocean, that meant hanging on to the dive boat's anchor line, lest they be swept away in the current and lost. It was far easier to decompress while resting on the bottom of a cave floor, or on a tree that had fallen into a cave's entrance, than on an anchor line. During calm ocean conditions, decompression was not difficult, and there was always enough marine life floating past to keep the Rouses occupied. But when the current was running, or the waves kicked up, their arms and shoulders got tired of holding on to the line.

It didn't take them long to adapt the use of the jonline, a nylon rope usually six feet long, to aid in decompression (it was named for its inventor, Jon Hulburt). They would wrap it around the anchor line and then hang on to a loop in the end of the jonline. If the current was strong, they would clip the line to their harness, so their arms wouldn't get sore. In high wave conditions, the anchor line would jerk up and down with the waves, but the jonline would take the stress, not their arms. The device was useful, but it was just another thing that had to be carried all through the dive, even though it might not be needed. And it had to be easily accessible, because if it was needed the diver must be able to reach it and tie it on while holding on to the anchor line; otherwise he could lose his grip on the anchor line and be swept away.

In cave diving, explorers can store anything not needed during the dive itself at whatever depth it might be used. If they require extra tanks for decompression, these can be "parked" somewhere handy and clipped on as the divers make their ascent. Thus cave divers are as streamlined and unencumbered as possible during the actual swimming portion of the dive. This is not possible in open-ocean wreck diving, where the cardinal rule is that every diver has to be self-sufficient at all times. The wreck diver cannot even rely on the dive boat's being there when he gets back, as it is not unheard of for the boat's anchor line to slip free from a wreck in seas that suddenly turn violent. In such a case, if the diver needs extra scuba tanks for decompression, it will do him no good to have those gases attached to the anchor line at the depths where he needs them. A wreck diver must carry all of his required gas bottles with him. Sometimes he places the extra bottles on the outside of the wreck before going inside so that he is more streamlined, carrying fewer items likely to get snagged inside the wreckage. On wrecks with large openings and interiors, the extra tanks can be worn throughout the dive, even during penetrations, but this is the exception rather than the rule.

Most northeast wreck divers—those who dive the plentiful wrecks off the U.S. East Coast north of South Carolina—seek trophies of their explorations, whether live lobsters to eat or shipwreck artifacts to bring up and display. The diver who brings up the largest or the most lobsters on a single dive will proudly reveal his take once back on the dive boat. For sheer impressions, size means everything, and the diver who brings up the biggest lobster is looked on as a very competent diver, even though very large crustaceans do not taste as good and sweet as their smaller counterparts. The diver who comes up with artifacts is seen to have a good eye—and maybe some luck thrown in. To retrieve artifacts consistently is the mark of the truly proficient wreck diver. But to get any of these trophies, a diver has to take a nylon-mesh goodie bag to contain his lobster catch, or a bag with tools if he wants to retrieve artifacts that might require removal. Sometimes, divers take a bag containing tools *and* a mesh bag, to be prepared for whatever they might come across. There is nothing better than to come up with a bonanza of both lobster and artifacts; in the eyes of the hard-core wrecker, hitting Lotto is a close second to such an experience.

The wreck diver who can capture still or moving underwater images is a curious breed, and many regard such persons as anally retentive masochists: The sheer number of things that can go wrong with underwater imaging equipment—and the attention to every detail required before, during, and after a dive—is staggering. Imaging equipment and water do not mix well, and large housings are required to protect each piece of equipment from the slightest drop of seawater. In spite of the heavy housings, it is all too easy to flood a camera, causing thousands of dollars' damage. Or for the camera to malfunction. Or for the diver to have the wrong lens for the underwater conditions or sea life he or she encounters.

By the late eighties, the harsh, unpredictable, cold-water wreck-diving environment had given rise to many different ways of wearing the various equipment that a diver might need during the dive. And also to impassioned arguments about the correct way to wear the equipment, as well as the correct way to conduct the dives themselves. This resulted in cliques of wreck divers who had similar philosophies and dived together. Clashes were inevitable as wreck divers hunted trophies and status.

Ken Reinhart's warning to Chris Rouse that cave diving was a tiger waiting to take a swipe should have included wreck diving. With no Grim Reaper warning signs in and around wrecks, as there had been in the Devil's Cave System at Ginnie Springs, the Rouses were unaware that the tiger also waited in wrecks.

4

Artifact Fever

Two years before John Chatterton discovered the mystery U-boat off the New Jersey coastline, dramatic changes in the world of sport diving were set in motion by a very unlikely candidate. The Californian Michael Menduno arrived on the diving scene full of energy, enthusiasm, and vision that would transform sport diving. With his long, dirty-blond hair, crooked teeth, and slim, nonathletic frame, he seemed an unprepossessing spokesperson for new and daring methods of diving exploration, and when the first issue of his magazine, *AquaCorps*, was distributed in 1989, it was to distinctly unimpressive reviews. But Menduno was a fast study, and his spirited presentations at diving shows across the United States gave voice to divers undertaking extreme dives and elicited curiosity among those who had been content to stay well within the relatively shallow confines of recreational diving.

Before long, *AquaCorps* found its footing, and its combination of attitude, cutting-edge information, dramatic underwater photography, and offbeat graphics made it the bible of diving's avant-garde. The Rouses were keen fans. Whenever a new issue came out—and no reader ever knew when that would be—if the Rouses saw it first, they would call their friends to brief them on the contents, and their fellow divers would do the same if they were the first who could get the word out. Finally, here was a diving publication that boldly probed the world of extreme cave and wreck diving, including the dives now occurring worldwide that were pushing the limits of how far below the surface or into a cave system sport divers could venture.

Like so many developments in diving that had come before it, *AquaCorps* cleaved old-time conservative divers from those who either recognized the sport's inevitable evolution or sought to know how to safely go deeper and stay down longer. Before *AquaCorps*, divers who worked at dive stores and who engaged in deep cave or wreck diving were often warned not to talk to the shop's students or customers about what they dared to do. Many dive shop owners were worried that the trend toward deeper, more complex diving would result in more deaths, which would bring bad publicity for the sport and a downturn in business. As the magazine became more slick in its graphics and presentation, and became more popular, it lent a legitimizing voice to those whom some viewed as diving's pariahs. Suddenly, it was cool to dive deep.

Menduno's *AquaCorps* was aimed at helping sport divers around the world share the information they needed, accelerating the development of underwater exploration. When he ventured to Florida from his base in California, where he dived with a group of marine biologists, Menduno was surprised at the level of diving sophistication he found in the cave-diving community. A trip to Key West, the last island in the chain stretching from the Florida mainland into the northern Caribbean, opened his eyes to the work of his fellow pioneer, Billy Deans, one of the world's leaders in teaching amateurs to dive ever deeper.

Like Glenn Butler, Billy Deans had inherited a passion for diving from his father, who dived recreationally in Florida, where Billy was born and raised. In 1965, the ten-year-old Billy took a scuba-diving course and was certified. He and his father enjoyed exploring the coral reef environment off the Florida Keys. Billy was fascinated by the brilliant colors of the reef and the fish that hustled for food and survival in a constant effort at life maintenance. Existence was elemental under the waves: It was either eat or be eaten, live or die—not so different from how divers themselves had to function in the alien world they visited.

In 1977, Billy started teaching others how to dive. As he became ever more familiar with the reef and its denizens, Billy took his place among them, spear gun in hand, and supplemented his living as an underwater hunter. He soon realized that the larger, more lucrative fish like grouper and yellowfin tuna were to be found in deeper waters, especially around shipwrecks. After diving to 200 feet using air, and then enduring long decompression, Billy and his friend John Ormsby noticed how tired they got as a result of the excess nitrogen remaining in their bodies even after they surfaced. There had to be a better way. They read the two available manuals—both published by the U.S. government—and found that they could make their deep dives safer by breathing pure oxygen at their 20- and 10-foot decompression stops. They religiously followed the U.S. Navy recommendations for in-water oxygen use to prevent toxicity. The oxygen made them feel much less tired after dives. Deans and Ormsby had uncovered intuitive evidence that their dives were safer because excessive nitrogen had been eliminated from their bodies much faster than when they breathed only compressed air during decompression.

Billy Deans read what little he could find, cultivated friendships with the military special warfare divers in the Keys, and learned some of the secrets of mixed-gas diving, which most sport divers knew nothing about. After finding out that Dr. Bill Hamilton and his colleagues at Ocean Systems, Dr. Heinz Schreiner and Dave Kenyon, had developed a computer program for calculating dive times and depths—which divers call dive profiles—using various gas mixtures, the soft-spoken Deans called Hamilton, explained what he was doing underwater, and asked to purchase a set of the proprietary mixed-gas diving tables for use on the U.S.S. Wilkes-Barre, a light cruiser that had been taken out of service and intentionally sunk off Key West in 250 feet of water to make an artificial reef. The idea was that it would attract big game fish and would benefit the local economy by providing sport charter boats with another fishing site. Hamilton was skeptical, worried that Deans's ambition had outstripped his sense of what could be safely accomplished. "Well, Billy, you know that deep diving is *real* dangerous, don't you?" asked Hamilton.

"Yes, I do," Billy replied respectfully, the polite southern boy his father had taught him to be. "We're diving wrecks in the two-hundred-to-two-fifty-foot range on air and we've learned how to make those dives much safer using oxygen during our decompression. We really need the mental clarity helium provides for greater safety at depth. And to do that, sir, we need your diving tables."

"I've been involved with research and commercial oil field diving for, well," Hamilton said with a chuckle, ". . . well, too long, really. And you know what? Those guys have all sorts of safety divers and safety protocols, which is far beyond what you guys are doing in recreational diving, and accidents *still* happen. Why do you think you can do it any better than the pros? And for what? Anything like teaching or catching fish you're getting paid to do, you can do at shallower depths, where it's much safer."

Deans expected to meet some resistance. Commercial divers always scoffed at sport divers, and even thought they were crazy and irresponsible for ever trying to go deep without surface-supplied gas and communications systems. Researchers—and Hamilton definitely fell into that category—were even more incredulous that sport divers would attempt deep diving, which they viewed as suicidal without the elaborate support network that commercial divers like Glenn Butler worked within.

Billy explained that he and Ormsby had developed a good safety system to use on the deep wrecks. Deans and his colleagues would dive in teams, which included in-water safety divers, who would monitor the divers and the dive times. If someone did not surface when he was supposed to, Deans would initiate a search right away. If a diver went low on gas during decompression, the safety divers would give him extra tanks to breathe from. All divers would have oxygen available underwater, supplied from the massive cylinders on the dive boat. From the cylinders, custom-made 50-foot regulator hoses, known as whips, would lead into the water, where they would be secured with clips onto a trapezelike decompression station constructed of ropes, which clearly marked the critical 20- and 10-foot depth stops.

Hamilton always tried to dissuade sport divers from deep diving. Once he was convinced either that the diver knew what he was talking about, or that the diver would go ahead and deep-dive even without his diving tables, Hamilton would give his support. But not without a fair monetary return for his effort. In the late eighties, there were very few people who had decompression tables for trimix (the oxygen-helium-nitrogen mix) diving, and of the tables available to the sport diver, the DECAP computer program was written by the men—Bill Hamilton, Heinz Schreiner, and Dave Kenyon—who had by far the most experience in deep-diving research. "I guess you've persuaded me," Hamilton told Deans. "Just don't be an idiot and get yourself killed. Prove me wrong and show that you sport divers can do it as good as the pros!"

Hamilton's trimix diving tables in hand, Billy Deans explored the *Wilkes-Barre* with the advantage of clarity that helium gases provided. No more five-martini dives for him and his crew. Slowly, over the course of the 1980s, he developed his own training program to teach other divers how to dive deep safely. Using a rigorous set of checklists and approaching the sport like a military commander—to the point of using phrases like "mission objective" instead of "dive plan" and "after-action review" instead of "postdive review"—Deans put his advanced students through a series of progressively more challenging tasks, first in shallow water, and then deeper. Borrowing a page from the military, Billy had students in one phase of their training black out their masks, stand up on the dock fully geared, and go through emergency procedures by feel alone: turn off the gas to a malfunctioning regulator, spit out the bad regulator and put another one in the mouth without using the hands or arms, turn on the gas supply for a scuba tank that had been accidentally shut off, unclip the extra scuba tanks slung under the arm to free them of entanglement, then clip them back on again. During one exercise, the instructors would shut off a student's gas supply, and the student would have to turn it back on. During these simulations on the dock, students usually found themselves "dying" several times. If they could not manage the task, the students would drop the breathing regulator from their mouths and gasp for air. On the safety of the dock, the students were spared the agony of breathing water as they groped for the right equipment knobs before their lungful of air was depleted.

Designed to help students react instinctively during an emergency, Deans's tasks also had the added benefit of humbling them as they came to realize just how easy it is to die underwater.

Deans had learned about death. In 1985, while he was still perfecting his deep-diving techniques, he had helped cut the body of his friend John Ormsby out of a shipwreck after Ormsby, at 210 feet, had rashly changed the dive plan (which had been that they would stay together and would not enter the wreck) and left Deans. Ormsby swam inside the wreck, where he got entangled in cables and drowned. It took several teams of divers two days to free the corpse and bring it to the surface. The sight of Ormsby's pale, death-stiffened body saddened and hardened Billy Deans, who now saw firsthand that survival underwater meant more than just eat or be eaten. Some people thought that Billy was too fanatic in his teaching style and that at five feet five inches tall, the man had a Napoleon complex. But those people hadn't seen John Ormsby's helplessly entangled body wrapped in thick cables, an image that would appear in the instructor's dreams if he fudged attention to any detail in teaching, no matter how small. Billy Deans had to struggle constantly to keep John Ormsby's ghostly image at bay.

Only after a student had demonstrated proficiency in the water and the right attitude did Deans have the confidence to take the diver down to the deck of the U.S.S. *Wilkes-Barre*, at 200 feet, or 50 feet farther, to the ocean floor, where the cruiser's steel carcass loomed surreally above them, bristling with underwater life.

Menduno was fascinated by the procedures and methodology used by elite sport divers like Billy Deans. It was what he needed to fill the pages of his magazine. He moved to Key West, where he relied heavily on Billy Deans and the knowledge he gained watching Billy at work. Ironically, although Menduno was not a sport-diving instructor, he delivered lectures about the art of what was coming to be known as technical diving. Tech divers used gas mixtures to go deeper safer, and they employed new equipment, sometimes inventing their own where standard off-the-shelf gear was deemed inadequate. Menduno duly reported the sport's evolution, and hastened it.

What tech divers were learning still came at the price of divers' lives, both within the sport-diving community and among professionals. Certainly the knowledge propounded by *AquaCorps* might have saved some lives, but the inevitable diving deaths—and the accounts of those deaths being published in *AquaCorps*—led many in the diving world to denounce the more extreme of technical dives as suicidal. It was no coincidence that the ones bad-mouthing these pioneering efforts had a vested economic interest in promulgating a public perception of diving as so safe that even your grandmother could participate—along with the rest of the family. To be sure, a dive to 30 feet in warm, clear water was relatively safe, and was far less demanding than exploring the depths of a cave or a U-boat lying at 200 feet, but even a warm-water social dive meant going into an alien environment using life-support equipment, which meant that even in those relatively benign waters divers occasionally died. Thanks to the loud voice of *AquaCorps* these facts did not drift under the seaweed to be lost in obscurity.

Chris and Chrissy Rouse were fascinated to hear veteran divers talk about the various wrecks they'd explored the way sailors would compare their ports of call. It reminded Chrissy of his friends talking about their favorite bars.

Chrissy started working at Underwater World, the dive shop in Horsham, Pennsylvania, where he and his father had taken their first diving course together. Mike Gucken, the store's owner, liked the confident, efficient way Chrissy repaired and maintained the store's equipment and the regulators brought in by the customers. Chrissy's skill and enthusiasm did not carry over to his work for his father. Although he had taken two years of vocational training to become a diesel-engine mechanic, Chrissy could not operate basic testing devices when his father asked him to trouble-shoot faulty equipment for their excavating business. This drove Chris crazy. Chrissy maintained that he couldn't tune up his own car and always asked his dad to do it, but the son effortlessly performed tune-ups of breathing regulators that had to perform flawlessly to keep their owners alive, and he repaired the buoyancy compensators that prevented divers from plunging into the seabed under the weight of their equipment. It seemed as though Chrissy wanted to be dependent on his father.

When they had returned home from Ginnie Springs in 1989 as full-cave-certified divers (which meant they could penetrate thousands of feet into an underwater cave and even explore new caves and passages), Chris and Chrissy Rouse brought with them new equipment configured in a way that made most divers at the quarry raise their eyebrows in bewilderment and disdain. As the Rouses continued to dive the quarry each weekend for the simple pleasure of diving and to maintain their skills, and as more instructors came with their students for the drudgery of final training, the Rouses stuck out like fresh carrots in a pickle jar. When divers surfaced after seeing the Rouses swimming underwater—Chris and Chrissy moving their legs and fins out and together behind them like frogs as they swam, in perfect cave-diving style—there would inevitably be remarks. "Did you see those guys with the double-tank setups? They must have really bad air consumption! What was that weird way they were swimming?" The instructors were at a loss to explain the Rouses to their students.

The swimming techniques the Rouses had learned in their cave training included the frog kick, which they now used exclusively; it was completely different from moving the legs alternately straight up and down in the flutter kick every basic diver is taught. When they frog-kicked, the Rouses moved horizontally under the water with their heads slightly down, and their legs bent at the knees so that their fins were actually above their heads. The traditional flutter kick encourages a diver to swim with his legs and feet hanging below his torso because it is a person's natural position on land to have his feet beneath him, and he has the same urge underwater. The force of the flutter kick is directed straight down, which stirs massive amounts of silt. So strong is the force of each flutter kick that from above it looks like an aerial view of a bombing run, with silt exploding in expanding circles at regular intervals behind each kicking diver, who leaves small kick craters in the silt. A properly executed frog kick directs the force of the kick up and away from the bottom, preventing silt disturbance and the curtain of blackness it causes.

Chrissy in particular was acutely aware of the differences between his techniques and equipment and those of open-water divers at the quarry, including the instructors: It made him different, just like the time he had to take special classes in school and the other kids teased him. The Rouses' cave-diving training had put them in the forefront of modern sport diving, but they were the only ones at the quarry who seemed able to comprehend that. As father and son swam comfortably about the quarry, refining their skills, they felt like *Homo sapiens* in a landscape populated with Neanderthals. "Hey, Dad," Chrissy once remarked when he surfaced, "did you notice how even the instructors have such terrible technique?"

Looking over at an instructor about to descend with his students, Chris replied, "Yeah, they make it look like a coal mine down there. No wonder we can't see anything underwater."

Just then, an instructor swam up and called out, "Gee, guys, think you've got enough gear on?"

Chrissy got instantly steamed. He and his father had seen the instructor underwater. With his clumsy and dated technique, the guy would be laughed out of Ginnie Springs. Chrissy let out a disgusted groan.

Chris Rouse was proud he'd given his son the best possible diving training and equipment in the sport, and disappointed that other divers—especially instructors—treated them like space aliens. It seemed that in this crowd, unlike at Ginnie Springs, they would always be oddballs. It was a shame, really. Chris liked coming here with his family. The quarry was a great place to keep their diving skills honed when they couldn't go elsewhere. And it provided a convenient, controlled environment to test their equipment, whether new, modified, or recently tuned up. Chris turned to his son and said quietly, "C'mon, Junior, let's go get something to eat. Mom'll have the grill ready." Avoiding the crowds of students and instructors gathered on the floating docks, the two men swam back to shore.

Back in 1987, before Michael Menduno launched *AquaCorps* and a year before the Rouses took their first diving class, what was then the world's most ambitious sport-diving expedition to date occurred at Wakulla Springs in northern Florida. The clear water gushing from the springs had long attracted tourists in glass-bottom boats that glided across the Wakulla Springs mouth, a black hole, looming below them, 300 feet in diameter and 200 feet deep.

Divers had ventured briefly into Wakulla Springs as early as the 1930s, but even as they discovered Pleistocene-era bones and a complete mastodon skeleton, their cumbersome hard-hat suits and their surface-supplied compressed air thwarted any serious exploration of the cave system. In the 1950s, a group of Florida State University students used Jacques Cousteau's newly available scuba apparatus to continue where the hard-hat divers had left off, but soon they too reached their safe diving limits. It was not until the late eighties that Dr. Bill Stone, a former astronaut candidate, fixed his sights on mapping the vast tunnel complex that lay beyond the black hole entrance to Wakulla.

Stone recruited a team of elite cave divers to undertake a concerted effort to reveal the spring's mysteries. In the fall of 1987, a small army of support personnel assembled a base camp on ground, near the water leading to the spring. They hauled in truckloads of huge supply cylinders of breathing gases, which Stone and his team mixed for the deep explorations that would take divers to 300 feet, and perhaps deeper. To help the divers make efficient headway, Stone's team would use diver-propulsion vehicles that resembled torpedoes. These scooters would also transport the multiple scuba tanks the divers required in addition to the many tanks—up to seven—that each one would carry on his person.

After such deep dives, the Wakulla exploration teams would have to endure up to thirty hours of decompression. This fact posed massive problems. Even though the water was 69 degrees Fahrenheit, divers exposed for such long times risked life-threatening hypothermia. Also, research by experts such as Dr. Bill Hamilton had revealed that divers could suffer decompression sickness when they did not maintain proper hydration and nutrition levels. Drinking fluids and eating during decompression was essential to allowing the body to function like a well-tuned machine, pumping out inert gas before painful, debilitating bubbles could form. Stone's solution was a vast, circular, gas-filled in-water habitat that looked like a science-fiction spaceship. Divers would enter the habitat from the open bottom during their decompression and sit on benches, eating, drinking, and making jokes with their colleagues to pass the time. Stone even installed two telephones so that divers could contact the surface support team. The habitat was designed so that the divers would enter at 60 feet and then it was gradually raised from within as they went through their decompression stops.

Even in the relatively calm spring water, nature had other plans for Stone's habitat. The engineer in Bill Stone labored over pages of calculations to figure how the habitat could be safely anchored at each depth. Because it would be gas-filled, the habitat would be buoyant and would seek to shoot to the surface like a balloon. Even chains and cables fixing the habitat to the bottom would be inadequate against the vast forces of lift, and they would snap like string. Cables could prevent the habitat from floating away in the spring's current, but Stone believed that nothing less than lead weight would take strain off the cables and keep the habitat at the desired depth. According to his calculations, it would take almost 19,000 pounds of weight to counteract the lifting force of the gas inside the habitat. As it turned out, he would need 2,000 pounds more.

Bill Stone's ambitious Wakulla Springs project was the manifestation of his vision—many would say obsession—to build a self-contained life-support breathing apparatus that would allow a twenty-four-hour dive on a single breathing unit, including multiple gas switches. Usually, a diver had to carry at least one scuba tank with an attached regulator for each gas required, and he had to replace the regulator in his mouth with the one attached to the gas supply he wanted to breathe next. This required concentration at depth and also meticulously labeling the gas content of each tank before the dive, and then placing those tanks properly either on the diver's person or in the cave. Even then, mistakes were still made, and divers sometimes accidentally switched to the wrong regulator, breathed a gas toxic at that depth, and drowned. A rebreather could help prevent such accidents. The rebreather was a unit that could take the diver's expelled gas and feed it back into the breathing system to extend the time the breathing gas could be safely used. The standard scuba device vents exhaled gas—including carbon dioxide, the deadly by-product of human respiration—into the water, and the amount of time the diver could remain underwater was limited to the number of scuba tanks he could carry. A rebreather would use chemical pellets to absorb, or "scrub," the exhaled gas. Stone's idea was not new. Rebreathers had been around since the 1880s, when the Englishman Henry Fleuss invented the tool to rescue trapped miners. Soon, rebreathers were used in underwater exploration, and then by various militaries around the world. What was new was Stone's plan to build backup systems into all critical components of his rebreather and to use microchip technology to computerize his unit.

The first rebreathers used only one gas, oxygen, which had the advantage of being simple to scrub of carbon dioxide and allowed the largest margin of error; breathable oxygen did not have to have all of the carbon dioxide scrubbed from it in order to sustain human life. But the use of pure oxygen meant that divers were limited to depths of 60 feet for very short times; if they stayed too long or went deeper they risked suffering the toxic consequences of oxygen at depth, and drowning. Air, on the other hand, with only 21 percent oxygen, allowed deeper dives but did not provide enough of a margin for error during the scrubbing process.

Stone's vision of a unit that would allow multiple breathing gases relied on computer processors and sensors that would measure the percentage of each gas in the breathing mix and adjust the mix according to programmed instructions. For example, as the diver went deeper, the percentage of oxygen in his breathing gas would be reduced to prevent oxygen toxicity. Ironically, although the oxygen percentage in the mixture was lowered, the pressure on the diver—and therefore on the gas breathed by the diver—meant that the pressure exerted by the individual gas components being breathed, including oxygen, increased with depth, essentially making the gas a higher-strength, concentrated version of what it was on the surface.

Bill Stone dubbed his rebreather the Cis-Lunar MK-1. He usually awoke at 5 A.M. to work on it before going off to his full-time engineering job. When he returned home he went back to it, stopping long enough only to eat and shower. When exhaustion overcame him, around midnight, he would go to bed and dream about it. The long hours Stone spent obsessing over the MK-1 took a toll on his marriage: His wife left him, taking their children with her. Stone persisted until he had a prototype MK-1 ready for testing during the Wakulla Springs project. Although the bulky 160-pound unit resembled a science-fiction concoction from a fifties B movie—two large cylindrical scrubber canisters and several scuba tanks were mounted on the diver's back while two large, waterproof computer and sensor displays and pressure gauges protruded in front of the diver—it worked. Both underwater and in the decompression habitat, Stone breathed from the unit for twenty-four hours straight.

The Wakulla Springs project lasted several months, including the construction and then dismantling of the habitat. Participating divers, including Sheck Exley, penetrated thousands of feet into the system, to create extensive maps of the vast tunnels and rooms that they flew through on their scooters. In the process of mapping the system they went to depths of 360 feet. Although one of the habitat's internal telephones was used extensively for divers to call in their dinner order—which support divers delivered—the second, an emergency phone, which would be used in the event a diver suffered the bends, was never touched. But Stone was prepared for this eventuality. With the radical dive times and breathing gases, it would take consultation with many decompression experts—including Dr. Bill Hamilton, who was on call—to come up with an in-water method of treating the victim. A severely bent diver who returned to the surface from 360 feet would almost certainly die before reaching the surface.

Michael Menduno liked to call the Wakulla expedition the "Big Bang" of sport diving. With a perfect safety record and—thanks to Hamilton's and his colleagues' diving tables—no incidence of the bends, cave divers everywhere felt proud that Stone's elite divers could accomplish a pioneering endeavor worthy of any commercial or military operation. At Wakulla Springs, Bill Stone and his divers mapped a path to further, deeper cave explorations than ever before accomplished. Stories about the successful Wakulla expedition were confined at first mostly to cave divers themselves, and divers on the project were celebrated as superstars in a quiet, cave-diving way. They were even being given diving equipment by manufacturers so that other divers would see that the sport's best wore Brand X.

Two years later, when the Rouses heard of Stone's legendary exploits, they were fascinated, envious, and determined to win renown for themselves by diving deep.

In the caves, a diver could be Theseus, could dive the labyrinth, master the beast, and emerge victorious. But beneath the open seas, he could penetrate a mythic underworld and, like Aeneas or Ulysses, return to the sunlit realm a hero—trophied, wiser.

Talking to divers who had explored the shipwrecks in the northeastern United States since the 1950s, Chris heard grand tales of ghostly hulls, their cargo and accoutrements—such as portholes, the ship's bell, china plates, and silverware—spilled around them as if from an opened treasure chest. He studied some of the artifacts recovered over the years that were displayed at various dive shops. A few shops even had massive local lobsters, plucked from the ocean complete with their two gigantic claws, mounted as trophies. Chris met veteran divers who would hold out a gnarled finger or thumb and tell him about their underwater battle with the huge crustacean that had mercilessly crushed a finger of the hand that tried to grab them. With a smug, conspiratorial tone, the veteran would warn Chris, "It hurts when the bug grabs ya, but imagine how much worse it'd be if they grab one of your hoses!" Chris thought that it would surely be an adventure to capture one of these delicacies. There were plenty of dive boats that went out regularly all along the East Coast. The ocean seemed to Chris a treasure chest waiting to be relieved of its valuable contents.

With stories of artifacts and lobsters ringing in their ears, the Rouses loaded their several hundred pounds of diving equipment into their van and left Revere, Pennsylvania, at 2 A.M. on June 11, 1989, in order to get their equipment on Bob Burns's charter dive boat *Dina Dee* before its 6 A.M. departure time from Brielle, New Jersey. They headed out to the *Mohawk*, a passenger steamship that sank after a collision in 1935. Because she sank in relatively shallow water—the sand bottom was only 80 feet down—the wreck rose close enough to the surface that she posed a hazard to navigation and had been blown up by the Coast Guard; the explosion had scattered the wreck's hull plates in a haphazard jumble along the ocean bottom. On the ride out to the wreck, many of the passengers were seasick and emitted pained grunts as they vomited over the boat's side. The Rouses' stomachs churned with nausea and nervous anticipation; it was all they could do to prevent themselves from joining their fellow divers at the rail and vomiting.

When they descended 20 feet into the choppy Atlantic waters, the churning sensation in their guts stopped, and they could concentrate on what they saw underwater. As they neared the bottom, an underwater junkyard came into view before them; the wreck's steel hull plates lay mangled and twisted into bizarre shapes, scattered as far as the eye could see, which on this particular day was only 20 feet at best. The dark-green water made the scene more surreal. Their underwater lights, powered by the equivalent of motorcycle batteries, projected a search-light intensity toward the hazy shapes spread before them. Anything that lay beyond 20 feet faded into a dark blanket. Marine life was every-where; fish seemed to dance into and out of the spotlight, choreo-graphed by an unseen, underwater playwright. Whenever Chris or Chrissy approached a lobster lurking under a steel hull plate, it would defiantly move out from the plate, holding its open claws toward them, ready to crush the bubble-blowing invaders. Whenever Chris or Chrissy got close and shone his light directly on it, the bug elusively retreated backward into the wreckage and tightly wedged itself into its den, claws open and menacing. Catching a lobster by hand was not easy. With their forty minutes of dive time almost over, they swam back to the dive boat's anchor line and ascended. They were elated. It was a new world, and they had barely touched it. Their underwater experience and post-dive emotions were a stark contrast to the wretched feeling in their stomachs prior to their descent. Pavlov himself could not have designed a better positive-stimulus machine.

After several weekends spent diving wrecks off the New Jersey coast Chris proposed over dinner that all three of them go on a Caribbean dive trip to the island of Saba being offered by Underwater World. Because they would be living on a luxury dive boat, they could conduct many easy dives in a short period of time without a lot of effort, in brand-new waters where they would be unconfined by cave or quarry walls.

In the Caribbean's warm, calm water, the dive boat's crew mem-bers not only helped the divers get into their equipment before each dive but also replaced the spent scuba tanks between dives, attaching full tanks to their jacket-style harnesses. Instead of having to spend the time to replace their tanks, the Rouses were free to eat and drink the plentiful bounty laid out for the divers by the ship's chef. They felt like diving royalty.

"This sure beats the rockin' and rollin' boat rides to get to the Jer-sey wrecks," Chrissy said to his parents. "God, I never imagined a boat where people aren't getting seasick!"

■   ■   ■

As Chris flew in his small airplane above the Pennsylvania landscape, he could allow himself to marvel at his good fortune: He was his own boss, he had a loving wife and son, and almost as important, he had the time and money to spend scuba diving with his family and to witness landscapes and experience adventures most other people couldn't even imagine. The Rouses had invested heavily in working hard. Chris's successful excavation business had yielded a nice, modest-size house and a private, peaceful parcel of woodland, a plane, a garageful of diving gear, and the heavy machinery he required to stay in business. But Chris could not escape the laws of gravity, and he had to come down eventually.

As the nation's economic engine sputtered in the aftermath of the stock market crash of 1987, the recession glided into Chris's world. By 1990 his customers felt less inclined to install a new swimming pool, fix their driveway, or engage in expensive property upkeep they could delay until more certain economic times. Chris found that demand for his services dropped dramatically, and he struggled financially. He had dreamed of having an excavation business ever since his childhood, when he pushed toy trucks around in the dirt and declared to his older brother, "Wouldn't it be great to have our own *real* construction company? We'll call it Rouse Brothers Construction!" His brother had long ago traded that dream for the supposed security of a salaried desk position—"a *real* job," as their parents always reminded Chris—and now Chris wondered whether he had made the right choice. Though he and Sue had some savings, he never knew when the next paying job was coming in. And when would they arrive at a steady enough pace to pay all of the bills, maintain his heavy machinery, and buy all of the expensive diving equipment they craved? Soon, Chris had to make difficult choices. For lack of money, he grounded his airplane. It sat strapped down on the airfield, stranded for lack of cash.

With excavating jobs becoming scarcer, Chris kept himself busy during the day by replacing worn brakes, clutches, and tires, changing oil and hydraulic fluid, and tuning up the powerful engines of the bulldozer and dump truck. To Sue, he confided that things looked grim. How were they going to keep living if things remained at this slow pace? "Chris, don't worry," Sue reassured him. "Things will get better. We've always worked hard together, and things have always worked out for us."

Chris wasn't sure. "Maybe it's time to think about something besides the excavation business," he told her.

He sold the airplane. "It really hurts," he told John Reekie. "Well, at least I'll be able to pay the bills and keep diving!"

Struggling with his roofing business himself, Reekie understood just how difficult things were for Chris. "Well, at least you got some money for your plane, Chris. But what are you going to do for money once that runs out?"

"I think I'm going to go into the diving business," Chris told him, his voice edged with eagerness. "I love diving. There's got to be a way I can make a living at it. I'm gonna start fixing scooters and making a few pieces of diving equipment to sell."

Chris had faced difficult circumstances before—and he had surmounted them through grit and physical determination. One afternoon back in 1980, when the Rouses were still building their excavation business and living in a trailer home, Chris had gone out to his repair shop, a barn on his property not far from their home, and started to heat a fitting on his bulldozer's hydraulic cylinder so that he could remove and repair the unit. He knew that he had to be careful because the hydraulic fluid and the grease surrounding the fitting were combustible, yet there was no way around it: The fitting was on so tight that the only way to loosen it was by applying high-intensity heat from his welding torch. At first, things went routinely. Then, without warning, the cylinder exploded, sending machinery, tools, and debris in every direction. Chris was hurled across the workshop and slammed into the wall with such force he lost consciousness. The explosion was muffled by the dense woods.

Chris awoke to searing agony on his face and in both hands. Through a haze of pain, he gritted his teeth and inched his way to his home. When he opened the door, ten-year-old Chrissy looked in frozen fear at the apparition coming into the house. His father's face and hands were a mass of black, crumpled skin, and from his body emanated the strange, sickly smell of burned hair and flesh. "Dad, what happened?" he cried out.

"I had an accident, son. Call Henry, next door," his father said between pained grunts. He stumbled into the doorway and collapsed on the floor with an anguished cry. "Please, hurry, Chrissy! It hurts!"

Chrissy ran to the phone and called the neighbor, who arrived a few minutes later, took one look at Chris's face, and spirited both Rouses into his pickup truck. As the three blasted at top speed down the Rouses' dirt road toward Henry's house, Chris groaned in pain at every bump the truck bounced over.

Henry's wife met the trio. She immediately comforted Chrissy. Her young children looked on with wide eyes and open mouths as Chris was rushed into the bathroom. As Henry helped cut the layers of clothing away from Chris's body, his wife, their children, and Chrissy brought in as much ice from the refrigerator as they could carry. Henry filled the bathtub with cold water, and everybody dumped the ice into the tub. Chris was eased into the tub. The water and ice cooled his overheated body and face, and he screamed at the extreme temperature. His hands were now bloody, blackened clumps of flesh. His eyebrows and eyelashes had been seared away, and his mop of hair was singed.

Henry's wife phoned Sue, who was waitressing to help the family pay its bills, and told her what had happened to Chris, and that they were taking him to the emergency room, and to meet them there. In his hospital room, Chris looked at his concerned wife through a thickly bandaged skull. He could not touch her through the layers of gauze bandages on his hands and arms.

When Sue got back home that night after retrieving Chrissy from Henry's house, both mother and son were shaken. "Is Dad going to be okay?" Chrissy asked, crying.

Sue took a deep breath and hugged her child. "We need to help Dad when he gets home. He can't use his hands to do anything, and everything hurts him."

Chrissy looked up at his mother with his saddened brown eyes. "I want to help, Mom. I want Dad to be okay again."

When Chris was released from the hospital two days later, he came home an invalid requiring constant care. His pain was blunted only with regular doses of powerful painkillers that numbed both body and mind. He also needed antibiotics to prevent his first-, second-, and third-degree burns from turning into massive infections. Chrissy was old enough to tell time, and Sue drew a large clock on a piece of paper, indicating which pills Chris needed to take and at what time. She arranged her waitressing schedule so that either she or Chrissy was with Chris at all times. The elder Rouse lay in bed, obediently swallowing the medicine his wife or son put on his tongue. Chris also had to be assisted with every bodily function, and his family helped with that. At ten years old, Chrissy Rouse saw that even his father could need help and that he wasn't always strong. His father had always helped him, but now the child was father to the man. Chrissy's world had altered dramatically. It confused and frightened him.

When Chris Rouse recovered, two months later, he returned to work and went on to build his house three years later. As Chrissy helped his parents with the building project he saw his father as strong again. Things were back the way they should be.

As a young man pushing twenty, a high school graduate who hadn't gone to college, Chrissy appeared casual, laid-back, happy-go-lucky. But inwardly, he knew how fragile his world was, and how easily it could change in an instant. Just as his father had once needed him, so now he maintained a reliance on his father and a reluctance to become truly independent. For a long time he lived at home. A series of minor car crashes left him in debt to his parents, who always chided him for his driving accidents, but who nonetheless lent him money to pay for another vehicle and the resulting steep insurance increases.

Both Chris and Sue had driven with Chrissy enough to know that his attention would easily drift from the road. One time, with Sue as Chrissy's passenger, he completely turned his head to look at her and talk. She noticed that his full attention was now on her, and instead of just glancing in her direction, Chrissy seemed to have forgotten about the winding country road they were on. "Chrissy, keep your eyes on the road!" Sue screamed in alarm. She also noticed that her son's attention would completely turn to the radio or the tape deck when he wanted to change the music. Although frightened, she hoped that Chrissy's behavior was just a sign of an inexperienced new driver, not a young man who still had the symptoms of attention deficit disorder. After his car crashes, both parents hoped that their son had been shaken enough to pay greater heed to the necessity to focus on his driving.

Chrissy just shook off his crashes as freak accidents that could have happened to anyone. His blasé attitude and air of entitlement grated on his father. When he was Chrissy's age he already had a two-year-old, and now here was his shaggy son enjoying a freedom Chris had been denied.

Even Chrissy's choice of friends reflected both his carefree attitude and his dependence on older father figures. Two of Chrissy's pals, Tim Stumpf and Paul Curtin, were both about ten years older than he was. Stumpf was already divorced, and Curtin's marriage was in the midst of dissolving. Both older men lived in Tim's house, not far from Underwater World, where they all worked. Tim and Paul were aggressively making up for time they felt they had lost to the responsibilities of marriage. Tim's house was like a college fraternity, with people coming and going at all hours, and raucous parties long into Friday and Saturday nights.

Tim and Paul liked Chrissy's easygoing nature and were amused by his innocence. Both men arranged to get Chrissy some fake IDs, so that he could join them at the local bars, where the legal entrance age was twenty-one. Chrissy, feeling comfortable with his diving buddies, eagerly flashed his fake ID and joined in the beer drinking. One night early in their friendship, after Chrissy had swallowed several beers, Tim and Paul looked smugly at each other and suggested that it was time for Chrissy to meet some girls. "Sure, I'm up for that!" said a happy, grinning Chrissy. He eagerly went up to a girl they all agreed was attractive. From a distance, Tim and Paul watched Chrissy in animated conversation.

"Well, he sure has the right spirit," Tim said.

"Yeah, he's not shy, that's for sure," Paul agreed.

Soon Chrissy rejoined his friends. "Well, what happened?" Tim asked. "Did you get her number?"

"No. She has a boyfriend," Chrissy told him.

Both Tim and Paul agreed that it was just bad luck. They immediately pointed Chrissy toward another woman, and off Chrissy went to dive into the unknown. But over the course of the evening, Chrissy never seemed to get anywhere with the women he tried to meet. "Chrissy, not every one of these girls can have a boyfriend!" Paul exclaimed. "Tim and I have seen these girls in here a lot, and most of the time they're not with guys at all. What are you saying to them, anyway?"

"Well, I don't know. They don't seem to be too interested in diving," replied Chrissy.

"Diving?" Tim blurted out.

"You're talking to them about *diving*?" Paul asked.

"Yeah, what else is there to talk about?"

Tim and Paul both agreed that some coaching was in order. With the help of the older men, and thanks to his natural charm, Chrissy was soon meeting women successfully.

Because Tim's house was conveniently located not far from Underwater World, Chrissy started spending more time there, staying over after parties or after ventures to the local bars. Even though Chrissy tried to broaden his conversations with women beyond diving, it was still his main focus. And there were plenty of women to be met through the dive shop and the classes he assisted with. Most of the women who regularly showed up at Tim's parties were divers, and most of the time Tim, Paul, and Chrissy met those women through Underwater World. In spite of Chrissy's beer-induced eagerness to meet women at the bars, he had far more success when his passion for diving and women were combined.

"Bernie, I'd kill to do the *Doria* the way you guys did," Chris Rouse said to me when I called him in the summer of 1990 at Steve Berman's suggestion. Anyone who dives the North Atlantic has to be intrigued by the wreck that stands out above all others: the Italian luxury liner *Andrea Doria*, a magnificent and perilous carcass of a ship that has been proclaimed "the Mount Everest of scuba diving" since it went down in 1956, approximately eighty-five miles off Nantucket.

The *Doria* was not the fastest of ocean liners, but it was a floating monument to Italian artistry. The works of art commissioned specially for the vessel and its sleek lines earned it the nickname "Grande Dame of the Sea." Aesthetically, the *Doria* is to today's bulky, boxlike cruise ships what a Ferrari is to a garbage truck. On the night of July 25, 1956, on its one hundredth crossing of the Atlantic, it collided with another ocean liner, the *Stockholm*. Both vessels had seen each other on radar while they were over seventeen miles apart, and they had acknowledged each other in radio messages. But in the fog that lay off the Nantucket coast as the *Doria* made its way to New York City, the *Stockholm*, which had a reinforced bow, sliced through the side of the Italian liner. Fifty-six people lost their lives in the collision. As the *Stockholm* reversed its engines, tons of water rushed into the gaping hole in the *Doria*'s side and the luxury ship immediately began to list heavily. The captain gave the order to abandon ship. Other vessels came to the stricken liner's aid and rescued most of the passengers and crew. The *Stockholm* itself saved many passengers of the ship it had rammed.

The *Doria*'s demise was slow enough for photographers and television crews to hire planes and circle the mortally stricken vessel, capturing every moment of its death as it rolled over onto its side and sank. So great was the air traffic over the site that the Federal Aviation Administration had to set up a special zone around the *Doria,* and air traffic controllers slotted times when the various news agencies could have access to it. Never before had such a prominent ship been captured on film while it sank. Still and moving images captivated the public worldwide. Harry Trask of the *Boston Herald* captured a series of photos of the *Doria* in its very last moments, and his shot of the ship with only one propeller visible won him the 1956 Pulitzer Prize for news photography.

The legend of the *Doria* as a diving destination began just hours after its sinking when Peter Gimbel, on assignment to get photos for *Life* magazine, became the first diver to visit the wreck. The *Doria* represented the envelope of what divers could reach with relative safety because of its depth at 240 feet, water temperatures in the low forties, sharks, the currents around the site, and the unpredictable, rapidly changing conditions above, on the ocean's surface. Gimbel, the heir to a department store fortune, became obsessed with the wreck. He would eventually spend a great deal of money over the years in his quest to bring up the purser's safe and the treasure it was rumored to contain. He eventually hired a commercial diving company to cut a hole into the *Doria*'s side and bring up the safe, one of seventeen aboard the vessel. The expedition proved difficult and the safe was elusive, even to some of the world's most experienced divers with their elaborate support team and equipment. When the safe was finally retrieved and then opened during a live national television broadcast, most people were disappointed: Instead of fabulous jewels, the safe contained only clumps of sodden paper currency.

Sport divers view a wreck—especially one as large and prestigious as the *Doria*—as a treasure trove, even if it does not promise jewels and gold. At first, starting in about 1965, only a boat or two would occasionally go to the wreck. In 1970, Captain Steve Bielenda, the self-professed "King of the Deep," first began taking sport divers to the *Doria* on his boat, the *Wahoo*. By 1975, Bielenda on the *Wahoo* and then Bill Nagel on the *Seeker*—Nagel was the alcoholic captain who would later take Chatterton and then the Rouses to the *U-Who*—were going to the site regularly, twice a season each. In those days, a diver had to be invited by the boat captain to pay his money to go on the trip. Simply having the money to go was not enough to get on the boat. Usually, a captain watched divers as they dived progressively more challenging wrecks on the coastline, over a period of several years. If the diver was well liked and exhibited good skills and judgment, he'd get an invite. To dive the *Doria* was to enter an elite league.

The *Doria* offered not only bragging rights but trophies. Skilled divers brought up brass-framed windows from the promenade deck, or dishes bearing the crest of the company that had had the liner built, the word ITALIA with a crown over it. Chinaware from the first-class section were prized; the plates had a gold band running around the edge and an elaborate Chinese scene painted in the center.

There are many dangers in diving the *Doria*, some more obvious than others. Getting to the *Doria* in the first place is half the challenge. Blue sharks used to be common but today are rarely seen during dives. The larger sharks were cautious toward the newcomers blowing bubbles, but the smaller, younger ones were fearless, frequently bumping divers and charging them, seeking to establish a pecking order among themselves and the divers. Sometimes a diver has to press his back-mounted tanks against his buddy's, so that they were back-to-back and could use their heavy mallets or crowbars to fend off the most aggressive of the circling sharks. It would take a well-timed, well-placed blow on the shark's nose to stop the harassment. Luckily, no divers have ever been bitten while diving the *Doria*.

The dangers were such that over the years only a small group regularly dived the wreck, though many others were lured by both the challenge and the prestige among divers that would be granted after successfully visiting the ocean liner. For some, the lure proved too much, and they paid with their lives. This only lent the wreck more mystique.

Depth is one factor that makes the *Doria* challenging, just as height is for Everest. The shallowest part of the *Doria* rests in 165 feet, over three martinis. The deepest part, at 240 feet, is like having just under five martinis. The depth combines with the cold and the limited visibility to increase the narcosis effect; warm-water dives with clear visibility are much easier for the diver mentally and physically. Even the most experienced divers succumb to the effects of the Martini Law, and an individual diver may be affected to a greater or lesser degree from one day to the next.

Current is another danger, one far less obvious than depth. There is no way to know what the current will be like below the surface, or how it will change on the surface during the course of a dive. Divers have experienced currents on the *Doria* at different intensities—and even angles—at various depths during a single dive. Conditions can change within minutes. A diver struggling while fighting the current risks deadly levels of carbon dioxide buildup in his system, if he does not inhale and exhale deeply enough to purge the toxic gas from his body. At least one *Doria* diver has been swept off the anchor line, fought to get back, passed out, and drowned.

The *Doria* also has a way of inducing artifact fever, an obsession with retrieving a trophy from the wreck that leads a diver to take excessive risks. This is especially dangerous when diving deep. Yet the *Doria* does not give up its treasure easily. When John Ormsby came aboard the *Wahoo* with Billy Deans in 1985, he was a highly skilled warm-water wreck diver with many dives to 250 feet behind him. The experienced northeast-wreck–diving crew warned him to modify his equipment. He had lots of clips on his harness, which he used for all his backup equipment. He was told that with those clips all over his harness, he would get caught on a cable or on the fishermen's nets that were by now draped all over the wreck. Ormsby snapped back that he was an experienced wreck diver and liked the way his gear was configured. During his dive, even though he had not planned to penetrate the wreck, he swam inside the first-class section; when he did not reappear at the anchor line on time, the other divers there feared the worst. When word was relayed topside, a search team went down.

Ormsby was found at a depth of just over 200 feet, and about 30 feet inside the wreck. Apparently, a large cable caught on one of his harness clips, and when he turned to find where he was caught, the cable tightened around him like a boa constrictor. He ran out of air and drowned while hopelessly entangled in the cable.

The Rouses were especially intrigued by the stories Steve Berman and I told about our experiences on the *Andrea Doria*. When I first dived the *Doria*, in the summer of 1990, I had been full cave certified for a year and had been applying cave-diving techniques to northeast wreck diving for the previous two years. Steve Berman and I decided that we would treat the *Doria* as a giant steel cave, and use cave-diving techniques to penetrate deep inside the wreck. We dived from Bielenda's *Wahoo*. Gary Gentile was one of the crew members. Gentile had made over 100 dives to the wreck, and had written a book on this site, *Andrea Doria: Dive to an Era*. Berman and I had each read the book scrupulously and were excited that Gary was on board because we could double-team him with questions.

Berman and I jumped from the *Wahoo* and descended to the wreck. The strong current quickly wore me out, and although the intact vessel looked magnificently tempting resting on its side, I aborted the dive almost as soon as I reached the wreck. Berman seemed to have all his energy, but he ascended with me without question. When we were back aboard the *Wahoo*, I apologized to him. "Shoot, don't worry about that," he told me. "The first thing is safety. If anyone ever says anything negative to me when I abort a dive, I'll never dive with him again. Let's just focus on having a good second dive." I was relieved, and my respect for Berman increased.

On the second dive, we went inside the wreck, swimming horizontally at 202 feet. The wooden walls between cabins had disintegrated, allowing us to swim among the remaining oval steel cabin supports through what was once a row of adjoining passenger cabins. Lying everywhere was light-brown silt and debris—all that remained of cabin paneling and bed mattresses, sheets, and blankets. Electrical cables dangled in our way. Because the ship rested on its side, everything was skewed at a 90-degree angle. Bathroom sinks and bathtubs were attached to the wall on my left, which had once been the floor of this deck. In the distance, I saw a faint light and what looked like another diver. My heart beat faster. We were 50 feet inside the wreck, and I wondered who else would be this far in—and coming at me from the other direction. As I swam closer I saw my reflection in a mirror, and had to laugh. I turned to Berman and signaled our retreat. On the return, Steve picked up three dishes; since he had no "goodie bag," he deposited them in the all-purpose bag clipped to my harness. Back on the *Wahoo,* one experienced *Doria* diver looked at us, shocked. "Wow, you guys got some artifacts. Not bad for rookies!"

Bolstered by our initial success, Steve and I planned a more challenging third dive. We decided to drop straight down a passageway we had passed previously about 30 feet inside the wreck. The vertical passageway was huge, and our powerful dive lights did not penetrate the blackness to the bottom. Our descent took us to 238 feet—almost five martinis—and we then swam along a horizontal passageway, with Steve leading and paying out guideline from the reel, just as we would in cave diving. We were about 150 feet inside the wreck when I spotted glass and crystal trays and dishes scattered in the fine silt on the floor. Rather than signal Steve before reaching for any goodies, the way I was supposed to, I allowed artifact fever to get the better of me. I kneeled on the bottom and in a frenzy proceeded to stack a number of trays and dishes, then put a wineglass on top of the stack for good measure.

As soon as I settled into the bottom, and then again when I grabbed the artifacts, the fine silt on the passageway floor billowed around me like a brown, atomic mushroom cloud. I was working by feel. I unclipped my goodie bag and prepared to put the entire artifact stack into it. Just then, I felt a furious pull on my calf, which almost knocked me facedown into the silt. Turning, I moved into the direction of the tugging and when my mask came within inches of Berman's I could see him, and I heard him yelling, "Let's get the hell outta here!" I turned to try and grab a dish, to show him what I was doing, but he quickly grabbed my leg again, more insistent this time, and repeated the command. I gave up on both the artifact stack and my open goodie bag lying next to it. And then I noticed Berman swimming around me, frantically removing white guideline wrapped around my body. Apparently, when I had dropped down to grab the artifacts, one of the tank valves behind my head had gotten caught on the line, and as I moved around for the best spot to land on the bottom, I wrapped the line around myself.

Perhaps another, less experienced diver, or one of less fortitude, would have left me there. Something similar had happened to a diver on *U-853*, the German U-boat that lies off Rhode Island. He had gotten tangled in his guideline; he made it out of the wreck, but he was still tethered to the line running through the wreck. He signaled to his buddy for help. His buddy later said that the entangled diver had panicked and flailed wildly, which caused the unentangled diver to leave instead of cutting the line with his dive knife or disentangling him. On the boat, the buddy gave several accounts of the incident, and it could not be determined exactly where the entangled diver was. The only crew member on the boat refused to dive in a rescue attempt, saying that it was against recreational diving guidelines to dive without a buddy. Coast Guard divers were called in and eventually recovered the body, still tethered to the wreck, billowing in the current like a macabre flag.

Berman and I made it back from our third *Doria* dive safely. The stack of artifacts and my goodie bag still inside the wreck called for recovery. Back on the *Wahoo*, outside the boat's main cabin, Berman and I discussed the dive while we looked out over the ocean. Steve Bielenda was curious about our hushed conversation and came over to ask how our dive had gone. I briefly explained what happened. Bielenda listened intently, then gave us a big, knowing grin. "Well, you did the right thing, left the artifacts and got yourselves out. Sounds like you guys have some unfinished business on the *Doria*. Comin' back?"

When he heard our plans to come back with a team of divers and dive the wreck using mixed gas, he chuckled and said, "Yeah, the *Doria*'s got ya now. It does that."

The *Andrea Doria* was like Wakulla Springs in the sense that both dives were deep and challenging, and those who successfully dived these sites were held in high regard within the diving community. And they walked the earth with the self-assurance that they were different from the rest of humanity, in the same way that elite, military experimental test pilots knew they were different. In the diving community, mixed-gas diving was a shift in the way things were done among amateur divers, and gas divers were now the top dogs, just as the space program had provided a shift in who was top dog in the world of cutting-edge flying back in the sixties.

Over the next year, Berman and I put together the expedition we called Team Doria. We invited a group of divers to participate who brought to wreck diving the expertise they had gained in caves. When I invited the Rouses to join the Team Doria expedition, they jumped at the opportunity to use their skills on the prestigious wreck. Chris Rouse liked my plans, and he remarked thoughtfully, "A steel cave? What a concept! That's gotta be something to dive in! And a couple of those *Doria* dinner plates would sure look nice on my mantelpiece."

5

Team Doria '91

June 27, 1991. Captree Boat Basin,
south shore, Long Island,
midway between New York City and Montauk Point.

CHRIS AND CHRISSY ROUSE were avid divers who were increasingly applying cave-diving principles to their wreck diving as their skills and desires increased. When they had first taken the advanced diving class with Bob Burns and then ridden with him on his charter boat, the *Dina Dee,* to some of the wrecks off the New Jersey coast, they were content to mimic the gear configuration of the average recreational northeast-wreck diver, which consisted primarily of a wetsuit for insulation, a single tank of air, and a small emergency reserve tank, known as a pony bottle. This gear sufficed for the Rouses' dives to wrecks that lay shallower than 130 feet, the maximum depth limit recommended by diving certification agencies for recreational divers in the United States. As the Rouses grew more proficient and comfortable diving wrecks, they adopted the equipment configuration of the more advanced diver, wearing two primary tanks

of air on their backs to allow longer, deeper dives and provide an ade-
quate reserve in case of an emergency.

The Rouses' cave dives had always required that they use at least two
tanks of equal size because of the "rule of thirds," one of Sheck Exley's
ten most important cave-diving precepts: Divers should use no more
than one third of their gas supply to go into the cave, save one third for
the exit, and reserve another third strictly for an emergency. This meant
that the Rouses needed to carry very large scuba tanks to successfully
explore deep inside a cave. In the northeast-wreck–diving environment,
the double-tank configuration had been used for years by divers who
engaged in the open-ocean decompression required after exploring a
deep-water wreck, or after spending a long time on a shallow-water
wreck. At the maximum recreational depth limit the Rouses would have
had only ten minutes of bottom time before encountering mandatory
decompression, according to the U.S. Navy diving tables. A stay of fifteen minutes at 130 feet required only a one-minute decompression
stop at 10 feet. A twenty-minute stay required four minutes at 10 feet, a
twenty-five-minute stay required ten minutes at 10 feet, and a thirty-
minute stay required twenty-one minutes of decompression, with the
first three minutes of that time spent at 20 feet. The Rouses followed
the more conservative decompression schedules suggested by their
wrist-mounted computers, and their decompression times were longer
than the U.S. Navy tables, whose figures were based on the work done by
the Scottish physiologist John Scott Haldane for the British Admiralty
in the early 1900s. Haldane's work was a remarkable breakthrough in its
day, but modern research revealed finer points of human physiology
not reflected in his decompression tables.

Now, in the environment of a challenging wreck like the *Doria*, cave
divers, including the Rouses and me, would make the most of our experience in caves through what some wreck divers thought were radical
equipment configuration changes, especially the extra tanks of air that
we attached to our diving harnesses and wore under our arms. For a
long time, cave divers had carried extra gas for deeper cave penetrations.
The extra tanks were known as stage bottles because we would breathe
one third of their contents and then leave—or stage—them in the cave,
until we retrieved and breathed from them as we exited. Of course, we
couldn't "stage" them in open water, and had to carry them with us.

When wreck divers saw the Rouses or me gearing up on a dive boat, they looked at the extra tank of air we each carried under an arm and wondered what in the world we were doing. Some boat crew members who observed us suiting up thought that our extra equipment was too much for a diver to carry, and that we would get ourselves into trouble in the demanding and ever-changing realm of ocean wrecks. The worst comments came when other wreck divers saw us attaching green scuba bottles prominently stenciled in white lettering with the word OXYGEN; "This guy's an accident waiting to happen," I would hear. Most wreck divers were unaware that breathing oxygen at the 20- and 10-foot decompression stops is extremely beneficial because it allows the body to eliminate the excess nitrogen more efficiently and quickly. Carrying oxygen during a dive was voodoo, according to wreck divers. They thought it invited accidents because it was too easy for a diver to grab the regulator attached to the oxygen bottle by mistake and breathe the gas at depth; the convulsions from oxygen toxicity would inevitably cause drowning. But the cardinal rule in wreck diving had always been self-sufficiency: A diver was supposed to carry everything he needed during the dive, including all his decompression gases, which for wreck divers usually meant just air. Pure oxygen was a gas most wreck divers did not understand, and they were afraid of it.

The Rouses, like the rest of the Team Doria '91 divers, had readily embraced new approaches to the sport of wreck diving, even though the new methods remained controversial—even to our crew members, as we soon found out. Besides carrying oxygen during the dive for decompression, all of us believed in using guidelines when we were exploring a wreck, a practice that caused more conventional wreck divers to voice vehement opinions about whether using a guideline was safe or suicidal.

"If there's a line in my way, I'm gonna cut it," the crew member Hank Garvin announced as we prepared to set off toward the *Doria* on a cool June afternoon. I knew his view, if not his vow, was shared by the crew members on the *Wahoo*, not to mention most other veteran northeast-wreck divers. I had chartered Steve Bielenda's 55-foot *Wahoo* for the Team Doria expedition, even though I knew exactly what Hank and the rest of the boat's crew believed about using guidelines on wrecks.

Over the past year, the burly Garvin and I had already survived several heated debates about the use of guidelines inside wrecks. Garvin, with thirty years of diving experience, had seen too many deaths among wreck divers, and recovered too many bodies, not to have forceful opinions about every aspect of the sport. He knew first-hand how precarious wreck diving was; he knew that a diver who had too much to contend with—including the rapidly changing underwater environment and all of his equipment—could easily get overwhelmed and make suicidal, even murderous, mistakes. To him, a guideline was another piece of equipment for the diver to manipulate, something else that could malfunction, entangle, or strangle a hapless diver.

"Look, Hank," I said, glaring at Garvin as we watched the *Wahoo*, being loaded with provisions, "we've chartered the boat to do it our way. We've been planning this expedition for a year. Whatever you think about guidelines, it's our call on how we choose to dive."

"Yeah, sure, you can dive the wreck any way you want to," said Hank, nodding grimly. "You know that I think everything can have its place. Most times a guideline is just a crutch. It's a way for a diver to bypass the time and the number of dives you need to get the experience to know a wreck so well you could get out of it with your eyes closed without relying on a guideline." Garvin had repeated this viewpoint to divers so often it had become his mantra. Now, the older Garvin sounded almost fatherly. "And Bernie, you know what happens when someone relies on a line and it gets cut, don't you?"

"Yeah, Hank, we've been over this before."

"Yeah, well, then you know that the guy relying on the guideline that's not there will end up *dead.*" Garvin paused for effect. "You're okay, Bernie. I'd hate to have to recover your body. It'd ruin my day. It really would."

I chuckled. "Thanks for the sentiments, Hank. But you won't be needing to recover my body."

"Really? What you and Berman did last year on the *Doria* was crazy! How far did you go in? One hundred feet? Two hundred? On your *first dives*?"

"You still don't get it, do you, Hank?" By now I was frustrated. "To us, the *Doria* is a giant steel cave."

Hank raised his chin toward the heavens and shook his head. "You and Berman may be very comfortable and have lots of experience inside of caves. But the *Doria* is *not* a cave. And the open ocean is not as predictable as a cave. And now you've got a whole *team* of guys to do this silly stuff?" Garvin let out an exasperated breath. "Man, there's gonna be a spider web of guidelines inside the wreck. Maybe one of you guys won't get caught up in it. But what about the rest of us?" Garvin and the other crew members would be diving the old-fashioned way, alongside Team Doria.

"Hey, if there's a guideline you feel is in your way, go somewhere else on the wreck," I told Garvin. "We're paying for this jaunt, and the dives are for us—not for you and the crew!"

Garvin, like most other northeast-wreck divers, preferred to use the dive strategy known as progressive penetration. This entailed venturing into a wreck only one body length, making yourself totally familiar with the area before moving two body lengths inside on another dive, and getting familiar with that area before going farther. In theory, it would take many dives before a person got far enough inside so that he could no longer see the light filtering in from the hole where he had entered. For longer penetrations, some divers teamed up: One diver would swim in to the point where he could barely see the exit, then would remain there and shine his light toward the other diver, who would continue farther inside the wreck. The first diver acted like a lighthouse, guiding his buddy back to safety with his beacon.

Because most wreck divers did not have training in the use of a guideline, they were likely to shun its use. Recreational instructors teaching the sport usually had limited experience with guidelines, and most were adamant in teaching that wreck penetration was far too advanced and dangerous for sport divers. That was the official stance of recreational-diving training agencies. Those who wanted to use a line usually had to experiment without benefit of an instructor. Under such circumstances, unpleasant guideline experiences were inevitable. It was just too easy for the line to slip over its reel, get caught in the spinning mechanism, and jam. The braided nylon line could also swell as it absorbed water, come off the reel, and float in the water like a big wad. Waves on the surface and surges underwater could toss the diver and his guideline around like clothes in a washing machine, which also caused the line to unravel and float in the water like a net threatening to snare the diver. Rather than train in the use of the line at a shallow site, such as a quarry, and make modifications to the reel, most wreck divers gave it one or two tries in the challenging wreck-diving environment and then quit in frustration. A guideline is a tool toward safer and more efficient underwater explorations, not an end in itself. Even a diver trained in its use might decide not to use this tool on a particular wreck dive. Sometimes the line presented more of a potential problem than it was worth, especially when you were digging for artifacts in a tight area of a shipwreck.

At its best, a guideline is not just an aid but a lifeline. I found out just how important a guideline was to me when I decided *not* to use one during a dive for some artifacts. In 1989, I was diving on the U.S.S. *San Diego,* a World War I armored cruiser that sank off Long Island's south shore in 1917 after hitting a mine laid by the German submarine *U-156.* The 500-foot-long *San Diego* lies upside down in 110 feet of water and is one of Long Island's most popular wrecks. Most divers do not venture inside the wreck, nor do they have to if they want to get an impressive experience of the warship. The first time I dived the *San Diego* I was struck by the 50-foot visibility, the vastness of the wreck, and the large schools of fish that swam around and into the hulk. Swimming above the ship, and along its side, I was captivated by the massive steel hull plates that swung out from the top of the wreck as if on a hinge and then back again, propelled by the water's powerful surge. Some divers in the water with me did go inside the wreck, and their exhalation bubbles combined with the rhythmic movement of the hull plates to make it seem like a breathing dragon lying on the ocean bottom. With a sight like that, many divers did not need to go inside and risk their lives. But the chance to retrieve artifacts proved a great lure for others of us to venture into the vast interior.

After diving the *San Diego* several times and making gradual penetrations into it, I overheard one of the dive boat's crew talking about the dish room. Intrigued, I asked about it. The crew member told me that it was 30 feet inside the wreck at a depth of 90 feet. He described how I could get to it. I took the advice of the experienced wreck diver and elected not to use my guideline reel in spite of my basic cave-diving training. Instead, the crew member advised me to hold on to the side of the room's entranceway when I swam in so that my other hand would be free to dig for the dishes. When I dug for my prizes and created the inevitable silt-out, he explained, it would be easy to get out of the room because my hand would be resting at the opening. He felt that a guideline would only get me entangled.

When I swam into the dish room, I found myself several feet above the silt-covered floor. Dropping into the room, I moved away from the entrance while digging for artifacts with my left hand. I moved my right hand to a collapsed beam inside the opening. As soon as my digging arm plunged up to the elbow into and out of the thick, Jell-O–like silt, the room turned black. I put my dive light against my mask and could still see nothing, including any sign of the light. I kept digging and found the remnants of a ceramic water pitcher, which I recognized by feel from having seen a number of these artifacts displayed at dive shows and in a museum. It was a worthy prize.

When I went to exit the room, I felt my way along the wall for the hole. It was not there. I suddenly felt very much alone, and very far removed from the safety of the dive boat. I heard a loud pounding over my metallic exhalation: My heart was beating faster and I had to concentrate on controlling my breathing rate lest my precious air run out too soon.

I remembered Marc Eyring's words, during my basic cave-diving training, about silt-out emergency procedures: "Don't keep your eyes open in a silt-out. Your mind will only want to make up things for you to see. Keep your eyes closed and concentrate on where you think you are. Just open your eyes occasionally to see if you've swum out of the silt."

With my eyes tightly closed, I swam slowly and used my hands to feel the room's interior. I had to keep fighting the fear that I would stick my hand into the face of one of the wreck's many resident eels, and get bitten. I worked my way along the wall of the room, and then along another wall. Opening my eyes, I could see that the silt was not black here but only a dusty brown, which allowed me to see a little. I checked the air in my primary tank, and noted I had enough to continue searching without having to breathe from my smaller emergency air tank. My depth gauge read 90 feet. The only problem was the tight area I now found myself in; it seemed like a steel coffin, and the thought made me shiver. Was I still in the dish room, or had I somehow swum into another area, or even to a different deck level? I forced myself to focus, turned around, and faced a wall of black silt suspended in front of me like a curtain. With dread, I knew I had to go back through the curtain because it was the way I had come: The black silt indicated where I had been digging.

I closed my eyes and slowly swam forward with my right hand pressed against the side of the wreck. I knew that if I lost physical contact with the wreck, I would get completely disoriented and could end up getting turned around, making my exit virtually impossible. With my right hand on the side of the wreck, I waved my left hand around to try to feel something. I recalled hearing a crew member tell his dive buddy about this room, explaining that there would be a bunch of wooden shelves to one side of the opening leading out of the room. Now, my left hand came into contact with the shelves and my heart jumped. Carefully, I felt the space between shelves, and continued to move along slowly. Then, I felt nothing with my left hand, and I made a big circle with it. Still nothing. This had to be the exit! Excitedly, I swam forward and my head crashed into the back of what had been a large wooden dish cabinet. I could hear the dull thud.

I groaned in bitter disappointment and cursed in anger. I stopped what I was doing, allowing myself time to think and get control of my emotions. Pressing my right hand against the side of the cabinet, I backed up and continued my search, waving my left hand about, trying to feel for another shelf. I remembered that I had dropped into the room when I came in, and decided to swim higher up, and after I went about two feet up, I again continued searching for the exit, moving to my left. With my right hand pressed against the wall of the room, I came to a spot where my left hand felt nothing. I swam forward very slowly this time and alternated between putting my left hand in front of me like a football player stiff-arming a would-be tackler and then waving my arm in a circle. I still felt nothing. I kicked twice and moved forward without hitting anything. I opened my eyes and saw that I was in the passageway leading out of the wreck. A faint glow of green light from the water-filtered sunlight outside the wreck illuminated the escape route from the steel tomb. My heart jumped. Nothing had ever looked so beautiful.

Not long after my close encounter in the *San Diego,* an experienced wreck diver found himself in a similar situation in the hulk when he recovered a World War I–era rifle and then tried to exit the wreck. He was not as lucky as me, got hopelessly lost inside the silted labyrinth, and drowned. The victim was a crew member on a dive boat, and when his body could not be found, other boats came on the scene and their crews searched the wreck. After almost a week of searching, Hank Garvin calculated he knew where the body was, although it was in an area that initially seemed unlikely. Garvin found the victim, his body an unpleasant sight; the exposed facial flesh had been eaten away by various sea creatures and grossly distorted by the gases trapped under the skin, which had expanded and stretched the rubber dive suit. It took several more dives to cut an opening so that the distended body could be removed in one piece.

In spite of this fatality, and others like it, Hank Garvin and the rest of the old-time northeast-wreck divers still remained opposed to the use of guidelines inside wrecks. In Garvin's mind, the only way to ensure a retreat from a shipwreck was to be thoroughly familiar with it. The dive-boat crewman who had died in the *San Diego* did not have a lot of experience inside the wreck, and he had never before been to the area where he had recovered the rifle. When he had tried to exit, he missed a key turn, and swam into another deck level that dead-ended.

When Chrissy Rouse and I spoke about this particular death and the other wreck divers' refusal to consider using guidelines, Chrissy found it hard to believe. "The old boys think that more experience would have gotten him out of the wreck?" He scoffed in disgust. "Haven't enough guys died inside of wrecks relying only on experience? A guideline's the only sure way out. I don't get why wreck divers are so closed-minded about using guidelines inside a wreck."

Like me, Chrissy had experienced the value of a guideline first-hand, on a dive with his mother. At Ginnie Springs there is a thick, gold-colored permanent guideline into the Devil's Cave System. Chrissy and Sue Rouse followed it and went through a restriction, a tight area, that required them to take off their tanks, push the tanks through the opening, and then wiggle their bodies through, to don their tanks again on the other side. Their struggles severely reduced the visibility. Soon, they could not see the line leading out of the cave.

Chrissy and Sue hovered in the water, peering everywhere to see the guideline. They did not see it.

During their cave training, Chrissy and Sue had conducted lost-line exercises, both on land and in the water; the training gave Chrissy supreme confidence about what to do next. Using hand signals, he told his mother to hold the side of the cave while he went looking for the line. She obeyed, waiting in the low-visibility cave as her son deployed his emergency reel, tying it off on a rock outcrop next to her, and swam off with it. She believed Chrissy would find the guideline that would lead them both back to sunlight, yet she still felt an intense loneliness; her only company was the sound of her exhalations and the bright glow her light reflected in the sandy silt suspended in front of her.

The beauty of the lost-line drill is that it does not require that you find the entire way out of the labyrinth. Chrissy needed only to find the guideline he and his mother had followed in. By methodically searching the area, he was sure to come across the permanent line.

When Chrissy found the nylon line that led out of the cave, he tied off his emergency guideline reel to the permanent line and followed his emergency line back to his mother. Sue's heart jumped when she saw her son materialize like a ghost from out of the glowing silt curtain in front of her. Chrissy flashed an "OK" sign with his hand and Sue automatically returned the signal. Chrissy signaled his mother to follow the line. Sue Rouse made a gentle O with her left thumb and forefinger around Chrissy's emergency line so that she would have physical contact with the line, and she swam slowly but deliberately along its path. As she swam, Sue made sure to sweep her right hand over her head and in front of her like a windshield wiper, to prevent hitting her head on a rock. Chrissy followed his mother as she swam to the permanent line and found the way out.

To the nineteen-year-old it was a great adventure. Chrissy relished the stunned look on people's faces whenever he told the story. People not familiar with cave diving and the lost-line drill were startled at Chrissy's cavalier attitude and wondered if he was just displaying machismo to cover his fear. But Chrissy's reaction was not machismo. It was the security of his belief in his own youthful immortality—combined with the rational confidence imparted to him by his dive training. He could not conceive of his own death inside a cave.

"God, Chrissy, that was scary!" his mother said when they got out of the cave.

"No, Mom, there was nothing to it." Chrissy concentrated on taking his fins off so he could climb the wooden steps leading back onto land. "I know I'm not going to die in a cave. I'm gonna die wreck diving."

Sue was horrified. "What? Don't say that! I don't want to hear that sort of talk!"

Later, Chrissy would tell me, "After what I've learned in cave diving, I can imagine how scary it would be deep inside a wreck without a guideline. It's stupid to not run a line inside a wreck." But that he insisted on saying that he would die wreck diving was odd. After this incident, Sue heard Chrissy repeat the assertion that he would die wreck diving. Why would he keep telling her such a thing? She brushed off her concerns. Perhaps it was just his childish way of getting her attention.

When the Rouses arrived at the *Wahoo*, I helped load their equipment onto the vessel. They had brought forty tanks with them, mostly scuba tanks they would wear during their dives, but also several five-foot-high green oxygen-supply cylinders that they would use to mix more gases if they needed them, or to transfer more oxygen into the tanks they carried for their oxygen decompression. This would be the first sport-diving expedition to the *Andrea Doria* using mixed gases—one of several reasons that the Team Doria expedition aimed to be significant for divers everywhere.

The scuba tanks that we loaded onto the *Wahoo* contained various gas mixtures, and each tank with anything other than compressed air was marked with special stickers that listed the gas contents of the cylinder. The tanks with high-oxygen-content gases or pure oxygen were specially color-coded: green for pure oxygen, yellow and green for nitrox (a high-oxygen-content gas that also contains nitrogen), and orange for the small bottles of argon that we would use as an insulating gas to inflate our drysuits. Each tank's sticker listed not only the composition of the gases in that tank but also the maximum operating depth at which the gas in that cylinder could be breathed. This helped prevent divers from breathing a high-oxygen mixture at too great a depth, then convulsing and dying from oxygen toxicity.

The most radical gases were the trimixes—helium, oxygen, and nitrogen. Helium-oxygen mixtures, known as heliox, had been used successfully for over sixty years by both commercial and military divers, but the use of trimix was something very new. Few divers or researchers had extensive knowledge of trimix gas or much practical experience in using it. Although mathematical calculations designed to predict its effects were theorized, what actually happened to the body during a trimix dive was still open to scrutiny. Theoretically, trimix gas was logical for breathing underwater, and made sense to me and the other divers I had asked to be part of Team Doria. Besides, the Rouses and I had been trained in the use of trimix gas by Sheck Exley, and if he could survive dives down to 867 feet using this technology, that was good enough for us. As we saw it, researchers would spend a lot of time coming up with a precise explanation of the physiology of how the gases were absorbed and eliminated from the body, but even then there would remain many mysteries, just as there remained mysteries having to do with the use of compressed air. If we waited until the scientific community got around to agreeing on the protocols for trimix gas, we would be old and gray and would have long since lost any chance to make deep diving safer or extend the depths at which we could dive.

Although Bill Stone and his team at Wakulla Springs cave had successfully used trimix on many long dives at depths down to 360 feet in 1987, it was still not completely clear which decompression tables worked and why, or how exactly the body reacted to these gases. Researchers wanted to know how the body would react to absorbing and dispelling two inert gases, nitrogen and helium. The different molecular weights of the gases could be input into computer models to generate decompression tables. But how effective would the decompression actually be in the field when it was applied to human bodies? And how effective would the decompression schedules be in the open ocean, where a diver might not be able to hold precise depths during decompression because of rough surface weather?

Researchers generally thought divers were crazy to risk the ravages of the bends, but at least two—Karl Huggins and Mike Emmerman—were eager to document the effects of the Team Doria dives on me, on the Rouses, and on the rest of the expedition divers. Huggins, who had monitored other groups on live-aboard dive trips, was a research associate in the Department of Atmospheric and Oceanic Science at the University of Michigan, served on the university's Diving Safety Control Board, and was internationally known for his research on decompression theory. He had written the decompression algorithm that was used in the first widely popular diver-carried decompression computer, the EDGE, manufactured by Orca Industries, which came on the market in 1983.

The EDGE computer sensed the diver's depth at frequent intervals, then calculated the amount of time that the diver could stay at that depth without having to decompress, based on the algorithm Huggins had developed. The EDGE used a microprocessor, a forerunner of the computing chips behind today's powerful desktop computers. If decompression was required, the computer indicated the shallowest depth that the diver could ascend to—called the diver's ceiling—without violating the decompression model. The original EDGE did not show all of the depths where ascent stops had to be made, nor did it show the time required at each stop. But it did show the total time required for ascent, and when the diver could go up to his next decompression stop, the ceiling indicator told the diver where to stop.

The EDGE made conducting dives much easier because it measured the diver's actual depth in real time; it provided a custom decompression schedule based on the theoretical gas absorption calculated by the decompression model on that particular dive. Although the EDGE was a bulky piece of diving equipment—its rectangular casing easily took up the entire length of the forearm—the average diver was won over by a clever graphic display that showed how much nitrogen gas had theoretically been absorbed. At first, divers were leery of relying on electronics to make decompression calculations in the harsh underwater environment. The high price tag was also enough to make most of them sit back and observe the problems other divers might encounter when using the computer before taking the plunge to purchase one.

By 1986, there were more than five thousand EDGE computers in use by divers worldwide. It was a modest beginning, but soon the EDGE's continued strong sales prompted other manufacturers to make use of evolving technology and bring smaller, more powerful diving computers onto the market. As the price tag on the EDGE dropped, its one real drawback, besides its bulk, was that it could only calculate dives down to 165 feet on which divers were breathing compressed air.

Huggins had become interested in researching the dives on the Team Doria expedition when his friend Mike Emmerman explained the scope of the project. I had invited Emmerman, a partner at the Wall Street–based investment firm Neuberger Berman, to participate in this expedition and conduct research. During the day Emmerman managed hundreds of millions of dollars in investment funds. His weekends, evenings, and vacation time revolved around diving. He conducted his own research on dive computers, focusing on the effects of diving after flying in commercial airplanes, and working to determine when it was safe to fly after diving. A commercial airplane cabin is pressurized to seven or eight thousand feet above sea level—less than one atmosphere pressure. This means that a person whose body is adapted to sea level is actually eliminating nitrogen during a flight. A diver who flies too soon after diving risks getting bent, even if he had no symptoms of decompression illness before takeoff.

With Chris, Chrissy, and me among the guinea pigs, Huggins and Emmerman—both trained Doppler technicians—would use the nonintrusive device called the Doppler ultrasonic bubble detector to record the sound of blood flowing through our bodies. It could detect any substantial postdive buildup of inert gas bubbles, which might lead to decompression sickness. The bubbles could be heard as chirps and rumblings, where the sound levels are categorized according to four degrees of severity. Generally, the more bubbles, the greater the potential for the bends. However, research had already shown that for some mysterious reason inert gas bubbles could be present in a diver's body without any overt signs or symptoms of the bends. One theory about this phenomenon was that bubbles could form directly in the tissues, and would not be detected by the Doppler device, even though causing the bends. Therefore, the theory went, bubbles in the bloodstream were less important than bubbles in tissues. By documenting with Doppler the dives being done on the Team Doria expedition, our researchers hoped to begin building a database of actual trimix dives that might allow them to get an idea of the decompression stress divers were placing upon themselves. They would also make comparisons against dives where only compressed air was used at depth, and rate these with recordings made by other researchers on other expeditions.

On this expedition, we hoped there would be ample opportunity to compare numerous dives conducted with different dive tables, some of which were based on competing theories. Huggins had based his computer algorithm on a combination of John Scott Haldane's early 1900s decompression theory and the updates that the U.S. Navy and the Pennsylvania Analysis of Decompression for Undersea and Aerospace group had made to Haldane's theories, along with Doppler-based no-decompression limits proposed by Merrill Spencer at the Institute of Applied Physiology and Medicine in Seattle. Some of the more recent theories competed with Haldane's, whereas others expanded on his work. The Schreiner Model—a mathematical decompression model named after the man who had been Bill Hamilton and Glenn Butler's boss at Ocean Systems—was one of those theories. Some divers would be diving using tables generated by Bill Hamilton's computer decompression model, which were based on the research done by Schreiner, Hamilton, and others at Ocean Systems.

Randy Bohrer would be diving using tables generated by the computer algorithm he had written, which was based on the theories of professor and medical doctor Albert Bühlmann, at the University of Zurich, who had taken up the complex issues of decompression modeling as a hobby. Bohrer, an aerospace engineer who worked for Grumman during the day and researched computer decompression modeling in the evenings and on weekends, had run into the inevitable problems that decompression modelers run into, which led him to an alliance with Bill Hamilton. Bohrer had been retained as a consultant for a number of big dives, and had written the decompression tables for Sheck Exley's world-record cave dive to 867 feet.

Earlier in the year, I had brought Randy Bohrer in on the diving-computer project I was working on as a consultant for the Japanese trading company Inabata. I had proposed creating an air computer first, then modifying the basic programming and tooling for that computer to manufacture a more sophisticated device that could calculate dives using nitrox—otherwise referred to as oxygen-enriched—gases. Eventually, I foresaw a third computer, which would calculate dives using trimix gases, but not before the sport—and the market—

progressed and more divers used these sophisticated deep-diving tools.

I had my own theories about the body and its ability to decompress efficiently, as well as its tolerance for cold water. These theories were not couched in scientific or theoretical terms. Instead, they were practical because they had to be: My life and well-being were on the line every time I dived. What worked worked, regardless of the exact physiological mechanisms in play. Essentially, I believed that the body trained itself to eliminate the inert gas by repeated exposures. Cold water changed the body's circulatory characteristics, reducing blood flow to the extremities and closing off blood flow to the skin, reducing the body's heat loss. This changed the way a diver absorbed excess inert gas and—more important—eliminated it. Yet I believed that cold water was more of a mental obstacle than a physical one: Only by repeatedly exposing the body and mind to long cold-water dives could a diver keep his body and mind conditioned for cold-water decompression. A recreational diver, a diver who by definition avoided decompression diving, was limited to ten minutes at 130 feet. Typically, an experienced wreck diver planning a decompression dive to 130 feet would plan to stay on the bottom for no more than twenty minutes, and then decompress for four minutes if he or she followed the U.S. Navy decompression schedules, which were based on the work done by Haldane. Diver-carried decompression computers were a bit more conservative than the tables based on Haldane's work and, depending on the computer being used, indicated decompression of about half an hour after an exposure of twenty minutes at 130 feet.

For divers contemplating diving deep wrecks, like the *Andrea Doria*, the mental and physical conditioning they needed to tolerate longer in-water times meant that they had to gradually dive deeper and deeper. With each dive they had to extend their times so that they would be prepared to endure potentially long decompressions. I had gradually extended my in-water exposures so that I was diving as deep as 238 feet, breathing air for various times on the bottom, and then regularly enduring two- or three-hour decompressions with the Bühlmann-based algorithms in the computers I used. To safeguard against computer failure, I carried two identical computers on each dive, as did every serious diver, including the Rouses. The time I was spending on the bottom at

130 feet—a depth I now considered shallow—was up to fifty-three minutes. To minimize the number of scuba tanks I would need to carry for these long dives, I exercised diligently as I had throughout my life, participating in sports ranging from track to street hockey, ice hockey, boxing, karate, and rugby. My physical regimen on land combined with my lifelong sporting interest resulted in a strong body and efficient lungs that allowed me to conduct long dives with only three scuba tanks, which surprised fellow divers on dive boats, who thought that I would require several more tanks.

The Rouses agreed with my decompression theory, although they did not believe in my training regimen. They thought that the best way to condition themselves and avoid the bends was by diving. Chris and Chrissy had extended their dive times and decompressions in much the same way I had. Further, when we used oxygen to decompress, we could reduce the duration of our actual decompression stops because oxygen allowed the body to eliminate inert gas more efficiently. But instead of reducing our in-water time, we used the oxygen to add a greater margin of safety to our dives, staying in the water as long as recommended by our computers, which calculated only air. After long, deep air dives, we breathed oxygen during decompression, and noticed how much more energy we had than after dives in which we used only air during decompression. We could feel the effects of eliminating more inert gas during decompression. Though the Rouses and I could not explain definitively what happened inside the body during a dive, which is what scientists were seeking to do, our bodies could feel that our methods worked. Theories were fine, but what we knew was that we didn't get bent after our long, deep dives.

As the *Wahoo* struggled against an unrelenting assault of waves and a fierce crosscurrent, we edged our way closer to the *Andrea Doria*, hugging Long Island's south shore on our way to Nantucket to avoid the punishing sea conditions farther out. The boat was packed with twelve Team Doria members, two researchers, a reporter, a crew of eleven, and so much equipment it was difficult to move about on the deck. With everyone gathered in the main cabin trying to stay warm, I handed each of the Team Doria members the most recent team list, including everybody's contact information and a brief biography of each diver. Not everybody on board knew one another: I had recruited team members from around the United States, Canada, and even Switzerland. I handed out polo shirts and sweatshirts, the TEAM DORIA '91 logo embroidered on them, to all divers, including crew members. Hank Garvin accepted his shirts and then pointed to the list. "What's that?" When I handed it to him, Hank looked it over and asked, annoyed, "Where's my name? Why aren't any of the crew listed?"

"Ask Bielenda," I replied. "He wouldn't tell me who was going to be crew even after I asked him a bunch of times, so I couldn't include that info."

"Yeah, Bernie," someone chimed in, "Bielenda didn't want you to know how many crew members he was stuffing the boat with!" A number of people laughed, and others grunted in agreement. Then, some of the bigger Team Doria divers complained that their bunks were far too small—and didn't all these crew members have such spacious bunks?

I had to clamp down on the carping right now. "Yes, we're a bit crowded. We are on a boat and that means there's limited space. Also Bielenda told us to bring all of the tanks and gases we'd need for all of the dives because he's not guaranteeing air fills from his compressor, so it's even more crowded than usual. Plus we've got extra guys on board to do research and report what's going on. Let's deal with it."

Hank took the list I had given him and waved it at Sally Warhman, another crew member, who had just wandered in. "Hey, check this out. We don't even rate on the great diver list." Hank shook his head and walked away.

Though she stood only five feet five inches, Sally's body was built on a bigger plan, just like Janet Bieser, who at the moment was putting her three-hundred-pound-plus form to use to steer the vessel; Janet's massive frame was matched by her extensive boat-handling experience. Everyone respected Janet's diving ability, and her strength was legendary: She could easily pull a fully suited diver who was in trouble back onto the *Wahoo* with one hand. The large size of these crew members had long prompted mutterings in the diving community about "the women of the *Wahoo*." But what mattered to the

Wahoo's owner, Steve Bielenda, when he chose his crew members was not the size of their bodies, but the size of their hearts and the depth of their experience, both of which Sally and Janet proved to have in abundance. Sally looked over the team list and grunted. She looked around, and then leaned over to me. "You know, a friend of mine hangs out at the quarry in Pennsylvania. She tells me the Rouses are there all the time. These guys are quarry divers!"

To call someone a quarry diver was a huge insult. It meant that they did not have the skills or the courage to dive in the ever-changing open ocean, and that they preferred the safe, protected environment a quarry afforded. The Rouses were outside, making sure their equipment was safely stored. I couldn't let this insult to my friends go unanswered. "The Rouses dive everywhere," I told her. "They always want to be diving, whether it's a quarry, a cave, or a wreck. I think more divers would be better off if they spent time practicing at a quarry once in a while."

"I'm just telling you what I heard, that's all," Sally said curtly and put the list down on the counter.

Unfortunately, the team list that I had created as a useful tool had further separated the team from the crew members, creating an us-versus-them situation. As it was, Hank's talk with me before we had left the dock had emphasized the differences between team and crew: We were the new guys on the block, with newfangled ways of doing things. Steve Bielenda had put many of the most experienced northeast-wreck divers on the boat as his crew, adding to the usual number of crew he carried. And many of those divers, including Bielenda himself, gave the impression that the *Doria* was their wreck. Who were we to come along and dive their wreck using new methods? I wondered if Steve Bielenda and his crew were waiting for our team-based deep penetration to fail. Or was I just being a paranoid expedition leader?

The mounting tension made me even more nervous with anticipation than I would have been otherwise. This was by far the most ambitious diving project I had yet undertaken, a huge step up from leading the occasional Caribbean trip for the Manhattan dive shop for which I worked part-time as an instructor, or from running independent wreck-diving day trips or long-weekend diving excursions.

I had been lucky thus far; I'd never been on either a day trip or an expedition during which a diver was lost, though many of the veteran divers on board the *Wahoo* had not been so fortunate. I hoped my luck would hold for the sake of us all.

I knew enough to worry in a particularly informed way. My research with the National Underwater Accident Data Center at the University of Rhode Island made me very familiar with the details of every wreck-diving tragedy involving an American diver. The accident tales that divers told and retold showed me how the loss of a diver at sea affected those on board: profoundly, yet differently, depending on the exact circumstances, the mental toughness of the survivors, and how well the victim was liked by his fellow divers, among other things. One dead diver who had displayed arrogance before a dive and who in the process of killing himself nearly killed one of the crew members underwater when he collided into her in his rushed descent—sending her spiraling 60 feet down to the bottom at 240 feet—was subjected to a postmortem beating by the crew member: She kicked his body repeatedly, spat on it, and issued a torrent of curses at the recklessness that had taken his life and nearly her own. In another incident, a victim's buddy collapsed in hysterics on the dive boat immediately after enduring a decompression he had spent haunted by the image of his friend, drifting lifeless along the ocean bottom, whom he had not been able to bring back with him to the surface. When he was back on the dive boat, the surviving diver was reduced to shrieking, crying hysteria as the crew—which included at least one war-hardened former soldier—questioned him and tried to ascertain what had happened. Veteran divers looked on the buddy's behavior as poor form: Going into hysterics is fine *after* you tell the crew where the body can be found.

Sometimes during an expedition to the *Andrea Doria*, diving is more important than death, especially when prized underwater trophies are on the line. For example, a rumor circulated among hardcore wreck divers about a diver who was not very well liked and who died on his very first descent. Rather than call the Coast Guard immediately to report the fatality, everyone on the dive boat pressed the captain to wait until the scheduled expedition was over, in three days' time. They had each paid the captain over $800 to go on this trip and they were enjoying optimal diving conditions. The death, if reported, would end the expedition because the Coast Guard would demand that the boat captain return to shore immediately with the body. No one wanted to head back to shore, lose their opportunities to gather trophies and rack up bragging rights, and lose their trip fees. The captain supposedly agreed to the diver's demands. The victim's body was placed in the sleeping bag he had occupied in life. The bag was then filled with ice from everyone's coolers, to slow down the body's decomposition, and placed back on his bunk.

Chris Rouse had manufactured some of the equipment cluttering the *Wahoo*. He had gone ahead and started the diving company he had fantasized about when his excavation business kept sputtering under financial strain. John Reekie had suggested the name of the company, Black Cloud Scuba, because it seemed to John that a black cloud was always hanging over the Rouses. Reekie especially noticed this when it came to equipment: The Rouses' gear, although meticulously maintained, was always breaking down. During dives with the Rouses, Reekie realized that their gear—and even his gear—would uncannily malfunction with amazing regularity. I had to agree—the Rouses had a black cloud hovering right above their tousled heads. Their company logo depicted a single black cloud releasing rain. More ominously, the cloud was simultaneously releasing three black lightning bolts.

In spite of their uncertain financial footing, the Rouses poured generosity on their friends, freely sharing anything they had. Even as Chris struggled with his new diving business—repairing diver propulsion vehicles and manufacturing diving reels himself, using the lathe and drill press in the workshop he had previously used exclusively to maintain his excavation machinery—he would give samples of his self-made diving equipment to his friends. On board the *Wahoo*, Steve Berman, John Reekie, and I each had the upline reels that Chris had given us. We would carry the three-foot-long reel wound with three hundred feet of sisal rope, along with a lift bag for use in an emergency. If we could not find the anchor line during the dive—either because of disorientation or because the line had come free from the wreck—we would deploy the upline reel and a device called a lift bag to create a line to the surface and a floating buoy. The lift bag was filled with air from one of the tanks, and the bag with the upline attached rose to the surface like a helium balloon. When the line no longer spooled from the reel, we would know that the bag had hit the surface, and we would cut the line from the reel and tie the end to a piece of the wreck. Making a controlled ascent on the upline, we would be assured of not drifting away from the wreck in a current and getting lost at sea.

As we made our way out to the *Andrea Doria,* the two researchers Huggins and Emmerman were busy at work in the cabin of the *Wahoo.* They carefully marked audio cassette tapes with each diver's name. Working quietly but efficiently, they started the process of using the Doppler ultrasonic device to take baseline measurements of each diver's blood flow, which they would compare with postdive measurements to see if they could detect any bubbles in our bloodstreams. I stripped off my sweat jacket and shirt so that they could apply the Doppler's transducer, which was like a small microphone, first over my heart, then over the area where my left shoulder joined my torso. Listening to my blood flow through headphones, they shook their heads, and then made small adjustments to the transducer's location. When they were satisfied that they had the transducer positioned where they could get the strongest blood-flow soundings, they marked it with a circle, using a pen. I did a few deep knee bends while they recorded my blood flow.

When I looked down at my body with one circle drawn over my heart and another drawn at the shoulder, I thought I looked strangely like a target that decompression sickness could aim at. Just before a dive I didn't pay much attention to the potential danger. If I had trained, eaten, and slept properly, my body should function as I wanted it to, and I would be able to eliminate the excess gas accumulated during the dive without problems. But what if I was wrong? What if I did everything right and still got bent? I had heard about divers who had been permanently crippled even though they had supposedly done everything correctly during their dive. Like everybody else, I wanted to believe it couldn't happen to me. But what if it did?

While I put my shirt back on, the diver Wings Stocks went through the same testing procedure. Although it was no nickname, Wings was a fitting moniker for the beefy, muscular man who looked like a Hell's Angel, complete with long, flowing beard and tattooed forearms like tree trunks. Yet he always wore a disarming smile, which, combined with his round, wire-framed eyeglasses, vibrant personality, and soft voice, made others relax and trust him. Pushing aside Wings's beard, the researchers marked his body as they had done mine. Soon, all our bodies were marked with the two targets.

Moving outside the cabin, I braced myself against the doorway to survey the rolling waves and the overcast sky. Everything beyond the *Wahoo* was a dull gray that contrasted sharply with the colorful scuba tanks crowding the deck. Billy Deans was bent over his torpedolike scooter, tightening the rope holding it fast along the inside of the gunwale. Billy Deans had come after all, as a crew member. Many of the *Wahoo*'s regular crew didn't think he would return to the wreck that had claimed his friend John Ormsby in 1985. Yet Billy's friendship with Steve Bielenda and the chance to be part of a technical-diving expedition had brought him up from Key West. Michael Menduno had accompanied Billy on the long ride up the coast. Menduno wanted to cover this expedition for his magazine, *AquaCorps,* and he was busy gathering information from Captain Steve Bielenda.

Catching Bielenda's eye, I said, "Remember, we want to anchor into the stern section."

"We'll do our best, but I can't guarantee anything," Bielenda told me.

His reply disturbed me. I had made plans based on diving the stern section of the *Doria,* because this area had numerous large doorways and windows that would allow access to any of several deck levels. The plans called for each two-person dive team to run permanent guidelines along the long horizontal passageways on several decks, at 202 and 238 feet. Vertical lines could be run along the smaller passageways that connected the horizontal passageways, and the lines would be connected. If a dive team came across an area with a lot of artifacts, that team would indicate the way out by attaching a line arrow to the guideline at the spot where the artifacts lay. The other dive teams could then work in shifts to retrieve the artifacts. But if Bielenda did not anchor into the stern section, our plans would be far more difficult to carry out because of the way the wreck lay on the bottom and the access it provided to various deck levels.

Anchoring is a tricky business. First, the captain has to navigate to the wreck. In 1991 that involved using Loran-C, a radio positioning system that employed a receiver to mathematically triangulate radio signals sent from a series of installations along the U.S. coast. The receiver produced two sets of numbers that corresponded to nautical charts' longitude and latitude. If you had the Loran-C numbers for a wreck, you could key in that data and use it to steer to that location in a way similar to—but more precise than—using a compass. Loran-C is accurate to about fifty feet of a precise location. (Today, most boating professionals prefer the greater accuracy of GPS—the global positioning system, which uses signals from satellites and can get you to within three feet of your desired location.)

Once in the general vicinity of a wreck, the captain of the boat commands a crew member to toss overboard a bright, floating object, such as a large plastic bottle, to which is attached a weighted line. The makeshift buoy marks the location around which a search pattern is conducted to try to find the wreck with the bottom scanner, which looks like a small television set except that it shows only the contour of the bottom, and sometimes schools of fish. The outline of a large wreck that comes high off the sea floor, like the *Andrea Doria*, is clearly visible with a bottom scanner when the dive boat is directly over the hulk.

Once the bottle buoy has been deployed, the captain now has to judge several things at once: the speed at which the dive boat is moving, the strength and direction of the current and waves, the force of the wind against the dive boat, and finally how long it will take for the anchor to reach the bottom. Steering the boat into position so that the boat will drift with the current over the wreck, the captain calls out to the crew standing on the bow of the boat the moment when the anchor should be dropped. Most often used is a clawlike grappling-hook-style anchor, which is usually attached directly to ten or twenty feet of chain. The chain, in turn, is attached to the anchor line, a thick braided nylon rope. With luck, the anchor will drop down and be carried over the wreckage as the dive boat drifts with the current, so that the hook holds fast on some part of the wreck. If the anchor does not catch the wreck, it is hauled to the surface and the procedure is begun anew.

When the captain is convinced that the anchor is secure, two crew members dive down the anchor line and decide whether the anchor has snagged at a good spot. If not—which is the case most of the time—the crew members grapple with the anchor to free it from the wreckage and swim with it to the spot where the captain has asked them to secure it. Then the anchor is secured on wreckage, and a rope is tied around both the anchor and the wreckage so that the anchor does not come loose and cause the dive boat to drift. During overnight or multiday offshore trips, rope is considered too weak to keep the anchor in place reliably, so a massive steel shackle—which looks like the letter C until a thick rod is screwed into the holders at the open ends to make it look like a letter D—is used to hold the anchor firmly to the wreck. The shackle is usually reinforced with a rope, which acts as a backup in case the shackle's rod comes loose. Getting the anchor out of the wreck at the end of the trip requires divers to free it by hand.

John Reekie stood nearby. The crew member John Moyer walked over to the Canadian and asked, "I noticed you have on an *Empress of Ireland* shirt. I'm interested in diving that wreck. Have you been on it?"

Reekie frowned. "Been on it? I run expeditions to it!"

The *Empress of Ireland* was a passenger liner that went down in the St. Lawrence River on May 29, 1914, not far from the shores of Rimouski, Quebec. The loss of 1,012 lives made it second only to the *Titanic* in the number of lives lost in a peacetime disaster at sea. Many people referred to it as the Salvation Army wreck because a large contingent of passengers were on their way to a meeting of the Salvation Army in England. The cold Canadian water, strong currents, and the wreck's crumbling interior made the site formidable—which, when combined with its elegant artifacts, made it one of the world's top wreck-diving sites.

"I've heard so much about the *Doria*. I have to see if it's anything compared to the *Empress*," Reekie remarked to Moyer. The two men went on to discuss the details of diving the two wrecks, their mutual interest in sunken ocean liners enabling them to establish a friendship.

Moyer had been part of many wreck-diving expeditions, both as a crew member and as a paying diver. A Coast Guard–certified captain, he was one of the most experienced deep-wreck divers in the northeastern United States. He had also experienced a serious case of the bends back in 1985, while he was preparing for an expedition to retrieve one of the *Andrea Doria*'s two bells. Because they believed the bell would have to be cut free of the wreck, Moyer practiced on land with Bill Nagel, the captain of the dive boat *Seeker*, to get experience in underwater metal cutting using a welding torch. Moyer then went with the rest of the team to practice their metal-cutting techniques on a 200-foot-deep wreck off the New Jersey shore. The *Goulandris* was a 362-foot-long freighter that sank in a collision in 1942. Its proximity to shore and familiarity to the divers made it a great testing ground, and its readily accessible large brass spoked steering wheel provided a lucrative trophy divers were motivated to liberate.

When Moyer came up from welding to board Bill Nagel's boat, the *Seeker*, the normally strong man felt extremely fatigued and had to be helped up the ladder. He was so confused and lethargic he could not take off his own equipment, including his diving suit. Gary Gentile, a Vietnam veteran who had suffered severe wounds from the Vietcong's bullets, knew what it was like to feel helpless and hurt; he immediately assisted his friend Moyer and coordinated his efforts with others'.

When he was fully unsuited, Moyer was led belowdecks, to his bunk. He lay down and told the others he had pain, first in his shoulders, then in his elbows, wrists, and hands. Gentile, who had himself been bent years earlier, knew that it was critical for Moyer to be administered oxygen to help the stricken diver's body eliminate the nitrogen bubbles. Unchecked, the bubbles would leave Moyer permanently crippled or worse. Gentile rushed to get Moyer a cylinder of oxygen.

A Coast Guard helicopter hoisted Moyer from the *Seeker* uneventfully and flew him to a hospital, where he underwent recompression therapy. Although Moyer showed no outward signs of injury, he was told not to dive for several months so that his body could completely recover.

During the expedition to recover the *Doria*'s bell, Moyer decided to join the team even though he could not dive. Moyer was a true team player and was content to assist topside with the dive boat's operation, getting divers into their gear, helping them get back on board the boat, and offering suggestions for retrieving the bell when it was found. Moyer helped hoist the 500-pound brass artifact, bearing the inscription *ANDREA DORIA,* onto the boat. He continued to dive with Nagel and even worked on the boat as a crew member. Yet over the next two years, Moyer saw Nagel drifting further and further into an alcoholic abyss. By 1987, Moyer felt that Nagel had given in to the urge to drink uncontrollably, which left him seemingly unconcerned with the divers who paid to go on the *Seeker*. When a diver did die during a *Seeker* expedition to the *Andrea Doria*, Moyer perceived that Nagel barely reacted. Moyer quit working on the *Seeker*, and avoided any association with Nagel at social functions. But Moyer loved diving and divers, and still wanted to work on a dive boat. He approached Steve Bielenda about working on the *Wahoo*, and Bielenda was happy to have another proven veteran on his crew.

As the roar of the *Wahoo*'s diesel engines faded to a low hum and the boat slowed, I knew we were close to the *Andrea Doria*. Chrissy walked over to me, looked at the waves, and said sarcastically, "Great day for diving!" We all had a lot to prove.

6

The Steel Cave

JUNE 28, 1991.
Aboard the dive charter boat *Wahoo*,
over the site of the *Andrea Doria*.

THE ROUSES HAD BEEN SURPRISED at the recognition that greeted them when cave- and wreck-diving aficionados found out they were part of the Team Doria '91 expedition. It was their first real taste of general admiration and acclaim, although they had already developed a solid reputation for their diving abilities and enthusiasm.

As they contemplated what lay beneath the steady six-to-eight-foot waves, punctuated with the occasional large, rolling waves up to twelve feet, that rocked the *Wahoo,* Chris and Chrissy Rouse started to see firsthand why the *Andrea Doria* had earned the title "the Mount Everest of scuba diving." The wreck lay at 240 feet and rested on its starboard side, its hulk rising to 165 feet. At its shallowest point, the hull was 35 feet beyond what recreational scuba-diving agencies in the United States recommended as the deepest safe diving depth. Situated at a particularly nasty patch of ocean where the weather could change rapidly both on the surface and underwater—just as it had that foggy night in 1956, when the *Andrea Doria* was sent to the ocean floor after a collision—the wreck lay alluringly below us, a siren calling us to high adventure and high risk.

Deep in the *Doria* lay many works by famous Italian artists that had been specially commissioned for this liner. Some of the artists had since died, and their paintings, sculptures, ceramic murals, and vases were now far more valuable than when the liner sank. Some of the artworks on the *Doria* were one-of-a-kind, and were priceless. Even such seemingly mundane items as dinner plates bore special meaning when divers retrieved them from inside the ocean liner that had been dubbed the "Grande Dame of the Sea." Her sleek, graceful lines recalled other Italian masterworks created in the near and distant past, from sculpture and paintings to architecture, motorcars, and fashion.

Chris and Chrissy Rouse knew that simply by diving this wreck they were entering an elite league of divers: Steve Bielenda estimated that only about five hundred people had dived the wreck since the luxury liner sank in 1956. Some of those had died just 200 feet below us. Others, who wanted to minimize their risk but still have bragging rights, had never recovered an artifact from the wreck: They were content to go down briefly, touch the wreck, and come back up, their only trophy the adventure itself. Those who sought to recover artifacts usually spent many dives building up the experience they needed to go inside safely and bring something out. If Chris and Chrissy could not only dive the wreck but bring some artifact out of it, they would go to the head of the class, the pioneering cave-diving techniques allowing them to trump most of the serious divers in the world. They would feel like accomplished sportsmen.

Standing in the cabin, I watched Sally Warhman peel potatoes for a salad that would be part of the food left out for everyone to snack on after their dives. Her eyes on her work, she said, "Hey, Bernie, what's this I hear that some of your divers are talking about the huge passageways inside the wreck? It sounds like they think they could drive a truck through there. It isn't that big. I hope you've warned them about the dangers of cables and silt-out."

"Yeah, they know about the dangers. But once you've dived caves, the passageways are large enough for running lines, and making deep penetrations," I replied.

Sally stopped peeling the potatoes and looked up at me. "I don't get it. Why would you want to swim through the wreck when you could just find an opening close to where you want to go and then drop right down to where you want to be?"

"Hank asked me the same thing," I said. The crew member Hank Garvin could not comprehend our fascination with swimming through the wreck. He believed you spent as little time inside the wreck as you could, and those terror-filled moments were solely for the purpose of gathering artifacts. Lingering inside a wreck for any other reason was, to Garvin, an unnecessary flirtation with danger. Sally apparently felt the same way. "Sally, there's something about just swimming through caves and wrecks. Sure, the artifacts are nice, but it's great to just see what's there."

Sally looked as if I'd told her there were a lot of great restaurants in purgatory. She shrugged and turned her attention back to the potatoes. "Whatever does it for you. Just be careful."

Steve Bielenda climbed down the ladder from the *Wahoo*'s wheelhouse deck and walked briskly into the main cabin. "Bernie, we're anchored in first class."

I was disappointed. We were anchored hundreds of feet away from where we had planned to start our dives. Steve Bielenda and his crew were very experienced, and prided themselves on being able to anchor wherever they wanted. "What happened to anchoring into the stern section?"

"We're lucky we're out here at all, never mind the stern section. Haven't you noticed? We've got some real weather out here, we're rocking like crazy, and we've got a bit of current. You should be happy we hooked the wreck!"

Asking the captain to try to move the anchor would delay our expedition dives another day. That was not a good idea, given the weather, which could easily get so severe that we would have to make a hasty departure. Although I wasn't happy with this development, we would have to make the best of it and start our dives along the *Andrea Doria*'s first-class section.

I turned to the Team Doria divers seated in the cabin. "Okay, guys. We're in the first-class area, not third class like we planned. For now, let's just go and see what it's like down there and orient ourselves for our next dives."

The dive boat underwent a methodical scramble as the Team Doria divers started searching for their dive bags among the piles that had been shoved aside on the platform where the crew members were suiting up. Usually crew members assisted the other divers with their gear and then, after they were in the water, the crew would dive. Today it seemed to be every diver for himself. In order to make room on the platform for many divers to suit up at once, the dive bags had been tossed into a heap at the stern of the boat, which was already packed with diving-equipment boxes. Lashed to the gunwales were scuba tanks several rows deep, taking up to three feet of precious deck space along the *Wahoo*'s perimeter. The Rouses alone had brought forty tanks, along with multiple boxes of gear, which included several of each piece of equipment for backup purposes in case anything broke. They didn't want to give the black cloud hanging over them the opportunity to thwart a dive on this prestigious wreck. The Rouses would have been more than embarrassed if an equipment failure prevented them from diving the wreck. Beyond the fact that word would spread among divers, and apart from the damage that news of an equipment failure would do to their budding diving business, it would have been a defeat, and that was not allowed.

I would be diving with Steve Foreman, who had been part of Bill Stone's team at Wakulla Springs cave. Steve Foreman held cave-diving instructor card number 106, the lowest number among those actively teaching cave diving, with the exception of Sheck Exley. Foreman was very soft-spoken and humble about his many cave-diving accomplishments. He did not have extensive cold-water wreck-diving experience and he asked Hank Garvin, Steve Bielenda, Janet Bieser, and Sally Warhman to give him pointers about the best strategies to dive the *Andrea Doria*. The crew members all appreciated Foreman's attitude and wondered why the other Team Doria divers did not display the same obvious respect—or should it be reverence?—for the wreck, and for the crew members' considerable experience on it, even if Garvin and the other crew members wouldn't be using guidelines for deep penetrations the way Foreman would. The cave-diving instructor left a lasting positive impression on the *Wahoo*'s crew.

I was further along in suiting up than Foreman, and the rolling boat made it difficult for me to remain seated while fully geared up. "I'll meet you on the wreck," I called out to Foreman. He agreed to let me go ahead and lay out the guideline on the wreck, which he would follow to find me.

As I descended the anchor line, I could soon make out the vast outline of the ocean liner as it spread in all directions before me, resembling a toppled skyscraper with portholes. No matter how many times I behold a shipwreck underwater, I am always amazed that I can actually swim through something that once floated proudly on the surface. *Andrea Doria* had been an entire floating city; now, sprawled on the ocean bottom, its size meant I could not swim the entire length of the ship on one dive, which always left a piece of the puzzle to explore on another dive.

The anchor line was attached at the shallowest point of the wreck. I looked around to establish my bearings. The visibility was a good 40 or 50 feet in all directions. The water was a light green and contrasted with the wreck's rust-red steel and the white blanket of anemone tentacles that waved hypnotically at me. Anemones are creatures that affix themselves to shipwrecks; they look like plants, but are actually animals. They feed by catching in their tentacles the plankton and fish eggs that float past with the current. Whenever I swam close to an anemone, its tentacles quickly retracted into the body of the animal, which looked like a soft, brown mushroom stem. The anemones' defensive reaction reminded me that I was an intruder to their world.

Because the visibility on the outside of the wreck was so good, I decided to swim toward the bow and look at the bridge, the ship's control center where the captain had stood commanding his vessel. As I swam along the outside of the wreck making my way forward, I could see rows of portholes everywhere. The wreck seemed to stretch on forever. When I saw the bridge wings jutting out perpendicular to the hull, I knew I was nearing my destination. The officers and lookouts would stand on the bridge wings to get a clearer view of any objects that their ship might run into. I swam past the bridge wing and looked to my right. The front of several decks sloped gracefully downward. I stopped, hovering in the water just in front of the bridge. I looked inside and tried to imagine exactly what had transpired here to have caused the vessel's fatal collision.

Steve Foreman swam up to me and gave the "OK" hand sign, which I returned. He had found me by following my guideline, which I had paid out from the anchor line. We both floated 30 feet in front of the bridge, admiring the ship's graceful, curved lines and the contrast of colors. We dropped halfway down the outside of the bridge to a depth of 200 feet, and then stopped. Time passed quickly as we admired various parts of the wreck's exterior. Soon, Steve gave me the thumbs-up, meaning he wanted to ascend, and I nodded. Then I signaled that I would stay on the wreck and he could ascend alone. He signaled "OK," turned, and swam away.

I looked for an appropriate place to enter the wreck and found a large opening that led into the first-class ballroom. Everything seemed so still and the ballroom itself was very large, like Ginnie Springs cavern. Unlike Ginnie Springs, however, sunlight filtered in through the openings where there had once been plate-glass windows. I dropped down, avoiding tables that were affixed to what had been the wreck's floor but now, because the wreck lay on its side, was the wall on my right. I wondered which famous people had sat at these tables, amusing themselves as they crossed the Atlantic Ocean, heading to and from their business and social commitments. As I dropped down, I liked the feeling of floating through the room where people had once danced and laughed the night away. I came to a large mound of silt. Pipes protruded through it.

My head buzzed from the effects of narcosis: I had chosen to dive using air, which I was comfortable with at this depth. Although breathing trimix would have given me a clearer head, it would also have meant carrying more bottles, including a separate bottle of insulating gas for my drysuit, and two decompression gases. When I considered the extra load I would have to carry for diving on gas, and factored in the uncertainty of trimix decompression schedules, I decided to keep things simple and not change what had worked for me in the past; I breathed air and would use oxygen for decompression. The cold penetrated in spite of the thermal insulation I wore under my drysuit. I checked my depth gauge. It read 237 feet. Almost five martinis. I felt fine, bolstered by the martini-induced confidence.

As I swam along the bottom, I saw the faint outline of a bottle. I opened my goodie bag, gently grabbed the bottle, and put it in the bag. I then stuck my hand in the silt, reaching for another artifact. The silt was soft and so light that my motion immediately created a cloud of swirling brown particles around me. During this dive, unlike my dive into the U.S.S. *San Diego*'s dish room, I had a guideline with me, and felt secure that I would find my way out easily in spite of the curtain of silt drawn by my digging for artifacts. When my arm sank up to my elbow in the silt, I felt another bottle and retrieved it. My third stab into the silt netted a jar. On my fourth stab, I felt a large, round object. I could not lift it with one hand. Putting the guideline reel down next to me, I grabbed the object with two hands and pulled it out of the silt. I did not know what it was, but put it in my goodie bag and positioned it on the bottom with the bottles and the jar on top.

I could not see my diving gauges, but I knew instinctively that it was time to go. I grabbed my reel and started swimming while reeling in my guideline. I had no problem finding my way out and back to the anchor line. As I started my ascent, I checked my two diving computers. I had been underwater for thirty-nine minutes. My first decompression stop was at 60 feet. The decompression timers indicated ninety-nine minutes, but ninety-nine minutes was the maximum number the computer could display externally; internally, the decompression register was in three digits—my decompression time was at least one hour and thirty-nine minutes.

I slowly swam up the anchor line, pulling on it with one hand while I ascended. I did not want to unexpectedly encounter a current and get carried away from the anchor line. If that happened I would have to decompress while drifting in the ocean, and then, when I sur-faced, I would be out of sight of the *Wahoo* and would be very lucky if I was found alive. I kept checking my computers during the ascent, and when I came to 60 feet, I tied my jonline around the anchor line, then slipped my left wrist through the loop at my end of the line and grasped it with my hand. The anchor line tugged up and down, but I stayed at 60 feet, thanks to Jon Hulburt's neat invention (as a matter of fact, Hulburt was a *Wahoo* crew member for this expedition). I was required to decompress at this depth only for four minutes, and then the computer display showed me the number 50; next to it was an arrow on top of which rested a horizontal line. This meant that I had a ceiling of 50 feet and could ascend to that depth, but no shallower. I loosened my jonline's knot and slid it up the anchor line. When I got to 53 feet, I again tightened the jonline's knot and allowed the slight current to carry me backward, like an astronaut at the end of his tether. I lay facedown in the water, parallel to the unseen sand bottom that lay 190 feet below me.

My strategy for enduring the upcoming several hours of decompression was to relax, and enjoy the feeling of floating weightlessly, while I put my mind into a state of meditation. It was important for me to stay awake and I could not let myself relax to the point of falling asleep. If that happened, my blood flow, breathing, and general body functions would slow down and would not effectively remove the excess inert nitrogen gas from my system. But if I concentrated on my breathing rhythm and watched the marine life floating past me, I could be both awake and content. Unlike Steve Berman and John Reekie, I did not need an underwater stereo and I avoided using one. Perhaps that was because I lived in Manhattan, where I seemed to be surrounded by noise. Underwater, I was comforted by the soothing sound of my steady breathing: first, *swisssshhh,* as I breathed in and pulled air from my regulator, and then the *blub, blub, blub, blub* of my bubbles as I exhaled.

My only real concern during decompression was being stung by jellyfish. Although the jellyfish could not sting through my neoprene rubber drysuit, gloves, or hood, my lips were exposed to the water and were vulnerable. Sometimes, long trails of jellyfish tentacles floated toward me, and I would have to gently fan the water to create a current that would move the stinging tentacles away. When the body of a jellyfish pulsed toward me, I would sometimes catch it in my open hand and admire the beauty of its translucent body and the powerful contractions it made trying to thrust itself forward. After a few moments of this, I would gently move my hand to one side with the jellyfish still pushing against it, and then let the jellyfish go, where it pulsed onward, toward its destiny. The anchor line itself often became a snag for jellyfish tentacles and I had to watch out that I did not pull on the anchor line, get a jellyfish tentacle on my glove, and then rub my lip, which could happen when I needed to change regulators to breathe from another tank. Even though these tentacles were no longer attached to the jellyfish, the stinging cells, called nematocysts, were still active and they would burn my lip. In severe cases, my lip would swell and turn very red, as if stung by a bee. Jellyfish stings on the lip were not uncommon, and other divers faced the same discomfort. I spent three hours and fourteen minutes underwater, then surfaced, swam to the *Wahoo*'s stern, and climbed out of the water.

"Your research pals don't feel so great," Steve Bielenda told me first thing. It turned out that Karl Huggins and Mike Emmerman, the decompression researchers, were incapacitated by seasickness. They lay, sea-foam white, on the floor in the *Wahoo*'s cabin and got up occasionally to stagger out of the cabin and to the railing, where they vomited into the sea. They were far too sick to measure me for signs of inert gas bubbles in the bloodstream, and they had only been able to measure a few other divers—between bouts of vomiting—before they gave up and went into the cabin to lie down. I was disappointed but knew that this was the nature of diving and research. Nothing was guaranteed. In spite of advances in technology, human beings were still often held captive by their own physical and mental limitations, from their guts to their lungs to their motivations.

Unknown to Team Doria members, the *Wahoo* crew member John Moyer had been reconnoitering the *Doria*'s first-class area for two important artifacts: the vessel's second bell, and a wall frieze by Guido Gambone, who had been influenced by Picasso. The frieze was the largest artwork the late renowned artist had ever created. Made of ceramic, which was his favorite medium, the frieze covered an entire wall within the ship and recalled the art of the ancient Etruscans; the meaning of the work was still a mystery to experts. The artwork was near to priceless in value, but it was not because of money that Moyer searched for it. Rather, he wanted to rescue the frieze to preserve something of beauty that would be lost forever when the steel wreck succumbed to the combined effects of storms and the chemical reactions of steel with salt water and completely broke up.

Moyer's ultimate goal was one he shared with many diving enthusiasts: He wanted to start a permanent *Andrea Doria* museum, where people could see the artifacts recovered and learn more about the wreck, its fatal voyage, its design elegance, and its art. Moyer hoped that the second bell and the art frieze would become centerpieces for the future museum.

While I knew of the diver's general ambitions, I didn't know that he was scouting out the *Doria* on this expedition. As noble as Moyer's intentions were, he could not reveal what he was doing: Competition for artifacts among wreck divers was fierce, and someone else could come along and snatch the prizes that Moyer had sought long and hard. The competition for *Andrea Doria* artifacts was especially strong between Bill Nagel's boat *Seeker* and Steve Bielenda's *Wahoo*. During one of the *Seeker's Doria* expeditions—when Moyer was working for Nagel as a crew member—John Chatterton and other divers found a cache of dishes spilling out of a supply closet in a corridor. Although the *Seeker's* divers recovered hundreds of artifacts from this closet during two expeditions, they did not have enough time to gather everything.

Word got out about the bonanza when the *Seeker* returned to port between expeditions. The *Wahoo* already had an expedition scheduled, and when the *Wahoo's* crew heard about the dish closet, they planned to get their share of the artifacts. But the *Seeker's* crew had other plans for the artifacts: Chatterton descended to the wreck and welded a metal bar across the hole at the point where divers could most easily penetrate the wreck and drop right down to the dishes. Not content with blocking the entrance from the *Wahoo* divers, the *Seeker's* crew went a step further: They brought down a sign and affixed it to the barred hole. The sign read CLOSED FOR INVENTORY. THE *SEEKER*. As Nagel's boat departed the scene, everyone on board had a good laugh while they carefully stored their prized artifacts to prevent damage during the long ride home.

The *Wahoo's* divers were undeterred by the welded bar blocking their path. The sign only made the divers more determined to thwart their rivals' efforts. Hank Garvin and Richie Kohler dived to the hole. Kohler took off his tank, and wriggled past the metal bar into the wreck. Garvin then passed Kohler's tank through the low opening, where Kohler strapped his breathing unit onto his back and proceeded to the artifact area. When he recovered a goodie bag full of dishes, Kohler swam back up, handed the artifacts to Garvin, took off his tank again, passed it through the opening, and then crawled through himself. Garvin helped Kohler put the tank back on and the two ascended, smug in the knowledge that they had foiled Chatterton's and the *Seeker's* efforts. On their next dive, Garvin and Kohler took the *Seeker's* sign to add to their trophies and put their own sign in its place. It read INVENTORY COMPLETED. THE *WAHOO*.

Before our Team Doria '91 expedition, Moyer confided his plans to his boss, Steve Bielenda, and to Billy Deans, whom he had worked for at Key West Diver, the technical diving facility Deans owned in Florida. Billy Deans had brought along his Aqua-zepp, a diver-propulsion vehicle that looked just like a torpedo with handles on each side and a T-bar welded on top, three quarters of the way back. Once underwater, Deans lay face-forward on top of the Aqua-zepp and held the handles, positioned like a high-speed motorcycle racer. The bullet of a device propelled him so forcefully through the water that he needed the T-bar to hook his legs onto so that he would not flutter and lose control. Moyer held on to Deans's ankles and was pulled along. He signaled with a tug when he wanted Deans to stop and park the Aqua-zepp on the wreck. Once parked, the divers entered the wreck and searched the first-class area. Though they did not find the *Doria's* second bell, they did find the Gambone frieze. Its enormous size and weight meant they would have to bring their own team out to recover this treasure.

After I got out of my diving gear, Chris Rouse walked over to me and said, "You should talk to Wings. He's really pissed off."

"Why?" I asked.

"He's not happy with a bunch of stuff, but he's really mad about getting an artifact busted because the crew didn't help him."

I walked over to Wings, who was clearly agitated, judging by the scowl on his face. "Wings, what happened?"

"Fucking crew. All they care about are their dives. I thought they were supposed to be here to help. When I came up and was on the ladder, I was hollering for someone to help me, but nobody came."

"Maybe they couldn't hear you?"

Wings glared at me. "It's the crew's responsibility to *see* a diver when he comes up. Somebody should have been there and I shouldn't have had to yell." Wings's long beard quivered in indignation. "The whole attitude here *sucks*. Man, these guys would never stay in business if they were in California! And look at *this*." Wings reached into his goodie bag and pulled out a few pieces of long, curved, white glass and an oddly shaped piece of brass.

"Wow!" I exclaimed. "It looks neat. But what is it?"

"It *was* a wall-mounted flower vase in the men's room. I took it off the wall intact, but it broke when I got tossed around on the ladder. If one of the crew were there to help me, I'd have a nice, intact artifact." Wings grunted. He bent over the platform we used to gear up for our dives and laid the glass down, joining the pieces like a jigsaw puzzle. "See. It went like this," he said. "Oh, well, I guess I can glue it together, but it won't be the same." He sounded like a boy with a broken toy, and I understood his feelings completely.

"Yeah, you're right. But at least you got something. Let me talk to Bielenda and see what we can do so this doesn't happen again."

Bielenda listened to Wings's complaint and said simply, "I'll make sure someone's at the stern to help out. Someone should have been there for Wings, but it sounds like they were off helping somebody else. You can't be everywhere at once."

"There's enough crew on the boat that manpower shouldn't be a problem," I replied.

Bielenda looked me hard in the eye. "Bernie, don't forget, the crew have to work in shifts, so we have one or two people at the radar all night, and to make sure we don't start taking on water."

I wasn't sure I had made my point, but I noticed that when John Reekie came up from his dive, the crew members Hank Garvin and Jon Hulburt were there to help him.

As Reekie climbed the rocking ladder, he handed his goodie bag to Garvin. "Be careful with that!" shouted Reekie. "There's a glass bowl in the bag. Don't bust it!"

When he was safely back on board and out of his equipment, Reekie walked over to the plastic drum where Garvin had left Reekie's goodie bag for safekeeping. Reekie pulled the glass bowl out. It was large and looked ideal for punch, with the top rim cut to look like a series of connected semicircles. But he was disappointed that it did not have engraved in the glass the word ITALIA with a crown above it, the emblem of the company that had owned the *Andrea Doria*. Hulburt examined the bowl. "Where'd you get that?"

"The kitchen," Reekie answered gruffly.

"You went to the kitchen?" asked Hulburt, sounding more than a little surprised.

"Yeah, I looked at the deck plans and then went in. This wreck's bigger than the *Empress*, but it's still built the same way," Reekie said, referring to his baby, the ocean liner *Empress of Ireland*, which lay in the Gulf of St. Lawrence.

Hulburt admired the bowl and exclaimed, "Wow! It took me five years of *Doria* diving before I was comfortable enough to go where you just went on your first dive."

"Well, it sure helps having a line," Reekie told him. Garvin, listening to the two men, rolled his eyes at Reekie's mention of the guideline.

Chris Rouse peered over Reekie's shoulder. "I wish we'd have gotten something."

Chrissy Rouse frowned at his father. "We might have if you hadn't gotten spastic and tangled up!"

"So, guys, what happened on the dive?" I asked, a little alarmed.

Chris had gotten tangled in monofilament, the transparent fishing line used by fishermen that becomes attached to the wreck when fishermen snag their hooks on it and break their line. Monofilament is on every wreck and entangles even the most cautious diver. As Chris tried to cut the fishing line away from himself, he got tangled in his guideline. Chrissy helped his father, but it took some time to resolve the situation. In the confusion, they had abandoned their guideline reel, which lay on the wreck not far from the anchor line. I offered to retrieve the lost reel on the next dive.

"Nah, we'll get it. You can't just leave your gear on the bottom," Chris said indignantly.

I was reminded of Steve Bielenda's comment to me a year earlier when I complained about leaving my goodie bag, which contained a reel and light, inside the *Doria* during my third dive with Steve Berman, when he had wanted to leave the wreck and I had been entangled in the guideline. Bielenda had chuckled and remarked matter-of-factly, "If ya ain't left nothin' on the bottom, you ain't doin' nothin' underwater! We all got plenty of stuff left behind in the ocean."

Reekie looked at the Rouses and quickly threw in, "Why can't you guys leave a reel on the wreck? You have all sorts of shit on the bottom. What's the difference if you left a reel there to add to the other stuff?"

Seeing an opening, Chrissy decided to launch his own attack on his father. "Yeah, and you left that stage bottle down there. Why didn't you bring that up? That tank and the regulator are worth a lot more than a reel."

Chris set his jaw and turned to face his son. "What? You got some nerve!" He jabbed a finger in Chrissy's direction. "*You* were supposed to bring the tank up. *You* left it there. Don't try and blame it on *me!*"

The bickering was heating up quickly. I stepped between the two divers. "Okay, okay. Forget it. Get the tank on the next dive. Hell, I'll get it if you want."

My ploy worked. Both Rouses were diverted from clawing at each other by the thought of someone else recovering their gear, which was unacceptable. "No. No. We'll get the tank," Chris told me. "Thanks anyway, but we can retrieve our own stuff."

I wasn't very happy as I walked away from the Rouses. Their wild underwater antics gave me one more thing to worry about. The weather was miserable, and if it was not for the fact that everyone on board was very experienced, Steve Bielenda would not have even considered coming to the site once he had seen the water conditions offshore. As it was, he and I conferred regularly about the weather. With his many years as a sea captain, I trusted him to avoid unnecessary risk. Even then, we were both pushing it in our shared eagerness to have this expedition work out for the best. The boat was being violently rocked from side to side, and that afternoon, as I tried to eat the meal Sally had prepared, I was frustrated that my sweet peas rolled off my plate and onto the cabin's floor like scattered marbles. Although all of the Team Doria divers had a good laugh that Sally would serve peas in this sort of weather, the rolling food underscored the sea's roughness. I looked away from the peas and out the cabin window. When we were in the trough of a previous wave and the larger waves bore down on us, all I could see was a wall of water towering over the boat. I was reminded of the scene in the movie *The Poseidon Adventure* where a giant ocean liner is hit broadside by a massive, rogue wave and capsizes.

As the Rouses joked that the peas could always be eaten by our seasick researchers, Bielenda related that the weather report indicated that the sea would not get worse and would probably calm down. We elected to stay above the wreck that night. The crew would take turns watching the radar to make sure no other ships would collide with us. The area of the ocean we were in was known as the separation zone because it separated the sea lanes into and out of New York Harbor. They are marked on navigational charts as light-brown lanes; resembling highways cutting across the dark blue of the ocean south of Long Island, the northern light-brown lane is the route designated for ships of all sizes and descriptions from around the world to take when coming into U.S. territorial waters from the east; the southern lane is for ships outbound to Europe from the United States. Even though large freighters and tankers were not supposed to be in the separation zone, we often saw these behemoths steaming close to our relatively puny dive boat during the day.

The crew's vigilance at the radar was vital. Nobody wanted the *Wahoo* to end up on the ocean floor next to the *Doria*. On one night watch, Janet Bieser repeatedly called over the radio to a freighter on a collision course with the anchored *Wahoo*. While we divers slept in our bunks, unaware of the oncoming danger, the freighter continued on its course, until Janet angrily snapped commands into the radio microphone while simultaneously shining a spotlight toward the oncoming vessel. When the freighter was only a quarter mile away Janet saw on the *Wahoo*'s radar that the massive vessel had begun to make its course change. She breathed a sigh of relief and knew that if the rapidly moving freighter had not begun its course correction at that time, she would have had to cut the *Wahoo*'s anchor line to avoid being rammed and sunk. If the men on the freighter's bridge were asleep, the ensuing collision would not disturb them because it would be an unnoticeable bump, like a great white shark crashing into plankton.

I had slept undisturbed in my sleeping bag on one of the large, double-wide bunks below the main cabin, where the crew also slept. Steve Bielenda always reserved these spacious bunks for his crew and assigned me a bunk here because I had put the expedition together. I usually slept in the stern sleeping quarters that were accessed via a hatchway resembling a doghouse and a set of steep wooden stairs. Although the forward bunkhouse was more spacious, I was superstitious and preferred the small wooden bunk in the stern that everyone dubbed "the wine rack" because it was so narrow and enclosed. The wine rack had been my bunk when I'd dived the *Doria* with Berman in 1990, and we had good luck on those dives.

When I awoke after Janet's battle with the freighter, the sea was still rocking the *Wahoo* with the same intensity as the day before. Although the waves had not gotten smaller, they had not gotten larger either. I chose to look on things optimistically. Even then, I was concerned. These were not good conditions to be diving in. I did not want anyone getting hurt or killed because I pushed things and allowed the dives to continue. I knew that some divers, even though they might not feel totally at ease with the sea conditions, would not want to lose face; they would dive if given the chance. The least experienced diver among us was the one that I was concerned about. He had not been able to conduct all of the planned, necessary preparatory dives for this expedition and that left him woefully unprepared for anything but the best diving conditions. Sally told me that during his dive yesterday, he had problems with the rough surface conditions; when he descended to 20 feet, he realized how difficult his decompression would be, and aborted the dive without descending to the *Doria*. When he told me about his dive, I felt bad that he had not been able to see the wreck, but was also relieved that he had made the right decision and was back safely on board the *Wahoo*. Now I spoke to him, asking if he planned on diving today.

"Are you going to go in?" he asked, his voice a little tremulous, the brave little boy ready to emulate whatever his big brother would do. I didn't want him diving, but couldn't really expect him not to if I planned to go in. "No, I think it's too marginal today," I said. "I'll play it safe and stay on board."

"I guess I will too," he said. I could tell by his face how relieved he was. I was relieved too. However disappointed I was to give up my own opportunity at more artifacts, I didn't want this green diver to dive in these conditions, which he had never before experienced, and risk killing himself because he followed my lead.

The Rouses went about gearing up, the rolling boat forcing them to concentrate extra hard on moving cautiously among the cluttered deck to get all of their equipment together. They would stop what they were doing occasionally and one would ask the other how much longer he estimated it would take to finish suiting up. At least the weather was good for something: It prevented the Rouses from bickering before their dive. I helped Chris with his equipment, wished them both a good dive, and watched them jump into the water. When the Rouses were underwater, I again conferred with Steve Bielenda about the weather. He fixed his ice-blue eyes on me and said, "It's right on the border. We could be in for a rough night if we stay out here. It's your call."

I looked out over the waves, and then back at the white-haired sea captain who now sported several days of stubble on his chin. If it was going to be any rougher than it had been last night, I wanted no part of it. But if we left, the decompression research data would definitely not get recorded. Huggins and Emmerman, now pale and exhausted after a solid two days of nausea, would never get their sea legs and test out the targets they had marked on my body. I wouldn't get any trophies beyond the few bottles I had picked up yesterday. And as leader of this shortened expedition, I might get a good reputation for caution and sense, but I would not return home waving my guideline and trophies in triumph, with useful research in hand on the worth of mixed-gas–diving techniques on wrecks. On the other hand, the conditions were so severe that we were not anchored into the area of the wreck where we had planned to dive, which left us diving in teams of two and not coordinating our efforts overall to lay guidelines in the major passageways as we had planned.

Although it was a difficult decision, there was really only one thing to do. I turned to Bielenda and declared, "Okay, that's it. Let's wait for our guys to come up and then head to Block Island."

"Okay. But if we do that, we won't be coming back to the *Doria* tomorrow. There won't be enough time or fuel. We can go to another wreck, closer to shore, if conditions are better there."

I agreed.

As I walked away from the salty-faced sea captain, I breathed a sigh of nervous disappointment. I had done only one dive, and most of the other guys were just finishing their second. Yet aborting the expedition was the right thing to do. I hoped.

The Rouses surfaced an hour and a half after they had descended—a relatively short dive for them. During that time, the sea had gotten calm, and even the sun was shining. I feared that I'd made a bad decision to leave. There was only one more diver in the water. When the crew member Jon Hulburt surfaced, the other crew members told him we were leaving. Through his mask, I saw his eyes register shock. As the veteran diver climbed the ladder to get into the boat, he looked right at me and said, "What? We're leaving now? Great timing, just when it gets calm. Who made *that* smart decision?"

I didn't say anything. I hoped that time would vindicate my decision to leave.

As the Rouses took off their gear I heard them arguing, just as they had done after their last dive. "Now what happened?" I asked, though with the sun cheerily warming the back of my neck, I was in no mood to hear.

Chris turned to look at me. "We *were* having a nice dive. We penetrated about ninety feet. When we came out and swam on the outside of the wreck, Junior here decided to drop the reel and it fell to the bottom."

Chrissy rolled his head and his long, wet hair flopped up and down. "I didn't *decide* to do anything! It was an accident."

Chris shot his son a disgusted look. "Yeah, well, you could have found a better spot for the accident. You dropped that reel into the wreck right next to a nasty fishing net. And then you got tangled in it when you went to get the reel."

Chrissy apparently didn't want to be outdone by his father, who had gotten entangled during their previous dive. This time, instead of the elder Rouse getting tangled, it was the son who needed help to be pulled free.

Cave divers to the core, the Rouses knew the guideline reel helped preserve their lives underwater. With a more than sentimental attachment to the reel, instead of ascending and abandoning it, they would risk their lives to retrieve the reel. I was alarmed. "You got tangled in netting?"

Chrissy answered casually, "Yeah, it sucked. I had to cut myself free from the netting, and when I did that, I got caught in the line from our reel, and had to cut that too."

"Why didn't you just leave the reel? It's only a piece of equipment. And you make those things anyway for the business. How much can they cost? Five or ten bucks? And what's your life worth?"

"Every piece of equipment counts," answered Chris somberly.

The sun didn't feel so warm anymore. When I heard the Rouses' story, I was glad to be leaving the wreck before anything more serious happened.

That night, after six hours traveling from the *Andrea Doria* site to the nearest landfall, Steve Bielenda tied the *Wahoo* securely at the dock in Block Island as a wind blew so fiercely it threatened to rip flags from their poles. I was glad we were not at sea; I knew I had made the right decision.

During the expedition, Michael Menduno had been busy on board the *Wahoo* taking photographs and notes for *AquaCorps*. He knew Team Doria was the first real convergence of the cave- and wreck-diving communities, which made it a landmark expedition. That meeting had turned out to be rougher in more ways than the waves tossing the *Wahoo* around above the *Doria*. Menduno knew that those on board included many of the most advanced amateur practitioners of the complicated sport that he had dubbed technical diving. These divers' use of technology as a tool to overcome the limitations and dangers of the deep—including their development of mixed gases and other techniques to dive into shipwrecks and caves—set them apart from the rest.

The diving certification agencies were still adamantly opposed to sport divers' engaging in deep diving, and they were aghast that sport divers even contemplated undertaking complex dives involving mixed gases, or even air dives involving decompression. The agencies reasoned that if professional and military divers encountered difficulties even with their elaborate support network, then sport divers would surely encounter problems that would translate into more diving deaths, bad publicity for the sport, and a drop in business. Ever the optimist, Menduno believed that technological advancement was the natural order of things. It seemed logical to Menduno that sport divers should embrace mixed-gas technology and extend the depths they could dive. He also had a vested commercial interest in greater numbers of divers becoming enthusiastic about technical diving because that was what his magazine was all about. Menduno mused, "Bill Stone's Wakulla project was the Big Bang of technical diving. Team Doria was a collision of some of the forces set in motion by the Big Bang, before those forces merged in harmony."

Overall, I felt that the expedition had been disappointing. There was nothing that could be done about the bad weather; the uncertain elements, I knew, were part of diving. But the initial tension between the wreck divers and cave divers had deeply discomfited me. The discord existed beyond what my limited experience allowed me to effectively moderate. Gradually, over the course of the trip, the tension had eased, and some divers, like John Reekie, had impressed the older wreck divers with the application of cave-diving techniques to recover artifacts. The decompression research, especially the comparison of air to mixed-gas diving, had been unfruitful. Huggins and Emmerman had done their best and that was all anyone could ask, yet their seasickness prevented them from carrying out the research they had intended. Even after thousands of years of technological innovation, the sea still posed a formidable obstacle for humans, whether they chose to work on top of or under the water.

The artifacts I had recovered were nothing more exotic than a few soda bottles from the mid–fifties and the base of an ashtray. Even though Steve Berman and I had recovered some dishes from the *Doria* the previous year, quantities of the wreck's prized artifacts had eluded me again. It left me feeling unfulfilled yet determined to try again.

The Rouses had not recovered anything. Although they would be able to go back home secure in the knowledge that they had conquered the Mount Everest of scuba diving, they did not have the trophies that would really set them apart from the crowd. More than anything, they wanted some tangible proof of their outstanding diving skills. The challenge still loomed large, and they had not met it on this expedition.

And they would not let sleeping trophies lie—as I would find out almost immediately. When the *Wahoo* got back to home port Chris

Rouse said, "Bernie, we've decided to run our own expedition to the *Doria*, next year. We hope you'll be part of it." I didn't say yes and I didn't say no—but I was amused, and a little perturbed, that after just two contentious and fruitless dives into the *Doria*, father and son saw themselves as ready to lead an expedition, when they had never before led any sort of diving trip.

For the Rouses—as well as for me—the lure of the *Andrea Doria*'s artifacts propelled us to push our diving limits even further.

7

Triple Vision

WHEN THE ROUSES WENT to Underwater World, the shop where they had learned to dive and where Chrissy now worked repairing equipment, they held their fellow divers rapt with stories of their dives on the *Andrea Doria*. A dive that deep, that far out in the ocean, was well beyond the skills and aspirations of most of the shop's customers and employees, which served to turn Chris and Chrissy into local heroes—the Horsham, Pennsylvania, equivalents of astronauts returning triumphant from the Moon. Then came the inevitable question: "What did you get?"

The question was not intended to hurt, but still it cut like a knife. The Rouses both had wanted to return home with some artifacts, and they would have liked to come into the dive shop proudly displaying their trophies, the deep-sea equivalent of Moon rocks, tangible proof of an accomplishment shared by only a few hundred men and women around the world. Yet they were left with second best: They had dived the Mount Everest of scuba diving, but they wanted to be among those fewer still who returned home waving evidence of their dives. Trying to remain upbeat, Chris replied, "We didn't get anything—this time."

"Not any dishes or anything?" a weekend diver remarked. "People get dishes from there, right?"

"We'll get something next time," Chrissy said tersely. "We're putting together our own expedition for next year."

As the Rouses started planning their next foray to the *Doria*, they also kept up a steady pace of diving, returning each weekend to the quarry where they had completed their initial certification. After the challenge and excitement of diving a great ocean liner, this venue was a bathtub. Sure, it was nice to help out the instructors with their classes, and the Rouses could maintain their diving comfort and skills, but assisting during pool sessions was now as mundane as being a kindergarten teacher at nap times. Even if they were tethered to their jobs, to landlocked Pennsylvania and the need to make money, there had to be a way to get their pulses pumping and recover that adrenaline high they had known at the *Doria*—taking some risks, remaking the rules. And having something to show for it.

One night, over dinner, Chrissy suggested to his parents, "Wouldn't it be neat if we could find caves around here? There's got to be some. Maybe we can even find new forms of life and stuff like that!"

His father's face lit up. His son was on to something. "Yeah, it sure would be nice to do some real exploration around here. I'm just sick of the driving to get to either a dive boat or the caves in Florida."

"Yeah. And caves have no waves. Man, that *Doria* expedition was nasty. My stomach didn't feel so good."

"Mine either," Chris Rouse agreed as he lifted another forkful of food to his mouth.

At the end of July, only one month after they had dived the *Andrea Doria*, Chrissy called and said to me, "You can't tell anyone about this, but we've found a cave near us! It's on private land. You start the dive in a well house on the property, and you enter the water by taking out some loose floorboards. We had one-hundred-foot visibility and we even found some pottery on the bottom at sixty feet. Bernie, we'll let you know if this thing really goes, and you can dive with us. Right now, it looks like it's pinching out about a hundred feet in."

My heart leaped. This was great news. An undived local cave! It was a dream come true. "Let me know if you need any help with anything, even carrying tanks and stuff," I said. In the wake of the *Doria* mission, a mixed blessing of an accomplishment for me, I too was feeling landlocked. And I knew how rare an undived cave was and how the significance associated with it could bring a diver more accolades and acclaim than a thousand dishes. Such an expedition could really make a diver's name.

"Bernie, wouldn't it be cool if we found some new life forms and we got to name them?"

"Yeah," I breathed. "What a rush that would be."

Chrissy wasn't just being grandiose. In the past, divers had made startling discoveries inside caves and had even brought back specimens of completely new and previously undocumented species. As had long been the tradition, when someone discovers a new species, or a new, previously unexplored area above or below the earth, the honor of naming it is theirs.

One of the most dramatic discoveries of new life forms in recent years had occurred in Romania, at the edge of the Black Sea. In 1985, while starting the foundation for a new power plant, workers revealed an opening in the earth's crust. The government needed to know what lay underneath the great yawning vein where the foundation was to be laid. Christian Lascu, a geologist from the Emil Racovita Speleological Institute in Bucharest, was called in to inspect the opening, which he called Movile Cave. Lascu used a rope to rappel into the shaft, then found a maze of cave passages. He crawled 328 feet through one passage until he was stopped by a body of water. Further exploration would require diving gear. Lascu called on his friends in the Group for Underwater and Speleological Explorations, which he had helped form in Bucharest in 1981. Among its founding members was Serban Sarbu, a local high school biology teacher and cave diver. After preliminary exploration and measurements of the cave passages, Lascu and Sarbu rappelled into the cave in 1986, accompanied by their teammates, who carried the diving gear.

Lascu and Sarbu's discovery became the stuff of the most fanciful dreams of people like Chris and Chrissy Rouse, me, and cave divers everywhere. The two men dived into the water, swam a short distance through a tunnel, and then came to an air bell, an area where the tunnel was not completely flooded but partially filled with air, resembling a half-flooded subway tunnel. There was not much of interest to the divers here, but the air bell indicated the possibility of other cave rooms. They swam farther, through another completely flooded tunnel, and entered a second air bell. Here they found an alien environment unlike any they had ever witnessed, or even read about—except in science fiction: an environment whose walls and water literally crawled with strange insects. As they looked around in awe, they saw a bug smaller than a pea with numerous legs and long antennae crawling along the cave's wall, probing the rock surface for something to eat. One of the bug's antennae brushed against the antennae of an exotic-looking centipede, which was unfortunate for the bug: The two-and-a-half-inch centipede lunged at the bug, caught it in its jaws, and shredded it. In the water near the two men, an aquatic scorpion swam toward them. They watched as it sought out a bug in the water, grabbed it with its two long front legs, impaled the bug on its beak, and sucked out the bug's blood and other juices while the victim struggled in its death throes.

As Sarbu and Lascu turned to look at each other in astonishment and exultant triumph, they saw that they were each covered with a thin, white film, like wet toilet paper. Clearly, this cave was special. It warranted sustained inquiry, and it would establish the two divers as celebrated pioneer-naturalists. On subsequent dives, the two men documented forty-seven species living in the air bell, including thirty-two species previously unknown.

Further research unveiled something else: The gas in the second air bell was not air as we know it on the surface. It consisted of only 10 percent oxygen and contained over 3 percent carbon dioxide and a little under 1 percent methane. Surface life forms would not survive under these circumstances, yet an entire self-contained ecosystem thrived in air bell number two. Not only that, but a high concentration of hydrogen sulfide and methane rose to the water's surface from a hot-water vent leading deep into the earth. These gases were actually metabolized by a micro-thin film of bacteria—the substance that covered Lascu and

Sarbu whenever they ventured into the cave. The bacteria's metabolic processes released hydrogen sulfide, an acid that reacted with the limestone walls, eating away at them to create the cave. Though speleologists had speculated that such a process of cave formation was possible, it had never before been documented. Movile Cave was proof of a chemoautotrophically formed system—that is, a self-contained cave created as the direct result of the interaction of chemicals and life forms with the rock.

In addition to the acid they emitted, the bacteria produced glucose, an organic compound that was used as the building block for the rest of the organic compounds: carbohydrates, fats, and proteins. The microbial mat was at once the catalyst for the cave's formation, and the base of the food chain. Lascu and Sarbu became the first surface dwellers to enter the sealed cave system since its formation over a five-million-year period.

The discovery breathed new life into Sarbu. In 1987, he defected from then Communist Romania and made his way to the United States, where he used his work in Movile Cave as the basis for his doctorate in cave biology at the University of Cincinnati. He received a Fulbright scholarship, and after the Communist government fell in Romania, he returned periodically to continue his study of Movile Cave's fantastic world. He has become a legend among the cave-diving elite, who are inspired by Sarbu's discoveries to press on in the hopes that they, too, can make startling discoveries like Movile Cave.

Although Serban Sarbu's discoveries were significant, they were not widely known to the general public until the mid-nineties. Twenty years earlier, the discovery of new life forms along deep ocean vents had made headlines and captured news spots around the world. At that time, Robert Ballard—the man who would later go on to discover the deep-water resting places of such famous ships as *Titanic*, *Bismarck*, and *Yorktown*—was working on his doctorate, trying to show the usefulness of deep-submersible vehicles, minisubmarines that could go far deeper than their full-size military counterparts. During two National Geographic Society research expeditions, he and other scientists discovered several unique phenomena at the bottom of the Pacific Ocean, west of Ecuador. Here, one and a half miles below the surface, a vast vent in the ocean spewed forth molten lava, augmenting the ocean floor. Further research revealed an entire ecosystem that included giant clams, tube worms, and crabs from a family of previously unknown crustaceans. At the base of the food chain were bacteria that metabolized hydrogen sulfide spewed from the earth's core. This was the first discovered example of chemosynthesis, life forms' use of chemicals instead of sunlight to produce energy. Scientists had previously thought the deep ocean too inhospitable for extensive ecosystems. But the National Geographic expeditions brought back still and film images and specimens of creatures that thrived on the edges of the deep ocean vent.

The discoveries invigorated people who believe that life in our universe takes many forms. Some people had been smug in the notion that unique life forms would be found only in outer space, but we now had proof that our own planet still concealed many mysteries of life. What else would we discover underwater?

Even as our technological development allowed us to put a man on the Moon in 1969, in 1991 we still could not put a man in a suit on the bottom of the ocean because of the crushing water pressure. Exploration and research in the deep ocean was possible only inside highly specialized minisubmersibles. But diving-suit design was progressing: The Newtsuit, designed by Canada's Phil Nuytten, could now take divers down to 1,500 feet surrounded by a surface-pressure environment, which meant they could rise immediately back to the surface without having to decompress. For deeper explorations, humans had to content themselves with brief forays in submersibles, where the best they could do was peer through small, thick glass portholes at the alien world outside the vehicle. If they wished to touch something, or retrieve a sample from the outside and bring it to the surface, they had to do so through painstaking movements of a mechanical claw attached to the submersible.

Closer to home and far more accessible to sport divers than either the work or person of Serban Sarbu or Dr. Robert Ballard was Rob Palmer, a British cave diver whose 1990 book *Deep into Blue Holes* described his scuba explorations of Bahamian caves. Palmer frequently gave talks at various diving conferences, where the gregarious Englishman mingled with other divers at social events. He enjoyed the admiration of the masses attending the conferences, and he glowed in the spotlight. Rob Palmer stood in contrast to Billy Deans and Sheck Exley, two men who felt more comfortable in very small group settings and who shied away from the attention offered them at the large diving conferences.

Palmer's book cover showed divers in a deep cave system, the distances obviously vast as they swam through a massive underwater room. "Did you get Palmer's book?" Chris asked me over the phone one day. "Oh, did you *see* that great cover shot? Wow, what a cave that must be! Wouldn't you just *love* to explore it?" I agreed. Chrissy, Chris, and I were all equally enthralled.

Both of the Rouses and I were impressed with the spirit of exploration that had guided Palmer from the cold, murky caves of his native island nation to the fantastic discoveries of caves and life forms in the warm-water, clear caves throughout the Bahamas. Many of the life forms found on Palmer's expeditions were thought to have been extinct for centuries and offered scientists a chance to examine these creatures, as well as learn more about how life developed on the planet and how it continues to adapt. The caves themselves offered enormous and—in scuba-diving terms—often very deep systems to explore. Oddly, tides seemed to move through these caves—another phenomenon neither obvious nor previously known.

Inspired by discoveries of new life forms and by divers like Exley, Deans, Dr. Bill Stone, and Rob Palmer, the Rouses went back to Lahaska—the cave that started underneath the Pennsylvania well house—several days after they had first dived it. The visibility was only 10 feet: The silt remained suspended from their previous exploratory probing of the dark-brown, mud-covered walls to find passages that led farther. There was no current to carry away the silt as there was in the spring systems in Florida. Undeterred by the low visibility, the Rouses pushed on. Chris and Chrissy decided to split up, with each of them exploring different areas of what they dubbed "the Big Room." They each found passageways that led them out of the room, and they extended their maximum penetration into Lahaska Cave to 200 linear feet. It was slow going, but promising, just as Florida's cave-diving pioneers had experienced in the systems they discovered in the fifties and sixties. The Rouses' explorations were yielding new passageways, which elated them and raised their hopes of finding ever more extensive tunnels. Maybe they would find new life forms somewhere in this cave after all?

Lahaska's low ceilings meant that the two explorers would need a different equipment configuration to allow at least one of the Rouses to continue pushing the discovery forward. The lack of large tunnels filled with crystal-clear water meant that their diving in Lahaska Cave would be safer if they dived alone, and they decided that each one would explore a different area of the cave and independently probe for continuing passageways. During their second exploration of the cave, Chrissy used an advanced tank setup known as sidemounting, where the tanks are worn at the diver's side and not on the back, as they normally are. This was perfect for wide but low systems, such as Lahaska Cave.

Sidemounting had itself been developed by British cave explorers, who frequently encountered sumps, bodies of water blocking their progress in otherwise dry cave passages. The sidemount rigs allowed the cavers to penetrate the sump and swim to another section of dry cave passage, where they would continue exploring. Rob Palmer was well versed in this form of diving, and pictures of him in sidemount configuration appeared in his book.

Chris and Chrissy were excited about their new cave, but the adrenaline rush it provided them would soon be shut off, and for mundane reasons: The cave's water supplied a seasonal motel, and when the owner opened one of the faucets in the motel after the Rouses dived it in late July and found murky water flowing out, he was understandably frustrated. The silt that the Rouses stirred in Lahaska Cave was not filtered out of the well system. The owner did not want his guests to experience muddy-water showers, so he told the Rouses that they could explore the cave only during the winter, late fall, and early spring.

Luckily, cave systems' water temperatures do not change drastically from season to season the way the air temperature does, but remain within a few degrees of the region's average yearly temperature. In late July, when the Rouses first dived the system, the water temperature was 52 degrees Fahrenheit; the Rouses could comfort themselves that even in the dead of winter, the water temperature would not drop drastically lower than that. Still, their high aspirations were thwarted, at least temporarily, and they were both back at their jobs and at the quarry, with nothing to show for their efforts but words and hope. That was not easy for men whose ambitions—and competitiveness—kept pushing them further and deeper.

With Lahaska Cave exploration cut off until the late fall, the Rouses made time for their instructor friends at Underwater World, and they often continued to assist classes during final checkout dives for certification at Dutch Springs quarry. Cathie Cush, one of the instructors who worked for Underwater World, had been teaching since 1986 and had met the Rouses when they first started diving in 1988. When the store's owner asked Chrissy to help Cathie with her students during spring checkouts in 1989, her first impression of Chrissy indicated a generational difference between the eighteen-year-old and the woman who was closer to his mother's age: She thought Chrissy was overimpressed with himself, strutting with the confidence of youth.

In spite of her first impression, Cathie grew to value Chrissy as an excellent assistant because he was always willing to lend a hand and efficiently helped the students with their equipment. As Chrissy's diving skills developed, Cathie came to rely on the younger man's expertise, and she appreciated his examining her equipment and fixing anything that did not work flawlessly. She especially valued the way he suggested changes to her setup that made her more streamlined and efficient in the water: He never made her feel that she was inadequate or that he was trying to show her up in front of her students. She now felt so confident with Chrissy's expertise that she actually felt uncomfortable if the young man did not inspect her regulators and gear setup before she went in the water.

Cathie had developed a good friendship with all three Rouses, including Sue, who liked Cathie's relaxed, trustworthy, and non-threatening manner. Cathie admired the Rouses' passion for the sport, as well as the confidence that the wife and mother displayed in her two men, who engaged in such a daring exploit as cave diving. Cathie also identified with Sue's participation in cave diving, and marveled that the three of them enjoyed such a hazardous sport as a family activity. The Rouses' passion for diving especially came across whenever they told any story about their diving adventures. When any of the Rouses told a story, they were as enthusiastic as children telling their friends what they got for their birthday. During one party, Chris sat next to Cathie and proceeded to hold her spellbound with his stories of cave diving. Chris casually recalled swimming at night on the surface, toward an underwater cave, and asking his buddy what all the red lights on the shore were. Chris simply nodded and smiled as he told Cathie that his friend had answered, "Gator eyes." Cathie couldn't imagine being so casual about swimming at night with alligators onshore—even if it was in full scuba gear. She was also moved by the story about Chrissy searching for the lost line while his mother waited alone for her son to return and bring her to the line leading out of the cave. Cathie could only think how anxious Sue must have felt. That night with Chris, even though Cathie knew she should be sociable and talk with the other guests, she was glued to her chair, unable to get up even for another drink or to visit the bathroom.

Cathie's friendship with Chrissy developed as much out of fascination with his passion for the sport as it did out of admiration for his youthful self-assurance and masterful diving skills. She also enjoyed the flirtatious interaction with a younger man. One evening, after Chrissy helped Cathie at the quarry, he drove her home in his car, a beat-up Volkswagen Beetle whose backseats he had removed to make room for the racks that secured scuba tanks. As they arrived at her house, Chrissy parked the car and casually reached into the back. From among the melee of scuba tanks and bags of diving equipment, he pulled a slice of pizza out of a box. It was frozen pizza—but it had defrosted and had never been heated. Cathie looked at him with alarm. "You can't eat that!"

"Why not?"

"Because it's frozen pizza right out of the box. You're supposed to heat it, that's why!"

Chrissy contemplated the pizza. "Nah, it looks fine. It's been sitting in the car over a week. It's not frozen now." He took a bite and moaned in appreciation.

Cathie was shocked, amused, and a little worried. Her young friend wasn't disgusting her—he was recklessly courting food poisoning. Chrissy swallowed his pizza, looked at Cathie, and blurted out, "You know, I've always had this fantasy of being with an older woman."

Cathie was stunned more than ever. She didn't know what to say. Chrissy's youthful, long-haired look and nonchalant manner belied his seriousness, but she knew a come-on when she heard one. "Chrissy, your mom would tear my eyes out!"

Chrissy's face drooped into sadness. He looked away briefly. Suddenly, he turned to look at Cathie, his eyes sparkling like a child's on Christmas Day. "Yeah, but my dad would say, 'Go for it!'"

Cathie could only laugh. As she opened the car door she remarked, "I've got to go, silly. Alone. See you soon."

Chrissy had told his friend Tim Stumpf about his desire for an older woman while they were hanging out at a local bar, drinking beer and telling stories about women, as young men do. Chrissy was spending more and more of his spare time at Stumpf's house, partying with his somewhat older friend, enjoying a newfound freedom and identity that he lacked at his parents' house, where his father had an opinion about everything, from the flavor of Chrissy's bagel to the length of his hair and his lack of any life ambition. The one thing that Chrissy needed more than anything was something that his parents could not easily give: independence. It was something he had to take when he could grab it, and earn long term.

Chrissy told Tim over a beer how things had gone with Cathie Cush. "I really like Cathie, you know? She's fun to be around, she likes diving—"

"And she's an older woman," Tim interrupted. "So, cut the shit. Did you get down, or what?"

"She did come on to me," Chrissy lied. "But you know, she's like my mom's age, and they're friends and all. I mean, what would my mom think?"

Tim made a disbelieving face. "You're kidding, right? Like you said, 'No.' Sure!"

"No, man, really. No kidding!" Chrissy insisted.

Better for Tim Stumpf and his drinking buddies to think Chrissy Rouse lied about turning Cathie down than to know that she had considered his advances a youthful prank.

Chris and Chrissy were bored. They were both eager to teach more advanced subjects and not just help out with the basic diving class.

Sue still enjoyed assisting students, and she found that the people who faced the greatest challenges during the pool sessions were the ones most rewarding to help. Sue remembered her own difficulties during training, and the discomfort she had felt when she went to the quarry for her final training, the checkout dives to get her certification. She was determined to help others avoid discomfort—and possible injury. Sue was also there during checkout dives, assisting with the class and at the same time keeping her diving skills up-to-date. This was important if she was to dive the *Andrea Doria* next summer on the expedition her husband and son were planning.

Meanwhile, I returned to the *Doria* six weeks after our disappointing expedition. The few dishes I had recovered with Steve Berman in 1990 and the soda bottles I retrieved on the Team Doria expedition served only as an appetizer: I hungered to recover a large pile of dishes, like experienced *Doria* divers such as Hank Garvin and the crew of the *Wahoo*.

This time, I dived with John Griffith, who had been a member of Team Doria. Griffith had short hair and thick glasses and confided the details of his projects as if relating vital state secrets. "Bernie," he would say, leaning closer while looking quickly over both shoulders to make sure nobody was listening, "I'm going to tell you something, but only if you *promise* not to tell! Promise?" I'd consent, and then John would unveil his latest engineering masterpiece to create some sort of better diving equipment. He would always punctuate his revelations with "Bernie, I swear I'll never talk to you again if you mention this to *anyone*!" One of his secrets was his plan to start his own specialty diving business, just as the Rouses had done. Griffith would do things a bit differently than the Rouses, who had plunged into their diving business not just out of love of the sport but out of financial desperation. Griffith was doing well financially as an industrial lighting salesman, and he lived comfortably with his wife and their two children in a New York City suburb. With his finances on solid footing, Griffith had the time to meticulously set up manufacturing and importing contacts for the gear he would sell, with his company logo affixed to it. Griffith was still in the planning stages, and I kept his secret, as I had promised.

The thick prescription lenses built into Griffith's diving mask made his eyes look bug-huge and gave him a cartoonish apperance. It was hard for me not to laugh whenever I looked at him underwater, but if I did laugh, water flooded my mask and I had to go through the simple but annoying procedure of tilting my head back, holding the top of the mask, and blowing air out of my nose to displace the water, which was usually enough to stop my laughter, until Griffith would swim up to me and stare into my mask with a concerned look on his face, which distorted his eyes even more. Nevertheless, Griffith's methodical, serious approach to diving seemed sensible to me, and he was a very willing team player. He was also easy to get along with and I liked diving with him.

Also spurring me to ally with him as a diving partner was our shared hunger for trophies. Together we could make a killing on the *Doria*. Griffith had a plan to recover numerous artifacts from a dish closet inside the *Andrea Doria*. He knew where the room was because he had dived there recently with Steve McDougall, who earned his living as a New Jersey state trooper, with special duties on the bomb squad. The powerfully built policeman shaved his head, and looked very much like Mr. Clean. McDougall's diving skills were impeccable; he and Griffith had worked as a team, with McDougall going inside the small closet, filling up a goodie bag with dishes, then relaying the bag out of the room to Griffith, who then handed him a second bag to fill. When McDougall was done filling the second bag, the two divers dragged their heavy haul out of the wreck and rose triumphant to the surface. It was a proven plan, and other skilled wreck divers, including Hank Garvin and the crew of the *Wahoo*, had successfully carried it out after Gary Gentile—the diver who wrote the book on diving the *Andrea Doria*—discovered the closet.

"Bernie, can you dig?" Griffith asked. "Because I really don't like the idea of going into a tiny room at over two-hundred-foot depth and stirring up all that silt." My heart raced with anticipation. Yes, yes, I could—and would—dig while Griffith waited outside the dish closet holding the guideline leading out of the wreck. Although other wreck divers, particularly the older veterans, felt a guideline was unnecessary, Griffith shared my belief that we could too easily get disoriented in the silt-out and end up losing our lives for a place setting. To complicate matters, the closet was next to a stairwell, which itself was at a ninety-degree angle because the wreck lay on its side. Without a guideline, disorientation, combined with a four-martini nitrogen buzz, would probably cause us to change deck levels when we made our retreat from the silted passageway.

After we descended, Griffith led the way into the gaping hole, letting the guideline spool out from his tie-off near the anchor line, which was only 20 feet away from the opening. I admired the still intact teak decking, now covered with a thin film of silt. The wreck's rusted steel frame was overgrown with anemones, the plantlike animals whose tentacles catch nutrients floating past in the current. The anemones thinned as we penetrated farther into the wreck, where water did not flow freely. Griffith swam to his left, around a steel wall, and disappeared completely, as if the wreck had swallowed him. I followed his guideline, rounded the steel wall, and caught a glimpse of his swim fins as they disappeared into another hole, to our right. I followed and noticed the stairway to our left as we swam to the closet. Griffith waited, hovering in the water next to the wall on our right, looking at me through his mask and large eyes. He pointed to an opening in the wall. It was the closet. I nodded, swam past him into the opening, and found myself in a tiny room. I dropped a few feet to the bottom of the room, my heart pounding with excitement. I made sure to keep my fins up as I stuck my arm into the silt, which felt fluffy and offered no resistance until my arm was in up to the elbow. With my buried hand I could feel the solid bottom of the room. I craned my neck upward to prevent my mask and regulator from being enveloped by the silt. If that happened, my regulator might clog and malfunction. I moved my hand slowly around the bottom and felt a cup, which I grabbed and pulled out of the silt. The room was now pitch black and I could not see Griffith's light, which I knew was only a few feet away. I put the cup into my goodie bag and then plunged my hand into the silt again. The room was littered with artifacts, which made a muffled clinking sound when I dropped them into my rapidly filling bag. I swam toward Griffith, holding the goodie bag in one hand and waving my free hand in front of me as I had done inside the U.S.S. San Diego, when I was lost and had to search for the opening of the dish room. Griffith saw my hand come out of the black curtain of silt that billowed from the closet, and he grabbed my arm to let me know he was there. I thrust the goodie bag in his direction. He took the bag and pressed a second bag into my hand. I turned around, dropped back down to the room's floor, and continued to gather artifacts.

Griffith and I worked well as a team and in three dives gathered over 120 artifacts, including hand-painted flower vases, dishes, saucers, and various-size cups. The china sported a deep-blue band and a separate band of gold running around the inside of the rim of the dishes, or on the outside of the cups. They also carried a distinct deep-blue logo depicting a crown over the word ITALIA, the name of the company that had owned the *Andrea Doria*. I was elated. Finally, I had achieved a significant haul of the *Doria*'s prized artifacts.

The artifacts themselves weren't so important to me that I needed to hoard them, the way many other divers did, and I eventually gave most of my share away as gifts to friends. What was important to me was the satisfaction of carrying out the dive plan in one of the most challenging wrecks in the world. I now felt that I had "arrived" in wreck diving. The Rouses had not been able to make it on this expedition and I knew they would groan in disappointment and envy when they heard about my success.

The weather was outstanding on our expedition, the water calm, and the visibility underwater good. The only drawback was a stiff current during decompression, but I managed this easily with the jonline tied to the anchor line and then clipped to my harness, which allowed a hands-free decompression where I was free to relax and admire the marine life that was propelled swiftly past me in the current.

There was time for a fourth dive during the expedition. Griffith urged me on. "Come on, Bernie, let's go to the room again and *really* clean it out!" he exclaimed as we celebrated our hoard. Even without his mask, his eyes were huge with excitement.

I was amazed. How many artifacts did we need? I wanted a new challenge, and looked forward to a long swim through a new area of the wreck. Maybe I could even cut through the second-class area where we were anchored and probe the third-class passageway. I wanted to recover the goodie bag, reel, and light that I had abandoned during my overly exciting third dive with Steve Berman in 1990. They lay next to a pile of artifacts, and were abandoned when I got snagged in the guideline while recovering artifacts and Berman untangled me so that we could both swim out.

Griffith contemplated my plan, then shook his head. "Bernie, two hundred and forty feet is too deep for me. I can't safely do that kind of dive with only one set of tanks. I know you're comfortable with it, but I'd just get us both in trouble. You go alone, if you want." I appreciated my friend's honesty. And now I could look forward to the heady freedom of a solo dive.

When I entered the *Doria* at the now-familiar opening that led to the dish closet, I swam the 20 feet to the stairwell that lay beside the closet. Instead of making a right turn into the stairwell, I swam to my left, down a corridor that passengers and crew once traversed to get to other parts of the ship. I tied off my guideline here, away from the entrance leading into this area, and away from the stairwell. It was far enough away that somebody else diving from our boat would not accidentally follow the line, thinking that it led to the dish closet. I had been in this area enough to know my way out from here without a guideline. My technique was a combination of the old-time wreck diver's method of progressive penetration and the cave diver's guideline method.

The once horizontal passageway now lay vertical, its path still leading to the opposite side of the *Andrea Doria*, but now it was a drop straight down to the bottom instead of parallel to the ocean surface. I followed it, looking for another connecting passageway to my right, one that would take me into the third-class area of the ship. Behind me, the green-tinted sunlight, which had filtered down to the wreck and into the opening I had entered, was now fading, and soon I had no ambient light at all. In the pitch blackness, only my powerful dive light could reveal the interior's secrets. The water felt noticeably colder, perhaps because of my exposed lips, but the low temperature actually seemed to penetrate my drysuit and thick underwear. My narcosis-clouded mind registered only cold. I neither cared where it came from nor paid much attention to any discomfort it was causing me.

Now, I was warmed and caressed by my solitary experience inside the wreck. Nobody else was here to disturb this moment for me, to interrupt whatever I felt like doing on this dive, or to dictate what I should or should not be doing at any given moment. On this dive, I did not have the responsibility of watching out for my buddy, nor was I a burden on anyone else. It was a situation as liberated from daily existence as any I had ever experienced, and I lapped up the peaceful pleasure of a solitude that had sometimes been a curse for me growing up an only child.

As I descended the corridor headfirst, my exhaled bubbles ran along my body and then up the path I had come down. Sometimes the bubbles from a diver's mouth would end up trapped inside the wreck, converging to form air pockets inside an enclosed room or passageway. The oxygen in the expired air bubbles would react with the wreck's steel, creating rust and eating away at the metal, weakening it, making it easier for the water current and storms to act over time as a sledgehammer pulverizing the *Doria* into the bottom of the Atlantic Ocean. Eventually, no trace at all would remain on the ocean floor of the floating art palace.

I could not find the passageway into third class. When the vertical passageway ended, I could make only a left-hand turn, toward the bow of the vessel, deeper into second class and heading toward first class. I checked my depth gauge, although I did not need to: I knew my depth was 238 feet and the gauge only confirmed it. My pressure gauges indicated a comfortable margin of life-giving air in both tanks. I switched regulators so that I would breathe the tanks down evenly. With this necessary dive maintenance taken care of, I swam along the horizontal passageway, my guideline spooling easily off the reel, my light revealing dishes and glassware buried to varying depths by fine silt. I frog-kicked down the passageway so I would not disturb the silt, and passed up the dishes. I could get these on my return, if I did not come across something better.

Ahead of me, the passageway came to an abrupt end in a mound of silt from which protruded pipes and cables. It looked like a landslide. I turned around and swam back, slowly inspecting the dishes I had previously disregarded, as if I were shopping. I knew that as soon as I touched something, the visibility would very quickly be reduced to nothing, so I wanted to make sure that what I did grab was worthwhile; I already had plenty of artifacts on this trip and I had the luxury of being picky. I plucked up a dish and put it inside my goodie bag, silt billowing around me. I kicked twice to propel myself farther along the corridor in the direction I had come, slipping out of the silt cloud. As I moved along the passageway, I wound in my guideline reel while inspecting the bottom for more trophies. The ITALIA crest was distinguishable on a second plate, and I put the dish in my bag, then proceeded on my way. I came to an interesting, delicately shaped white ceramic creamer. I had never seen one of these before. I carefully picked it off the bottom. As I lifted the creamer up to the small goodie bag I carried especially for delicate items, a plume of silt trailed from it like a jet engine's exhaust. The artifact looked intact and I was pleased with it.

After I had safely put the creamer into the bag and made sure it was securely closed, I checked my dive computer, which indicated that I had already been underwater for twenty-two minutes. It was time to go. I swam quickly along the corridor while reeling in the line, then propelled myself rapidly up the vertical passageway. My computers beeped with warnings that I was ascending too fast, which could cause decompression sickness. I ignored the warnings; I felt that a fast ascent from 238 feet to 200 feet was justified, because each minute I stayed at depth added dramatically to my required decompression, which now would clock in at over two hours. I slowed my ascent when I got to 200 feet, and I came to my guideline tie-off point. I unclipped the line, reeled it all the way in, twisted the knob that prevented the line from unraveling, then put the guideline reel into my all-purpose bag, which contained some tools, backup printed dive tables in case my two computers failed, a lift bag, my jonline, and extra knives in case I needed to cut myself free from an entanglement and either lost or could not reach the two knives I wore.

I swam out of the wreck, shut off my dive light and clipped it off on my harness, and kicked toward the anchor line, where I had tied off my oxygen decompression tank and another decompression tank that contained air. I found these tanks and clipped them onto my harness shoulder rings. As I slowly ascended the anchor line, I grabbed each tank's bottom clips and attached them at my harness hip rings, so that the tanks lay under my arms and did not swing about dangerously, which could injure me or other divers on the anchor line, especially during the long decompression.

After three and a half hours underwater—most of which was spent decompressing, during which time I examined my artifacts, relived the dive, and allowed myself the luxury of thinking how lucky I was to be able to explore underwater—I surfaced and climbed aboard the

Seeker, elated with my three finds. And I had done it all on my own. The winner of trophies, the entrepreneur of the deep, I felt like a lone cowboy on the planet's last frontier.

Solo diving had become one of the more controversial aspects of the sport. Only recently had the subject been openly discussed in the community, spurred on by Michael Menduno's magazine *AquaCorps,* whose first issue, in 1989, was titled "Solo." The recreational training agencies held as their motto "Always dive with a buddy," yet many divers have chosen to dive alone on occasion. Both Chris and Chrissy Rouse had conducted many solo dives in caves, and most divers, especially cave explorers, had the skills and guts to dive solo all the time, just as northeast-wreck divers had shown themselves to have years earlier. Cave and wreck divers knew that self-sufficiency and self-reliance were the best methods to prevent an accident. If you knew what you were doing you could learn to go it alone. The confidence that came from successfully conducting solo dives was a tremendous asset. But there were drawbacks also.

Having another diver close by was considered a way to ensure safety, so that if one diver encountered problems, the other could assist in overcoming them. This viewpoint was a direct result of the YMCA's swimming program, which taught that people should always swim in the ocean or in lakes in pairs, so that if one swimmer got cramps, the buddy would be able to get the afflicted swimmer back to safety.

At their most rational and sociable, which was most of the time, even very daring divers would agree that having a buddy could not only be useful but sometimes meant the difference between life and death. When Chrissy Rouse and his mother lost their visual reference to the guideline leading out of the Devil's Cave System, the buddy system worked because Chrissy had the skills and confidence to conduct the lost-line search and find the guideline that led out of the cave. Although Sue could have undertaken the search herself, her fear was eased by knowing that her son and diving buddy was doing it for the team. She knew that Chrissy would be back for her. Chrissy's dive to find the reel was essentially a solo dive because his mother had to wait while holding on to the side of the cave wall.

The psychological effect of having another diver nearby was

often extremely calming, especially to those new to cold-water, limited-visibility conditions, or when divers explored inside wrecks or caves. To be alone in an alien world could often be overwhelming, leading a diver to panic and death. Perhaps the effects of nitrogen narcosis enhanced the human mind's primitive fear of the dark and of enclosed spaces, triggering the survival "fight-or-flight" response.

The urge to flee when you are underwater usually leads to irrational behavior. A diver's most common impulse is to swim rapidly to the perceived safety of the surface. Unfortunately, a panicked diver fleeing to the surface has a tendency to hold his breath. When this happens, the compressed air he has breathed from his scuba tank expands in his lungs as he ascends to a level where there is less surrounding pressure. The expanding air rips through his lungs' walls in a process called air embolism. The released air bubbles may enter the bloodstream, where they continue to expand, eventually reaching the heart and causing it to stop pumping. Or the bubbles enter the brain. There, they cause death by damaging the sensitive brain tissue, and also by shutting off the supply of oxygen as the expanded air bubbles get so large they block blood from getting past. A diver with air embolism is extremely lucky if the bubbles do not enter his bloodstream and instead rip through the tissues and collect under his skin, usually around the shoulders and neck. Subcutaneous emphysema swells the skin and feels like pressure on the neck; the swollen skin crackles to the touch, like Rice Krispies soaked in milk. Although the fight-or-flight response may have helped primitive man survive, it is deadly to the diver. Underwater problems have to be solved underwater.

Although the dive-training agencies officially believe that having a buddy would help in any situation, the primitive urge to flee is sometimes so great that a panicked diver endangers the diver who comes to help him. For example, if a diver runs out of air, and his buddy attempts to share his air, they can end up fighting for the regulator: The urge for self-survival can become so great that one diver irrationally refuses to give the life-giving regulator back to the other. Numerous double fatalities have occurred in this manner. In spite of the dangers that a panicked diver can pose to a buddy, recreational dive-training agencies still insist that divers dive in pairs.

One of the ways that a diver can help his buddy avoid or overcome panic is with the use of voice communications. Even in a frightening, blackened, silted-out environment, hearing another person's voice can be calming; it also can facilitate the formulation of a rational, coordinated plan to safely complete the dive. In an environment where all of your senses are muffled, shrouded, absent, or at risk, being able to speak can make a huge difference. Although commercial divers like Glenn Butler use voice communications as part of their standard equipment, sport divers for the most part have gone without this potentially life-saving apparatus. An exception was Jim Baden, an ex-marine, masterly diver, and pioneer technical-diving instructor.

The Rouses and I had a chance to see Baden's voice communications system at work during our Team Doria expedition. Baden had flown from California for this expedition, as had Wings Stocks. Baden, like Stocks, owned a dive shop in California and taught everything from recreational diving to mixed-gas technical diving. But that was where the similarities between the two men ended. In appearance and temperament, Baden and Stocks were opposites. The former U.S. marine sniper was as tall as Stocks, but his frame had the wiry musculature of a swimmer as opposed to Stocks's bulky, football lineman build. And Baden's angular face was always clean-shaven, his hair cut short, quite a contrast to Stocks's bushy, Hell's Angels look. Baden reveled in military precision, dispensing with smiles and chitchat. His no-small-talk philosophy and his teaching methods were more distant from Stocks's gentle, mentoring training than his dive shop in the hills east of Los Angeles was from Stocks's shop in a suburb of San Francisco. Of those dedicated—some would say masochistic—few students who had stuck with Baden's rigid, militaristic training program, there was only one, Chuck Schmidt, whom Baden had deemed ready for the challenge of the *Andrea Doria.*

Both Baden and Schmidt had trained together extensively using full-face masks, which cover the entire face, unlike conventional scuba masks—referred to as half-masks—which cover only the eyes and nose. The full-face mask has an oral-nasal piece built into it, the same type of device a dentist uses when administering gas to a patient. The single regulator was affixed at the base of the oral-nasal mask and did not require Baden and Schmidt to hold their regulators in their mouths. This feature afforded them the advantage of using communications gear so that they could talk to each other and to the surface. And the gear itself was a big technological advance, because, rather than use umbilical cables to hard-wire their communications system to the surface, as commercial divers had done for over a hundred years, Baden and Schmidt employed radio waves to transmit their voices.

As a commercial diver, Glenn Butler approved of the fact that Baden and Schmidt used communications for sport diving: "I couldn't imagine not using communications gear underwater," he has told me. "It keeps you focused. It's also invaluable if you encounter any problems down there." Commercial divers frowned on the usual procedure of sport divers, which precluded communications capability between divers and topside personnel. If something went wrong underwater, commercial divers reasoned, it was so much easier to prevent a tragedy if everyone could speak with one another. The ability to communicate verbally makes it far easier to summon divers into the water to help search for a lost diver, or help bring up an unconscious diver. Their argument has plenty of merit. How many sport divers' lives could have been saved if they had been able to call for help?

One tragic father-son incident could have been avoided with the use of communications equipment. The dive pair planned to penetrate the wreck of the U.S.S. *San Diego*—the armored cruiser sunk off the south shore of New York's Long Island during World War I—and look for artifacts. The son followed his father inside the wreck, but swam too close behind and got his mask knocked off his face by his father's leg. Visibility was severely reduced by the father's flutter kicking—the motion where the legs move alternately up and down and the force of the kick is directed downward, stirring up silt—and when the son got his mask back on, he could see nothing. With no visibility and no communications equipment, he could not locate his father. The seventeen-year-old boy swam back to the dive boat *Wahoo* and told the crew that he had gotten separated from his father. A search was initiated, and the boy's father was found, inside the wreck, dead. Did the father expend all of the air in his single tank looking for his son? Or did he get disoriented and lose his way out?

The boy was devastated. He told the *Wahoo*'s crew he believed he had caused his father's death. The youth gave up diving permanently and still carries the psychological burden of the responsibility he feels for his father's death. No amount of consolation from the *Wahoo*'s crew could bring back the boy's father, or the boy's enthusiasm for the sport he had shared with his father.

For the Rouses, communications equipment posed the drawback of letting them say too much underwater. They did not need to extend their verbal bickering capabilities any further. Underwater, the regulators in their mouths created a self-imposed bickering moratorium which made their dives more enjoyable. Though they thought Baden's idea was innovative, the Rouses wondered about the safety of having only one regulator and were uncertain how they would efficiently switch breathing gases during a dive. Baden overcame these problems by wearing a backup half-mask around his neck with a separate regulator unattached to the full-face mask and within easy grasp. If he encountered a breathing problem with his unit, Baden would take off the full-face mask underwater, put the spare regulator in his mouth, and then don his backup mask. Baden also used this procedure when he needed to switch to decompression gases. The Rouses thought this cumbersome. Also, the full-face mask used more gas than the standard scuba setup.

Not that this father-son team wasn't laden already. The Rouses' cave-diving training specified that they carry at least two of every piece of life-support apparatus during a dive. In a cave, when the only way to the surface was usually a long swim back in the direction they had come from, regulator failure or light failure could be deadly. Unlike divers who swim in open water, cave and wreck divers cannot swim straight up to the surface when they encounter equipment problems. The Rouses also took down with them copious quantities of breathing gas to allow for an emergency reserve; they knew that every breath of gas is a potential lifesaver. They did not welcome anything that limited their breathing capability, even if it could reduce the possibility of panic during an emergency. The Rouses preferred to rely on their training and the instinct for each other's habits they had honed by diving together constantly. As Chrissy knew from his experience with his mother when they lost the guideline in the Devil's Cave System and he successfully conducted the lost-line search, training and well-honed instinct were better than relying on technology.

What the Rouses did not take into account—and what Baden instinctively knew—was that savvy and smarts could be combined with audio technology to take the sport of cave and wreck diving to new levels of safety. I was as guilty of this omission as the Rouses, and so were the majority of sport divers. Why? Not only was the new equipment unwieldy and expensive, but for sport divers it trespassed on our desire, even when we dived in teams, to go it alone—to be enterprising underwater and not to rely on technology we didn't need and that seemed like a challenge to our trust in our skills, experience, and singular courage.

Chrissy Rouse had impressed Billy Deans during the Team Doria expedition. Both Rouses paid attention to details such as dive planning and dived with a well-thought-out equipment configuration, and Deans liked that. In fact, he knew he could use it. Unlike his father, Chrissy was free to relocate because he had no commitments, like a wife, a house, and a business, and his obvious excitement about diving, knowledge of the sport, and impeccable skills made him a perfect candidate to be a trainer at Deans's Key West Diver center.

Deans saw how technical diving was growing. Demand from the uninitiated for his courses in mixed-gas diving was increasing. He was also fielding a rising stream of requests from experienced divers for charters to the cruiser *Wilkes-Barre,* the 250-foot-deep wreck that Deans and his buddy John Ormsby had dived in their spearfishing days, and the wreck that had pushed Deans to obtain Dr. Bill Hamilton's new trimix dive tables so he could continue to explore it safely. Chrissy had mixed-gas experience, having been trained by the master, Sheck Exley, in a class that he had taken with his father and mother in October 1990. Chrissy's cave-diving training also helped instill in him the right attitude about how critical it was to plan every aspect of a dive. The longer Billy pondered, the more he knew that Chrissy Rouse's combination of knowledge, skills, and youth would be an asset to his business.

Dive-shop owners were now paying Deans to come from Florida and teach mixed-gas diving in the Northeast. While conducting open-water dives with students on deep wrecks off New Jersey, Billy

Deans encountered Chrissy Rouse aboard the *Seeker* and suggested that Chrissy consider working at Key West Diver.

Chrissy was elated. He called me when he got back home. "Bernie, guess what? Billy asked me to come down and work for him! I can't believe it! I mean, this famous guy is asking *me* to work for *him*."

"Great," I replied. "Are you going to move down there?"

My question stopped Chrissy's excitement cold. He hadn't, it seemed, gotten past the high of just being asked.

"I don't know. Nothing's set yet," he said, sounding abashed. "But I don't like that it's so far away from the great wrecks we have up here."

"Billy's shop *is* closer to Florida's caves," I pointed out.

"Yeah, but now that my dad and I have found this cave up here, maybe I should stay up here and help him out diving it. If this cave doesn't go anywhere, then maybe I'll go down and work with Billy."

Chrissy's life was so full of diving promise. I found myself wondering whether it made sense for his career or his feeling of his own adulthood to remain tethered to Pennsylvania and his father's projects and temperament. I and other divers had noticed how Chrissy was always being berated by his father over the smallest thing, from the way Chrissy configured their equipment on a boat before a dive to his alleged lack of mechanical skills—even though Chrissy was far better at fixing diving equipment than most professionals. Although Chrissy always fell short of his father's expectations, I admired Chrissy's knowledge and skill with diving equipment. But Chrissy had time, and with the explosion of interest in diving, his opportunities would only bloom in the coming years. And maybe that cave would end up making the Rouses' name, turn them into heroes of the sport.

I wanted to include the Rouses on another charter I had planned. "Hey, Chrissy, why don't you guys come out and dive the *Northern Pacific*?"

"Naw. We're broke."

"You're broke? You can't be!" I said. "Let me talk to Chris!"

I heard Chrissy yell to his father to pick up the phone and when Chris came on the line, I asked, "Hey, Chris, come on—you can't be so broke you can't dive the *Northern Pacific*? I've got a charter to it. It'll be great. We'll bring back some portholes."

Chris sighed. "Chrissy's not kidding, Bernie. We're really broke. The excavation business is almost dead. And the dive-gear business, well, that's just starting up. I even had to sell my plane and my life insurance!"

I was shocked. "You sold your life insurance? What will Sue do if anything happens to you?"

"Hey, I had to do it!" Chris protested. He didn't like my question.

"Did you sell your dive gear?"

"No way! We need the dive gear! I'm hoping to make money selling the dive gear I make, and I've got to have my own dive stuff to get in the water and test out the stuff before I start making lots of 'em and sell 'em."

I understood what the man was saying—after all, his diving equipment represented both his love and his hopes. Yet I wondered that he had sold his plane and his life insurance but not any of his diving equipment, which he had in overabundance.

Sue Rouse was supportive of her husband, as she had always been. If Chris had to sell his plane and even his life insurance, well, that was the way things were meant to be. Although she had enjoyed Chris's success in the excavation business, she knew their good luck could not hold out forever. They had always been pessimistic, and even during their good fortune they braced themselves for what they felt was the inevitable string of bad luck that haunted them. It was as if they were living a dream from which they would awaken to face the dark reality of their lives.

Now that the economic recession was taking firm root in Bucks County, they again struggled to make ends meet. Chris handcrafted specialty equipment in his workshop next to their house, and he sold the gear to the dive-shop owners with whom he had developed a personal relationship. Some dive shops started carrying Chris's equipment at their customers' insistence. The most profitable aspect of Chris's Black Cloud Scuba business was the repair of diver-propulsion vehicles, which help divers penetrate much farther into caves than they can by swimming, and allow wreck divers to blow away vast areas of sand to uncover buried artifacts. To enhance his repair capability, Chris had gone to the trouble and expense of having machine molds made to his specifications so that he could have propeller blades manufactured out of metal instead of replacing broken blades with the plastic ones currently on the market. The metal blades were far stronger than their plastic counterparts, and were nearly impossible to break.

Word spread among the small, tight-knit community of divers who needed a proficient and reliable repairman when their vehicles broke down. Chris built his business primarily on word of mouth. It had worked for his excavation business, and he was sure it would work for his diving business. Chris Rouse rapidly gained the reputation of being the best in the country at repairing scooters. Vehicles were shipped to him for repair and overhaul from all over the country, and also from Canada. Yet he still wasn't making enough money to support himself and his family.

Sue could only think back wistfully on their early success in the excavation business, which seemed so distant and the details of which she struggled to remember. Sue would stick with her man in sickness and health, for richer and for poorer, until death parted them. And right now it was poorer.

Sue's vow was not just an idle promise: It was something she lived by. She knew that Chris lived by it also. Over twenty years they had developed total trust in each other, and neither had given the other any reason not to have and maintain that faith. If anything, Chris's earlier business success—which had seemed like so improbable a wish at the beginning—had bolstered Sue's confidence that her husband's plans would always come out well in the end, including this scheme to have a specialty diving equipment and repair business.

While Sue stood by her husband once again, some of their friends wondered whether the Rouses' relationship wasn't stuck in their high school years. Chris criticized not only his son at every turn, which led to their incessant bickering, but also his wife: The food she prepared wasn't perfect, both the house and their clothes were not clean enough, and her diving was not sufficiently aggressive to suit her husband. Perhaps the family contentiousness was just a continuing adolescent struggle among all three of them, to establish the kind of pecking order that high school sophomores seek. At the very least, all of the Rouses were stubborn, it seemed, and none of them would give way.

■   ■   ■

While I was preparing to leave for a three-day trip to the wreck of the *Northern Pacific*, an ocean liner that had been converted to a troop transport and in 1922 had sunk off the coast of Delaware in 150 feet of water after a mysterious fire, my three-year-old son watched me pack my dive bags. He had watched me many times before. Unlike all of the other times, though, this time he asked, "Are you coming back, Daddy?"

He said it in such a strange way that I stopped what I was doing and looked at him, wondering whether he knew something I didn't. "Of course I'm coming back, Gil. Daddy always comes back." Gil just looked away, as if he needed more convincing, and that afternoon, I hugged him extra hard before he and my wife saw me off as I drove to the *Seeker*'s home port in Brielle, New Jersey.

I had contracted with Bill Nagel to charter his boat *Seeker* for this expedition. Although Nagel had cautioned me against making a trip this far from the *Seeker*'s home dock in October—late for the northeast dive season—I persisted and put the charter together. Although I could have left the charter to the *Northern Pacific* for the next diving season, with greater odds for good weather, I was determined to complete my best diving year to date with at least one brass porthole, many of which were known to remain on the ocean liner, underneath steel hull plates that lay on the sandy ocean bottom. Bolstered by my success on the *Andrea Doria*, I was obsessed with adding another unique prize to my rapidly growing artifact collection.

We chugged to Delaware, just south of New Jersey. We had excellent weather, which was a pleasant surprise after a week of storms. I hoped that the storms had shifted the sand around the *Northern Pacific* to reveal artifacts, especially the portholes we craved. Among the people who had signed on for the charter was Peter Thompson, who had been one of my students, and who had brought me into the diving computer project as a consultant for the Japanese trading company he worked for, Inabata. Kevin O'Brien and Cliff Herbst had also both been my students. Dennis Anacker and John Harding aspired to dive the *Andrea Doria;* they were friends from the New York City Sea Gypsies, the dive club I had joined in 1987. Ed Dady, an avid and experienced diver who had gotten in touch with me through Steve Berman, would be my dive buddy. We would all work as a team, laying guidelines on the outside along each side of the upside-down wreck and searching for artifacts. I missed the Rouses, even though their bickering could get crazy and distracting at times; I knew they would have loved this weather and this wreck.

On my first dive I found an area of the ship where the sand formed an unnatural shape, as if covering something, and I dug into the sand, recovering shards of dishes and two intact eating utensils. When I came up after two and a half hours underwater, one of the dive teams reported having seen several portholes lying underneath a massive steel hull plate. After assessing the situation, I decided to take down a jack with two-ton lifting capability and see if I could raise the hull plate to allow us to retrieve the portholes. I dived again that night and followed the guideline that led to the portholes, where I deployed the heavy jack under the hull plate. When I cranked the handle, the hull plate didn't move. I tried to find out what the problem was.

My vision was limited not by silt but by countless tiny creatures that swarmed all around me, like an aquatic version of Hitchcock's *The Birds*. They were so numerous and so small that I couldn't make out exactly what they were and decided that they were either lobster or shrimp hatchlings. They were attracted to my diving light, which I needed in the pitch blackness of the nighttime dive. When I exchanged my regulators to switch between my two primary air tanks, I swallowed countless hatchlings. I enjoy seafood as much as the next person, but this was a little too fresh for my taste. When I moved my dive light farther away and then placed it on the sand, the hatchlings followed it. The mass of creatures actually reduced the bright beam from my light, and their forms cast eerie, rapidly shifting shadows on the hull plate I was trying to move.

I looked under the hull plate and saw that the jack could not exert upward pressure because the sand was so soft that the jack became buried ever deeper in it the more I cranked the handle. It was as if the wreck itself had taken on a will to deny me the portholes that lay maddeningly—tantalizingly—close.

I continued with my task in spite of the hatchlings and went searching for a piece of wreckage to put underneath the jack to give it purchase. Although the *Northern Pacific* is largely intact, I saw wreckage scattered all around the massive hull rising 40 feet off the sand, and I quickly found some metal to complete my task. After situating the jack on top of the metal, and tensioning it against the hull plate, I ran out of dive time and groaned in disappointment. I swam back to the anchor line for the long decompression.

It was after midnight when I climbed back onto the *Seeker*. My muscles ached, I felt weak, and my throat was sore. I'd had a frustrating dive and now I was coming down with the flu.

My sleeping area on the *Seeker* was damp and cramped and I did not sleep well. I decided not to dive again and took two ibuprofen pills to ease the muscle aches. I knew that if I was feeling ill enough to take medication, I should not be diving, but as I lay there achy and fitful I kept visualizing those portholes. They seemed almost close enough for me to grab from my bunk, and I imagined the polished brass artifacts on display in my Manhattan apartment.

When I got up that morning, my dive buddy, Ed Dady, wanted to get into the water. I told him I did not feel well, but he persisted. I took some more medication, including pills to clear my sinuses, and lay down again as the boat pitched gently beneath me. Strange, I mused, that Ed was so insistent on being in the water with a buddy when he was an experienced solo diver. Besides, when we went into the water together, we usually split up, and then would see each other again only on the anchor line during decompression. This method of diving was jokingly referred to as "same-ocean buddy diving," and many experienced divers engaged in it, if only to placate the captains of the dive boats they dived from.

After resting for several more hours, I felt better from the combination of medication and food. I decided to go in for a twenty-minute dive, letting Ed and others know I didn't feel so great and that if I felt uncomfortable underwater I would abort the dive early. If that happened, I told Ed, I didn't expect him to end his dive. It was only a 150-foot dive, I reasoned; the weather was great and I had already made two dives to the wreck in the past day, so I knew what I was dealing with.

When I descended, I felt new energy, the lure of the portholes and the pleasant buzz of nitrogen flooding me with fresh adrenaline. I tied off my oxygen decompression tank on the anchor line and then swam to scout for other portholes—the other divers had encountered no better success raising the hull plate, even with the metal I had placed underneath the jack—and we had given up on those particular artifacts. I swam to the area just to see the tempting prizes anyway, and to try and figure out another way to get at them. After twenty minutes, I still felt great, had ample breathing gas, and decided to continue the dive and make it a standard long dive. My previous two dives had each lasted forty-three minutes at 150 feet, plus decompression, and I could do that easy, I thought.

I swam toward the bow of the 500-foot-long wreck, even though we were anchored high at the very stern of the ocean liner where I was planning on descending. When the vessel sank, its massive weight caused it to plummet bow first and upside down into the sand; the abrupt arrest of the 8,200-ton ship's forward momentum had caused tremendous stress on the steel hull, and it cracked in two, leaving a 10-foot gap between the bow section and the rest of the ship. I was fascinated to be able to see every deck level clearly defined as I ascended from the sand to the top of the hull. It was like looking at a cutaway drawing, only this was real.

I dropped down to the sand again and penetrated the bow section, looking for lobsters. If I couldn't get a porthole, at least I could get something huge and edible as a prize. As I was bagging the second of my crustaceans, I saw Ed's dive light at the large crack leading into the bow, where I had entered. I finished putting the lobster into the bag and swam toward Ed. When I got close to him and swam out of the bow section, Ed signaled that we should ascend the upline, a secondary line tied to the split in the hull left by a *Seeker* crew member, Dan Crowell. I returned the signal, agreeing.

As we ascended, I checked my gauges, noting the time required for decompression. Then I remembered that I had left my oxygen decompression tank tied to the anchor line at the wreck's stern. I would need the oxygen to add safety to my decompression after my third long dive within twenty-four hours to 150 feet.

We had ascended only 10 feet above the wreck, to 100 feet. I signaled to Ed that I wanted to descend, swim to the other line, and ascend there. He looked at me quizzically. I turned away from him, making my way back down, and started swimming on top of the wreck's keel, at 110 feet, toward the anchor line at the stern. The current had picked up and I started breathing hard as I kicked vigorously to make headway. I knew that time was important, and I was eager to get to my oxygen bottle and start my decompression as quickly as possible. With no handholds on the bare keel, I had to use my leg muscles to propel myself rather than using the pull-'n'-glide, which would have required far less breathing gas because the arm muscles are smaller than the leg muscles and don't need as much oxygen to fuel them.

I looked down at my gauges as I swam, breathing hard. At this level of exertion, carbon dioxide was rapidly building up in my system and caused me to breathe even more rapidly. If I kept breathing this hard, I would pass out well before I reached the stern, which was about 350 feet from where I had begun my swim. I realized I had to come up with another, less physically demanding way to get to my oxygen bottle.

I dropped over the wreck's side and down to the sand. Although my decompression time would accumulate more rapidly the longer I spent at 150 feet than if I were at 110 feet, I was now out of the current, and I could pull-'n'-glide using the wreckage strewn about the bottom to hang on to. But my exertions had already taken a toll.

According to our interpretation of the Martini Law, 150 feet is the equivalent of three alcoholic drinks. The carbon dioxide buildup and my weakened state from what I thought were flu symptoms were increasing the narcotic effect of the air I breathed. I felt as if I had instantly gulped another martini. My head spun when I turned to look for Ed. I saw him following me, but he seemed some distance away. I stopped long enough to catch my breath, and then proceeded to pull-'n'-glide toward the stern.

The closer I got to the stern, the murkier the water became and the harder it was for me to see the hull, even though it was only 20 feet away. Or was the murkiness the result of my exertion, the carbon dioxide buildup, my weakened state, the medication, and the increased narcosis?

My heart thumped as I searched for the anchor line in the area where I knew it should be. It was suddenly so black I had difficulty distinguishing things. I swam toward the wreck's massive hull, away from the wreckage strewn on the bottom, and waved my light up and down as if it were a paintbrush and I were painting the hull. The anchor line should be here, yet I could not see it. I also could not see

Ed. If I had had communications gear, I could have asked him where he was, and he could have guided me to the anchor line, which it turned out he had found, not far above where I was searching.

Although the communications equipment would have helped, better judgment on my behalf would have been even more effective: I should not have changed my decision not to dive after I started getting ill. In my obsession for more artifacts I had pushed my body too far and had not respected either the ocean or the difficulties of diving deep. I realize that now. After numerous dives conducted at over 200 feet, I had regarded the 150-foot depth as shallow and had taken the danger of depth for granted. I was now in serious trouble.

I swam on and continued to search. Why could I not find the anchor line? This was an easy wreck to navigate and I had not encountered problems on my previous dives. Maybe I should have run a guideline after all?

Time was becoming critical as I swam harder to get to the anchor line faster. I was swimming near the wreck and did not have any wreckage to grab on to for pull-'n'-glides. I was breathing hard again. I swam past familiar-looking landmarks, but could only wonder why they looked familiar without putting any connections together. When I swam past a huge crack in the hull, I marveled that there were two of these on the wreck. I swam up to 110 feet and swam on top of the wreck, expecting to find the anchor line that had been attached at this depth at the stern. Then I came to the bow of the wreck, unmistakable by the arrowlike point that the hull formed here.

And then I realized what had happened, like a drunken man whose thoughts were suddenly focused by a splash of freezing water to the face: I had swum underneath the anchor line and gone around the stern, then proceeded back toward the bow on the *opposite* side of the wreck. I had swum 1,500 feet, most of it at a depth of 150 feet.

I was now not only physically but also mentally exhausted. I could swim back to the secondary line that I had started to ascend with Ed, before I fixated on my oxygen decompression bottle and headed for the anchor line. But how far away was that? Eighty feet? Or maybe 150 feet? And what if I missed that the way I had the anchor line? The thought of swimming against the current again wore me out further. I had enough breathing gas in my tanks to make the swim to the secondary upline, but I would not have enough to complete my required decompression. My computer indicated ninety-nine minutes, but that was merely the maximum amount of time it could show on the external display. The time required for decompression was probably closer to two hours, the total time tracked on the computer's internal register.

If I kept swimming around underwater searching for the upline, I would drown. The upline reel that Chris Rouse had given to me as a gift was attached to my tank. I could deploy the line by attaching a lift bag and sending it to the surface, then tie the line off on the wreck, swim up the line as I would have the anchor line, and decompress without drifting away from the wreck and the dive boat. But deploying the upline would take me a few minutes, and the current was pushing me away from the wreck. And without my oxygen bottle I did not have gas to complete decompression.

I stopped swimming, breathing hard, and concentrated on taking several long, deep inhalations to steady my breathing rate. I looked toward the stern and saw the wreck's grayish-black keel merge with the color of the water 30 feet away. I looked upward and started ascending, using my exhaled bubbles as a guide to my ascent rate; I stayed underneath the bubbles.

I breathed normally, making sure not to hold my breath so that I would not get an air embolism. I knew that too fast an ascent rate could cause the bends on a regular dive, but I was going to get bent anyway. Even so, I did not want to ascend too fast and make matters worse. I would go to the boat and they would get me onto a Coast Guard chopper, and then I would be fine once I got into a recompression chamber. I really screwed up this time. But at least I would be alive.

As I ascended, I waited for the pain that I knew was sure to hit. Where would it start? I did not even consider that I might become paralyzed and not be able to swim back to the boat. I knew that everything would work out fine. It had to.

When I broke the surface, I was relieved that the weather was flat calm. I was surprised that I did not feel any pain. I turned toward the *Seeker*, which was several hundred feet away, and waved my arm in the diver's distress signal.

Nobody was on deck to see me. I shouted out, "Hey! Hey! *Seeker*!"

Captain Bill Nagel walked out from the main cabin. I shouted again and waved my arm. Nagel looked around the deck, then casually out to sea, toward the yellow lift bag attached to the crew's secondary upline. It turned out that he could not hear my shouts, but my arm, waving in my reddish-orange drysuit, caught his eye.

Dan Crowell was starting to climb the *Seeker*'s ladder after completing his dive. I saw Bill say something to Dan, who was just stepping over the stern of the boat, onto the deck. Bill helped Dan off with his tanks and soon he was swimming out to me, holding a line attached to the boat that could be used to haul me back. I pulled my snorkel out of my goodie bag, put it in my mouth, and started swimming slowly toward him. Crowell stopped when he reached the end of the rope, waiting for me to get to him.

"What happened?" Crowell asked as he grabbed on to the webbing of my tank harness to prevent me from drifting away.

"I fucked up. Pull me in." My chest had started to hurt and I wanted to get back on board the *Seeker* and then into a recompression chamber as quickly as possible.

"Did you do your deco?"

"No."

Crowell's eyes widened. "You didn't do *any* deco?"

"No. Pull me in."

"Are you in pain?"

"No," I lied. "Just get me back in."

"Do you have gas?"

"Yeah, I got gas."

"Okay, grab this line," Crowell said as he handed me the line he had swum out from the boat, "and descend. I'll go back and we'll bring you more tanks and oxygen so you can do your deco."

I deflated the air in my drysuit and tried to descend, but could not. The pain was already getting intense, and I was having trouble breathing. The nitrogen bubbles were overwhelming my body. I came back up. "Dan! Forget it. Pull me in. Hurry. Please."

Crowell swam over to me. "All right. Hold on tight." He turned and motioned Nagel to pull me in, while he swam toward the boat, holding the line. Others joined Nagel on deck and soon it looked like a tug-of-war with everyone pulling on the rope. I could feel myself moving faster and faster toward the *Seeker*.

Every breath was harder than the last, and I kept swallowing water through my snorkel, even though there were no waves. I spat the snorkel out, let it sink, and grabbed one of my regulators, which I put in my mouth. The pain was now searing my lungs, and I alternated grunting and screaming through my regulator as I was pulled in.

When Dan Crowell, Bill Nagel, and my dive buddies had pulled me to the *Seeker*'s ladder, they looked down over the stern at me. Dennis Anacker asked, "What happened? Did you have an equipment problem?"

"No. I fucked up," I said between pained breaths.

"Okay. Climb up the ladder."

I felt far too weak. And now my vision was being affected: The word SEEKER painted on the stern of the vessel was in triplicate.

Triple vision. I knew I was suffering neurological decompression sickness, the most severe form of the bends.

I felt nauseated. "I can't climb," I whispered. "I'm too weak."

My friends stared at me, disbelieving, while Dan Crowell, still in the water next to me, caught his breath from the exertion of the swim out to get me and then helping to pull me back. When nobody moved to help me, I panted in pain, "This isn't a drill, guys. Get me up!"

Crowell immediately tried to unclip my tank harness, but he was not familiar with the cave-diving equipment I wore. He moved my gauges and hoses with a brush of his arm and cursed as he tried desperately to find a buckle to unclip me from my tanks. He unclipped my goodie bag, looked at it, and tossed it aside to sink to the ocean bottom. Crowell seemed flustered. The pain focused me. I tapped my left hand against my right shoulder. "Relax, Dan. Here. The buckle's here."

After Crowell unclipped the harness, several people climbed down the ladder. I felt Anacker's hands under my armpits and then somebody else grabbing my arms, then I was hauled up and onto the gratefully hard surface of the boat. "Can you walk?" Nagel asked.

"I think so."

"Good! Go lie down on the table," Nagel commanded as he

pointed to the large center table where all the divers sat and geared up before their dives.

Once I was lying down, Nagel took my two diving computers off my wrist. He gasped when he saw the decompression indicator showing ninety-nine minutes. "Jesus Christ! Look at this missed deco!" he shouted. "What happened? What did you do? *What the fuck did you do?*"

I just looked at him, too tormented to feel guilty or angry. One of my friends gave me some water to drink. But I felt too sick to drink anything and was afraid I would throw up. Dave Dannenberg, an instructor who owned a scuba shop, came over to me and draped the hose leading to an oral-nasal mask over my hand. I knew what would come next. I had taken the "Oxygen Administration" course for divers and knew that he would recite a statement to protect him from a lawsuit if one were brought against him. "This mask is attached to pure oxygen, which is thought to be very beneficial to someone suffering a diving injury, and to their chances of recovery," Dave recited. "I suggest you breathe the oxygen, but the choice is entirely yours." The most important thing from a legal standpoint was that I grabbed the oxygen and placed the mask on my face, because oxygen was considered a prescription drug if someone else administered it. Even while trying to save my life, Dave had to worry about protecting himself legally. Only in America.

I grabbed the mask even before Dannenberg was finished with the statement, and I breathed the oxygen. One of my friends told me they had to remove my diving suit so that I would have better circulation. "Don't cut it off me!" I panted, not wanting to destroy my $1,500 investment. Even in this dire circumstance I was convinced that I would be diving again soon, and I would need my suit for that. I cried out in pain as I twisted and turned to get out of the snug-fitting suit. The effort made me sweat and groan with pain. Every part of my body now hurt with my slightest movement. My insides felt as if they were being forcibly rearranged. I imagined the dinner scene in the movie *Alien* when the gestated creature ate its way through its human host's stomach and popped out.

Dave Dannenberg began the field neurological examination. I knew what he was doing because I had also taken this advanced course, and I knew how important it was for everyone to track my medical condition carefully. All of my vital signs and general condition were recorded on a slate, along with the precise time each had been taken. This slate would be sent with me to the hospital so that attending medical personnel would be able to determine the best treatment for my condition.

I was slowly losing my ability to function and the feeling was leaving my extremities. My pulse steadily weakened. I went deaf in both ears, which was actually a relief because now I could no longer hear Bill Nagel screaming about how badly I had screwed up. The pain reached a new level of intensity. I closed my eyes and drifted off. But Bill did make a call for me to be evacuated by Coast Guard helicopter.

When I was in the water and had made the decision to ascend, I had reassured myself that everything would go well, and that I would be fine once I got to a recompression chamber. Now, the pain was so great and my symptoms so severe that the full realization of the seriousness of my situation dawned on me. I was facing death. Yet I knew that I did not want to die now, not here, not on the dive boat *Seeker*. My life couldn't end like this. Could it? Surely, my life had to have more meaning than it already carried. I now knew that if I lived I would probably never dive again and would be lucky even to walk. And I accepted that, letting go of the dream I had. "Good-bye, Lucy," I thought.

Lucy was not my wife. Lucy was short for the *Lusitania*—the luxury British ocean liner sunk by torpedoes fired from the *U-20* during the First World War. Its sinking was controversial, and evidence points to Winston Churchill's having ordered the *Lusitania* to an area where a German U-boat was known to be operating. Churchill—who was then Great Britain's First Lord of the Admiralty—desperately wanted the United States to enter the war on the British side, but with the strong pacifist and isolationist movements in the United States, American public opinion kept the country neutral. Churchill knew that the sinking of an ocean liner by the Germans with the subsequent loss of American lives would inflame U.S. public opinion and hasten American entry into the war to fight alongside Britain. The *Lusitania* sank off the southern Irish coast in 325 feet of water and took 116 American lives, and its destruction turned U.S. public opinion from isolationist to angry, leading to the entry of the United States in the war, as Churchill had hoped. Because of its depth, Lucy was an even greater challenge than the *Andrea Doria* and I had started thinking of the possibilities of diving it over a year earlier. Even now, even on my way to death, I was a diver.

Though the evacuation helicopter had been called, everyone on board the *Seeker* wondered if I was going to live long enough for the chopper to arrive and take me to a hospital equipped with a recompression chamber. Nagel himself did not hold out much hope. He had seen divers permanently crippled when they missed only a few minutes of decompression, and I found out later that he doubted there was any hope for someone who had omitted over an hour and a half of decompression. He monitored the situation from the wheelhouse, listening to the radio for instructions from the Coast Guard. He cursed as he imagined the tangle of paperwork and the questioning he would have to undergo when I died.

Dave Dannenberg continued to monitor my vital signs, calling out his findings to someone who wrote down the time and took notes. My pulse was hardly detectable. My skin was ashen white, the blood drained from it as my plasma thickened with nitrogen bubbles and my circulatory system fought to keep my critical organs supplied with oxygen. My friends—some of them had been diving with me for years, and some of them had been my diving students—looked on in shock.

I drifted off, my eyes closed. The pain was overwhelming. I wanted to leave it behind. Gradually, the pain eased and went away completely. Happiness and a feeling of well-being washed over me.

A bright, white light appeared before me, even though my eyes were closed. My body drifted upward, and from above I could see the *Seeker*, everyone aboard, and my sorry self lying on the gearing-up platform. I went into a white tunnel. I had never felt happier. I only had to float to the end of the tunnel and all my problems, all of the pain and frustration in my life, would be over. I wouldn't care about diving anymore.

As I drifted closer to the end of the tunnel and the light got ever brighter, I suddenly heard the soothing chimes of my son's crib merry-go-round. I remembered my wife, Diana, and our son. They needed me. And I had told Gil that I would be back.

I stopped my drift toward the end of the tunnel and struggled to turn around. I had to get back. The white light dimmed and then went away completely. I opened my eyes. Searing pain racked my body. I clenched my teeth and knew that I had to put up with the pain and fight for survival if I was ever to return to my family.

8

Voice from the Deep

OCTOBER 13, 1991. ABOARD THE DIVE BOAT *SEEKER*,
26 miles off the coast of Delaware,
over the wreck of the *Northern Pacific*.

A S I LAY ON THE PLATFORM BENCH where all of us had geared
up, I was struggling just to keep on living, praying for the Coast
Guard helicopter to come fast. The U.S. Coast Guard station that
patrolled this area, in Cape May, New Jersey, received Bill Nagel's call
for my emergency evacuation. The call had gone out over marine
radio, which meant the message had been overheard by other boat
captains and crews and murmured about among the various dive-
boat captains, crews, and customers, uncomfortably reminding them
what was at stake every time they jumped into the water. News of an
accident like mine not only serves to reinforce caution among divers;
it also means that if someone else gets hurt, one potential recompression chamber is already going to be in use. If a diver in southern New
Jersey, or in Delaware, was injured right after my accident, he would
have to be airlifted to an alternative recompression site, farther away

than the one I was heading for. The chances of a diver's making a full recovery decrease the longer it takes to get him into a recompression chamber.

I was in luck. As I would find out later, a chopper was already fueled and warmed up, its crew having just returned from an exercise patrol when Nagel's distress call crackled over the air to the Coast Guard dispatcher in Cape May. Although my anguish made it feel as though hours elapsed before I felt the wind disturbance of the chopper's blades overhead, the response time was only forty-five minutes. If the chopper and crew had not been ready to go when the call came in, I would have had to wait about another half hour for the chopper to arrive at the *Seeker,* which would have given the nitrogen bubbles even more time to trample my organs.

As I felt the strong gusts blowing over me, I looked up and saw the white helicopter with its blue and red insignia stripes and large, bold black lettering, USCG. Although the sight was welcome, I was struck by how unnatural it was for a helicopter to be hovering only thirty feet above the *Seeker*'s stern. The only things we divers normally see when we are this far offshore are the occasional boats in the distance; airplanes and helicopters are something that we might see as tiny dots in the sky, not machines hovering off the stern. My hopes soared at the sight of the rescue chopper, which would whisk me to the recompression chamber that promised me a chance at recovery.

I had held out this long by focusing only on the arrival of the chopper. Now I would focus on surviving until I got to the hospital. This was the same philosophy I used when I dived: If I visualized the dive in its entirety, I would be overwhelmed at how complex it was, how much effort was required to accomplish the task. When I segmented tasks—first into getting geared up, then getting into the water, then down the anchor line, and so on—I could complete a dive that might require three or four hours of risky actions and decisions. Now that I was fighting to stay alive, when I did think of the whole process, and how long it would take for me to get into the recompression chamber, I quickly found myself despairing, my energy and will to survive draining rapidly. "You only need to hold out a little longer," I began saying to myself. "You're on your way. The pain's not that bad. You can do it!"

The *Seeker* remained at anchor, even though the Coast Guard radioed Nagel to get under way and head into the wind. It was easier to hold a helicopter precisely in place over an object when the helicopter had wind traveling over its blades. Bill Nagel refused to move. He had his reasons. My dive buddy, Ed Dady, was still in the water decompressing, and Nagel felt that moving the boat would have put Dady's life in danger by possible contact with the *Seeker*'s churning propellers. Also, Nagel reasoned that the weather was so calm that the helicopter pilot could hold the chopper precisely over the stern of the dive boat without danger of crashing due to a sudden wind gust. What Bill Nagel did not appreciate was how difficult he was making things for the helicopter pilot, who now had to use much more power and fuel to keep the chopper hovering in place. A helicopter hovering in place for a long time also risks a downward drop because of the dynamics of the wind turbulence created by its own blades. If that happened, the helicopter would crash into the *Seeker*, most likely killing everyone on board both the helicopter and the boat, and putting me out of my misery for good.

Dennis Anacker and John Harding—my friends from the Sea Gypsies dive club—got me upright, but my legs felt like cast iron and I could walk only with my arms draped over their shoulders. The three of us shuffled over to the wire basket the chopper had lowered to retrieve me. I dumbly looked at the basket, which resembled a cage uncovered at the top. How was I going to climb into it? It seemed a task requiring superhuman effort. I felt very tired, which was, like my confusion, a symptom of decompression sickness. Anacker and Harding lifted me up so that I only had to swing my legs over the top of the basket to climb in. That I managed. I slumped into a sitting position at the bottom of the basket.

I felt cramped, and the wind from the helicopter's blades made me squint. I watched my friends and the dive boat get smaller and smaller as the basket and I were winched upward. The closer I got to the chopper, the more difficult it became to breathe; the air was so turbulent—like sticking your face out of the window of a speeding car—that I had to tuck my head down to get a breath. When the top of the basket was level with the chopper's floor, a man in a flight jumpsuit and a dark-green helmet reached out to me, grabbed me under the arms, and pulled me into the machine. In front of me, I saw two seats side by side, both occupied by men who were also dressed in flight suits and helmets. The man to my left gave a thumbs-up signal, which was returned by the man who had dragged me aboard. I lay behind the seats, on the chopper's metal floor. I could feel the machine's increased vibration as it lifted upward and sped off, away from the scene of my stupidity.

At last, I was finally on the way to the hospital. I could relax. But the Coast Guard man attending to me seemed to be shouting something.

I shook my head, pointed to my ear, and said, "I'm deaf."

"What happened?" mouthed back the man.

"I fucked up."

He looked at me, frowned, then nodded his head.

I made a shivering motion by folding my arms around my body and rocking back and forth. He got a blanket and covered me. Warmth. The first bit of comfort I had allowed myself to feel in a long time.

The chopper quivered fiercely as we flew and flew. Where were they taking me? I struggled to remember which recompression chambers were in the area. Duke University in North Carolina? New York City? Or maybe someplace else? The Coast Guard personnel attending to me saw that I was ashen white and listless, which indicated to him that I was in severe shock. He tried to inject me with adrenaline. When I saw him pull a syringe from his medical bag, I welcomed it, hoping that the injection would give me more strength and ease the pain and discomfort I felt. But I watched in dismay as the medic unsuccessfully probed my arms for a vein. Although I have been told by medical personnel that my veins are very good and easy to find for injections, the level of shock I was undergoing had caused the veins in my arms to collapse. The medic's face clouded over as he kept trying. Finally he shook his head while he mouthed the words "I can't find it. Sorry."

My hopes sank. I felt very weak. I looked longingly at the syringe in the man's hand. How much energy did I have left? I forced myself to breathe in and out, fearing that if I did not make this conscious effort my body would quit trying. I looked at the Coast Guard man and mouthed back, "It's okay. Thanks anyway."

The effort to make the words poured gasoline on my pain. I reached out and held his hand in street-style greeting, trying to gain some life-giving energy from him, as if he were a newly charged battery and I were a fading flashlight. It must have looked as though we were arm-wrestling for life.

At last, after what seemed a generation, the helicopter landed. The Coast Guard man attending to me opened the doorway and I looked outside, trying to figure out where I was. All I saw was blue sky and a low brick wall. I learned later that we landed on the roof of the Hospital of the University of Pennsylvania. Several medical personnel ran toward the machine with a gurney, and rolled me onto it. The Coast Guard man went inside the building with me and handed the nurse the slate which the guys on the *Seeker* had used to keep track of my medical condition. I was wheeled into the hospital's emergency room and then into an area that the nurse curtained off.

I lay bathed in bright white lights and waited. Nothing seemed to be happening. What was going on? I wondered. Why aren't they taking me to a recompression chamber immediately? Alarm came over me. Maybe they don't know how urgent it is for me to get into a recompression chamber.

I opened my mouth and croaked out something I couldn't hear. How could I manage to explain to them that I had to have the excess nitrogen bubbles in my system reduced so that my body could breathe them out gradually? They had to know that only recompression could help me. Then, suddenly, terror swept over me. What if the chamber was already in use? God, how long could I hold out? I'm not ready to die! I started talking in what I hoped was a loud voice, while I lay on my back, staring at the ceiling. Squeezing the words from my faltering brain, I gasped out my name and address and then said, "I've been injured in a diving accident! I'm suffering from severe decompression sickness! I need to get into a recompression chamber right away!"

A miracle happened. A nurse came over with a clipboard, writing down what I said. She peered at me, and her lips moved, but I still heard nothing. I told her I was deaf from my accident. She looked surprised and mouthed the words "You can't hear me?" I told her I could not hear a thing. She wrote the question down and gave it to me. Luckily, the oxygen I had been breathing on the *Seeker* and during the chopper ride had helped my vision, and I could read her writing, although the words kept moving off the page, as if I were looking at a television screen with an improper horizontal alignment. "Are you deaf?" she had written. I nodded. Someone brought over a tuning fork and the nurse put it in my face. Can you hear this? I shook my head no. Put me in a recompression chamber now! I tried to say, but I might as well have been trying to commandeer a nightmare.

After I signed the forms to release both the hospital and the attending medical personnel from legal liability, the nurse found a vein, and I was hooked to an intravenous unit which provided saline to combat dehydration, combined with adrenaline and a liquid sugar to give me more energy. But they could not both stop the pain and save me. I couldn't be given painkillers because the personnel treating me needed to know if the pain was being resolved by my treatment, or where in my body the pain, numbness, or paralysis continued after the recompression. I looked at the needle in my arm that fed me liquid from the intravenous unit and wondered—was I getting better already? What had given me an adrenaline surge, helped me to focus on getting treatment I desperately needed, and rushed blood through the collapsed vein that the Coast Guard man had not been able to apply the syringe to? Maybe it was the fear of death.

I was wheeled to the recompression chamber, a large, enclosed metal tube that looked about the size of a large van. There was a row of seats for several people, since this system had been built to allow recompression treatments not only for divers but for multiple victims of burns or puncture wounds. Increased oxygen pressure was found to be beneficial in both of these cases, and hospitals with recompression chambers were sometimes able to schedule patients for simultaneous treatments, which made the most efficient use of the chamber, which cost a medical facility over a million dollars to install and maintain.

Now the only ones in the chamber were myself and the male nurse attending to me. We would both be subjected to the same amount of additional pressure, as the doctor outside the chamber controlled the treatment. Because the U.S. Navy Recompression Table 6-A recommended a five-and-a-half-hour treatment, both the nurse and I would be subjected to a depth-pressure of 165 feet, and the nurse risked getting bent from the long, deep exposure. Although this was rare, it had happened before. In spite of the risk, at least one medical person was required to attend to me, provide drinking fluids, keep me comfortable, and monitor my progress. Also, if I had problems equalizing the pressure on my ears, the nurse would have to puncture my eardrum. An instrument designed for this purpose lay menacingly on a table within easy reach.

Now that I was in the chamber, I felt renewed hope that I would be well again, as I had first thought when I made the decision to ascend even though I knew I would get bent. Yet although I had known other divers who had gone through recompression treatment, I did not know exactly what to expect. Whenever anyone spoke about the treatment, it was usually brief. Cave divers like Marc Eyring, at Ginnie Springs, in Florida, would refer to their treatment as being put in "the pot," and they would shrug it off as something that just had to be dealt with on occasion, an occupational hazard like frostbite for mountain climbers. For a commercial diver like Glenn Butler, the recompression chamber was simply another tool that he routinely used after his deep excursions, so that he could complete his lengthy 20- and 10-foot decompression stops in the comfort of warm air instead of cold water. Divers like Gary Gentile and John Moyer had simply told me that yes, they had gotten bent, been treated, and were fine now. All of these divers exhibited a nonchalance about their recompression treatment that made me believe the worst was over. I was wrong to believe that. A new and more psychic pain was about to begin.

As the doctor outside the chamber started the treatment, I felt the surrounding pressure increase on my ears, just as when I was diving. I relieved the pressure on my ears, just as I did when diving. The air got very hot and uncomfortable as the compressed air rushed into the chamber, and I felt as if I were in a rapidly heating oven. I started to sweat. Although I was uncomfortable from the sudden rise in air temperature, my pain eased as I was put under increased pressure and the nitrogen bubbles that were attacking my body were reduced in size. Some of the excess nitrogen was forced back into my tissues.

There was nothing much to do but lie there and wait. The nurse looked at me and occasionally checked my vital signs. When he was persuaded that I was in stable condition, he read a Stephen King novel to pass the time.

The compressed air in the chamber cooled, and now I felt as if I were in a refrigerator. I signaled the nurse for a blanket. As the pressure was gradually eased and I was brought closer to surface pressure, the nurse put an oral-nasal mask over my face so that I could breathe pure oxygen. I knew this meant that we were at 60 feet depth-pressure. The pure oxygen helped flush out the excess nitrogen faster and also forced oxygen into tissues that had been cut off from blood because of the nitrogen bubbles blocking the way. Some of my tissues did get oxygen even while I lay on the *Seeker* and in the chopper, but my blood flow was severely restricted by the sheer number and size of the nitrogen bubbles. The bubbles also compromised my blood's ability to carry oxygen. Dr. Bill Hamilton, among others, has contributed to research showing that the nitrogen bubbles are treated as invaders by the body's immune system, which mounts a complex and not fully understood systemic defense. Part of the immune defense involves the creation of nitrogen-specific and helium-specific antigens—antigens are the marker cells that attach themselves to invading viruses and bacteria, targeting the invading cells for destruction. Even after a person recovers from the bends, specific inert-gas antigens lurk vigilant in the body against a future bubble attack.

The attending nurse monitored me closely for signs of oxygen toxicity. If I showed symptoms of seizure, he would immediately take the oral-nasal mask off my face and the seizures would stop as I breathed the surrounding air. In the recompression chamber, the greatest danger was not dying from a seizure, as it was when I breathed pure oxygen underwater, but having a seizure and biting off my tongue. To help prevent the onset of a seizure as I breathed oxygen at 60 feet, the nurse put down the horror novel at twenty-minute intervals and took the oral-nasal mask off my face for air breaks. My luck held out, and I did not have a seizure.

It now dawned on me exactly how lucky I was: I had risked everything in my obsession for artifacts, and I had come close to dying. I had been so comfortable in the water that I did not allow myself to think anything like this could really happen to me. But as I looked around, I knew that it was all too real. I did not know if I would recover completely. I still hoped for the best, but now I finally admitted to myself just how close I had come to going over the edge. Even though I had pushed myself too far, I was still alive. But now nagging questions flooded my mind like oxygen: How did I let things get so uncontrolled that I wound up struggling for my life? What motivated me to take the extreme risks that led to my predicament?

Suddenly, I heard ringing in my ears. Then other noises. My hearing was returning! I told the nurse the good news and he relayed the information to the doctor outside the chamber. A short while later, the doctor stood beside my gurney, inside the chamber. Even though we were now pressurized at 30 feet, the doctor could enter through a lock-in, lock-out chamber, essentially a separate compartment attached to the main unit. The doctor could walk into the chamber from surface pressure, seal it, then increase the pressure until it matched the main chamber's pressure. When the pressure in the two chambers was equal, the doctor could open the hatch connecting the units and walk over to me.

"Can you hear me?" the doctor asked, incredulous.

"Yes," I replied. "But everything sounds funny, and my ears are ringing."

The doctor's face showed shock. "You're lucky you can hear at all." He shook his head. With a tone indicating disbelief, he said, "You're going to walk away from this." It was as if he expected me to be in a wheelchair for the rest of my life and felt betrayed. He quickly added, "But your diving career is over."

With those words I felt robbed of breath. Even though I was getting better, and was happy I could hear again, I wanted to close my ears. I could no longer dive! The news was a gut punch. The doctor informed me that he would extend the treatment at 30 feet to see if the extra time under pressure would help my hearing come back more fully. The thought of an extra thirty minutes in the chamber bummed me out. Thanks to the nitrogen and then oxygen pummeling me from the inside out, my body now felt worse and more battered than during my college days when I sometimes played two games of rugby in a row.

Could I just sleep? No, I would not be allowed to shut my eyes because sleep would slow down my breathing and circulation, reducing the rate at which the excess nitrogen was eliminated from my body. I wearily resigned myself to staying awake and to the extra time in the chamber. I hoped it would make a difference but I also knew that even the doctor could not know for certain if the extended time would help. Because it could not hurt me, the extra time was worth the investment and, in the larger scheme of medical care, even the added risk of the bends to the nurse treating me.

When the treatment was over and I was wheeled to my hospital room, I was both mentally and physically exhausted from my ordeal. It was nighttime and the hospital was quiet, the hallways bathed in dim electric lighting. It seemed I had survived.

During the six hours I was undergoing my recompression chamber treatment, the Rouses were diving in Dutch Springs, helping with checkouts. They had dived the previous day from the *Dina Dee*—the boat co-owned by the Rouses' advanced-diving instructor, Bob Burns—on the wreck of a massive freighter, the *Ayuruoca,* off New Jersey, thirty-five miles north of the *Northern Pacific,* in a deep area known as the Mud Hole. Chris and Sue dived together to 170 feet and into the wreck, where Chris recovered two small bottles from the massive vessel, which sank in a collision in 1945, just after World War II.

The Rouses made post-ocean, freshwater quarry dives the way to rinse their gear of salt water, which was corrosive to the diving equipment. When the Rouses arrived home in the early evening from the quarry, they got a call about my accident from Steve Berman in Florida—the news had traveled quickly through the diving community—telling them that I was very badly bent and it was not certain that I would live.

All Berman knew at the time was that I had surfaced too soon and missed about two hours of decompression. Both he and the Rouses had a lot of questions about what exactly had happened to cause such an uncontrolled event. Maybe I had several equipment problems, one after the other? Maybe I had gotten trapped inside the wreck and used up my air trying to get out? But they also knew that whatever had happened to me could happen to them. Hearing my account of the accident would provide them with another bit of knowledge that might prove useful in keeping them alive underwater. Steve Berman, the Rouses, and I had all been trained by Marc Eyring—

the former Green Beret who taught cave diving at Ginnie Springs—and we subscribed to his philosophy of the sport that when we stopped learning we would become complacent, and die.

The Rouses knew, of course, that there were grave risks associated with diving—that significant threats lurked in any sports adventure. Less than two years earlier, the Rouses became painfully aware of the very real, deadly risks that they and their friends undertook in the world of sport flying when Chris's first flight instructor, Pete Miller, died in the air. Chris and Chrissy had heard about Miller's death after a day of diving, much as they found out about my accident. That night in July 1989, when Chris turned on the television he heard about a midair collision between two private airplanes just a few towns away, at Quakertown Airport, where Chris had learned to fly. Although the names of the seven victims had not yet been released, Chris Rouse's heart sank. With a few phone calls Chris and Chrissy unearthed the tragic details. During an air show, Pete Miller—he had lent his plane to Chris and Sue Rouse for their first trip to Florida, with the words "A crash is as good as a sale!"—had flown a group of skydivers to their jump zone. After all of the parachutists had leaped out of the plane, Pete headed back to the airstrip. During his final landing approach, Pete collided with another private plane that carried six people. Both planes tumbled twelve hundred feet out of the sky and those who hadn't died in the air were killed on the tarmac. Chris was rocked by that news: It was the first time he had lost such a close friend.

The red-haired Pete Miller was a large-framed man, missing several teeth, whose lips seemed permanently attached to a stale, pungent cigar stub. With his raunchy sense of humor, the Vietnam War veteran was a throwback to the barnstormers of the 1920s, pilots who performed aerial acrobatics and dazzled crowds with displays of what they could do with that new phenomenon, the airplane.

Chris understood that if a man like Pete Miller, who had survived the Vietnam War, could die doing something he was so proficient at, then so could anyone else, and so could Chris and his family die diving. The realization tempered Chris's actions, making him more cautious. But Chrissy was too young to see things the way his father did. Chrissy had not developed the kind of close friendship with Pete

Miller that his father had. Chrissy saw Miller's death as tragic, but he was able to shrug it off—sometimes your luck runs out.

The news of my accident brought to Chris's mind Pete Miller's tragedy, reminding him that both in the air and underwater, people who were proficient at their sport could make mistakes and die.

Chrissy's driving record reflected just how little Pete Miller's death affected him. Fast, careless, recklessly confident, he crashed his own car not once, but twice. He wrecked his father's car and then cracked up his father's truck. Chrissy's third accident, when he crashed his father's car, alarmed Chris and Sue concerning not only his habits behind the wheel but also his level of maturity. Their boy treated his life—on land, at least—with suicidal abandon. But no matter how much they yelled at him, Chrissy's parents backed him up, indulged him. The accidents served to leave Chrissy further and further in debt to his parents, who would always break down and lend Chrissy money for another vehicle and the increasing insurance rates he had to pay.

By late 1991, the twenty-one-year-old Chrissy was still firmly dependent on his parents. His car crashes only strengthened that dependence at a time when he should have been building a life on his own. Presumably Chrissy liked it that way—it must have made him feel more secure to be tethered to his parents. After all, when he was ten, Chrissy had been rocked by having to help take care of his father after his welding accident. Now, maybe he could erase the trauma of that event by making sure his father took care of him. His father unknowingly encouraged his feelings of immunity from danger behind the wheel. Insulated by his parents from the consequences of his behavior, Chrissy could believe he'd never get burned on land—or, perhaps, bent underwater.

When word of my successful recompression treatment was relayed via radio message to the *Seeker*, everyone on board was relieved, and even amazed. Someone suggested sending me a *Seeker* T-shirt on which they all wrote get-well messages. Each person took a turn writing on the T-shirt with indelible black ink. John Harding drew a cartoon which he labeled "Bernie's porthole." It depicted a person peering out of a round recompression chamber window, which resembled a ship's porthole. The message was clear: In my obsession to gather portholes from the *Northern Pacific*, I had only landed myself close to the recompression chamber's porthole.

The messages were an important way for my friends to express their anxiety, fear, and anger over what had happened to me. Some of the guys had been my students, and many of them had sought wreck-diving advice from me, such as the secrets to achieving successful dives on the *Andrea Doria*. On top of that, I was the sensible, earnest diver who had recently written guidelines on wreck-diving safety. To some of my friends, my accident was a huge disappointment, as if their favored sports team had failed to win an early playoff game. Others had to ask if their own confidence in their skills was misplaced. They felt vulnerable. If someone could cause nearly fatal problems for himself underwater after making nine successful dives to the Mount Everest of scuba diving—and bringing back the artifacts to prove it—where did that leave them? Was it worth the risk?

Once they got word that I was recovering, my friends aboard the *Seeker* chose to dive as scheduled the next day, on another, shallower wreck. Rather than think too hard about the risks involved, which might serve only to make them give up the sport and camaraderie they loved so much, it was better to jump right back into the water. I probably would have done the same.

When I awoke in the hospital the morning after my recompression chamber treatment, I needed to go to the bathroom. I swung my feet over the bed and stood up. Suddenly, the room spun and I had to hold on to the side of the bed to stay standing. I closed my eyes and shook my head, hoping to clear my focus. When I opened my eyes everything was still spinning, which made me feel nauseated. I groaned. What was happening? I tried to take a step and completely lost my balance. I fell into the side of the other bed in the room, and then I collapsed onto my knees, holding on to the side of the bed so that I would not tumble over completely. I could not walk. I was overcome with terror. Was I going to be a cripple for good? What had I done when I ascended without decompressing? I'd thought everything would be fine once I got into the recompression chamber. But now, reality threatened to flatten me.

Although my hearing had returned, the nitrogen bubbles had

damaged my brain in such a way that my balance was skewed, and this affected my vision when I did try to walk. It was as if I had consumed too much alcohol. I swung my torso toward my bed, leaned over, and grabbed the railing with my hands. I pulled myself over to my bed, and then heaved myself up and flopped back onto the mattress. The exertion made me sweat heavily, and now my stomach heaved as if I were going to throw up. Then, I remembered the conversation with the doctor toward the end of my chamber treatment. He had said that I would walk away from the accident. Did he misdiagnose the extent of my recovery?

I lay in my bed, frozen at the thought of being crippled for life. Then a young man with dark, Mediterranean features and a stocky build similar to my own entered my room and introduced himself. Dr. Ignaccio Mendagurin, who was foreign born, explained that as a neurologist and a former navy diver, he was interested in my case both professionally and personally. I liked his calm, smooth tone of voice, which sounded nonjudgmental. And I very much liked the fact that he was a diver, just like me—or just as I had been until yesterday.

As Dr. Mendagurin talked, he reminded me of my father, a scientist who held a doctorate in materials science and a master's in chemistry and who spoke English with a clear, crisp diction that underscored his British education. My father, who was born in India, spoke several languages, including German, my mother's native tongue. Though my father had a darker complexion and a thicker, fuller thatch of tar-black hair than Dr. Mendagurin, the two seemed alike in many ways. I felt that Dr. Mendagurin would be far more empathic than the doctor who had treated me in the chamber, the man who had told me in such an amazed tone that I would walk away from my accident, as if to say that fools like me should rightfully be crippled permanently.

Dr. Mendagurin told me that my being deaf in both ears from decompression sickness—inner-ear hits, as they were called—was a malady from which nobody had fully recovered. He was impressed that I had regained hearing in both of my ears during my first treatment. It seemed to him that I was a medical anomaly. Could he attend to me so that he could witness and document my progress? Although I was frightened that I might have suffered permanent damage from my accident, I was glad that something useful might come of it after all, and I welcomed Dr. Mendagurin's expertise.

The doctor seemed to have a genuine scientific curiosity about my case, the same sort of curiosity that I had seen my father display. I had greatly admired my father's determination to arrive at a formula for the efficient cultivation of penicillin, which was produced as a result of fermentation of a broth in which a specific bacterium produced the precursor of penicillin under optimum laboratory conditions. When I was eleven, I saw him work on this problem night and day for six months. He always carried a pad and pen with him, and incessantly wrote pages of chemical formulae, even at the dinner table, until he was successful. My father's methodology is probably still used by Bristol-Myers in penicillin production. My admiration for my father was further increased because when I was eight, I had seen the results of a chemical accident at my father's lab, and was frightened by the bandages he wore from the chemical burns he suffered on his arms, hands, and face. My father was undaunted by the accident, and he told me that if everyone gave up at the first obstacle, nothing would ever have been accomplished. Much as Chrissy Rouse remembered his own father's accident, I carried this memory with me and knew it influenced my motivations on land and under the sea.

Now, I hoped that my hunch about Dr. Mendagurin was right, and that he would show the same sort of determination I had seen my father display. "Doctor, I'm happy that I can hear again, but now I'm worried that I might never be able to walk again," I said, lying perfectly still in my bed to prevent the world from spinning.

"Listen to me carefully," the doctor said, his tone earnest but compassionate. "You'll be able to walk again, but it's going to take time and effort. Your brain will have to train itself to use a new neural pathway to send the required signals to your body to walk."

I perked up. "Wow, that's cool! What do I need to do? And how long will it take?"

"You have to force yourself to walk, starting today."

"But everything spins around, and I have trouble standing. And the whole thing makes me feel like throwing up," I said and groaned.

"Yes, you're going to have to overcome that. You'll do it a little at a time. But you *have* to do it if you want to walk again. You'll make progress in small steps, and it *will* take time. You've got to be strong!"

Dr. Mendagurin examined me for his records and then left. I was alone, faced with the trip to the bathroom, only about fifteen steps away from my bed, but it might as well have been on top of Mount Everest. Determined to follow the doctor's advice, I got out of bed, and banged into the side of it, holding on. The effort was already intense. My heart rate and breathing rate increased. I started to sweat. I could not lie down again this time because I urgently needed the bathroom. I took another step and reeled to the end of the bed and grabbed the railing. Objects were now spinning faster and my stomach churned. I lunged forward and then held on to the dresser drawer like a shipwrecked sailor in stormy seas grasping ahold of driftwood. I let go of the drawer and bounced along the wall toward the bathroom door. The spinning room made my steps feel surreal, as if I were floating. I grabbed the door frame to steady myself and catch my breath. My skin was now slick from sweat, which made the room feel cold. I careened toward the toilet and felt like an airman abandoning a spinning, plummeting airplane. I sat down and thanked God.

After a very long time, I gathered the strength and will to make my way back from the bathroom to my bed, and I retraced my stumbling steps. When I got to the bed, I fell into it, panting and sweating with the effort. I was exhausted. All I could do was sleep to regain my energy. Before I dropped off to sleep, I thought about Dr. Mendagurin describing what my brain could accomplish. I hoped that while I slept my brain would be working on the neural pathway I needed to walk normally again.

The next day after once again navigating the linoleum like a drunken sailor, I underwent a second chamber treatment, although Dr. Mendagurin told me that he was doubtful that another recompression would improve my condition any further. For him, time and continued efforts to walk were the most critical to my full recovery. I still had tinnitus, ringing in the ears, but Dr. Mendagurin thought that this would also resolve itself in time. And he was happy with my progress over the past day, during which I had forced myself to try to walk several times.

During my recovery at the hospital, I had plenty of time to contemplate my accident. How had I gotten into such trouble that it had nearly cost my life? Why did I dive when I was feeling so bad? In the past, I had respected both the deep and myself, and I had not dived when I did not feel well; even when I had been very physically fit, I had not dived if my intuition nagged at me and a dive did not feel right. Once, on the *Andrea Doria*, I decided not to dive one day even though I was physically feeling fine, and the weather was great. That day, the competitiveness for artifacts seemed misplaced and the risk to my life did not seem worth it. Gary Gentile was surprised. Perhaps that was because I had more respect for the *Andrea Doria*. The *Northern Pacific* lay much shallower. Yet I had the nagging suspicion that the reasons for my current trauma had to go deeper. Even though I'd pushed too hard and dived when I should not have, I still could—and should—have gotten myself safely to the surface without missing decompression. I knew that underwater problems had to be solved underwater. It was something I drilled into my students, especially the ones who had a tendency to look for the surface as a refuge when they had problems. I knew that there were underlying reasons for my accident that went far beyond what standard accident analysis could reveal.

I was no stranger to an explanation of the causes of accidents like mine. I had worked in my spare time in affiliation with the National Underwater Accident Data Center (NUADC) at the University of Rhode Island to conduct a wreck-diving accident analysis of all fatalities involving U.S. amateur divers. After I had taken my cave-diving training in the late eighties and had seen what Sheck Exley had done for the sport of cave diving, I wondered why no such analysis had been conducted specifically for wreck-diving accidents. In December 1990, when I took Exley's mixed-gas cave-diving course, I talked to him about my ideas for an analysis of wreck-diving fatalities modeled on his cave-diving study. Exley was very helpful and offered suggestions to make my task easier, which I appreciated. He worked in a spirit of cooperation, believing that whatever we learned and shared would benefit the sport overall. Exley's approach was far removed from the infighting among wreck divers and wreck-diving boat captains I had both heard about and witnessed. The analysis I conducted was published with the NUADC's yearly report. At its core was a breakdown of the major causes of wreck-diving fatalities into two groups, one involving exploration outside of a wreck, the other involving penetrations, and gave suggestions for divers to avoid becoming a statistic, just as Exley's cave-diving report had done.

After parts of my analysis were quoted in an article that appeared in a U.S. national diving newspaper, *Underwater U.S.A.*, Chris Rouse called me one day. "Hey, man, you're famous." I had no idea what he was talking about, and he seemed surprised because the article's direct quotes made it seem to him that the reporter had called and interviewed me. No, I assured him, they had just taken the published information and quoted me from that. Even then, he was impressed at the recognition that I had gotten. "Well, at least people know your name," he said. "I'm just another nobody."

As I lay in my hospital bed, Chris's comment echoed in my head and stirred a disturbing thought: Was my accident the result of my urge for recognition? After a great year of diving, including artifact collecting on the *Andrea Doria*, had I still needed to prove beyond a doubt that I was an outstanding diver by recovering a brass porthole, the symbol in my mind of a diving top gun? Did my urge to be somebody seduce me into disaster, or was it just in my nature to pursue things as intensely as possible? But wasn't it just human nature to push things as far as possible to reveal the unknown in our world and ourselves? Christopher Columbus and Vasco da Gama had done that in their lives as they used different approaches to explore the ocean route from Europe to India. People had pushed the envelope throughout history to come up with more efficient ways to explore underwater. Sheck Exley had pushed himself to advance the cave-diving frontier. My father had relentlessly pursued his scientific research in spite of setbacks.

Diana, my wife, appeared in the doorway, looking drawn and scared. She had been escorted to the hospital by Kevin O'Brien, a student who had taken several courses with me, and my frequent diving companion; he had been aboard the *Seeker* and witnessed my spiral into decompression sickness. I looked at Diana's beautiful South American face, framed by long, wavy black hair, and I shuffled gratefully toward her in my hospital gown. She couldn't take her eyes off my face, bloated from all of the intravenous fluids. Diana smiled from relief and happiness, and hugged me. I returned her hug, squeezing her tight. Diana had often resented my frequent absences to go diving, and I had minimized to her the risks involved, confident as I had been that I would come home safely. Now, having seen what the bends could do to me, not only could she be resentful about my absences, but she had fresh and plentiful reasons to worry that one day I might not come home at all.

I looked sheepishly at my wife, embarrassed that I had gotten myself into this situation. "What did you tell Gil?"

"I told him you got sick and had to go to the hospital, but that you would be all right and would be home soon."

What else could she have said to our three-year-old boy? "I'll call Gil, and let him know I'm okay."

My wife nodded tightly. "That would be very good."

"I'm sorry" was all I could say to her.

"I'm sorry too," Diana said.

I felt a little uncomfortable, not knowing what else to say. I turned to Kevin and asked about my diving equipment. Kevin's face showed surprise, and then he chuckled. "You're still recovering from your accident and you're worried about your gear? Man, you're hard-core!" We both laughed. Diana didn't.

"Well, do I have any gear left, or did it get dumped in all the excitement?"

"Someone brought your tanks on board. I packed all your stuff back into your bags and took everything to your apartment."

I was relieved. All of the expensive equipment had not wound up on the bottom of the ocean. I knew I would need my diving equipment again—no matter what that doctor told me.

The second chamber treatment had not improved my hearing, and the tinnitus remained. Walking remained a struggle, but I forced myself to take the steps as Dr. Mendagurin had instructed. Now, after four days, I could walk without banging into anything, although my vision was severely skewed whenever I turned my head while I was shuffling along. It was like watching a video shot by someone walking with a handheld camera. In spite of my imperfect physical condition, I was relieved that I could walk down the hospital's halls by myself, and that I could hear.

When I was twelve, I had read *Victory over Myself,* the autobiography of Floyd Patterson. Boxing's first two-time world heavyweight champion had been a very shy and withdrawn boy, and even though I was a very outgoing kid, I could relate to his sense of needing to overcome himself in order to achieve what he was capable of. Now, while I contemplated my situation in the hospital, I knew that I would need my own victory over myself if I was to come back and dive safely again. The words of another childhood hero, Muhammad Ali, served to motivate me and reinforced my desire to dive again in spite of the terrible setback I was now recovering from: After he lost his world championship to the underdog Leon Spinks, Ali simply smiled at his distraught handlers and said, "It's all just a test." In his next fight, Ali defeated Spinks and became the only man to win the world heavyweight boxing championship three times.

I knew about tests in the boxing ring. My own amateur boxing career had mixed results, the most disappointing of which were my two unsuccessful attempts to win a Golden Gloves state boxing championship, first at age fourteen, and again when I was seventeen. I related to the battered boxer who fought alone and would not let defeat or a bruised body derail the ambition to win—even though that ambition might lead to brain damage.

When I was about to be released from the hospital, after five days, Dr. Mendagurin stood over my bed. I looked at his face and realized it pained him to give me my discharge. "I know that giving up diving is something that is difficult if not impossible for someone who loves the water as much as you, but you need to consider that if you ever take another hit like this again, you'll never walk again. You've used up your extra neural pathways. You won't get another chance."

His words rang in my ears. If I was able to walk and hear so that I could go back and dive, I couldn't screw up again. If I was going to dive and live, I had to know why deep water lured me like a siren.

One person I knew could give me the facts and focus for my exploration. Dr. Jennifer Hunt had first called me a month before my accident. She explained that she was a psychoanalytically trained sociologist teaching at Montclair State University, in New Jersey, had a private psychoanalytic practice, and was interested in studying psychological and sociological issues in diving. As we talked, I was not clear about what exactly she wanted to study and thought that it had something to do with gender issues. I had the impression that she still needed to develop the questions her research would explore. I was skeptical, and not overly thrilled to participate in a study about gender issues in diving when I felt there were so many other, more pressing things to research in the diving world. I agreed to be interviewed and we set up an appointment for a later date. Then, I dived off the *Seeker* to the wreck of the *Northern Pacific* while experiencing flu symptoms. I did, however, see Dr. Hunt once I traveled from the Philadelphia hospital to my home in New York City.

First I had to get home from the hospital. Steve Bielenda and Hank Garvin of the *Wahoo*, the dive boat I had chartered for the Team Doria expedition earlier in the year, had both called me during my hospital stay, and both were concerned. Although Hank and I disagreed about wreck-diving techniques and equipment configuration, we respected each other and I appreciated his offer to come down to Philadelphia from his home north of New York City, pick me up, and drive me home, since my wife did not drive. She was home, taking care of our son. I knew that Hank was sincere and if I really needed a ride he would make the trip, which would take him at least three hours each way. Steve Bielenda also offered me a ride, and for him the journey would take at least five hours from his home in eastern Long Island. Both Bielenda's and Garvin's offers touched me as acts of friendship, although during the Team Doria expedition I thought that they could have anchored us where the team wanted to be, and had felt shortchanged when they didn't—perhaps because of their own desire to dive another part of the ocean liner. Even though we had our differences, we were all divers, bound by our intense passion for the sport to help one another, no matter what.

My parents lived not very far from the hospital, but they did not come and visit me, although we spoke on the phone. My father knew enough about loss to try to keep a cordial distance from it. I suspected that he had to deny the seriousness of my accident because it posed too great a potential disaster to him. His late childhood had brought a great deal of loss, including the death of his father, a medical doctor with a prosperous pharmaceutical business in India, and, according to my father, the subsequent mismanagement of the family business by his older brothers. My father could only watch as his future was squandered by his brothers. He left India when he was seventeen years old to find a new life in Europe and North America, where he would eventually start his own materials-analysis laboratory. During a phone conversation while I was at the Pennsylvania hospital, my father asked whether I could get a friend to drive me home. He knew that my wife did not have a driver's license. In the end, Dave Dannenberg, the instructor who had attended to me on the *Seeker*, made the four-hour drive from his home in Connecticut to Philadelphia and drove me home to Manhattan. I could spare my father the direct pain of my brush with death.

As I would find out later, Diana also could not accept the seriousness of my accident. During her one brief hospital visit, the only physical sign of injury she saw was my fluid-bloated face and my difficulty walking. The bloated face was, she knew, from the intravenous fluids I had been given, and she knew that would go away quickly with the use of diuretics that the doctors prescribed. She convinced herself that I had trouble walking mainly because I had been bedridden for a few days and my muscles were stiff. Diana would have been more sympathetic if I had dropped a bowling ball on my foot. It was all part of her denial of the risk I faced when I went diving.

Five weeks after my accident, Dr. Hunt came over to my apartment to interview me. My son, Gil, said hello to her with unusual shyness. Perhaps he had become overly suspicious of strangers: The day I returned from the hospital in Philadelphia, I had suffered what I thought was a collapsed lung, which made it excruciatingly painful to breathe, and I had been attended to by paramedics as Gil looked on. He had seen me taken away by ambulance to the local hospital by strangers. His three-year-old mind was probably haunted that his father might yet again be taken away from him.

Dr. Hunt was a tall, slim woman, with short, blond hair, fair features, and a businesslike demeanor. I judged her about five years older than I was, but found out later that she was a decade my senior. Dr. Hunt smiled warmly at Gil, and said hello in a very gentle, nonthreatening way. After Gil said hello, he turned and walked back to be with Diana, his mother, the parent in his life who didn't get sick and disappear.

Dr. Hunt turned to me with a warm smile. "He's adorable. He's probably wondering what I'm doing here." She pulled out a small tape recorder and placed it between us on the couch. "Has he been worried about you because of the accident?"

Her interview had already started. We discussed Gil and his worries. She briefed me about what she was doing and in what framework she wanted to work with me. She was informally gathering data about the world of diving, about how divers perceive themselves and the diving world. She was fascinated by people in high-risk environments. "My previous research was about police violence—what notions the police have of what constitutes violence, what they feel is reasonable and not reasonable, and why," she told me.

It seemed that Dr. Hunt's work encompassed more than gender issues in adventure sport, and that would be useful to me. "That's interesting," I told her. "I have a degree in criminal justice. Among other things. I'd like to read your police studies."

Jennifer, as Dr. Hunt insisted I call her, agreed, and promised to give me copies of her papers during our next interview. We went on to talk about my diving, the social dynamics of the technical aspects of the sport, and especially the resistance that new techniques and technologies had always encountered in the diving community at large. I filled her in on a lot of the history, and on how I had gotten increasingly fascinated, even obsessed, with the sport. We stopped the interview late in the evening and scheduled another meeting in three weeks' time. I knew that my interest in her work was in no sense academic. For my own sanity and safety I needed to be her guinea pig.

I was still homebound and had not returned to work; I was staying out on the disability leave my doctor had given me. Diana nagged me almost continuously to go back to work, even though my benefits paid my full salary. She could not understand that my hearing, vision, and walking were still compromised, and thought that I was just slacking. The nagging made my home life miserable, which probably did not help my recovery. Only many years later did Diana fully understand and accept the gravity of my condition, and she apologized for how she'd treated me.

At our second interview, Jennifer gave me copies of her published academic papers about the police research she had conducted in the seventies, which clarified for me her primary interest: the normalization of risk in the lives of her high-risk subjects. Her police research involved direct observation in the field, combined with unstructured interviews of police, just as she was now doing with divers. As part of her previous study, she had attended the Philadelphia Police Academy as a researcher and had graduated with the first one hundred women recruits. Although she was trained to shoot a gun, she did not have a badge. But she rode in patrol cars, taking regular shifts, and participated in police work and the social world of law enforcement professionals. She was able to establish how police justify the use of force to themselves and to their colleagues. Dr. Hunt's approach was as novel as it was controversial. Instead of applying only traditional sociological theories to explain social behavior, she also employed her training in psychoanalytic theory and what she had learned while treating patients in psychodynamic psychotherapy.

Her psychoanalytic training led her to conclude that there was an unconscious level of motivation within each of us. According to Dr. Hunt's training and beliefs, unconscious memory, thoughts, and feelings stem from earlier parts of life, including childhood, adolescence, and early adulthood. These unconscious recollections, notions, and emotions affect what we think, what we say, and how we act. Unresolved conflicts from earlier life experiences may be hidden in the unconscious and influence behavior, which is especially important to people such as divers, who engage in high-risk activities.

Even though I fully accepted my individual responsibility for the accident, I was intrigued that things of which I was not consciously aware influenced my safety—or lack of safety—on a dive. If this was true, then divers, and others in high-risk activities, could be safer if they looked deeper and examined their own motivations and their unresolved inner conflicts. I began a journey that continues today: to understand the siren call that lured me, Chris and Chrissy Rouse, and thousands of other divers to master deep and murderous water.

On an entirely conscious level, Chris Rouse had been motivated to take up diving when the other sport-flying pilots in his social group started planning a flight to Bermuda for a scuba-diving vacation. Chris thought that becoming a diver not only would be fun but would help him maintain the close friendship that he and Sue enjoyed with the other members in the flying group; diving would be something that eighteen-year-old Chrissy would be excited about; and Chris believed that it would strengthen the family bonds to share the same adventure among father, son, and wife. Teen fatherhood had curtailed Chris's natural youthful escapades; now, at thirty-five, Chris could experience some of the manly challenges he'd once had to forgo.

The social, even tribal, aspects of diving combined in Chris with his natural competitiveness, evident in the intensity of his diving. Chris welcomed underwater challenges from the outset of his diving—early on he took to cave diving, which was far beyond the skills and aspirations of most divers—and he pitted himself against the water itself as much as against any one person in particular. Underwater, he was free to be his own man, just as he was as a business owner. And underwater, the experience of adventure gave a new meaning to his life and made him feel very special because he knew he was doing something unusual.

Two years before my accident and only eleven months after Chris and Chrissy had begun their first class, the Rouse family had an adventure that went beyond what most divers experience—an exercise that manufactured challenge and risk in a way that arguably was foolhardy. The three Rouses took the "Advanced Diving" course given by Bob Burns. During that course, Burns taught the Rouses underwater navigation, as well as search and recovery of objects underwater. At Pennsylvania's Willow Springs quarry, Burns conducted an exercise to find a sunken Volkswagen in the cold, murky water. Using a rope, the divers swam a pattern until they found the vehicle. The search portion of their class proved easy enough.

Their next exercise proved far more challenging. Burns set forth an entirely constructed task involving real and completely optional risks: to raise the car without getting trapped, crushed, or drowned. The trophy offered by this endeavor was not a treasure that the world might venerate, like a porthole, or a *Doria* dish. Instead, the artifact to retrieve was a rusted Beetle, and the challenge was to survive.

Chris and Chrissy Rouse were delighted at the challenge. Bob Burns had instructed Chris Rouse to send up a lift bag attached to a rope, and then tie off the rope to the Volkswagen so that the bag did not float around the quarry. The bright-yellow lift bag floating on the water's surface clearly marked the location of the car, and the bag could easily be seen from shore while everyone took a break and ate lunch between dives. Burns announced to the class that on their next dive they would raise the Volkswagen they had just found. Chris and Chrissy were very excited and eager to get started right away. Sue and some of the other students thought the task was too risky and they were skeptical about trying to raise a car to the surface. What was the point? Chris and Chrissy wanted to do it, if only to experience something new and to say they had done it. Getting the rust bucket up from the bottom would give them some bragging rights.

Raising a sunken car carries risk usually taken on only by commercial divers like Glenn Butler, who get paid, or for police and fire rescue squads, which sometimes have to raise sunken vehicles as crime scene evidence, or to extract people who had the misfortune of driving into the water. Police and fire divers use underwater communications gear to coordinate their activities, so that when they raise a car it won't strike a diver as it comes off the bottom, or ascend to the surface improperly tethered, then break free of its bonds and plummet onto the unsuspecting divers. Without communications gear, the Rouses and their buddies felt more pressure to execute their plan so perfectly that no one got injured or killed.

In spite of the inherent risks, Chris and Chrissy Rouse welcomed the challenge of getting a car to the surface. From earning his private pilot license to starting his own excavation business to building his own house, Chris had always shouldered aside any obstacles, a trait that his son, Chrissy, imitated. Chris saw the raising of a car from the bottom of a mud-lined quarry as a mechanical problem, the kind he was very good at solving. It helped tremendously that, along with having the right attitude, the men had no idea how risky or dangerous underwater salvage can be.

Diving has a long history partly because of our ignorance of the risks involved underwater combined with our determination to bring something up. Some of us have welcomed the pure challenge of overcoming the risks of the unknown, but undoubtedly, many divers have been motivated to accept the risks of the deep out of greed: For millennia the driving force behind diving has been the lure of salvaging sunken cargo and treasure and obtaining natural resources.

One of diving's most remarkable examples of ignorance colluding with greed to expose divers to tremendous risks occurred in the 1920s, when the wealthy English businessman Ernest Cox was motivated to buy from the British Admiralty the entire sunken German World War I Navy as scrap metal, which rested underwater in the protected anchorage of Scapa Flow, in Scotland's Orkney Islands. To him it was a sunken treasure. He was undeterred that a previous salvage attempt by a commercial company had yielded only scrap metal from four lightweight destroyers, already dragged into shallow water and beached by the British Royal Navy. Marine salvage experts around the world were unanimous that the undertaking of raising completely sunken ships as long as 700 feet, as wide as 96 feet, and weighing as much as 26,180 tons was folly. They were convinced that no one—especially not Ernest Cox, who had no experience whatsoever in underwater salvage—could raise the great German battle fleet. Nothing on this scale had ever before been attempted.

During the Versailles peace negotiations, the German fleet had been interned at Scapa Flow under the watchful eyes of the British, who had stipulated that treaty negotiations could not begin until the Germans disarmed their navy and allowed it to be kept in an Allied port. The Allies reasoned that if the Germans knew they would not be able to use their navy in the event the negotiations failed, they would be less willing to risk such a failure and more willing to sign the peace treaty.

On June 21, 1919, eight months after the armistice that ended the First World War, it looked as though the Germans would not accept the harsh terms of the proposed Versailles Treaty and the war would resume. Admiral von Reuter, the commander of the German fleet at Scapa Flow, ordered his officers to sink their own ships so that they would not be captured by the British and turned against Germany. All seventy-four German warships went to the bottom—the very morning a group of Scottish schoolchildren was touring around them aboard a tugboat. Some of the younger children were delighted to see the massive ships sinking, and thought that it was a show put on for their benefit. The older children and adults present knew that the sinking warships could strike the tugboat and sink it, and they were understandably terrified. Luckily, the tugboat and its human cargo made it safely back to shore. What the children had witnessed on their school outing was the single greatest act of naval suicide in world history.

Unfortunately for the Allies, the scuttling of the German fleet proved a huge embarrassment: They had wanted to divide the ships—some of which were among the most powerful in the world—among themselves as prizes of war. When the British Admiralty had divers and salvage experts assess the situation, it was judged most economical to sell the ships where they lay for scrap.

Cox had perceived a business opportunity in raising the German fleet for scrap metal and was nearly killed when a chain underneath a sunken ship snapped and lashed the deck of the wooden floating dock where Cox was standing. Luckily, everyone escaped unscathed. The incident served only to warn Cox and his workers that they should find a more suitable way of raising the vessels, which they did, using heavy wire cables combined with compressed air pumped into the warships, which divers had welded closed. Cox's enthusiasm and refusal to bow to the risks of the deep were rewarded with the salvage of most of the fleet, including the 26,180-ton *Hindenburg*, the largest ship ever raised intact. Unfortunately for Cox, the salvage was not successful from a business standpoint and he suffered losses of over ten thousand pounds sterling. Greed spurred technical innovation, but greed did not win out.

On its own scale, what the Rouses faced in raising the Volkswagen at the quarry was almost as daunting as Ernest Cox's earlier undertaking at Scapa Flow, although it would have been practically pointless if greed, or even usefulness, had been their motive. But unlike Cox, the Rouses had a body of experience and a teacher in Bob Burns who had done this before. Burns outlined the plan: They would take down a heavy, reinforced nylon strap to put underneath the car, and then they would attach each end of the strap to a lift bag with a 1,000-pound capability. Unlike the small lift bag that floated on the surface marking the car's location, the 1,000-pound bag that Burns wanted his students to use to raise the car was completely sealed. A special valve would be used to connect the bag to scuba tanks so that the bag could be inflated, and an overpressure relief vent would let out excess air as it expanded when the bag floated toward the surface. They would fill the bag with air from extra scuba tanks they brought down just for this purpose. The air trapped in the lift bag would carry the car to the surface.

The Rouses worked hard to get the strap underneath the car. They had to do a lot of digging to make a tunnel through which they could snake the strap, just as the divers at Scapa Flow had done years earlier to raise the German warships. Chris and Chrissy Rouse were not bothered by working in the zero-visibility conditions they created by digging, and they successfully got the Volkswagen to the surface. Nobody died. Proud that they had accomplished such a major task so early in their diving careers, they had further confirmation that they could do underwater whatever they set out to accomplish, as long as they planned everything properly—no matter how daunting the risk or dubious the rewards.

During my second interview with Dr. Hunt, she started to ask me questions about my childhood, especially as it related to my developing fascination with diving.

Chrissy Rouse, Billy Deans, Glenn Butler, and a host of other divers who engaged in the more extreme aspects of the sport were spurred by their fathers. In my case, it was my grandmother, whom we all affectionately called Omi, the German term of endearment for a grandmother, who started my fascination with diving. I was seven years old and living in London, England, where I had been born, when I visited Omi in West Berlin for the summer. Although Berlin is seen as a big, cosmopolitan city—one that has played a critical ongoing role in modern politics—most people would be surprised at the city's many lakes and forests, which lend it a charm that a place such as New York can only wish for.

Omi lived in Wannsee, a district where the large lake called the Wannsee is located; connected to it is a smaller lake. Sailboats and powerboats dotted both the large and small Wannsee, and sight-seeing ferries would take passengers for trips all around the city, across various lakes connected by canals. Though the specter of the infamous Berlin Wall and machine gun–toting East German guards in their watchtowers loomed above us, Omi and I were undisturbed. During that warm summer, Omi and I would go to the nearby Stölpchensee, the same lake where my mother and her twin sister had learned to swim in their youth, and I would frolic in the water for hours, jumping on an air mattress and seeing if I could stand on it. Omi would sit at the waterfront café and chat with friends over coffee.

Seeing how much I enjoyed the water, Omi bought me a snorkel, mask, and swim fins. On our next trip to the little lake, I taught myself to snorkel. The fins made me feel like a fish as I glided rapidly, almost effortlessly, through the water. With fins on, I had a fresh confidence in the water and felt as though I belonged—a new feeling for a child who by birth and breeding had felt like an alien in every environment, a scout sent out to master the customs and language of a foreign territory. Although there wasn't much to see in the turbid lake, it thrilled me just the same when I dived a few feet down and saw a plant sticking out of the muddy bottom. Life could occur even in such a dark and unfriendly place.

Diving connected me in other ways to my German past. On my various trips to Germany as a youth, my relatives would talk after dinner about their experiences during the world wars. One of my distant relatives, an elderly lady, had a picture in her living room of her husband in uniform, and next to it sat his gleaming parade helmet from the First World War, complete with a spike protruding from its center. As the Germans say, he fell in that war. My other relatives had fought on both fronts, either in the air or on the ground. Omi told me that my grandfather, Alfred Krüger, had been an aeronautical engineer in the Luftwaffe, and had conducted high-altitude flight experiments long before the Second World War. She told me that the bonus pay he received for the risky altitude experiments brought relief from the restricted life caused by a depressed German economy. My grandfather fell in 1944, and I always felt pangs of loss that I never knew him.

My uncle, who married my mother's twin sister after his first wife died of cancer, had been a rear gunner on a Stuka dive-bomber. Even after the war he retained his enthusiasm for flight, and he loved to fly model airplanes with me. He would frequently come over during my visits to take me to the park, where we would fly our toys, like two little children. My great-uncle, who knew five languages, had been in the army, had fought on both the eastern and western fronts, and was wounded twice. When I was eighteen, he told me about his war experiences over a bottle of wine. His images of the bitter-cold Russian front—his putting motor oil on his nose and ears to prevent them from freezing—never left me. The stories I heard did not relate to the murderous Third Reich and its agenda of war and genocide; instead I was hearing stories of individual skill and survival.

Although I never met any of my relatives who had been in the German Navy, I was nonetheless fascinated to learn after I started diving that there were freighters and warships off the New York and New Jersey coasts, not far from my home, that had been sunk during the world wars. And I learned about the German submarines known as U-boats that lay offshore. I determined to get the skills and equipment to safely dive them, and in doing so I would be touching a piece of my personal history and of world history unchanged by human hands since they had gone to their doom, years ago.

Dr. Hunt observed that my experiences in Germany were the closest I had come to feeling as if I belonged somewhere; even though my Indian features clearly did not fit in with those of the fair-skinned German people, my language skills did. My grandmother loved me unconditionally, and as a result I felt closer to the German people than to any other people. Since I was a young outsider with a mixed background, Germany was as close to a country I could call my own as I had experienced.

After I taught myself to snorkel in Berlin, we moved from my native England to Canada when I was eight years old. The decline of the British economy during the sixties made my father decide that there were better opportunities to be found in other countries. We crossed the Atlantic to New York City on the *Queen Elizabeth,* the December voyage on the luxury ocean liner a great adventure for me, and settled in Kitchener, Ontario. In Canada, my London accent again set me apart, and once more I felt like an outsider. After I had finally developed a Canadian accent and started to fit in, we moved to the United States, and, as Dr. Hunt observed, I was again an outsider, struggling to fit in. Only many years later, when I took up diving, did I feel I belonged; my experiences underwater resonated with the childhood satisfaction I'd felt snorkeling in Berlin as Omi stood guard. Dr. Hunt had uncovered some of my personal puzzle, but I knew there was more that might help me avoid another underwater accident. At the end of our second encounter, I knew I still had a lot of exploring to do, as I worked to understand what motivated the magnetic pull I felt for the underwater world and how other divers and I might live to love it more.

My interview with Dr. Hunt was interrupted as Diana called out, "Excuse me. Gil wants to say good night."

Gil walked over to me and smiled at Dr. Hunt. This woman had been a complete stranger to him when she came to our apartment for the first time a month ago, but she had not taken me away on a stretcher, as the paramedics had, and he must have felt a little more confident that his father would not again vanish. I too had some fresh confidence that I might be hanging around. Neither Gil nor I could know that Dr. Hunt's interviews and intervention would drastically change our lives and bring my son and me much closer. She would help me save my life—although others would not be so lucky.

Gil smiled at Dr. Hunt, then turned to me and with a big hug and a kiss said, "Good night, Daddy. See you in the morning?"

9

Iron Coffins

T HE ROUSES WERE CONCERNED and intrigued by my accident. We spoke often on the telephone during the months I strove to walk like a normal person and test out my reflexes and my hearing. I told Chris, "When I was in trouble on the *Northern Pacific*, I thought to myself, 'Well, I can either try looking for the anchor line until I drown, or go up, get bent, and get choppered to a chamber.' I just figured everything would be fine once I got into the chamber." I hadn't counted on watching my spirit leave my body and having to decide not to die.

Chris was fascinated. "Man, what a decision. I would have done the same, though. I'd rather take my chances in the chamber than drown!"

His words would come back to haunt me.

Chris and Chrissy questioned me in detail about the accident and about my progress recovering, as if by recounting the story I could get past the trauma, and by hearing it they could inoculate themselves against my mistake. "Bernie, when you're ready to dive again, come

229

on over and stay with us," Chris Rouse said repeatedly. "We'll go to the quarry and dive with you to make sure you're okay." He told me that he imagined how psychologically difficult my first dive would be—returning to the scene of the crime, as it were, with every intention of returning as much as possible. Neither of us doubted I would dive again. "Whatever you need, any gases, any equipment, anything, don't worry about it," Chris reassured me. "We've got everything here. And what we've got, you've got!" I was touched by his offer.

I told Chris about Dr. Hunt's theories that unconscious unresolved conflicts in our past could be reenacted underwater, with possibly dangerous consequences. I didn't know if there was anything to her approach, I said, but after meeting with her I was starting to examine my own history to see what might have spurred me to dive when I shouldn't have, and to keep pushing it even when I was down there.

"Whatever it takes to make you a safer diver, Bernie, go for it," Chris replied.

"Do you think there's anything to the theory?"

"I don't know, man. It sounds like a bit of a stretch to me. But what do I know?" Chris Rouse's shrug of a response didn't surprise me. For better or worse, he was a man whose character was defined by how he acted, not what he thought about his actions.

In December 1991, six weeks after my accident, I was able to return to work, heading down Wall Street to put in a physically unsteady but mentally intense day doing staff analysis. At this point in my life my financial industries job still ensured my livelihood, notwithstanding the ever more magnetic pull I felt toward deep water. Just as Dr. Mendagurin had assured me, my brain was developing a new neural pathway to send the signals to my body that enabled me to walk without falling over. Gradually, I could walk and turn my head so that, for example, I did not get dizzy and lose my balance when I crossed the street. I could sit and work at my computer but had to take frequent breaks to avoid blurry vision, headaches, and lack of concentration. My manager empathized and assigned me a light workload so that I could continue my recovery.

But now, as a diving survivor, I viewed things differently. A year earlier, when I was a systems analyst supporting the technology needs of traders and commodities brokers, I had always marveled that they needed to compare their activities to being at war. Wall Street traders and businessmen like to think of themselves as locked in battle, but I knew that they did not risk their lives and that the worst consequence of a trade gone bad would be the loss of their jobs. And even that would happen only in the most extreme cases—for example, if they violated the company's trading guidelines, which were implemented to limit the company's exposure to excessive financial risk. Certainly a stock market crash affected people around the world, yet such an event was well beyond the control of any single trader. And even if the market did crash, people didn't die from that alone.

Unlike the Wall Street traders with whom I worked, my cave-diving instructor, Marc Eyring, had been a Green Beret, inserted behind enemy lines in Vietnam. Eyring knew what being at war meant; he had been in real battles, risking his life and seeing some of the men in his outfit killed. And I, as a diving instructor and deep diver, knew that every time my students and I went underwater, the risks included death and paralysis. I prided myself on teaching my students so thoroughly that they would all have the tools to survive while using their life-support equipment in the alien underwater world. Though my students frequently joked that I drilled them like a boot-camp sergeant, many of them came back long after they had gotten certified to talk with me after they had had some harrowing underwater event, and thanked me for my thorough training, which had enabled them to save their own lives. I felt that the traders, by comparison, were playing at risk, with little more at stake in their physical well-being than if they lost a game of Monopoly.

Now that I had come so close to death from the bends, I felt that the war analogy so frequently made in the business world was even more childish. I became resentful that I had to spend time playing at a game with so little at stake. And I knew that at my job I was only a cog in the wheel, easily replaced if I stumbled. As I looked around me, I knew that I could not make any real difference in this environment; I would not be increasing our collective knowledge about ourselves or our world by compiling silly reports about things like our division's spending on personnel, or the success of our college recruiting efforts. The way that I could make a difference in this world was by training people and motivating them to explore underwater, and also through my personal explorations. Like the Rouses, I wanted to find new forms of life underwater and participate in expeditions that would give us all more knowledge.

Now, while I struggled to make a full recovery from my accident, I took breaks from my mundane work to look out the windows and focus on the world seven stories below. If I could navigate the maze of New York City streets as well as I had before I got the bends, couldn't I penetrate deep water again, wisely and safely? For now, I could only wistfully look down from my desk whenever an ocean liner or freighter floated up or down the Hudson River and wonder whether I would ever again be able to see the likes of such ships that had met their fates underwater.

Chrissy Rouse's life was getting more and more wild as he struggled to forge his own path independent of his parents. He was spending less time at home and more time with his friend Tim Stumpf, who lived not far from Underwater World dive shop, where Chrissy worked. The atmosphere at Tim's was like a fraternity house, with people dropping by casually and partying during the week, as if to keep themselves in shape for the weekend-long festivities. Chrissy would often stay over at Tim's, and in the spring of 1992, he moved in. He had just turned twenty-two and was living apart from his parents for the first time.

The young men and women who regularly hung out at Tim's were, like Chrissy, mostly divers. They lived fast and hard, which Chrissy liked; life was meant to be an adventure in the water, on land, and in bed. Chrissy found he could easily meet and mingle with women, especially since most of them were interested in his diving stories, which gave him something to talk about. Being at Tim's house gave him a venue where he could connect with women more privately than he could with his parents just down the hall.

Still, he was enough his parents' child to make sure to call his mother every day. It was apparent to everyone who hung out at Tim's that Sue Rouse and Chrissy were a very close mother and son. Even in the middle of a raucous weekend party, Chrissy would withdraw from the proceedings long enough to call his mother, if he had forgotten to do so earlier in the day. Tim would hear Chrissy say, "I'm fine, Mom.

That's why I was calling you, to let you know that everything's okay. I'm just here with a few people, relaxing a little bit." He'd wind the phone cord around himself as he paced the floor, winking at a woman sitting amid the laundry and pizza boxes. "I've already had a few beers and, no, I'm not doing any driving, Mom. Don't worry about me!" He'd groan jokingly. "Yeah, I know, Mom. That's why I call you to let you know I'm okay. You don't need to worry about me. Yeah, I love you, too."

Chrissy had started seeing Julia, the flirtatious, leggy blonde whom he had met in diving class a year earlier while he was assisting the instructor during the pool training sessions. Although each of them had been in a serious relationship with someone else, their other romances had ended, and now they had started dating casually. Julia worked not far away from the dive shop, and from Tim's house, and she would stop over frequently both at the dive shop and at Tim's to see Chrissy; she was able to relax and have fun with him in a way she had not found in her previous committed relationship. Each of them loved the other's adventurous nature.

Chrissy's rigorous nonchalance was contagious. At first, Tim had found it a bit odd that his new housemate had the early-morning habit of walking into the bathroom, sitting casually on the side of the bathtub, and chatting while Tim was relieving himself. But even more curious was that Tim's girlfriend had picked up the habit. Then Julia would feel free to join in the group discussion, and soon it seemed that the whole house was crowded into Tim's bathroom while he was seated. It became so frequent an occurrence that Tim and the rest of the people in the house eventually thought little of it. Frat-style living, it seemed, could be a coed team sport.

The sport extended to fun underwater, where the terms of adventure were far riskier. Chrissy could be a casual gladiator. He loved to play a game called bumper scooter, in which he and another diver would try to ram each other with their diver-propulsion vehicles, maneuvering to knock the other off the controls and send him crashing to the bottom, like two knights jousting on horseback. John Reekie, the Canadian who loved to dive with Chris in Florida's caves, enjoyed the game with Chrissy whenever the two were at the quarry, or even to amuse themselves in a cave while on decompression. Whenever Chrissy tried to play the game with his father, the senior

Rouse did not cooperate, and only got annoyed, shooting his son a furrowed-brow glare from behind his diving mask. The elder Rouse thought diving was too serious and the consequences of missteps too great for divers to play around underwater. After all, someone could get knocked unconscious if he got rammed in the head with the scooter, or if he crashed into a hard object and hit his head. If that happened, he could drown before the other person knew what was happening. Chrissy shrugged off his father's cautions, even after John Reekie performed a deft feint in the quarry during bumper scooter and Chrissy crashed hard into a railroad car that had been purposely sunk to attract divers. When he surfaced, Chrissy figured that either he or his father could fix the broken scooter, and the bump on his forehead would resolve itself.

On June 25, 1992, Chrissy went diving with his housemate Tim Stumpf on a wreck called the *Double East*, whose scattered remains 61 feet below sea level seemed worse to Chrissy than a junk pile. In fact, he later noted in his logbook, "Biggest pile of shit in ocean. Clear and calm. Tried to kill Stumpf out of boredom." The maze of metal was no fun, and there wasn't anything worth retrieving on this, his 594th dive. To pass the time, Chrissy decided to make things more interesting. Spotting Tim rooting among the wreckage, Chrissy snuck up on his friend, grabbed his leg, and used his knife to start cutting a hole in Tim's drysuit. The hole would let the cold water in, which Chrissy knew would be harmless at this depth—in spite of what he wrote in his logbook—on a dive where they would not need to decompress.

Although another diver would have been furious, perhaps even worried that his life was in danger, Tim and Chrissy always played outrageous pranks on each other, and Tim knew immediately that Chrissy was playing around. Tim turned and slapped Chrissy's mask, which promptly filled with seawater, temporarily blinding him. When Chrissy's hands went to reposition his mask on his face and purge it, Tim drew his own knife and went on the offensive, sawing a hole in Chrissy's suit. His mask on and clear of water, Chrissy grunted and grabbed Tim's arm to stop him from cutting his suit. The two wrestled underwater, gasping and laughing, each holding a knife in one hand and spinning in somersaults like a scene from a James Bond movie. Soon, their antics winded them; they laughed at each other and headed for the surface. Back on board the dive boat, soaking wet from the holes they had cut into each other's suits, they kidded around about their new ventilation systems. The holes, they knew, would be easy enough to repair, and soon their suits would be almost as good as new. They'd had fun, and the risk wasn't big; they knew better than to accidentally slice each other's hoses or stab each other by mistake.

Chrissy's casual outlook on life carried over onto land—from diving to driving. Though he did follow his mother's admonition and did not drink and drive, his fast driving sometimes caused him to lose control on Pennsylvania's often wet, winding country roads, and scrape a guardrail or slide into a tree. Although they were not major accidents, the damage to his parents' cars still had to be paid for, and Chrissy did not have a lot of money. The second real accident broke his bank account, and after only two months with Tim he had to move back in with his parents. The accidents and his son's uncertain future did not make either Chris or Sue Rouse very happy. But what could they do with their only child except to lend him the money to fix the damaged vehicle, and let him move back in until he got himself back on his feet financially? Isn't that what good parents do—look out for their son, ease his way?

In July 1992, I was ready to take the plunge again. Nine months after my diving accident, I accepted Chris Rouse's offer to stay with him and dive at the quarry. No matter that the doctor had said during my recompression chamber treatment that my diving career was over. I'd never believed him. I knew that if I could learn to walk properly, I would have to dive. For me, not to dive was too great a loss even to imagine for very long. I felt too strongly identified with the world of divers like Steve Berman and Marc Eyring at Ginnie Springs; the Rouses in Pennsylvania; Steve Bielenda, Hank Garvin, and the crew of the *Wahoo;* my dive club in Manhattan; and the many other divers I had met over the years. The underwater world had given me so much more reward than anything I'd received on land, except from my wife and son. To lose my place and position as a diver would be like being uprooted again, just as I had been in my childhood, when my family moved from country to country, and right when I would get comfortable with the local customs and dialect, we'd move again. This time, I was determined to remain a fully accredited citizen of the underwater realm of divers. I wasn't about to stay stuck on the surface.

My wife saw how restless I was now that I had not gone diving for so many months. When I told her I would be returning to the water she simply said, "Well, go blow bubbles and be happy. I know that diving makes you happy. You know what you're doing. Just be careful."

"Yeah, diving can be a cruel mistress," I joked. Diana replied with a half smile and a quick "Hmm."

When Gil saw me packing my diving bags, he asked in a puzzled tone, "You're going diving, Daddy?" He seemed to be preparing himself for another loss of his father. Maybe he thought that this time the loss would be permanent. I hugged him. "Yes, Daddy's going diving. But I'll be really careful and I'll be back at the end of the weekend, in one piece. Okay?"

I had trained diligently for my return to diving and was comfortable that I was giving my body the best chance to function properly underwater. What I did not know was whether my severe decompression sickness would predispose me to another case of the bends, even if I did everything by the book. My philosophy had long been that I had to train my body to "in-gas" and "off-gas" the excess nitrogen it absorbed in the course of a dive—that is, to properly absorb and eliminate the gas so that I did not get bent. I figured that I would now have to recondition my body to diving and would need to give my body training slowly. It was the diving equivalent of learning to crawl before I walked. And now that I could walk again on land, I was again ready to crawl underwater.

For my first dive, I planned to breathe a 50 percent oxygen mixture and dive for twenty minutes to less than 30 feet in the freshwater quarry, which would put just under one additional atmosphere of pressure on my body. When I came up, I would stop for at least fifteen minutes at 15 feet and continue to breathe the high-oxygen mixture to help my body eliminate the excess nitrogen. I knew that this was probably so overly cautious that it would serve only to cut my risk factor of the bends to an absurdly low level, yet psychologically the plan was something I could deal with.

As Chris had suspected, my real challenge was to surmount the terror involved in coming back to diving after nearly being killed by the bends. There were too many unknown factors when it came to how the body dealt with the bends in a diver who had never suffered the malady, and far more uncertainties involving someone like me who had been bent. I needed the support of friends. Kevin O'Brien—who had been on the *Seeker* and seen the result of my accident—said he would dive with me and be there along with Chris and Chrissy to make sure that I didn't get bent or freak out—and that if I did, I'd get medical treatment fast. And if the underwater pressure jammed my nerves and spurred paralysis, my friends could drag me out before I drowned.

At the quarry, I piled all of my diving gear conveniently within reach next to a picnic table, just as I had done on a visit here with the Rouses a year earlier. As Kevin got dressed in his diving equipment and the Rouses looked on—they were already clad in their drysuits—I methodically donned all of my gear in my usual ritualistic fashion. I had found that getting into my dive gear in a specific, unhurried order helped me to remember everything and not omit something small but important like my ankle weights, which helped me keep my feet in position underwater by counteracting the air that would work its way into my drysuit's foot pockets. Today, the step-by-step discipline felt like a meditative insurance effort. Even though my dive would be extremely shallow, I strapped on the double tank setup that I had worn on all of my previous dives during the past several years. I didn't want to cut corners and use only a single tank because I felt like that would be cheating: If I wasn't strong enough to carry my double tanks on my back while I walked back and forth between the picnic bench and the water, or if I had difficulty swimming with the two tanks underwater, then I would know that I had failed to get my body ready to dive again.

Kevin was dressed before I was, but he sat patiently next to me and watched me finish putting my gear on. The Rouses had gone down to the water, where they waited for Kevin and me. I lumbered toward them, looking forward to getting into the water to buoy the weight I carried on my back. I was excited, but I also felt as though I were walking the plank.

Kevin and I waded into the water and put our fins on. Chris and

Chrissy Rouse, Kevin O'Brien, and I stood in a circle, waist-high in water, like participants in a total-immersion baptism. Kevin looked at me. "Ready?"

I took a deep breath as I finished adjusting my mask. Grasping the regulator in my hand, I nodded, put the regulator in my mouth, and ducked under the water. At first, I stayed still, just savoring the feeling of breathing underwater again. The Rouses and Kevin looked on. Chrissy flashed me an "OK?" sign, which I returned. He pointed into the murky water, indicating the direction to swim. I checked my compass and signaled "OK." I swam slowly, deliberately. My muscles had been away from diving for a long time and I knew that I could not possess the grace and fluidity of motion that I saw in Chrissy. This dive was so different from the last one Chrissy and I had done together in this quarry, when we were practicing various techniques to employ on our *Andrea Doria* expedition. During that last dive, Chrissy and I each held on to a diver-propulsion vehicle that Chris had modified; both of us jetted through the water, to a far corner of the quarry and a now-submerged building that had once served as the pumping station when the quarry had been worked for material used to make cement. Now, we would not venture anywhere near the underwater forest that Chrissy and I had scootered through at high speed, swiftly contorting our bodies to avoid tree limbs that appeared suddenly from the water's murky haze. Our destination today was far more mundane than an underwater building: We would be going to the shallowest of the many underwater platforms where instructors had students demonstrate their proficiency at various diving skills. Although I was not a student in the strict sense of the word, Chris, Chrissy, and Kevin were all acting like watchful instructors, making me practice the diver's equivalent of musical scales, checking to see how limber I was.

When we reached the underwater platform and swam around it for a few minutes, Chrissy signaled to ask if I was okay. I signaled back that I was fine. Chrissy pointed to himself and his father, then toward the water's haze. He made a question mark with his finger, then an "OK" sign. Chrissy was checking up on me, making sure that I was comfortable and then asking if it was okay for him and his father to go swimming off on their own, which would still leave me with Kevin to watch over me. I signaled back "OK" and then watched as Chris and Chrissy swam off with what seemed like total absence of effort, just as we had done together on some long cave dives in Florida, where they were leading.

I checked my dive computers; twenty minutes had already passed. I signaled to Kevin that I was going to ascend the line that went up from the platform to a surface ball buoy. Kevin signaled in agreement. As we ascended, I remembered my last ascent, and the pain from my missed decompression ghosted through my mind even as my body bobbed easily through the murk toward light. Although my short, shallow quarry dive with Kevin technically required no decompression, I still stopped at 15 feet, as I had planned, to start retraining my body to eliminate the excess nitrogen it had absorbed even during this training-wheels dive. The minutes passed slowly as I worriedly tuned in to my body for any signs of oncoming bends. Nothing. I could have been in an especially dirty bathtub. Kevin and I exchanged "OK" signals several times while we waited at 15 feet. I knew that I was being paranoid, but I also knew from what Dr. Mendagurin had told me that I had no extra neural pathways and that if I again suffered a bad case of the bends I would be permanently crippled.

When I surfaced, everything felt fine. After swimming back to shore, and then ambling like a drunken bear to the picnic table, I took off my diving equipment and felt relief wash over me with the cool summer air. As I slid out of my double-tank harness, I felt that more than just the weight of my tanks had been lifted from my back and shoulders.

When Chris and Chrissy returned from their dive, we sat at the picnic table, eating, joking, and basking in the warm summer sun as we exchanged diving stories. My fears about returning to diving, and about the increased risk of the bends I faced, had been partially overcome. I could now move on to a slightly deeper depth as my next step in returning to diving. In some way, I think that Kevin and the Rouses were also relieved: If I could come back from such a bad case of the bends, so could they, if decompression sickness ever ambushed them. Divers and others who participate in sports that carry with them a risk of being crippled or killed always like to think that nothing bad will happen to them. Psychotherapists like Dr. Hunt call it a defense mechanism, one that allows the sport's participant to get on with the game. However, it is also dangerous if it leads to unnecessarily high risk taking. In practical terms, the trick to successful participation in a high-risk sport is to acknowledge that bad things can happen, make every effort to prevent those things from happening, and be prepared to confront accidents when they do occur.

When we went back to the Rouses' house, Chris showed Kevin and me the new diving equipment he was making in his basement. His business, Black Cloud Scuba, was expanding by word of mouth, just as years before his excavation business had grown. Although Chris was making more equipment sales, he also had to reinvest the money to buy other tools, or even molds to make equipment such as metal scooter blades. He knew it would take time to build Black Cloud Scuba to the point where he and his family could pay all the bills, eat, and live well from its earnings. Right now, he was selling off his excavating equipment one piece at a time—a truck here, a bulldozer there—to cover the mortgage and put food on the table.

Chris had his massive collection of comic books neatly stored in easily accessible boxes on long tables in his basement, which Kevin had first noticed when we visited more than a year earlier. When Kevin asked about the collection, Chris remarked, "Yep, those superheroes are neat. You know, what the comics need now is a full-time diving superhero—not those guys who dive only when they have to save the world." I could see a new scheme germinating behind Chris's brow. Maybe DC Comics would never buy the Rouses' story, but Chris and Chrissy could use these heroic fighters of evil as their role models, be the Batman and Robin of the deep.

Chris, seeing Kevin's intense interest in the comics, remarked, "You can read any of the comics you want. Just be careful with them, and make sure you put them back in the *exact* spot you got them from."

"Thanks, but I don't want to mess up your collection," Kevin replied, as he examined the stacks of comic books, which were in perfect condition, more than a thousand of them, stored sequentially and in special, heavy plastic envelopes to prevent them from getting spoiled.

Right now, Robin was back home living in the Bat Cave, and when we sat down to eat, Chris pointed his fork at Chrissy and grumbled good-naturedly, "I thought I got rid of this guy when he moved out, but he's back, like herpes. I'll never get rid of this freeloader!" He smiled but he also meant it.

Chrissy groaned and shot back, "Yeah? You never complain when I bring up the lobsters!"

"Aw, you eat most of them with your buddies over at Tim's house, anyway. You'd have to bring us way more lobsters to pay your rent here!"

"I brought some lobsters home just the other day!"

Chris started to retort, but then abruptly stopped. His son looked embarrassed.

Sue cut in. "Now, now, boys, play nice. Bernie and Kevin are here. Let's eat in peace."

Almost immediately, stripped of the crutch of father-son contentiousness, all three Rouses grew morose, which I thought was odd, until a little later when I heard what images Chrissy's reference to his recent lobster catch had brought back for the family. Chris probably hadn't wanted to tell me any bad diving news before I'd dipped my toe back into diving, but now his bad news raced to the surface.

One week before I visited the Rouses, parents and son had dived the *Arundo*, a 412-foot Dutch freighter torpedoed during the Second World War by *U-136*. The *Arundo* rests on the bottom at 130 feet, twenty-five miles off the New Jersey coast. The Coast Guard wire-dragged the *Arundo* after it sank. Wire-dragging is done to clear a hazard to navigation: Two ships drag a huge wire cable over the wreck to flatten it so other ships cannot scrape or crash into the unseen hulk below. The wire-dragging spread the *Arundo* across the sea floor in a jumble of steel plates and debris, but two locomotives that the freighter was transporting to Egypt remained intact. The steel plates are perfect dens for lobsters, and Chrissy caught three of them.

Ed Sollner, one of the divers on the *Arundo* trip, had hung out regularly with Chrissy at Tim Stumpf's house. The three young divers' penchant for more extreme diving forged an instant bond among them. The trio stood in contrast to most of the other divers at Underwater World, who engaged in far easier diving than Chrissy, Ed, and Tim. Most divers would not even consider undertaking cave penetrations or dives so deep they required breathing gas mixtures other than air. Even though most divers could appreciate Chrissy's grace underwater, they thought that the trio's cavalier *Top Gun* attitude about diving, their long, deep dives, and their exotic gas mixes would lead them into serious trouble.

Ed fueled other divers' fears with his fierce tirades against some of the U.S. Navy's diving recommendations. They were for wimps, he declared. Ed was very knowledgeable about mixed-gas diving theory, although he had never taken a formal mixed-gas course. The U.S. Navy had steadily revised downward its recommendations for oxygen toxicity limits—the level of concentrated oxygen that a diver could breathe without encountering oxygen-induced seizures—but what did it know? Sollner had frequently violated the U.S. Navy's dive tables, omitting mandatory decompression stops, and he had never gotten bent, so what could the Navy know about oxygen limits, if it was so wrong about the dive tables? The Navy was now being too conservative, he told everyone who asked and even those who didn't. He regularly dived with a higher percentage of oxygen in his breathing gas than the Navy considered safe. Many divers thought that Ed was playing Russian roulette, and that one day he would suffer seizures and die during a dive. As casual as Chrissy was in his life—including in his diving—he did not believe Ed's theory; Chrissy dived with oxygen percentages in his breathing mix that followed the Navy guidelines.

On the *Arundo*, Chrissy was diving alone, looking for lobsters. At one point, he came across Ed; both divers were methodically sweeping their dive lights under the wreck's hull plates, trying to ambush the dark-brown crustaceans before they could scamper away. Chrissy and Ed quickly parted company as they continued their hunting. When Chrissy surfaced, he was greeted with the news that Ed Sollner had died.

Someone had come across Ed's lifeless body, floating facedown just above some wreckage, his mouth open, his regulator dangling in the sand. There appeared to have been no struggle. When the body was brought back on the boat and hoisted aboard, the three Rouses were stunned. Chrissy had seen Ed on the dive, and he had been fine. What had happened? They immediately suspected the high oxygen percentage in the gas that Ed himself had mixed: He had probably had an oxygen seizure and drowned.

The dive boat chugged solemnly back to port with Ed's stiffening corpse lying on the deck, covered with a tarp and lashed down to prevent it from rolling about the deck. His face was turned away from the Rouses and the other divers, who kept a numb distance. At the dock, an ambulance met the dive boat and the Rouses followed it to the hospital, where Ed was officially pronounced dead. Chris called Cathie Cush—Chrissy's instructor friend about whom Chrissy had harbored his older-woman fantasy—and told her the news. Though Cathie had long ago broken up with Ed, the two had lived together until Cathie had moved out; it had become apparent to her that Ed was taking too many risks with his diving. She had not wanted to be hurt when he died underwater, a death she felt was inevitable. But now that Ed was dead, Cathie felt the pain anyway.

Cathie asked Chris to analyze Ed's breathing gas, to help determine the cause of death. The analysis indicated that Ed's breathing gas consisted of 39 percent oxygen, a gas mixture the Navy recommended be breathed to a maximum depth of 102 feet. Deeper than that, less oxygen should be breathed. Ed was found dead at 135 feet. He had proved his theory wrong.

Chris knew that pushing diving limits as Ed had done was folly. And to do so in what they all considered shallow water, on a wreck that was fun to dive but otherwise had no glamour to it, was tempting fate unnecessarily.

For the Rouses and many other people, Ed's death served to underscore the need for formal training and standards in the use of breathing gases other than air. Military and commercial divers pointed to Sollner as proof positive that sport divers were not disciplined enough to handle the restrictions imposed by the use of gas mixtures; equipment used to breathe high-oxygen-content gases had to be specially cleaned to prevent combustion, the gases had to be mixed properly and then analyzed to ensure the correct mixture, depth limits had to be adhered to so that a diver did not die of oxygen seizure, and the gear had to be properly marked so that a diver did not inadvertently die from breathing the wrong gas mixture at depth. Recreational divers—those who did not breathe gases other than air, who stayed above 130 feet depth, and who did not engage in stage decompression diving—wondered why anybody would want to go through all of the critical preparations required for a gas dive when the underwater experience was supposed to be relaxing and fun, and they did not understand someone like Ed, who thought that diving with gases other than air was fun.

Ed Sollner's death was used by both sides of the argument to prove their point. Those in favor of amateur divers using gases other than air said it proved that sanctioned training for sport divers was needed to prevent other divers from dying as Ed had; everybody against changing the status quo said that Ed's death just proved that sport divers could not be trusted to properly use any gas other than compressed air. Above all, divers like Chris and Chrissy Rouse, Steve Berman, and me worried that deaths like Ed Sollner's would cause the U.S. government to step in and pass laws regulating the sport and banning amateur divers from using any gas other than compressed air. We all knew that if that happened, our activities would officially make us underwater outlaws, which none of us wanted to be.

Around the time of Sollner's death, the sport-diving establishment's attitude toward mixed-gas use veered from negative to prohibitive. The organization that represented sport diving, DEMA (then called the Diving Equipment and Manufacturing Association; now called the Diving Equipment and Marketing Association), sponsored the industry's largest trade show, which had grown steadily over the years as diving became more popular, thanks to television specials, better marketing, and easier training standards allowed by newer, more reliable equipment. With a market and an image to protect, for its January 1992 trade show DEMA tried to ban any company from exhibiting or distributing any material related to the use of gas mixtures. The most common of these mixtures went by several names, including nitrox, oxygen-enriched air, and safe air.

The proposed ban outraged a number of people in the diving industry, most notably those whose companies were training divers to use nitrox. Dick Rutkowski was one of those men; he had served in the U.S. Navy, where he developed expertise in hyperbaric medicine, mixed gas, and life support systems, and then went on to a distinguished career with the National Oceanic and Atmospheric Administration (NOAA), a U.S. government organization. Rutkowski helped develop nitrox for use by scientists who were conducting research for NOAA, as well as the nitrox-specific dive tables published by the U.S government in NOAA's diving manual, which the Navy had adopted (this was the manual that Ed Sollner had ranted against).

After Rutkowski retired from NOAA, he set up a hyperbaric training facility in Key Largo, Florida, where he taught people how to treat injured divers, burn victims, and puncture wounds in a recompression chamber. By the time I took Rutkowski's nitrox course in 1988, he had already been teaching the general public about the safe use of this gas for two years. But gas use was catching on slowly, partly because of negative reporting in the diving press—I was only the 177th person Rutkowski had officially trained in nitrox. And even after a person had been trained in their use, nitrox mixtures could be obtained only at a few shops in the world, including Billy Deans's facility in Key West. Rutkowski taught the use of nitrox as the preferred gas for dives to 130 feet and shallower—standard nitrox 32 percent oxygen mixtures were toxic beyond 130 feet. But Billy Deans, in addition, saw the use of various nitrox mixtures as efficient gases to use for decompression after deep helium dives, like the ones he conducted regularly to the *Wilkes-Barre,* which rested in 250 feet of water not far from his dive shop and training facility. The higher oxygen content of the nitrox gases he created could be used to accelerate his decompression and get him out of the water faster than if he breathed only compressed air. He also knew that he felt much better physically after a deep dive when he decompressed using various nitrox mixtures and then switched to pure oxygen at his 20- and 10-foot decompression stops.

If DEMA thought nitrox gas mixtures unsafe for divers, then helium was completely unthinkable. DEMA's nitrox ban stirred Michael Menduno—the maverick founder of the magazine *AquaCorps,* who reported on subjects like solo diving, which the large training organizations thought of as heresy—and brought his fledgling magazine into the spotlight. Just in time for the DEMA show prohibition, *AquaCorps*'s fourth issue—titled "Mix" and dealing with both nitrox and helium gas mixtures—was released in January 1992. Menduno organized a conference in conjunction with the 1992 DEMA show to educate the industry about nitrox. Participants were seen going back and forth between the conference and the DEMA show, as if sneaking out of a Prohibition-era speakeasy to a respectable club where the party couldn't quite sizzle because they didn't serve alcohol. Anyone who wanted to know about nitrox—or other gas mixes—circumvented the DEMA ban by going to Menduno's conference and getting educated. And much like the United States' 1920s attempt to prohibit alcohol, DEMA's ban on nitrox only caused more people to know about it, and to want to experience it. The official proceedings of Menduno's nitrox conference were released in June 1992, just one month before Ed Sollner's death.

Divers as savvy as the Rouses could stand back from the battle over mixed-gas use; they could go their own way and concoct their own gases, without waiting around for commercially marketed gases to be approved. Chris, Chrissy, and Sue thought that nitrox and helium gases might be useful tools; they were among the first sport divers to become trained in nitrox and helium-gas mixtures when they had taken Sheck Exley's mixed-gas course in October 1990. The Rouses did not let the unavailability of gas mixtures prevent them from using these tools: When business was good enough so that they could afford to buy the ingredients, they bought the equipment to mix their own gases—which they did following Navy standards.

Ed's death did not keep the Rouses from diving each weekend, in preparation for their August *Andrea Doria* expedition, which they had spent much of the previous year organizing. In their view, Ed had not just bent the rules but had broken them, and thus the Rouses could separate their own presumably sensible behavior from Sollner's extravagant riskiness, thereby cordoning off their friend's fate from their own prospective future. As both Jennifer Hunt's research and common sense show, this is how risk takers, from mountaineers to skydivers, push past fear and paralysis to persevere. Chrissy was now diving on wrecks every weekend, usually accompanied by his friends instead of his father as he struck out on his own more and more. He regularly caught lobsters weighing several pounds and also brought up all manner of artifacts. Sometimes he dived alone, at other times he dived with a buddy.

It was only two weeks after Sollner died that Chrissy's rescue of an unknown diver took place. Diving solo on a wreck in 170 feet of water, Chrissy saw another diver on the bottom, in the sand next to the wreck, signaling to him. Chrissy swam over and was surprised when he read the diver's gas pressure gauge and found the man's tanks to be dangerously low on air. The diver seemed confused, Chrissy thought, and he knew the man was in trouble. Chrissy immediately deployed his spare regulator, which was attached to a cave-diving-style six-foot-long hose, and gave the diver the regulator, which provided him breathing gas from Chrissy's ample supply. Next, Chrissy removed from behind his own tanks the large upline reel that his father had constructed, took his regulator out of his mouth, placed it underneath the lift bag, pressed the regulator's purge button to release air into the lift bag and inflate it, and watched as the bag shot to the surface. He put the regulator back into his mouth and tied off his end of the line to a steel hull plate that lay nearby. He signaled the diver to ascend with him, and they swam up together, like two aquatic Jacks in the children's beanstalk story. The two divers decompressed successfully, while breathing from Chrissy's tanks, and the man gradually grew clear-eyed and grateful.

Chrissy did not know the diver, but his own rescue response was automatic. In coming to the stranger's aid, Chrissy risked his own life without hesitation: There have been several cases where an experienced diver aided another, only to have the other diver panic and fight the would-be rescuer for possession of their life-giving regulator, with the result that both divers perished. Chrissy's logbook entry is succinct, in its stream-of-consciousness writing style: "Dived solo 19 min found diver on bottom signaling me found him low on air & confused, shot bag & decoed with him." Chrissy never bothered to write down the man's name, even though he had saved the victim's life and risked his own. For Chrissy, coming to somebody's aid when he needed help was all part of the sport, and the young man was sure that others would do the same for him if he ever needed it. Of course, he knew things would never come to that. If only he could have come upon Ed Sollner when he was in trouble, he could have saved Ed's life too.

Chrissy dived without his father from several boats, including the *Wahoo,* the boat we had used for our mixed-gas expedition to the *Andrea Doria* in 1991. He would choose a boat based on the scheduled wreck destination, and he meticulously planned his dives so that he experienced increasingly deeper and more challenging sites as he prepared for his return to the *Doria.* On the *Wahoo,* Chrissy's manner and helpfulness endeared the personable young man to the crew. The

Wahoo's owner, Steve Bielenda, had seen many divers over the course of a diving career that dated back to 1959. A diving instructor since 1962, Bielenda had developed a sixth sense about how comfortable someone was in the basic practice of diving, and the ability to make such an assessment was a critical skill for someone teaching the sport. He noted that Chrissy was much more relaxed and carefree when his father was not around.

Bielenda had raised three children to adulthood and knew the challenges fatherhood carried. Every man, he knew, had a slightly different notion about how to raise his son, and he doubted that in the history of the world there had ever been a boy who had been perfectly raised. Yet he was impressed with how polite Chrissy was, and how much concern for others the young man exhibited. It was clear that Chrissy's parents had made the effort to raise Chrissy to be a sociable and responsible young man.

What struck Bielenda most was the interaction he had witnessed between Chris and Chrissy Rouse during the several days they had spent together on the *Wahoo* while diving the *Doria* in '91. Chris had been very critical of Chrissy at every turn; the elder Rouse chastised his son for the way he set up their equipment, how he tied their tanks to the railing, the way he stored his gear bags, even how he ate. Bielenda knew it was not his place to step in and say something to Chris Rouse about how he dealt with his son. Yet Bielenda could not help but notice how much the persistent, petty critique put Chrissy on edge. Now, without his father around, Chrissy seemed to Bielenda to blossom into a different person, a man who was assured of his own skills to the point of being at ease in the world. And Chrissy's dives were without incident, unlike both of the dives with his father on the *Andrea Doria* in the summer of '91—no bickering, no stumbles or minor trauma that could cloud the atmosphere for all the crew.

Chrissy was without a doubt his father's son, for better and for worse. He was influenced as much by his father's perfectionist, swaggering stance as he was by Chris's courage and generosity. My continued interviews with Dr. Hunt were giving me insight into both my own upbringing—my father had brought me up in the same overly critical fashion as Chris had raised Chrissy—and the Rouses' interactions. I could relate to both of the Rouses: to Chris from my growing experience as Gil's father, and to Chrissy from my experience as my father's son. I also knew that Chrissy had been given a deep appreciation for and curiosity about the world from his father because of their shared cave and wreck explorations; my father had given me that same appreciation and curiosity through family vacations in different countries, and by moving from one continent to another. But as I reflected on my own conditioning, I began to work to revise my emotional reflexes and seek a more encouraging, supportive way of raising my son. If the apple of the next generation could fall farther from the tree, and get less shade from its parent, then the new tree might grow taller and healthier.

For their expedition to the *Andrea Doria* that August, all three Rouses boarded the dive boat *Seeker*—which Chrissy liked to refer to as "the *Seeker* of death." It was his casual way of acknowledging that his deep diving was dangerous, and that he knew the stakes involved. Chrissy's joking about the possibility of dying while diving was his way of taking the edge off his danger-induced anxiety. Just before a dive, some people get more sullen, some become rapt in concentration, and others talk a lot. Both Chris and Chrissy were on the extreme end of talking a lot before their dives; bickering was their way of relieving their anxiety in the face of danger. Although others perceived the Rouses' interactions as hostile, Sue always maintained that they "were just communicating." It was a big gap in perceptions. Was Sue in denial over the bickering? Or was it all really just communicating, in a particularly contentious way?

Sue Rouse had done most of the work required to put the expedition together, sending out confirmation letters when she received a diver's deposit, following up with legal waivers of liability, and then making sure that all the expedition participants had filled in the forms properly and signed them, and finally making sure all of the money was collected and paid to the *Seeker* so that nothing would derail their departure. Not just chief petty officer but chief cook and bottle washer, Sue also prepared the food for all three Rouses, while Chris and Chrissy busied themselves with the equipment logistics for the family. Although Sue was going to the *Doria,* she didn't know whether she was going to dive on the wreck, telling everyone that she would wait and see if the conditions were calm and she felt comfortable enough. She liked dives to be mellow and steady, not jagged with adventure.

Chris and Chrissy filled the expedition with their friends and with divers who came highly recommended to them from others in the deep-water fraternity, especially those who, like the Rouses and me, were advocates of using cave-diving techniques to explore ocean shipwrecks. In a way, the Rouses' *Doria* foray would be a follow-up to my venture a year before: It would employ some of the same strategies but without the researchers' study and, ideally, without the seasickness and severe weather. Steve Berman and John Reekie participated, as did my friends John Harding and Dennis Anacker from the Sea Gypsies dive club. The *Seeker* crew members Steve Gatto and Tom Packer had looked forward to the expedition with the Rouse gang; both Gatto and Packer had met the Rouses on earlier diving trips, and they knew that the Rouses would liven up the boat with their antics, as well as bring an interesting group of divers with them.

Even though I was invited, I had to decline because I was not yet confident that my body—or my mind—was in condition to meet the *Doria*'s challenges. I was envious of the Rouses and annoyed that I could not go, but my solace was the fact that I was both alive and not in a wheelchair. As a consolation prize, I had the *Doria* artifacts that Steve Berman and I had recovered two years earlier, as well as some of the many dishes, cups, and hand-painted vases that John Griffith and I had recovered in the summer of '91.

The question that hung in the air like the thunderstorm logo depicted on their diving business cards was whether the black cloud stigma would continue to haunt the Rouses on their *Doria* expedition. It turned out that the trip participants were pleasantly surprised: The weather over the *Doria* was excellent, unlike the conditions for our expedition the year before. Chris and Chrissy plunged in four times during their expedition, recovering glassware from the same area where John Griffith and I had found artifacts with which we filled our bags repeatedly. They knew that the folks back at the dive shop, whose idea of risky diving was pretty much limited to the deeper parts of the quarry, with its cold, murky conditions, would turn sea-green with envy at their hoard. Chris and Chrissy would emerge from the underworld with relics enough to share.

Although the weather was flat calm, the current was intense. Even the strongest and most experienced divers like John Reekie and Steve Berman were having difficulties dealing with the sea conditions. After their third dive, Chris and Chrissy wanted to do something even more distinctive than recover artifacts. "Come on, Mom, dive with us," Chrissy begged his mother. "We'll be the first mother-father-son team to dive the *Doria*!"

Sue had spent a lot of time watching the water rush past the dive boat. "The current's just too strong, Chrissy. I don't have a good feeling about trying to dive in these conditions."

"You can do it," Chris said. "That's what you always tell me."

Chrissy nodded vigorously. "Yeah, Mom, we can go down, take you around the anchor line, and then you can come back up. You don't have to do a long dive. Just a few minutes."

"Yeah, we don't want to dive real long on the outside of the wreck. That would mess up our dive," Chris threw in, pointing to Chrissy.

"Let me get this right," Sue pondered aloud. "You want me to dive with you in conditions I don't feel comfortable with, but you want to make sure I don't mess up your dive? No thanks."

No amount of persuasion would change Sue's mind. Chris and Chrissy were disappointed at a missed opportunity to be in the record books as the first family to dive the *Doria*.

Although she had put so much time and effort into helping organize the expedition, she did not want to get injured, or worse. Two experienced divers had already run into problems because of the strong current. One of those divers suffered severe decompression sickness and Sue had watched as he was evacuated by helicopter to a recompression chamber. The other diver missed only a few minutes' decompression and did not suffer symptoms because a registered nurse on the expedition had brought saline solution and had administered it intravenously, which helped rehydrate him and ensured that his blood could efficiently carry both oxygen throughout his body and nitrogen to his lungs for elimination; the oxygen he breathed also helped clear nitrogen before bends symptoms developed.

■　■　■

Chris and Chrissy Rouse returned triumphant from the *Andrea Doria* expedition bearing bags of booty, tangible evidence of their visit to the Mount Everest of scuba diving. Their chests swelled with pride as they displayed their trophies and related their adventures to the divers at Underwater World. In spite of other people saying that they were destined for trouble because of the deep, long dives and the exotic gas mixtures they used when diving, they had proved that they were masterly divers, that they belonged among diving's elite. And they hadn't even brought their black cloud with them, eluding the silt of misfortune that had fogged their earlier efforts.

For most divers, recovering artifacts from the *Andrea Doria* would have been the highlight of a career, allowing them to sit back, relax, and enjoy their triumph. For Chrissy Rouse the *Doria* was another stepping-stone: He knew that he was well on his way to far more glorious accomplishments that would make him a diving superhero.

One month after their successful dives on the *Doria*, the Rouses headed to Quebec to dive the *Empress of Ireland*, an ocean liner that many divers thought was even more treacherous than the *Andrea Doria*, even though the *Empress* lay shallower, in the St. Lawrence River, off Rimouski. Just as top mountaineers consider K2 a far more difficult mountain than the higher and more famous Mount Everest, so divers deem the *Empress* a deceptively dangerous shipwreck.

The black cloud of misfortune returned to the Rouses even before the *Empress* expedition left the dock: Upon arriving in Rimouski, Chris had to busy himself with obtaining parts to fix the failing brakes on his van. Chris did not speak French, and most of his day was spent trying to explain to auto parts dealers what it was he needed. When he obtained the parts, Chris set himself the task of repairing the brakes himself. At two in the morning, after laboring for hours, he crawled out from underneath his vehicle, confident that he and his son could drive home safely after their dives. Now Chris could dive the *Empress* with peace of mind.

The Rouses' forays to the *Empress* carried with them a literal black cloud of their own making. The interior of the ocean liner was collapsing dangerously, and an extremely fine patina of silt covered everything. When they entered the wreck, their exhaled breathing gas immediately reduced the visibility to only a few feet, as the bubbles disturbed the rust and silt precariously coating the inside of the wreck. And then Chrissy introduced another challenge to the dive. The Rouses had not run a guideline from outside the wreck, as they usually did. Their plan called for them to venture just a short way inside to see if they could spot a passageway that might lead farther. When Chrissy entered the wreck, he got excited when he saw an unobstructed side passage. Instead of signaling his intentions to his father, or waiting until they got back to the dive boat so they could discuss plans for a more ambitious dive, Chrissy took out his guideline reel and tossed toward his father the line with its heavy brass clip attached. Chrissy did not bother to wait and see if his father had grabbed the line; he just plunged deeper into the wreck, assuming that his father would secure the guideline that would lead them both out of the wreck even in the blinding cloud of silt.

Chrissy's action surprised his father. Left behind in the billow of rust and sea-dust, Chris could not see to grab the line, and as Chrissy swam farther into the wreck, the guideline was pulled with him. The shiny brass clip bounced along the bottom and Chris desperately swam after it, like a large fish after a trolling lure. Eventually, Chris managed to grab hold of the clip, and he secured the line onto some wreckage lying in the passage. But now, visibility was very close to zero, and the line was tied off some distance into the wreck. Chris knew that they would have to exit the unfamiliar wreck blindly, without benefit of a guideline for the last thirty feet. If they made a wrong turn, they would get trapped inside the wreck.

When Chrissy came back, Chris was able to grope his way free of the wreck, with his prodigal son tagging along. After they had decompressed for over an hour in the 38-degree water, they climbed back on board the dive boat that Reekie had chartered for this expedition. Chris had barely spat his regulator out of his mouth when he started screaming at Chrissy. "Hey, asshole, who taught you to dive like *that*? You could have gotten us both *killed*!"

Chrissy bobbed his head and rolled his eyes. "What are you moaning about now, you old geezer?"

Chris quickly unbuckled himself from his diving tanks and then stood over Chrissy, who was slowly undoing the various straps and buckles that held all of his equipment attached to his body. Chris's face was red with anger. "Get serious! You don't just toss the guide-line back like that. That's not the proper protocol. Nobody *ever* taught you to dive that way. I made sure you got the *best* training in the world, and now you take stupid chances like *that*?"

"Well, I knew you were backing me up, and that you'd get the line and tie it off," said Chrissy, defensive but sheepish.

"I barely grabbed the line after chasing you down that hallway. What if I didn't get to it? Where would we have been then?" Chris let out an exasperated breath, shook his head, and slumped his shoulders as if the thought of what could have happened deflated him.

But Chrissy had regrouped. "What do you mean?" Chrissy fired back. "It's *your responsibility* to get the line and tie it off! You screwed up! Don't try and blame this on *me*!"

"What? I oughta knock some sense into you. Just think about it and you'll see that I'm right! Whose son are you, anyway?"

The battle raged back and forth as John Reekie and Steve Berman looked on. Both divers expected the Rouses to bicker as they always did, but this incident went far beyond the divers' usual playfulness. Reekie and Berman knew how serious Chrissy's action inside the wreck had been; neither diver wanted to be faced with having to recover their friends' bodies, and they were alarmed. Why was Chrissy diving so recklessly?

Other divers also wondered about the Rouses. Evie Dudas, a fixture in the sport diving world, was on an expedition with them for the first time, although she had heard through the grapevine about the Rouses' enthusiasm, skill, and persistent bickering. Evie owned a dive shop in Pennsylvania, a few hours' drive from Revere, where Chris and Chrissy lived. A widely admired diver, she had been diving since 1963, became an instructor in 1970, and bore the distinction of being the first woman to dive the *Andrea Doria,* in 1967. But her life had also been marred by tragedy: In 1968, she suffered a case of the bends that left her completely blind while she was still in the water and gave her severe vertigo. Her recompression chamber treatment brought her eyesight back almost immediately, but it would take her two months to recover her balance. Fourteen years later, in 1982, she suffered the loss of her husband in a diving accident. John Dudas, whom many considered one of the finest wreck divers in the world, died during a solo dive on what for him was a routine exploration on a wreck off the New Jersey coast. Though it was in only 160 feet of water, Dudas had not been deeper than 80 feet in the previous two years. No one could figure out what killed him. His death left the seven-weeks-pregnant Evie to raise their three young children alone and prepare for the arrival of another child to feed and care for.

The Rouses' bickering alarmed Evie. But something else disturbed her even more: Chris seemed to Evie overly critical of Chrissy. She had to suppress her motherly instinct when she rode in the Rouses' van back to the hotel from the dive boat and Chris denounced every brake, acceleration, and turn Chrissy made. Evie was not raising her children that way, and she thought that the very public criticism that Chris constantly leveled had to be humiliating to Chrissy. Like Steve Bielenda a few months before, Evie Dudas noted that Chrissy was nervous and agitated when he was around his father. Evie's gut reaction was to be concerned for the Rouses in the underwater environment, which she knew firsthand could be cruel and unforgiving.

What Evie and the other divers did not know about was Chrissy's childhood learning disability, or the wandering attention he exhibited as an adult. Nor did they know that Chris had not allowed Chrissy to drive when he was first eligible at sixteen years of age because he felt that Chrissy was not bringing enough maturity and focus to the task. When Chrissy was a teenager, what most alarmed Chris about Chrissy's carelessness was where he placed his tools when he worked with his father. A wrench would be thrown on the ground, or put to the side somewhere and then forgotten about. A misplaced tool on the ground was one thing, but a tool left lying on a diesel engine could mean disaster if the tool got caught in a motor's moving parts. No matter how many times Chris explained to his son the necessity of putting tools back in the same spot so that they could be easily found, the young man forgot the lesson. To Chris, it seemed that Chrissy spent more than half his time looking for tools he had misplaced.

At first Sue thought Chris was being too harsh in denying Chrissy permission to drive, but she agreed with him when Chris described Chrissy's behavior to her, and when Sue herself thought about how inattentive Chrissy was around the house. Driving was clearly not something for which sixteen-year-old Chrissy was ready. But when he was seventeen, Chrissy did get his license; his parents could not keep him from driving because the prohibition would hold him back socially, just as when Chrissy had been taking a few special classes in school and other children teased him. Once he had permission to drive, Chrissy could go out with his friends and—more important—could also date more easily. Now, at twenty-two, Chrissy was still prone to lapses of attention while driving, as Chris and Sue found out when Chrissy had several car crashes. Chris wanted to make sure his son stayed focused behind the wheel.

Was Chrissy's increased recklessness on the *Empress* the result of his attention deficit disorder? Many people would dispute that, pointing out that someone who had difficulty focusing on book learning often excelled at a physical activity, as Chrissy did at diving. But if Chrissy was now losing focus underwater—for whatever reason—why would Chris still engage in deep, dangerous diving with his son? Did it represent a father's hope that his boy could overcome his disability and excel at something, and his denial of the problem?

In spite of the Rouses' bickering, Chris's constant criticism of Chrissy, and the treacherous nature of the *Empress of Ireland*, the Rouses did not run into problems underwater from which they could not extricate themselves. They successfully conducted eight dives on the *Empress*. With the *Andrea Doria* and the *Empress of Ireland* now safely behind them, Chris and Chrissy sought a new challenge. The U-boat Bill Nagel and John Chatterton had discovered the previous autumn remained unidentified, still calling to divers to uncover its mystery. Diving it was worthy of the Rouses.

The *U-Who* had been discovered only one year earlier, on Labor Day, 1991, by a group of sport divers. The discovery of the wreck was more of an accident than the result of purposeful research. The dive charter boat *Seeker*, out of Brielle, New Jersey, had headed for a possible shipwreck location revealed to the boat captain by a commercial fisherman.

Given Captain Bill Nagel's penchant for drinking, it might be said he was fated for the find, because it was rumored the U-boat crews numbed the horrors of war with legendary drinking bouts, such as those depicted in the popular German movie *Das Boot/The Boat*. Why wouldn't they drink to excess? Their war machine was a cramped space ill-suited to accommodate anywhere from forty-eight to fifty-seven men, all sharing one toilet. Shaving and showers were luxuries. During the first two years of the war, lucky U-boat crews patrolling warm waters could, on occasion, surface in relative safety and crew members could take turns swimming and even fishing. But mostly, they had to endure the stench of machinery and their unbathed comrades as they stalked enemy ships. On land, they drank to quell their fear and dull their senses.

The ships the U-boats stalked before and shortly after the United States first entered the Second World War in 1941, after the Japanese attack on Pearl Harbor, were easy prey—primarily the freighters carrying oil, aviation fuel, ammunition, planes, tanks, guns, food, clothing, and other wartime necessities to the British. Merchant ships sailed individually up and down the coast, silhouetted against a well-lit shore, where wartime blackout rules were not yet in effect: Entire communities had protested that blackouts would deprive them of tourist income, and the seaside towns were kept ablaze with light. To make matters worse, ship sailing schedules, cargoes, and destinations were still being announced over public airwaves. All the U-boat commanders had to do was tune in to the frequency, decide which ships would offer them the best targets, and then maneuver into position to wait for the ship; they called this period of the war "the Happy Time."

The Happy Time resulted in 495 ships sunk in the first six months of 1941. During the whole of World War II, U-boats sank a total of 2,603 merchant ships in the Atlantic. Thirteen and a half million tons of shipping was lost; 30,248 merchant seamen died. Allied naval vessels also fell victim to the stealthy marauders: 175 were sunk.

U-boats themselves didn't have it easy, even during the Happy Time. At any moment, they could be spotted by patrolling warships or airplanes, and then they would turn into the hunted, their crews enduring hours of mental anguish during depth-charge attacks, as large drums of explosives and bombs sought their target. A direct hit by a depth charge or bomb, or an accumulation of detonations close to the U-boat, would crack the steel skin of the vessel, allowing tons of water to flood the ship and crush and entomb the warriors inside.

It took luck and every bit of a U-boat commander's skill and cunning to escape an attack like that.

One enterprising commander, after hours spent under relentless attack, came upon a novel idea. He had one of the torpedo tubes filled with a combination of oil, the body of a crew member who had already died, sailor's clothes, and, for good measure, his own white captain's hat. The crew then fired the debris out of the tube, where it floated to the surface. Seeing what looked like remnants from a "kill," the attackers withdrew, thinking they had done their job. This U-boat lived to hunt another day. Others weren't so lucky.

As the war progressed, Allied technological advances gained on the U-boats and rapidly surpassed them. First, underwater sonar allowed naval vessels to "see" the U-boats as they tried to use their greatest weapon, the cloak of the ocean, when they snuck up on merchant ships, or stole away after an attack. Next, airplanes were equipped with extremely powerful searchlights that lit up the night sky and sea's surface like daylight. Because U-boats had to surface to run their diesel engines, which recharged their batteries, and to refresh the stale air inside their steel hulls, many of them would be found at night on the surface, where they were most vulnerable, and bombed into fragments.

Another new device, a forward-firing explosive bomb called a hedgehog, would be fired simultaneously in large numbers to form a wide circle in the vicinity of a suspected U-boat. Hedgehogs would explode only on contact, obviating the need to preset the depth at which they would explode, as in the case of depth charges. Kills against U-boats rapidly increased as the war went on. Of the 1,162 U-boats commissioned during World War II, 784 were lost, most with all hands. The U-boat branch of the German Navy lost 28,000 out of a total of 40,900 men, and 5,000 were taken prisoner. Herbert A. Warner was one of the few men who survived active duty during most of the U-boat war and he rose through the ranks to become a captain, with command of his own U-boat; his autobiography bears the fitting title *Iron Coffins*.

In the murky, greenish-brown haze that passes for water clarity along the ocean bottom off the New Jersey coast lies the boat the Rouses were determined to identify. They would probably need several dives to circumnavigate the 251-foot-long *U-Who* fully and safely. But once they penetrated the interior and made their way amid the shards, bones, and rust, Chris and Chrissy could be the ones to identify the mysterious submarine. They would be not just heroic divers but parties to history.

The condition of the *U-Who* tells the story of the Battle for the Atlantic, whose outcome the British wartime prime minister, Winston Churchill, once stated was his greatest worry in the war. The *U-Who* rests upright on the Atlantic's sandy bottom in three distinct pieces, almost like a large cigar with a section torn out of its middle and left to rest alongside. The section that was blown off is the heart of the U-boat: its control room and, originally directly above it, the large stack known as the conning tower, which protruded upward, perpendicular to the rest of the cylindrical vessel. The control room is shattered, and the conning tower lies derelict on its side. It doesn't take an explosives expert to figure out that the U-boat was blown apart and that the men inside didn't stand a chance. Sharp, jagged pieces of wreckage are strewn all about the sea bottom, and, though the wreck's maws offer entrance, such an undertaking is not for the faint of heart.

U-boats that sank in divable waters have gone from being wartime trophy hunters to being trophies themselves, war relics and graveyards ripe for exploration and plundering. Although divers regularly dive U-boats, their activities are not without controversy. At the start of every diving season, the German naval attaché to the German embassy in Washington, D.C., had his assistant send to charter dive-boat captains a strongly worded letter declaring that diving on U-boats should cease immediately because the wrecks are war graves. The Rouses, and many other Americans, thought this was the height of German audacity: They knew that U-boats had aggressively roamed the world's oceans to sink many ships and inflict a heavy toll of lives. Why shouldn't the onetime ship hunters be hunted and peaceably explored themselves?

Not only moral issues arose around diving the *U-Who*. Its location did not appear in any naval archive, German or otherwise. Was the *U-Who* on a secret mission? Perhaps some of the Nazi leaders had tried to escape via U-boat and were on Chatterton's mystery wreck. Rumors persisted that Martin Bormann, second only to Hitler in the Nazi party hierarchy, eluded prosecution at the Nuremberg war crimes trials and certain execution by escaping the Third Reich via U-boat before the German surrender. Although the Allies believed they had come across the bodily remains of Martin Bormann in Berlin, many people were not convinced that the scant body parts were Bormann's.

The escape scenario was not far-fetched. Other Nazis had managed to avoid immediate retribution, including the infamous Adolf Eichmann, the head of the Gestapo's department of Jewish affairs, which oversaw the transport of Jews to concentration camps and their execution. Eichmann was captured in Argentina by Israeli secret service agents in 1960, sent to Israel, tried as a war criminal, and executed in 1962.

Maybe the *U-Who* had been carrying spies. The theory was plausible. In June 1942, two U-boats had successfully landed German agents on U.S. soil. One group was landed on Long Island and another in Florida. In both cases, the spies were rounded up relatively quickly; six were executed and two who cooperated, Ernst Burger and Georg Dasch, were given lengthy prison sentences. After the war, in 1948, both Burger and Dasch were given clemency by President Truman and both men were returned to West Germany. Perhaps the *U-Who* had been trying to land spies and its mission papers were among the many records that were either burned by the Germans toward the war's end or destroyed in bombing attacks.

Valuable cargo could also have been concealed on the U-boat. During the war, several U-boats had gone back and forth between Germany and her ally Japan, carrying much-needed raw materials for exchange. Or could the *U-Who* have been on its way to South America with valuable material? Of course, if that was the case, why did the U-boat come so close to the North American coast?

There was only one way to remove all doubt about *U-Who*: recover something that would clearly identify the wreck, and then research that vessel's war mission from surviving U-boat records. Chris and Chrissy Rouse knew that whoever uncovered the mystery would become well known, not only among divers but to the world at large. Exploring the *U-Who*, they would dive for fame.

10

The Last Dive

Toll the bell, call up the ghosts, summon
out the lifesavers and the pirates.

The shoals are there still, the winds howl
loud, the rain beats down, the waves burst
strong. Some night, in the chill darkness,
someone will make a mistake: The sea will
show him no mercy.

JOHN T. CUNNINGHAM

**OCTOBER 12, 1992. NORTH ATLANTIC OCEAN,
approximately 60 miles offshore,
equidistant from the New Jersey and New York coastlines.**

CHRIS ROUSE DIDN'T NEED to watch his only child descending
the *Seeker*'s anchor line in front of him to know what he was
doing, what actions he was taking. Four years into their romance
with deep water, he had dived so often with Chrissy that father and
son had developed a sixth sense with each other when underwater.
Regardless of what was happening in their lives on land, regardless of
whatever difficulties they had at any given moment as father and son,
they each knew they could count on the other in the unforgiving
underwater landscapes they loved to explore together. They would

need that special skill today. The ocean surface snarled with waves, which piled a new set of challenges on top of the usual dangers of diving. Chris had over seven hundred and Chrissy over six hundred dives under their belts, valuable experience that they would need today if they were going to be successful in recovering the captain's logbook from the mysterious U-boat that lay 230 feet below the *Seeker*.

The *U-Who*'s captain's logbook was an artifact that would positively identify the U-boat for which information was missing from American, British, and German archives. That log would help settle the question of whether the U-boat had been on a secret wartime mission, or whether it carried high-ranking Nazi party members or valuable artworks. It would be the Rouses' chance to secure for themselves a place in the pantheon of underwater exploration as discoverers of a piece of martial history and sleuths who helped solve a mystery.

The Rouses had already dived this wreck before; they knew the contours of what they would be seeing and where to go. As wrecks go, U-boats are not hard to navigate if they sank relatively intact. Even with its totally destroyed control room and blown-off conning tower, the *U-Who* did not pose a great navigational challenge.

What did threaten to daunt them was the weather. Topside, the waves had increased and now ran three to six feet in height, making the 60-foot *Seeker* rock uncomfortably for the divers on board. After dives like this Chris would confide to friends that the extra work of diving in the open ocean made him feel every one of his thirty-nine years. The *Seeker*'s two captains, Dan Crowell and John Chatterton, had warned them and everyone else that the weather was only getting worse. This meant that when their dive on the U-boat was over, they would be heading home and would probably not get another chance this year to solve the U-boat mystery. They'd prepared for this dive for so long that they were determined to go ahead, questionable weather or not.

They had goaded themselves into this dive when they had awakened to the overcast, windy morning. When Chrissy informed his father that he did not want to dive in such rough conditions, his father verbally abused him, questioning his diving ability and his courage. When Chrissy accepted the challenge, it was Chris who backed down, not wanting to dive. The tables were turned: Chrissy verbally laced into his father, returning the insults about diving ability, and even questioning his father's manhood. Ultimately, both divers had to dive to prove that they were *real* divers. Their bickering had gone on for hours as the *Seeker* was continuously rocked by the waves. The Rouses fit right in among a world of often eccentric and egocentric participants, and they earned their Bicker Brothers nickname on every dive expedition.

The Rouses planned to make the dive breathing air. Only two weeks before this moment, Chris had said to me, "Bernie, don't worry, we'll be fine. We've gone deeper on air and we'll be able to handle it." There were better choices for a breathing mix than air, and as an experienced wreck explorer I was concerned when they told me their dive plan. To go inside the notoriously cramped quarters of a U-boat at a depth of 230 feet while breathing air was extremely risky. The rough wave conditions would make Chris and Chrissy breathe harder as they gripped the anchor line and fought to stay on the violently snapping rope to prevent themselves from being blown off the line and away from the wreck they intended to explore. The extra work involved in fighting their way down to the wreck would have a more immediate effect on Chris and Chrissy: The nitrogen in the air they were breathing would get even more narcotic because of their increased labor, just as it had done to me during the nearly fatal dive that had left me hospitalized and temporarily crippled a year earlier. The greatly increased pressure underwater would affect their brains like alcohol, as it does the brain of every deep-sea diver breathing air. If they had chosen to breathe a mixture containing helium, their narcosis would have been greatly reduced, even with the extra effort required to descend in such a raging sea. But helium gas is expensive. Chris could not afford it now that his excavating business was doing so poorly.

The increased narcosis would first make itself felt as fuzzy vision. Their peripheral vision would also be affected, and their field of vision would get ever narrower as they got closer to the wreck, as if they were entering a dark tunnel. After a dive he and his father had done to 300 feet on air, Chrissy had once described sounds being weirdly distorted, as if vibrating in different pitch intensities. When he related that story to me, twenty-one-year-old Chrissy had laughed like a young boy who had discovered something mischievously satisfying. In an amazed tone, he told me, "Being at three hundred feet on air, I felt like I was hallucinating. It was really weird being underwater and all buzzed out."

Because both Rouses had experienced extreme narcosis at depth, they felt they could manage the nitrogen narcotic equivalent of the four-and-a-half-martini buzz they would encounter during this dive. What they did not take into account was the increased narcosis that their efforts in rough seas would bring on, and the effect this would have on their reactions to unforeseen problems. They had become too familiar with the underwater environment, too comfortable with its nuances, and too confident in their own excellent diving skills. Just the way I had only the year before. Our cave-diving instructor, Marc Eyring, always warned us that whenever complacency took hold in our diving careers, disaster was sure to follow. I had found out the hard way just how true that was, and now the lesson would be taught more severely to Chris and Chrissy.

Narcosis would further distort Chrissy Rouse's memory of the events on the dive. His postdive ranting, combined with John Chatterton's video images, our familiarity with the Rouses, our knowledge of the underwater world, and the equipment analysis of their diving gear, allowed his friends to piece together the story of that foray into the U-Who. The series of problems the two men encountered is the stuff of abject terror. It is the diver's worst nightmare—the last dive.

New Jersey state trooper Steve McDougall had finished his dive and was decompressing alone on the Seeker's anchor line when Chris and Chrissy Rouse entered the water and then descended past him, down the thick rope. McDougall, an instructor who had been diving for eighteen years, noted how smoothly and quickly the Rouses descended, like the confident, experienced divers they were. Chris and Chrissy tugged their way down the thick rope, which snaked through 230 feet of sea, its distant end tethered to the wreck of the U-boat below. The rope snapped violently as the dark-green waves slammed the dive boat. For the Rouses the water turned from green just below the surface to mourning black, as clear and cold as a moonless autumn sky.

As the Rouses dropped farther down the line and away from him, McDougall saw their exhaled bubbles expand into silver oblongs, like flying saucers. To get his body safely back to surface pressure, he had to spend over an hour coming up slowly so that his body could eliminate the excess nitrogen it had absorbed during his dive. He knew that he would be seeing the Rouses again when they began their own lengthy decompression, which would start well before his deco was over.

Topside, *Seeker* captain Dan Crowell turned to John Chatterton, the second captain on board the boat, and said, "I just checked the forecast on the radio again. The weather's not looking good at all."

Chatterton nodded, looked quickly at the ocean, then replied, "I'll go make sure everything's secure." Chatterton left and moved quickly around the boat, checking the equipment, making fast anything that was loose so that the boat would not get damaged and the divers on board would not get injured by debris tossing about on deck. Chatterton saw Steve Gatto and Tom Packer, both of whom were kneeling on the deck, bracing themselves for support as they hurried to finish putting away all of their equipment from the dive they had completed just before the Rouses had gone in the water. "Make sure everything's real secure," Chatterton reminded them. "We're gonna get going back as soon as the Rouses are on board, and it won't be a smooth trip." Gatto and Packer nodded.

Barb Lander, the only woman on board, reached into the boat's large cooler, just outside the main cabin, and grabbed her fifth diet Coke since waking up four hours earlier. Seeing Chatterton, she said, "I'm set. All packed and ready!"

"Let's hope the Bicker Brothers cut their dive short," Chatterton muttered.

Below, hovering just above the U-boat, Chrissy would have been trying to focus on what had to get done: when he reached the wreck, unclip the two extra scuba tanks he carried, one at each side of his body, and lay the tanks down on the U-boat's deck in such a way that they would not get swept over the side and drop into the sand. Then he would unclip his guideline from his harness while he swam toward the opening of the wreck.

Chrissy had always swum faster than his father, and since Chrissy had led down the anchor line, the distance between the two men would have grown as Chrissy saw the U-boat and fixated on his mission, just as he had done only a month earlier when he dangerously swam ahead of his father to recover artifacts inside the notoriously treacherous ocean liner *Empress of Ireland*. With his father still lowering himself toward the sea bottom, Chrissy wouldn't have bothered to wait but instead swam a short distance alongside the cigar-shaped vessel, his powerful dive light stabbing the water's blackness with a spotlight beam that played along the curved steel hull.

Particles of dirt and sand would have still been hanging suspended in the water from Steve McDougall's foray into the warship. Chrissy would probably not have paid much attention to the fish, jellyfish, and translucent, primordial, otherworldly-looking matter that made the U-boat their home, nor would his nitrogen-clouded brain even have fully registered the creatures seemingly dancing in his dive light's glare. Chrissy was so familiar with the underwater world that he would have immediately looked past the white, brown, and red living, breathing organisms—which resembled plant life and clung to the wreck's side like dense foliage on a hillside rock garden—so that he could make out the contours of the wreck underneath. The experience he had gained in the course of over six hundred dives enabled him to propel himself efficiently and forcefully, without much effort. He knew even before the dive that he would need to be economical and precise if he was going to find that logbook, or anything historically significant, in the precious twenty-minute span of the dive he and his father had planned.

The dive probably went well at first, and they should have reached the warship's heart, the control room, within four minutes of beginning their descent. The control room was completely shattered, with sharp pieces of the hull protruding at odd angles from it. A gaping hole had been blasted in the U-boat as it sank, and its jagged metal mouth made it look like a strange deep-sea fish poised to swallow the unwary. Even though he had been here before, Chrissy would have verified where he was by turning to his left and seeing what resembled a large oval metal tube, six feet in diameter, lying in the sand alongside the hole in the control room. Having encountered all of this before, he must have recognized the conning tower, the sailors' entryway to and exit passage from the body of the boat, which had been blown right off the submarine. It was his landmark, indicating that the hole in the submarine to his right was where he planned to enter.

Chris no doubt was breathing hard as he swam along the U-boat, trying to keep up with his son. Although the nitrogen buzz would have clouded his mind, he would have focused on getting into position outside the *U-Who*. They had planned that Chrissy would go inside and look for the logbook, while Chris would wait outside, in case Chrissy needed any assistance.

Chrissy swam into the wreck. Although veteran wreck divers scoffed at the cave-diving technique of paying out a guideline to lead them back to open water when penetrating a wreck, the Rouses' cave-diving training and their experiences on some of the most challenging wrecks in the world convinced them that the only sure way out of a wreck was to use a line. Chrissy would have nonchalantly tossed back to his father the brass clip attached to his guideline, just as he had done a month ago when they had gotten into a bitter argument after their dive about acceptable team protocol in using the guideline. The line would be Chrissy's safety device inside the U-boat; it would guide him out of the wreckage in the zero visibility caused by the silt and sand that filled the bottom of the warship. When the particles billowed up during his dig for artifacts, he would be blinded.

Chrissy probably did not bother to tie the line off to a piece of wreckage, as he should have done, because that would have only taken up precious time that could be used to look for the U-boat captain's logbook. The young diver always knew that his father was there to back him up, and in his haste to gather artifacts, Chrissy would cut corners, which infuriated his father. Even before the dive, John Chatterton, who was credited with the discovery of this wreck, had warned Chrissy against being overzealous in his quest for the logbook. In fact, Chatterton had tried to dissuade Chrissy from the ambitious dive, seeing in the younger man an artifact fixation that could only spell disaster, just as it had with other overly fixated divers in the past.

Chrissy would not be talked into changing his dive plan or his diving techniques, even if those techniques involved cutting corners: He was obsessed with getting inside the wreck and starting the search. As he had told others before the dive, he assumed his dad would tie off, as he'd done on previous dives, saving Chrissy valuable search time. His father grabbed the clip affixed to the guideline Chrissy tossed to him, wrapped the line several times around some wreckage, and then used the clip to secure the line to itself.

Chrissy had to crawl his way into the wreck. Cables hung everywhere, torn loose by the explosion that had ripped off the conning tower. Metal fragments, pieces of instruments, and rusted machinery marked the jaws of the U-boat. Chrissy later ranted that he felt he was swimming down a monster's gullet, into its stomach, a sure sign of nitrogen narcosis. When he entered the wreck, his exhaled bubbles would have loosened fine particles of silt from the ceiling almost immediately. Rust flakes would start their slow fall. Unlike a snowstorm that brightens the sky and landscape, the rust storm makes everything darker: The flakes themselves are dark red, and when they hit the bottom, they send up swirls of silt that curl upward slowly, like smoke from smoldering embers. With a narcosis-dulled mind, the swirling silt would seem like inflamed tissues of the U-boat's throat closing, further narrowing the already tight tunnel.

One of the frustrations Chrissy later expressed was that no matter how carefully he tried to move through the U-boat, he inevitably came into contact with some part of the wreckage. If he moved a leg, his fin would touch something, maybe a dangling cable or a slab of torn metal, he could never quite tell. When he turned from one side to the other, he would rub his shoulder or the hose to his breathing apparatus against some piece of debris. Every movement, every exhalation, caused silt to billow from the bottom and rust particles to flake from the ceiling.

Chrissy would have stopped kicking to reduce the silt he stirred up and instead would have pulled himself along the wreckage with his hands, using the technique called the pull-'n'-glide. As he reached out and grabbed indistinguishable objects, some would shift, and crumble, causing dark-red rust to mix with dark-brown silt from the sand and organic debris.

At this point, the adrenaline rush of exploration that divers feel would have made Chrissy's heart start beating faster, causing him to breathe more quickly. When he turned in the course of working his way into the captain's quarters, his tanks would have struck something, producing a dull, metallic twang that echoed in varying pitches inside his head. His powerful dive light would be useless, serving only to fix a fuzzy circle in the dark brown-red blanket surrounding him. As he felt his way farther into the wreck, past the silt he had stirred, he would have been able to see a few feet ahead.

In order to get into the compartment where he planned to dig for artifacts, Chrissy had to wiggle through a round hatchway that separated the damaged control room from the captain's quarters. He would have entered by crawling over the bottom of the hatchway so his tanks could clear the opening. Some of his equipment no doubt caught on the hatchway, but he'd made it this far before and would have known for a fact that he could make it in. His struggles to maneuver his various attached accessory equipment over the lip of the hatchway would have increased his frustration, and further enhanced his narcosis as he pulled himself all the way through.

Once inside the hatchway, he could dig into the silt, hoping to find the trophy that would identify this U-boat. His plan was to probe the area underneath some shelving, where, he had told friends, he was sure to find more objects. Ideally one of them would tell a more complete story about the U-Who, maybe settle all the unanswered questions once and for all. Everyone would praise Chrissy Rouse, intrepid diver, and celebrate his find. The discovery would put him in another league, he thought, alongside other legendary divers like his hero, Sheck Exley. Settling on the bottom, Chrissy would have started digging with his right hand while his left maintained a firm grasp on his guideline reel, which led to the outside of the wreck, and to his father.

The silt inside the warship meant that Chrissy had to dig up to his elbow in order to retrieve any artifacts that lay on the bottom of the wreck. Neither Chrissy nor anyone else realized that the shelving was no longer attached to the hull, but was held upright only by the sand and a few metal objects at its base. Pressed for time, Chrissy probably dug feverishly, feeling for anything that he might put into his bag to examine later. Brown silt and sand would have risen, mixing with the red rust particles knocked loose by his exhalation bubbles. His labor would have caused him to breathe harder and his exhaled bubbles' force would have further agitated the silt, sand, and rust mixture that surrounded Chrissy like a tornado. The digging would have quickly occluded all visibility, leaving him to rely on feel alone.

At this point in the dive, we imagine, eleven minutes had passed since he had left the surface with his father. The water here was reported to be only 41 degrees Fahrenheit, which a diver feels even through his thick drysuit and the ski-suit-like layer of underwear. But Chrissy's artifact fixation and the adrenaline rush of getting into the cramped U-boat would have helped his mind adhere to the task, even as his body felt fuzzy, drunken. Because of the zero visibility Chrissy now encountered, he could not even have noticed the tunnel vision brought on by the nitrogen narcosis.

Later, Chrissy told divers that his hands bumped into an object, and although he could see nothing through the silt tornado, he knew what he held was large. Chrissy's heart would have jumped at this point, as he would have fantasized that this was the box where the captain kept his logbook. The thought would have made Chrissy struggle and pull hard at the box with both hands.

When Chrissy managed to move the object from the resting place where it was tightly wedged, the shelf unit to his left started to fall slowly. Chrissy could not see it tumble, but he later reported suddenly feeling a crushing weight, which pinned him to the bottom. Getting trapped underwater is a terrifying situation, and the sudden scare would have increased his narcosis as if he had swallowed a huge drink of hard alcohol in one gulp. The level of his narcosis at this point would have put his mind into a hallucinatory state. This was completely unlike an earlier dive Chrissy had told me about, where he and his father dived to 300 feet depth breathing air in a warm, clear-water cave. Although Chrissy told me he had experienced heavy—even hallucinogenic—narcosis on that 300-foot dive, he did not have the many problems to deal with that he now faced inside the U-boat. Chrissy's narcosis inside the cramped, silted-out quarters of the U-boat must have been enhanced by the cold water, and his situation would not have been manageable had he been alone.

Their dive plan was for Chris to wait outside the wreck, keeping his eyes on Chrissy's guideline. The line had once been white, but had dirtied in places from their many wreck dives, where silt had infested the nylon. There was no need to replace the line because the divers could still see it. Suddenly, silt would have come billowing out of the wreck, as expected, when Chrissy started digging for artifacts. But Chris would have realized after a few breaths that something was wrong; the rush of silt would have been accompanied by a banging noise. Chris knew that, underwater, noise is muted and heavier, and vibrations are felt more dramatically. Holding on to the side of the opening where Chrissy had entered, Chris would have held his breath so that he could hear something other than his own exhaled bubbles.

He definitely would have been able to hear Chrissy screaming, but would have checked himself to make sure it was not an auditory hallucination brought about by his own narcosis. Chris's heart probably raced as he suddenly realized that it *was* Chrissy screaming.

Inside the wreck, Chrissy was in trouble. The narcosis would have quickly escalated as Chrissy's panic started winning its battle over rational thought, yet rational thought is especially necessary in this increasingly dangerous circumstance.

Chrissy later asserted that he tried to steady himself, tried to focus. He attempted to do a push-up and lift himself off the ground and out from under whatever was trapping him. These efforts would have made him breathe even faster and harder and use up more of the rapidly diminishing precious air in his back-mounted tanks. He would have heard what sounded like heavy drumming, and perhaps he would have known at some level that the sound was his own heart. But maybe he thought that the sound was the monster's heart beating, as his postdive, pain-induced ranting suggests. Chrissy was probably well beyond holding back the hallucinations at this point.

Acting on instinct alone, he likely reached out with his left hand to start banging the metal guideline reel against the steel hull, as a signal to his father that he was in trouble.

Outside the wreck, the banging would have gotten louder, more frequent, more urgent as Chrissy's desperation escalated. Chris took off his extra scuba tank and left it at the entrance to the sub, and then moved into the wreckage. He grabbed the line and followed it, and probably found that there was far too much movement on it. He might have thought that Chrissy had gotten himself entangled in the line, which he knew from previous experience he could get his son out of.

The crumpled interior was only five feet high, and less than ten feet across, because of all the protruding machinery in the way. Chris didn't really need the line to find his son: All he had to do was follow the deafening noise. He would have been able to hear Chrissy screaming into his regulator, in addition to the banging against the wreckage. But instead of letting go of the line, Chris would have wisely chosen to utilize his training and follow the guideline handgrip by handgrip, at the end of which he was sure to discover his boy. Brownish-red silt would have continuously billowed out of the hatchway like smoke from a raging fire. When Chris moved through the hatchway he would have bumped into Chrissy, struggling and screaming. Though he could not see his son, Chris was able to reach out and grab him.

One imagines that Chrissy felt the hand on his shoulder, felt his father's firm grip, and closed his eyes. He tried to calm himself. Between breaths he probably screamed through the regulator, "Dad, I'm stuck! Get me out, Dad!"

His father likely moved his head closer, and probably answered through his regulator, "Stop moving! I'll get you out. Get your shit together."

Chrissy's heavy breathing and screaming would have further heightened the hallucinatory narcosis, and as we know from his later ranting, he thought he was under attack by a monster. He would have tried to get away and probably flailed wildly.

Although Chris would also have been laboring under the weight of narcosis, his head was probably much clearer than his son's, and he would have moved slowly, because he had to rely on feel alone to determine what was trapping his son. He might have grabbed Chrissy and pulled him forward, as if he were a lifeguard wrestling a panicked swimmer into safety. Chrissy would have kept struggling to free himself, grunting into his mouthpiece with his anguished effort and screaming for his dad to help him. The elder Rouse would have known that he had to calm his son down if they were to get out alive, so he would have tried to calm the boy down by talking through his regulator with reassurances. This probably made Chrissy stop struggling only until the boy's hallucinations again got the better of him, and the procedure started all over again. Chris would have needed to move behind his son to find the shelves that had fallen on Chrissy. With an adrenaline-fueled fury, he would have grabbed the shelving and heaved, bracing himself on the floor for leverage.

A week after the Rouses' dive, John Chatterton, Steve Gatto, and other divers were the first to enter this compartment since the Rouses had been in it. Chatterton and Gatto reported seeing shredded, rubberized canvas from one of the warship's life rafts throughout the area; the shredded remains had not been seen by other divers before the Rouses entered. The life raft might have self-inflated on top of the shelves, further jamming Chrissy in place beneath them. This is not as hard to believe as it might seem: A life raft had previously been recovered from U-853, which also rests in U.S. waters; its automatic inflation system worked on the surface even after more than forty years underwater. Chrissy himself later screamed incoherently about a life raft. If the life raft had inflated on top of the shelves, Chris Rouse's efforts to free his son would have proved useless until he took out his knife and shredded the material. If that was not the case and he was able to lift the shelves, then perhaps the pair came across the life raft and shredded it like two knights in armor battling a dragon.

As if the two divers did not have enough to contend with, a postdive analysis of their equipment revealed that bits of rusted metal had lodged in Chrissy's primary regulator, which would have caused water to enter along with air during each breath. Chrissy would have had to spit the malfunctioning unit out of his mouth and replace it with his secondary regulator. Whatever level of narcosis Chrissy was experiencing, he still managed to focus on his life-giving equipment to make the regulator exchange.

When Chrissy was freed, the two divers faced yet another problem: They had to exit the compartment in which they were now both trapped and then make their way out of the wreck. Chrissy apparently tried to use his cave-diving training and follow his guideline, which should have led them straight out of the wreck. But the guideline was later found strung back and forth across the debris littering the bottom of the U-boat's compartment, and parts of it were buried, indicating that the two had difficulty finding the way out. The line leads out of the wreck through a different opening than the one they had entered, which provides further confirmation that they had difficulty getting out of the steel coffin that had entombed its complement of German sailors.

Once the two got out of the wreck, they must have been grateful that their way to the surface was now unhindered. Their minds must have relaxed a little as they realized they were now out of immediate danger. But what had been planned as a twenty-minute dive had now taken over thirty minutes and time was racing.

Chrissy would not have wanted to go back into the wreck to retrieve his line, which was attached to the metal reel he held in his hand. He dropped the reel. His father probably watched it plummet and land in the debris of the control room, where it was later found by Chatterton. The elder Rouse would not have made an attempt to retrieve the reel, unlike his reaction on their first dives on the *Andrea Doria*. They had to do something far more pressing now: retrieve the scuba tanks they had left on the U-boat's deck at the beginning of the dive. They would need them to surface safely. Without the extra tanks, they did not have enough breathing gas for their decompression.

Chrissy Rouse later told divers that he and his father searched along the U-boat's deck for eleven minutes, trying desperately to find their extra tanks. Though the U-boat is easy to navigate, the narcosis both divers must have been feeling probably disoriented them. They never found the cache of three scuba tanks that lay on the deck. Because they had exited from a different hole than the one they had entered, they were inadvertently on the opposite side of the U-boat. When Chris found the one scuba tank he had dropped off just outside the opening he had swum through to rescue his son, he clipped the bottle to his son and signaled for them to ascend. Chris must have known they did not have enough gas for both of them to decompress, and he would have sacrificed his own chance to decompress in order to save his son. Chris probably thought that he could surface and direct other divers from the *Seeker* to bring them more gas so that they could complete their decompression.

Somewhere, 230 feet above them, floated the dive boat and an end to this ordeal.

When they started their ascent, they had not found the anchor line, but they had no more time to spend looking for anything. Their decompression obligation was about three hours, which meant that they should slowly ascend, stopping at various depths during their stage decompression. If they did not decompress, their bodies would be like soda cans that are shaken, then opened in one brutal motion, their blood vessels blasting bubbles of nitrogen. If they could not find the anchor line during their ascent, they would drift underwater with the current while decompressing, and would most likely be lost at sea. Even in calm waters, it was a challenge to find people floating on the surface. But with the wind mounting and waves five to six feet high— the conditions an age ago when father and son had last been on board the *Seeker*—they would have to be extremely lucky to be found by Captains Crowell and Chatterton.

As the needles on their pressure gauges rapidly dropped toward zero, the Rouses ascended. They would have kept looking up, as they had been taught, to avoid the possibility of hitting their heads against floating debris. They would have turned slowly, looking for the anchor line, knowing it couldn't be far away. It is not clear whether the Rouses found it or not. If they did, it was their first turn of good luck. Ascending the anchor line would allow them to come up off the bow of the boat.

As they slowly ascended, they would have automatically checked their pressure and depth gauges, and then their forearm-mounted diving computers. Chrissy later said that the computers indicated they had been underwater for forty minutes.

Steve McDougall was still decompressing on the anchor line, and he had now ascended to a depth of 15 feet. He wondered where the Rouses were and knew that he should have seen them already. Although he did not know it, the Rouses were below McDougall's visibility in the murky green water. If he had seen the Rouses and they had signaled to him, he might have been able to help by providing them some of his breathing gas. Unlike commercial or military divers, sport divers do not routinely use underwater verbal communication equipment. Without that, the divers could not talk to one another, and the Rouses had no way of letting others know how desperate their situation was. McDougall, though he wasn't far from the Rouses, had no idea where they were, and as a consequence he could not help them.

Chrissy now switched to the scuba bottle that his father had clipped to him after they escaped the wreck. But instead of breathing air, only water came through the mouthpiece. Postdive analysis revealed a torn mouthpiece that would have allowed water to enter.

What happened next is another matter for conjecture; two different scenarios were reported by the divers on the scene. Some believe that Chrissy tried repeatedly to purge the regulator so that he could get air instead of water through the unit. Each time he pressed the purge button it would have released a large quantity of air from the tank. The postdive analysis of this tank revealed a 60 percent oxygen mixture and the tank slightly less than half full. If Chrissy had started out with this extra tank at full capacity, then the half-full tank can be explained by Chrissy's repeatedly trying to purge the regulator of water. According to this theory, Chrissy headed for the surface after trying unsuccessfully several times to get breathing gas from his regulator, and his father followed him.

Others believe that Chris Rouse did not have much gas left and headed to the surface on his own, knowing that he had to get more gas for himself and his son so that they could complete their decompression. The analysis of his tanks revealed that he had almost no breathing gas left, perhaps enough for one or two breaths at seventy feet, though we have to take into account the consumption of breathing gas while Chris was swimming to the dive boat, and later while he waited in the water. In this scenario, Chrissy would have seen his father ascending, and then followed him to render assistance. The question this raises is whether the father tried saving the son until the very end, or whether the son sacrificed his decompression and tried to save his father. In either case, the diver who ascended second knew that he risked crippling decompression sickness by following the other to the surface.

If it had been any other dive team—say, even two very close friends—one diver would never have followed his buddy to the surface, neglecting several hours of necessary decompression. Using up your strength getting a stuck diver out of a wreck, at 230 feet, breathing only air, would have been considered more than doing your duty. Risking paralysis or even death in surfacing after the ordeal went beyond what could reasonably be expected of a dive buddy. But the Rouses were no ordinary dive buddies.

Regardless of which ascent scenario you choose to believe, the two divers surfaced. Steve McDougall, who was still decompressing on the anchor line at fifteen feet, did not see the Rouses underwater again after they descended past him on their way down to the wreck.

On the *Seeker*, preparations were already under way for departure as soon as McDougall and the Rouses were back on board. Captains Crowell and Chatterton had been listening carefully to the weather reports with some anxiety. Yesterday's manageable two-to-three-foot seas had bulged up to six feet, with occasional waves as high as eight feet, which Chatterton knew was on the very edge of what any sane person wanted to be diving in. When he had awoken that morning, Chatterton had decided he would not do a pleasure dive, but would go down only to free the boat's anchor line so that they could depart when the divers who had braved the weather were done.

As the two captains surveyed the worsening weather front from the bow of the boat, Chatterton saw the Rouses pop up one hundred feet in front of them. Chatterton had the impression that the Rouses both looked scared. He thought to himself, These guys fucked up.

Chatterton cupped his hands around his mouth and yelled into the wind at the divers, "Get down! We'll drop more tanks to you and send in a safety diver." Both captains instantly knew that the Rouses should be doing decompression, not surfacing. They had been down for only forty-something minutes.

But the Rouses weren't getting ready to descend again; they were both pressing their power inflator buttons to put more air from their tanks into their back-mounted buoyancy compensators so that they could float on the surface with all of their heavy equipment.

Chrissy bobbed up and down in the waves, the current carrying him toward the *Seeker*. He had hit his limit: So much had happened on the dive, there had been so much chaos down below, he could handle no more. He looked at Chatterton and shouted back, "I can't breathe off my regulator. I'm coming aboard."

"Did you do any deco?" Chatterton shouted.

"No!" Chrissy replied.

Before Chatterton could respond, Chrissy stuck his face into the water and started swimming toward the *Seeker*'s stern, 160 feet away. Chris Rouse did the same. To Chatterton, it looked as though Chris

Rouse was struggling to swim. When Chris got a little closer to the boat, Chatterton saw the elder Rouse roll to one side in the waves; Chatterton thought that Chris's eyes already looked glassy, and knew that this was not a good sign.

Chatterton was stunned by what he saw. He knew that the Rouses had not conducted any decompression and that they were in deep trouble. He set the timer bezel on his watch and raced toward the stern as fast as the rocking *Seeker* would allow.

Steve Gatto was on the wheelhouse deck, above Chatterton and Crowell, and he had a commanding view of the two Rouses. Gatto raised his right hand over his head, bent his arm, and put his hand on his head to form a large O, one of the diving signs for "Are you okay?" A diver who is not in trouble would respond to the signal by putting his own hand on his head, which says, "I am okay." If a diver is in trouble, he waves his outstretched hand and arm back and forth in a wide arc, which is the call for immediate assistance. The Rouses did not respond at all, which Gatto—a very experienced diver who often crewed on dive boats—at first thought was due to the heavy seas and the Rouses' not wanting to waste time getting back on the boat. He knew that sometimes divers were so focused on getting back to the safety of the boat—especially in rough weather—that they often ignored hand signals. As the Rouses got closer, Gatto could see that they were not swimming normally, even given the high waves. He instinctively knew that something was wrong.

Gatto rushed to grab a throw line that Chris and Chrissy could hold on to so they could be dragged back to the boat. "Here," Gatto called out against the wind as he tossed the line, "grab hold. We'll tow you in!"

Inside the *Seeker*'s main cabin, one deck below where Gatto stood, Barb Lander looked out the windows and saw the line being tossed to the Rouses—by John Yurga, she thought. She rushed out to help pull the divers in. Things were moving fast now.

Chris and Chrissy Rouse floundered in the waves, but both managed to grab the line. The stocky, well-muscled Gatto strained to pull the two men toward the boat. He climbed down the wheelhouse ladder to the main deck, where Chatterton, Packer, Lander, Yurga, and Kohler helped pull the rope.

When Chris neared the *Seeker*'s stern, he let go of the rope and swam around the heaving boat to the ladder. He was breathing hard when he put his feet on the bucking ladder's bottom rung and held on as if he were a cowboy trying to ride a wild bull. Chatterton was leaning over the rail, looking down the ladder in anticipation of Chris's climbing up. Chatterton shouted, "Climb up the ladder!"

Chris replied, weakly, but without hesitation, "No. Take Chrissy first."

At this point, the excess nitrogen that Chris had absorbed during the extended dive, and had not had a chance to release slowly through decompression, now bubbled in his system. His body probably hurt as if someone were trapped inside him, trying to punch and scratch his way out. His breathing was labored. In spite of his pain, Chris still thought first about his son.

Just then, the younger Rouse, still holding on to the throw line, was dragged around the *Seeker*'s stern. A large wave hit and the surface current pushed Chrissy toward the boat's massive stern, which now hung in the air several feet above and perilously close to him.

Meanwhile, Chris Rouse stepped backward, off the ladder and into the waves, looking for the trailing line to grab onto. He found the nylon line floating on the surface, attached on one end to the stern of the boat and on the far end to a large, orange ball buoy. He swam backward, floating on the surface while holding on to the trailing line so that his son would have room to get onto the ladder.

As the wave continued to carry Chrissy forward, the hull came down hard. It missed Chrissy's head by inches. The manifold bar connecting his back-mounted tanks took the blow from the stern's abrupt drop. The strong metal manifold cracked under the stern's weight. In a loud, constant, high-pitched hissing, compressed air from the tanks was released through the crack, harmless but adding to the stressful situation.

The *Seeker* had no swim platform for the rescuers to climb down onto so that they could help get Chrissy away from the boat's heaving stern. Instead, Gatto, Chatterton, Packer, Lander, Yurga, and Kohler all hung their bodies over the *Seeker*'s stern, trying desperately to grab hold of Chrissy and pull him away from the boat so that the next wave did not result in his being crushed.

Somehow, they managed to get Chrissy over to the ladder without his being struck. He started to climb the ladder, but the combination of more than 150 pounds of equipment, the wildly rocking boat, and the onset of decompression sickness robbed him of the ability to climb farther. Chatterton commanded, "Climb up the ladder, Chrissy."

Chrissy replied faintly, "I can't move my legs."

The bends was wasting no time doing its devastation. Chrissy was already paralyzed from the waist down.

The Rouses were undergoing "explosive decompression," just as I had suffered only one year earlier. Father and son could try to conduct in-water recompression, which would require them to descend immediately and conduct their missed decompression. Now it would have to be extended several hours because they had surfaced and allowed massive bubbles to form in their bodies. But with a storm moving in, Chatterton knew that an extended in-water decompression would put the dive boat and everyone on it at risk. The only real option now was a recompression chamber. Commercial and military divers dive from vessels equipped with chambers; if there are any complications of the bends, they are immediately treated in the chamber on board the vessel.

The Rouses would have to be evacuated. Once inside the recompression chamber, if all went well, they would recover, as I had. If it did not go well, they would end up crippled, even after multiple chamber treatments. There are no hard-and-fast rules about who will be lucky with the bends and who will not.

But Chatterton, fighting the truth and attempting to motivate Chrissy, barked, "This is no time for joking around. Get your ass up the ladder."

"I'm not kidding," Chrissy pleaded.

Everyone realized how dire the situation was. The Atlantic Ocean was kicking and rocking the 60-foot boat like a child's toy in a bathtub. One of the most dangerous parts of a diving rescue at sea was now under way: getting the stricken diver safely aboard the boat during rough seas. Chatterton, Gatto, Packer, Lander, Yurga, and Kohler scrambled to hang over the stern to help get Chrissy on board. Six sets of hands grabbed at him, trying to get hold and pull him up the ladder.

Chrissy was dragged, powerless, into the boat. He fell headfirst to the *Seeker*'s deck. Chatterton was reminded of fishermen landing a tuna.

The hard fall stunned Chrissy. He blurted, "I've got to go back down and decompress, or I'm gonna die."

But it was already too late to get Chrissy back underwater. Lander, Yurga, Kohler, and Packer all worked frantically to unclip his extra tank—the one his father had clipped to him underwater—his artifact goodie bag, and his lights, and then they unbuckled the harness that held his two back-mounted tanks in place. When they had stripped off his equipment, they picked up the partially paralyzed diver and carried him to a large wooden platform in the middle of the after deck. Here the Rouses had suited up before their dive. Now, the suiting-up platform had become a makeshift hospital bed, one that had nearly been my deathbed a year earlier.

Lander put a regulator in Chrissy's mouth. "Here, breathe this—it's oxygen," she said.

Chrissy spit the regulator out. "Everything hurts so bad."

"Of course it hurts! You're bent. What did you expect?" Lander said as she put the regulator to Chrissy's lips again. "The oxygen will help ease the pain. You'll get better. Just breathe the oxygen!"

Lander was a registered nurse and could legally administer oxygen. Because she was a medical professional, she did not have to recite a legal statement about the perceived value of oxygen to an injured diver, or make sure that Chrissy put the oxygen regulator in his mouth himself as Dave Dannenburg had done with me. Chrissy knew the value of oxygen and he eagerly breathed from the regulator.

While Chrissy was being assisted up the ladder, Chris looked on from the water, where he was still hanging on to the trailing line, which prevented him from being swept away from the boat. When he saw that his son was on board, Chris swam to the *Seeker*'s ladder and stood on the bottom rung.

Chatterton and Gatto turned their attention to Chris. Behind them, Chrissy was shouting something, but Chatterton and Gatto knew that Chrissy was being attended to by the other divers, and they focused on getting Chris back on board.

Lying on the platform, Chrissy labored to produce words as he shouted to Barb Lander, who knelt over him, "Couldn't breathe . . .

couldn't . . . breathe. Only water . . . only water. Reg . . . broken . . . needed . . . air . . . had . . . to . . . surface."

Even though she was right next to Chrissy, Lander struggled to hear exactly what he was saying. She lowered her head so that her ear was right next to Chrissy's lips. In order to hear Chrissy, she had to filter out the background noises of the *Seeker*'s diesel engines and Chrissy's tanks, which still emitted the high-pitched hissing of compressed air escaping from the cracked tank manifold.

Lander tried to calm the frightened diver. "Okay, Chrissy, we can hear you. You're back on the *Seeker* now. What happened?"

Tom Packer handed Lander a large plastic cup filled with water. Lander cradled Chrissy's head in her left arm, paying close attention to his breathing, which seemed to be labored and getting shallower. Lander noticed that Chrissy seemed to be relaxing. She knew that he would need not only oxygen but also water to keep his body properly hydrated so his blood could efficiently carry the nitrogen bubbles through his system to his lungs, where they would be expelled during exhalation. "Here, drink some water," she said. As Lander held the cup to Chrissy's lips with her right hand, he drank eagerly.

As soon as he finished the water, Chrissy started screaming, trying to say something. His face was ghostly white. Sounds came grunting out of the stricken diver.

Lander tried to determine what Chrissy was saying, and she tried to get information about what had happened to Chris and Chrissy underwater. Packer leaned closer, pencil and clipboard in hand so that he could write down what Chrissy said.

Steve McDougall had finished his decompression and now surfaced off the *Seeker*'s bow. He started swimming toward the stern so that he could climb back on board.

As Chrissy screamed out words, Chatterton was leaning over the stern, shouting to Chris, who had wrapped his arms around the ladder's right rail. To Chatterton, it looked as though Chris had lost the ability to use his hands. Chatterton commanded, "Okay, Chrissy's on board. Now you get up the ladder."

Chatterton implored Chris to hurry, to get back on board. Chris's response was weak. He knew his child was safely aboard the vessel, and he lost his ability to continue the fight.

Chris looked at Chatterton through glazed eyes. "I'm not gonna make it," Chris said, his words barely audible, his body limply riding the ladder up and down with each wave motion.

Gatto, leaning over the stern next to Chatterton, thought that Chris was saying he was not going to be able to climb up the ladder by himself. Gatto leaned down and tied a rope securely around Chris's tank manifold, then assured Chris, "Sure you're gonna make it. I've got ya. I'm gonna haul your ass right on up the ladder."

Chris Rouse went limp. The wave action that rocked the boat and the ladder threw him into the water. Gatto held on to the rope that he had attached to Chris's tank manifold so that Chris's body would not drift away.

McDougall rounded the stern of the vessel just after Chris went limp. McDougall backed off and held on to the trail line, just as Chris had. He could see that others were attending to Chris. It was protocol to stay away from someone who was either on a ladder or about to climb onto a ladder, so that if the climber fell, he would not injure anyone who was stupid enough to wait beneath. McDougall bobbed in the waves, the *Seeker*'s stern coming into his view as he rode the crest of a wave and then disappearing as he fell into the wave's trough. He could tell that the diver at the ladder was Chris Rouse by his distinctive helmet and its attached array of dive lights. McDougall could see that Chris was in serious trouble. And where was Chrissy? he wondered. He didn't know that Chrissy was now safely on board. McDougall's heart thudded when he concluded that Chrissy was probably still underwater, dead from some accident that had caused Chris Rouse to come up early.

Chatterton was stunned when Chris went limp in the water. He instinctively jumped into the water, followed immediately by Richie Kohler. Both men wore only street clothes. The cold water shocked their systems, but adrenaline surged through them, combating the cold and galvanizing their actions. Chatterton immediately lifted Chris's head out of the water.

"I'm dying," said Chris weakly, and very calmly. "Tell Sue I'm sorry and that I love her." Chris's head fell to his right, his body relaxing completely. Life drained from him as the nitrogen bubbles overwhelmed his body and the sea continued its relentless pounding.

Chatterton and Kohler knew they had to get Chris out of his heavy diving equipment, but were bewildered by the array of hoses, lights, battery pack, the cave-diving harness, and all of the other equipment, including tanks and reels, bobbing up and down with the water's motion. Spotting one of several knives that Chris wore, Chatterton grabbed the shoulder knife and tore it from its holder. The waves kept pushing the two men toward the stern of the boat. Kohler grabbed Chris's tank valve, holding both Chris and Chatterton away from the boat. The large steel ladder swung dangerously toward the three men. They were being carried up and down the waves as if on a roller coaster.

Gatto scrambled down the ladder to act as a human buffer so that none of the three men in the water would get struck by the boat. Gatto shouted, "Okay, cut Chris out of his gear." He reached down and pushed Chatterton away from the boat. "I'll make sure the boat doesn't hit you."

Chatterton sawed away at Chris Rouse's shoulder harness. The knife was sharp and cut through the thick nylon strap quickly. Chatterton ducked his head below the water and grabbed Chris's waist belt. With one smooth pull, Chatterton disconnected the quick-release buckle. He then yanked on the crotch strap that was attached to the bottom of Chris's harness in back and to the waist strap in front. After a few pulls, Chatterton managed to undo the buckle that held both the crotch strap and the harness in place on Chris's body. He worked Chris's left arm free of the other shoulder strap and then pushed the harness with its attached tanks and equipment away so that it would not hit Chris. The tanks floated on the surface, supported by the air in the buoyancy compensator. Gatto tied off the rope in his hand to the ladder so that the tanks would not float away.

Chatterton threw Chris Rouse's limp body over his shoulder in a fireman's carry and struggled up the ladder. Kohler stepped onto the ladder's bottom rung, which was beneath the water, and braced himself so that he could give Chatterton a boost with one arm. Gatto grabbed Chatterton and helped him up the ladder. When Chatterton made it to the top of the ladder, he got purchase on the railing, then stood upright on the swim platform and dumped Chris's body into the boat. It landed with a dull thud. Chatterton scrambled over the stern, keeping his eyes fixed on Chris Rouse. Kohler ran up the ladder, and McDougall swam from the trail line to the ladder, so that he could climb up in full gear.

Chrissy Rouse was still lying on the wooden platform, his head cradled in Barb Lander's left arm. He shook his head and started screaming again, his voice muffled by the regulator in his mouth. He spit out the regulator and shouted out, "Something . . . something . . . fell on me . . . inside the . . . the . . . the . . . wreck. I was . . . pinned! Help! . . . Help!" While the rest of Chrissy's body lay limp he shook his head and screamed repeatedly for help.

Lander looked into Chrissy's dilated eyes. He was only a few years older than her son. She tried to establish eye contact with him, to help calm him down. As she looked deep into Chrissy's terror-filled eyes, she spoke firmly, trying to break his thoughts and get his attention. "Chrissy. Chrissy! You're on the *Seeker*. You're on the *Seeker*! We're giving you help! Stay calm."

Chatterton, leaning over Chris Rouse on the *Seeker*'s deck, thought for a quick instant of his battle experiences in Vietnam, where he had served as a field medic with an infantry division. During combat, he had treated several injured men at once, and his training and experience as an Army medic returned to him. He blocked out of his mind the screaming coming from Chrissy, who lay only a few feet away.

Chatterton quickly positioned Chris's body, then checked for breathing and a pulse. He shouted out, loudly, "Victim has a weak pulse, no breathing. I am initiating CPR. Call the Coast Guard and request an immediate evacuation."

Steve Gatto kneeled beside Chris's body, prepared to assist Chatterton with two-man cardiopulmonary resuscitation if Chris's heart stopped beating.

Captain Dan Crowell was already on the wheelhouse deck, looking down at the scene on the *Seeker*'s stern. He was waiting for information from Lander, Gatto, Yurga, Packer, or Chatterton as to either of the Rouses' condition. When he heard Chatterton's pronouncement, Crowell ran into the wheelhouse, grabbed the radio's handheld microphone, and urgently spoke into it. "Mayday. Mayday. This is the vessel *Seeker*, calling U.S. Coast Guard. Two divers facing imminent loss of life. CPR started on one. Requesting immediate evacuation by chopper. Repeat: Mayday. This is *Seeker* to Coast Guard. Imminent loss of life. Requesting immediate chopper evacuation. Please acknowledge."

While Crowell was on the radio, Chatterton felt Chris's pulse stop. The former Army medic called out the situation as John Yurga stood by, taking notes. Chatterton began heart compression, which alternated with Gatto's deep breaths into Chris's mouth: One breath was followed by five heart compressions, then one breath, then five heart compressions, in an exhausting ritual to sustain life. Chatterton had worked as an anesthesiologist after leaving the Army and he noted the fast changes to Chris's body caused by the massive number of bubbles forming. Each compression was meeting with more and more resistance, and Chatterton knew that Chris's blood was clotting. Even Gatto's breaths were meeting with resistance, although Gatto made sure he had Chris's head tilted back so that his airway was unobstructed by his tongue. Chatterton thought about intubating Chris, but he knew the problem was not in getting breaths into the airway—the problem was in Chris's lungs. They were now overwhelmed with nitrogen bubbles that his body had absorbed with each breath during the dive. Now, the nitrogen had come out of his tissues, had entered his circulatory system, and was being carried to his lungs for elimination during breathing. But there was too much nitrogen, and it had formed bubbles that overwhelmed Chris's ability to breathe it out. His blood had turned to sludge. Heart compressions couldn't move the blood, so even if the lungs could be filled with air, there was nowhere for it to go.

When the two men had been at CPR for some time, Richie Kohler kneeled down to relieve Gatto and assist Chatterton with the CPR. Between compressions, Chatterton asked Kohler, "When did you do your CPR course?"

It was over a year since Kohler had done the lifesaving class, and his certification had now legally expired. Chatterton did not hesitate when he heard the date of Kohler's certification. "Don't touch Chris. Your CPR is expired. Go over and get information about what happened from Chrissy. And write it down." To administer CPR without a valid certification could have serious legal consequences for Kohler.

Kohler went over to Chrissy, and motioned to Packer for the clipboard and pencil. Packer went over to Chatterton and Gatto, his diving buddy. Packer relieved Gatto.

McDougall climbed over the top of the *Seeker's* ladder and into the boat. To his right, Chatterton was working on Chris Rouse. Chrissy's howling was muffled by the oxygen regulator, but still McDougall knew how grave the situation was. He took his tanks off at the foot of the ladder. Quickly, he tossed his mask into an open box, then did the same with his fins. He lay the tanks down so that they would not crash into Chatterton, Packer, and Chris Rouse. And then he kneeled down to help. Chatterton knew that the state trooper's CPR training was current and he directed McDougall to relieve Packer and perform the breathing.

A few feet away, on the wooden platform, Chrissy still clung to life. His mind had trouble processing the situation, and he ranted like a madman, "My dad . . . my dad . . . came . . . in . . . and got . . . me . . . out. I . . . was . . . trapped. It . . . felt . . . like I was . . . going . . . going . . . to . . . be eaten. Monkeyfuck! Monkeyfuck! It was a Monkeyfuck! The monster got me. My . . . dad . . . saved . . . me. We couldn't . . . we couldn't oh, Monkeyfuck! We couldn't . . . find . . . deco . . . bottles. Help! Help! The monster's got me!"

As Barb Lander—the only woman on board, whom Chris had poked fun at earlier that day—attended to Chrissy, the young man asked between screams, "How's my father?"

Lander looked over at Chatterton, who was still performing chest compressions on Chris. Chatterton saw Lander looking at him. He stared somberly at her. Then, Chatterton slowly shook his head. He knew that for all intents and purposes, Chris had died when he said, "I'm dying. Tell Sue I'm sorry and that I love her."

A wave of exhaustion hit Chatterton. He looked from Lander to Steve McDougall, who was still clad in his rubber diving drysuit as he continued to breathe into Chris's mouth, trying to force air into his lungs. Even though Chatterton thought Chris Rouse was already dead, it was their obligation to continue CPR and to do all they could to try to keep the man's vital functions going until they were either relieved by a higher medical authority or a doctor declared him officially dead. They would not fail their fellow diver.

"Your dad's okay" was the reassurance Lander gave Chrissy. Why tell the boy that his father lay dead only a few feet away? Why burden him with the horror that his plight had probably killed his father—who had overextended his dive time and died trying to rescue his son—now, when he needed to fight for his life?

Chrissy had lain still for a while, but now he started ranting again. He complained of burning pain, then of feeling nothing, then of pain again. There was nothing Lander, Kohler, Gatto, or anyone else could do right now. And then Chrissy shook his head violently back and forth and cried out with an anguished scream, "It hurts too much. PLEASE GET A GUN! SHOOT ME! PLEASE!"

From the wheelhouse deck, Captain Dan Crowell called out, "Okay, the Coast Guard's on their way. We've got to secure everything on deck and get ready to get under way. You know the drill!"

Kohler, stunned by what he was seeing and had just heard from Chrissy, rose to his feet and stood next to the younger Rouse and then went to check that all equipment was tied down.

On board the Coast Guard rescue chopper, the pilot spotted the *Seeker* in the distance and alerted his Search and Rescue swimmer to be prepared. The SAR swimmer nodded solemnly. He would be lowered onto the *Seeker* by cable from the winch system, and would not have to jump into the water.

On the *Seeker*'s wheelhouse deck, Captain Dan Crowell engaged the *Seeker*'s propellers and headed the boat northeast, into the 20-knot wind, as he was ordered by the Coast Guard. Because of the sea conditions, Crowell followed a compass course of 320 degrees. The helicopter followed the *Seeker* and hovered above the boat's stern while lowering the swimmer.

When he was on board the *Seeker*, the rescue swimmer quickly assessed the situation in front of him on the boat's stern deck. He looked at Chatterton, then at Chris Rouse's slate-gray face and lifeless eyes. He pointed to Chris Rouse, pronounced, "He's dead!" and walked toward Chrissy Rouse, who was moving his head.

Chatterton was stunned at the finality of the pronouncement. He had seen death before, both on the battlefield and on the dive boat. But he had hoped for some effort on the Coast Guardsman's part to attend to Chris. Chatterton knew from his Army medical training and battlefield experience that the Coast Guardsman was only one person, with limited resources. The medical term for his quick decision was triage, which was developed during the First World War to treat wounded combatants: You attend to those who are definitely living first—Chrissy Rouse fell into that category—and put aside those like Chris Rouse, whose lives you probably cannot save even if you attend to them immediately.

The swimmer took from his waist pouch a waterproof radio. He spoke into the radio and requested that the helicopter drop a basket so that Chrissy could be airlifted to a hospital. "Put on your life vests!" the swimmer barked to everyone on the *Seeker*. "Prepare for basket drop!" Everyone scrambled to obey orders.

Above the *Seeker*, the helicopter moved in closer, and a metal basket was lowered to the tossing boat. On board the *Seeker*, the helicopter-induced wind turbulence caused soda cans, paper wrappers, bags of pretzels, lines, and cooler lids to be whipped around the cluttered stern of the vessel in spite of Chatterton's and Kohler's earlier efforts to secure all loose objects. Water spray whipped everyone's faces, no matter in which direction they turned.

The basket was lowered and allowed to touch the *Seeker*'s metal railing to discharge the powerful static electricity that would severely injure anyone who came into contact with the basket before the charge was dissipated.

Chrissy Rouse was paralyzed from the nipples down and had to be carried to the basket. While he was being hoisted upward, Chatterton leaned close to the SAR swimmer, so that the man would be able to hear him over the roar of the *Seeker*'s engines and the noise from the helicopter. Chatterton pointed to Chris Rouse. "You've got to take him."

"We can't risk another basket drop for a dead guy!"

"Are you a medical doctor?"

"No."

"Then you can't tell me he's dead for certain! You've got to take him."

"NO!"

"Look, the kid thinks his father's still alive. We've been telling him that so that he keeps on fighting to live. He's got to see his old man on the chopper with him, otherwise he'll know he's dead!"

The swimmer stared at him. "Do you have any idea how risky a basket lift is? We just can't do it for a dead guy!"

"I was an Army medic in 'Nam. I know all about dust-offs! Nobody's shooting at you here! Stop fucking around! Get this guy off the boat! NOW!"

The SAR swimmer knew they were wasting valuable time that could be better used in getting the crippled diver to the hospital. The swimmer turned from Chatterton and spoke into his radio. "Requesting a second basket drop," he shouted.

When both Rouses were on board the helicopter, the line was dropped down one last time. Instead of a basket at the end, it had a thick, padded strap. The SAR swimmer put the strap around his waist, secured it, walked over to the *Seeker*'s transom, and stepped up onto the wooden rim of the hull. He looked upward at the spotter, pointed his right index finger upward, and waved it in a circle. The helicopter rose. To Kohler, Chatterton, Yurga, McDougall, Gatto, and Packer, it appeared that the SAR swimmer stepped off the stern and was flying. The swimmer dangled from the helicopter as it flew upward and away while the spotter winched him back on board.

As Chrissy Rouse was flown off by Coast Guard helicopter to the hospital and a recompression chamber, those left aboard the *Seeker* were mentally and physically exhausted. One of their number was now dead, and another clung at the very edge of life, his survival still in doubt. It was all divers' biggest fear: that some event, or combination of events, would ultimately turn their most beloved activity into the instrument of their deaths. In a rough and unforgiving sea, the divers on the *Seeker* had a long ride home.

11

Eulogy

OCTOBER 12, 1992. ABOARD A COAST GUARD RESCUE
helicopter, flying northwest toward New York City from the dive
boat *Seeker*, 60 miles off the New Jersey coast.

CHRISSY ROUSE STILL STRUGGLED for life as the Coast Guard
helicopter sped him toward a recompression chamber. Chrissy
was unaware that his father's lifeless body lay not far away. According
to John Chatterton's watch timer, one hour and twenty-seven minutes had elapsed from the time Chris and Chrissy surfaced to the
time the helicopter arrived. That precious time allowed the nitrogen
bubbles to continue to expand inside the Rouses' bodies. Although
the helicopter was moving as fast as the pilot could coax it, several
hours would elapse from the time that Chrissy surfaced to the moment
that he would be put under pressure in a hyperbaric chamber.

The helicopter was heading to Bronx Municipal Hospital, also
known as Jacobi Medical Center. Glenn Butler, the former commercial diver, was the safety director of the recompression chamber facility. While Chrissy was en route to his facility, the Coast Guard

291

apprised Butler that two injured divers were being flown in for treatment, and gave a summary of their symptoms. Although he did not know the exact details, Butler had enough information to tell that the case was severe, involving a significant amount of omitted decompression. He marshaled his staff resources and braced himself for a long, grueling treatment. After Butler had put his staff on alert, waiting for the arrival of the helicopter, he called his old boss, Dr. Bill Hamilton, the physiology expert who had been part of the team at Ocean Systems that exposed Butler and other divers as their human guinea pigs inside a hyperbaric chamber, testing new gas mixtures and decompression schedules. Hamilton agreed to be on call for consultation with the bends cases coming in.

When the helicopter touched down on the landing pad at Jacobi, medical personnel rushed Chris and Chrissy into the emergency room, where they were met by a medical team including doctors, Butler, and his staff. Chris was ashen white, his body already rigid, and there was nothing that could be done for him. A doctor officially pronounced Chris Rouse dead at 13:48, or 1:48 in the afternoon. Only six hours earlier he had been joking with Barb Lander and the other divers on the expedition, teasing Barb about not doing the dishes that piled up in the *Seeker*'s sink. Now he was gone.

Chrissy still did not know his father was dead; the gurney that held Chris Rouse's body was quietly wheeled away to the morgue. As nurses worked on Chrissy, recording his vital signs, hooking him up to intravenous liquid, and cutting away his diving underwear so that they could put him into a cotton hospital gown, Butler asked Chrissy what happened so that the medical team could figure out how best to try to save his life. "Were you diving mix?" Butler asked, referring to a helium gas.

"No. We couldn't afford it," Chrissy said. "We were on air. We were very narced." (Chrissy used divers' slang for narcosis.)

Chrissy was paralyzed from the nipples down and now felt little pain. Butler assessed Chrissy's speech and concluded that the diver was in pretty good shape, considering the circumstances, because he was still able to think dimensionally, to put cause and effect together. This was an important piece of information for Butler because it indicated that Chrissy's brain had not yet been overwhelmed with nitrogen bubbles. But the other information Butler heard was not good: The two divers, breathing air, had gotten trapped inside a U-boat, managed to free themselves and get out of the wreck with no gas left, and then had made a direct ascent to the surface. Butler was aghast. No decompression. He knew that such a situation could possibly have been successfully treated if there had been a recompression chamber on the dive boat and if Chrissy could have been gotten into the chamber almost immediately. But under the current circumstances, successful treatment after such a delay was a daunting task.

The team needed to know the condition of Chrissy's blood and had a sample taken. The results were not good. Instead of normal blood, the syringe contained foam. There were so many nitrogen bubbles in Chrissy's system that his body could not expel them quickly enough through exhalation. With nowhere to go, the nitrogen bubbles fizzed in Chrissy's circulatory system. Chrissy's blood could not carry oxygen to his muscles, and his brain would be more and more affected. While he was being slowly killed by his deep dive, the depth of that dive was also the only thing that was keeping Chrissy alive: Because he had been under increased pressure, the oxygen in the air he had breathed underwater, as well as the pure oxygen he breathed after he surfaced, caused the oxygen in his system to be at a high surface tension, and it was this oxygen that Chrissy's body was now metabolizing.

"We couldn't get the debris out of our way inside the wreck, and it was all silty, so we couldn't see anything," Chrissy told Butler, as he grew increasingly breathless. "Then we saw the outside light every once in a while. It was so confusing. It felt like I was dreaming, and like I was hallucinating. It was like the wreck was grabbing me, trying to pull me further back into it. We were just crazy to dive this thing on air. It was the air, it was the air."

"You mean the air was bad?" Butler asked. Maybe the air in Chrissy's scuba tanks was contaminated with carbon monoxide. This can happen if the compressor used to fill the scuba tank does not have the proper filter on it, or if the air intake is improperly placed so that the exhaust from either the compressor or another internal combustion engine gets sucked into the compressor and then into the scuba tank. Even a small amount of carbon monoxide can kill a diver.

"No. No. The air was good. It was just crazy to dive this wreck on air. Crazy!" Chrissy lamented.

The nurses attending to Chrissy worked fast to get him out of his diving garments. They needed complete access to his body and could not put him into the chamber wearing anything but cotton, because clothing made from synthetic materials could create static electricity, which could cause a fire or explosion in the high-pressure air environment inside. According to Butler, Chrissy was inside the chamber within fifteen minutes of his arrival at the hospital. Butler worked the outside of the chamber, while a doctor and a nurse attended to Chrissy within the chamber. Butler decided to keep Chrissy on pure oxygen and take him down to a pressure equivalent to 60 feet, then see how the diver responded to that treatment. The increased pressure would start to reduce the nitrogen bubbles in Chrissy's system, and would even force some of the nitrogen back into a dissolved state in the blood, muscles, and other tissues. The increased pressure would also force pure oxygen into the bloodstream and then into the tissues. When Chrissy got to depth, he cried out in pain, a common occurrence at this stage of treatment because the circulation was returning to Chrissy's body as the nitrogen bubbles in his bloodstream were reduced in size. It is like the feeling of pins and needles when the circulation returns to your arm or leg after it has "fallen asleep," only much worse.

Although a bent diver's pain can be excruciating, it is also a sign to medical personnel that the treatment is progressing well. For the first time, Butler began to feel hopeful that one member of this diving team might survive. After a few minutes at 60 feet, the team decided to send Chrissy down to a pressure equivalent to that at a depth of 165 feet. According to the theory of bubble mechanics, this depth should reduce the size of the nitrogen bubbles to a little more than half their original size. Butler turned the knobs that released compressed air into the chamber, and watched the pressure gauges as the needles moved rapidly to the 165-foot pressure mark.

The scenario that transpired over the next few hours is one that Glenn Butler has since gone over repeatedly with as many hyperbaric experts as he could. All of them have given Butler the same answer: Because Chrissy had been diving at 230 feet depth and he was now at a pressure equivalent to only 165 feet, the bubbles would be reduced only slightly; nothing short of a recompression to extreme depths—anywhere from 300 to 400 feet—and a long saturation treatment lasting several days, as well as a complete blood transfusion, could effectively have eliminated the nitrogen bubbles in Chrissy's body.

But medical technology has its limits, and one of those limits is the pressure rating of the hyperbaric chamber. Applying too great a pressure to the hyperbaric chamber would have been blown out the chamber's seals, causing deadly explosive decompression to Chrissy and the medical staffers attending him. There were simply precious few chambers in the world equipped to take a diver down past 165 feet, and the Jacobi facility was not one of them. Even if the facility could take Chrissy below 165 feet, such a treatment was entirely experimental. The team was following published diving treatment protocol. Chambers that could take a diver deeper were specially constructed for navies, commercial diving companies, or researchers; they were generally not available for the treatment of a bent sport diver. The most advanced chamber in the country belonged to the U.S. Navy's Experimental Diving Unit, at Panama City, Florida. Butler knew that even they would have had their hands full with the complexities of treating a patient who was as far along with the ravages of the bends as Chrissy. Plus, Chrissy would probably never have lived long enough to be airlifted to Florida. For Chrissy, it was all or nothing in the Jacobi chamber.

At two-thirty in the afternoon, Chrissy regained movement and feeling in his lower extremities. "Where's my father?" he asked, grimacing in pain.

"He's being treated in a separate chamber," the doctor lied. The young man needed his strength to fight the bends. If Chrissy knew that his father was dead, he would probably be so overcome with grief that he would not have the resolve to keep the battle going.

Chrissy's pain was incredible. He screamed. Then he screamed more as his blood pulsed through his body, further awakening his senses to the abuse his body had endured. To Butler and his team, Chrissy's hideous cries were excruciating, as if their healing chamber had been converted to a medieval torture device. Butler ordered the overhead communications between the inside and the outside of the chamber to be turned off. The medical personnel switched to headset communications. They could not bear to do otherwise.

Sue Rouse had been contacted by the Coast Guard and informed that her husband and son had been in a diving accident and were now in the hospital. She was told nothing further about their condition. As she was driven by Denny and Eleanor Willis the three hours across Pennsylvania and northern New Jersey to the hospital, she thought that she would be reunited with her loved ones—hurt perhaps, but alive. She had always feared this would happen. They were tough, healthy, vigorous. They would beat back the bends or whatever else had ambushed them. They had to live.

As Sue Rouse headed to the hospital, the pressure on Chrissy's body was being reduced, according to the schedule prescribed in U.S. Navy Recompression Table 6-A, a treatment I had successfully undergone only one year earlier. After five and a half hours in the chamber, having successfully gone from 165 feet to the pressure equivalent of 60 feet, Chrissy now breathed pure oxygen and was gradually brought up to a pressure equivalent to 30 feet. But the team could see that Chrissy was not responding well to the decreased pressure. There were no more cries from the young man, who lay still on the gurney. Chrissy had passed out. The team decided to take Chrissy back down to 60 feet. But before they could do so, Chrissy's strong, young heart failed. CPR could not revive him. Chrissy was declared dead at 19:50, or 7:50 P.M.

Sue arrived at the hospital only moments after Chrissy died. When she got to the emergency room, she was told that her husband and son were both dead. It was completely unexpected news and it shattered her.

As Sue was being comforted by Denny and Eleanor, the doctor informed them that somebody had to identify the bodies. Through her tears, Sue gasped, "I'll do it. Let me see them."

"You don't want to do this, Sue," Denny said. "Let me take care of this for you." Although identifying his friends' bodies would be difficult enough for him, he knew it would be far worse for Sue. Denny was a diving instructor and had gotten interested in cave diving through the Rouses' enthusiasm for it and their insistence that he go down to Ginnie Springs and take the cave-diving classes. After his first trip, Denny was hooked on cave diving, the Rouses' high-energy spirit, and what seemed to him their slapstick humor.

"No, Denny. I need to see them."

Chrissy's body had been wheeled out of the hyperbaric chamber and now lay on a gurney inside a curtained section of the emergency room. As she walked toward her son, it looked to Sue as if he were merely asleep. She gently reached over and touched his hand. It was still warm. Though she stood frozen in grief, she had an urge to grab Chrissy, shake him, and say, "I'm here, Chrissy. I'm here. It's all right now. Wake up!"

She remembered the time when she was pregnant with Chrissy and just married. She and Chris watched a movie on television called *Angel in My Pocket*. During the movie, Chris reached over and gently rubbed Sue's stomach. "You've got an angel in *your* pocket," he said. Now her angel was gone.

Her husband's body had already been taken to the Bronx morgue. Denny again offered to spare Sue the ordeal, but again she refused his offer. The morgue was now closed and they would have to return to New York City the next day to accomplish that grim task.

In her husband she had lost her best friend, someone she had literally grown up with, known since high school, even before her adult life began. Although many people perceived the Rouses as bickering all the time, Sue thought of it merely as communicating. It was their style of interaction, the way that they had grown accustomed to dealing with each other over the course of their well-cemented, long-term relationship. She knew that Chris loved her deeply and would do anything for her, including building a house with his own hands and putting her desires before his own, instead of buying the airplane he had wanted. And his willingness to work hard made him a good provider. Chris went diving often, but he also included the family in his activity whenever they could all go. Sue thought that as a husband and father, Chris was far better than many men who would go off and frequently spend time alone with their buddies, or at a bar. And with Chrissy she had had the challenge of motherhood, which she had not thought would come so early in her life but which she had nonetheless embraced.

One of the questions that divers still ask today is this: Would the Rouses have been able to save themselves if they had been breathing mixed gas, which would have given them clearer heads at depth? Chrissy's statements to Butler indicated he had gotten trapped inside the U-boat, and that his struggle to get out of the wreck led him to hallucinate underwater. As Butler understood it at the time, Chrissy's problem was one of survival while deep and breathing air. Some divers think helium gases would have helped father and son survive; they argue that if Chrissy had been breathing mixed gas, which he had been trained to use and which he had experience deploying underwater, his mind would not have been as clouded as the interior of the wreck itself. Possibly he would have been able to extricate himself. In that case, the theory goes, Chrissy would have been able to exit the wreck without his father's even having to come in and get him out, and the two men would have been able to find their extra scuba tanks on the U-boat's deck and then conduct their full decompression. They might have been rattled and scared, but they would have survived unscathed.

Other divers disagree, pointing out that even though breathing mixed gas would have given Chrissy a much clearer head, it would not have ensured that he would have been able to rescue himself. If Chris had had to heft the shelf off of his son while the two were breathing mixed gas, they would have consumed their gas at a much faster rate because it was lighter than compressed air and offered less breathing resistance. Panting with exertion, they might well have run out of breathing gas and died inside the wreck. Also, if they had ascended without any decompression after breathing mixed gas at 230 feet, the molecularly lighter helium gas would have bubbled in their bodies even faster than the nitrogen did, and they both would probably have died even sooner.

As it was, Chrissy survived for three hours and did make it into the recompression chamber, where over five hours his symptoms even started to abate: The feeling returned to his legs, and the paralysis he experienced from the nipples down seemed resolved as he moved his legs and hips. Why, then, did he die in the recompression chamber? Was there a better treatment he could have been given? Or perhaps some medication? The sad truth lay in the autopsy. When doctors removed Chrissy's heart and then opened it underwater, the ventricles released foam, not blood. There were simply too many nitrogen bubbles that Chrissy's body had to eliminate before foam formed in the heart.

As Dr. Bill Hamilton describes it, Chrissy's heart experienced "vapor lock." Hamilton explains it this way: "The heart is a pump designed to push fluid through it. Like any pump, if air gets into the system, the pump just squeezes on the vapor over and over and nothing happens; it just can't function. That's what happened to Chrissy." But was there some other treatment that Chrissy could have been given? Hamilton muses briefly about the answer. "I've thought about that a lot. In theory, you might have been able to put him down under far greater pressure, perhaps even using helium as a recompression gas. But in reality, there are so few chambers in the world, and so few hyperbaric technicians or doctors—even today, forget 1992—that could handle a deep helium recompression treatment, that no, I don't think it would have been possible, unless everything had been planned way in advance. Realistically, there's nothing that could have been done to save him, under the circumstances. Both Chrissy and his father were dead when they hit the surface. The only thing that surprised me was that Chris died as quickly as he did and that Chrissy lasted as long as he did."

It's a lesson for the many divers who today are plunging deeper than the Rouses ever did, and taking greater risks. Yet even today, deaths still occur while divers use mixed gases, and also while they dive breathing air; deaths still occur in both deep and in shallow ranges. The water is still an alien, unforgiving world, just as it was when humans ventured into the depths thousands of years ago, first out of curiosity and then out of greed.

What might have saved the Rouses—even after everything that had happened to them—was underwater communications equipment that would have allowed them to talk to the surface, and also to Steve McDougall, who was not far away, decompressing, when the Rouses ascended. If they could have let crew and buddies know what was going on, extra scuba tanks could have been lowered to the Rouses. Then, no matter what happened to them inside the U-boat, they would have been able to decompress in the water and avoid the bubble buildup that killed them both. As it was, they essentially died deep and alone.

The news of the disaster swept like a typhoon through the diving community even before Chris and Chrissy had been declared dead. The emergency radio call that Seeker's captain, Dan Crowell, had made to the Coast Guard, as well as the radio messages back and forth between the helicopter and the *Seeker*, had been picked up by other boat captains in the area. When the *Seeker* returned to port, divers from another dive boat that had gotten back earlier lined the pier, and extended their condolences and offers of help to those on board.

When the *Seeker* pulled into port and docked, Barb Lander, John Chatterton, Steve McDougall, John Yurga, Steve Gatto, Tom Packer, Richie Kohler, and Dan Crowell could only sit on the vessel, in shock. Instead of the usual, almost festive mood among divers that accompanies the successful completion of an expedition, the atmosphere was somber, and everyone was quiet, lost in their own thoughts. Though many of them had seen death before—on a dive boat, on a battlefield, or in the course of police work—it was still numbing that two of their fellow divers had been struck by catastrophe at the same time.

At Tim Stumpf's house in Horsham, Pennsylvania, where Chrissy had lived periodically when he had enough money to live free of his parents, a small crowd of men and women began gathering on the lawn, trying to gain solace from one another. When word reached them that both Rouses had died, everyone was stunned. Now, three of their top guns, including Ed Sollner, who also used to hang out at Tim's, had died within four months. Everyone who gathered that night on the lawn thought about their own diving, and many of them decided to put an end to their dreams of diving deep to recover artifacts, or to find new forms of life, or just for the sheer thrill of it.

Chrissy's girlfriend, Julia, was there, as part of the impromptu wake. Her romance with Chrissy had taken her by storm; it was even a bond they had both sought to avoid for some time, before they gave in to their mutual attraction and started dating. It had blossomed into such a relaxed and rewarding relationship that it seemed they had always been together, a bond as sturdy as that of Chrissy's parents. Julia could only recall how sensitive and giving Chrissy had been to her; he had never forced or rushed the relationship as other young men had tried to do. Julia found Chrissy's approach refreshing, his attentions as direct and soothing as a trade wind over a fertile island. How could her perfect relationship have ended this way? She wanted to believe Chrissy's death was a nightmare she could awake from and tell him about. But the nightmare went on and on, and she did not awake. She consoled herself with the fact that she had not taken Chrissy for granted—she had known how special the relationship was, although she had never been able to admit to herself he could be stolen from her by the deep: She always thought Chrissy's skills were far too good for anything bad to happen to him underwater.

Chrissy's old, beat-up car stood in Tim's driveway. Somebody had to drive it back to Sue Rouse's house. Julia decided to return it herself, as if being in the car could somehow put her in touch with Chrissy again. As she drove toward Sue's house, she played Chrissy's favorite song, "Even Flow," by Pearl Jam. It was difficult for her to see the road; it was as if a black cloud hovered over the car and emptied tears over the windshield. When Julia arrived at Sue's house she was amazed that she had not skidded off the road and ruined the car, as Chrissy had done several times with his vehicles.

The Rouses died on Columbus Day weekend—the same national holiday weekend when I had nearly died a year earlier. I found out about the Rouses' deaths at work, where I was taking a computer networking class to upgrade my skills. During a break, I called Ginnie Springs to speak to Steve Berman about some equipment I needed repaired. The woman who answered the phone was distraught. When I asked her what had happened, she said tearfully, "You don't know? We've lost Chris and Chrissy." Her statement didn't register until she gave me a vague description of the Rouses' accident.

Why did I live through my accident and they did not? Although they had been deeper by 80 feet, I had been down longer. Did they remember our many discussions about the choice I had to make—either a direct ascent to the surface without any decompression, or drowning—when I had foolishly pushed my dive beyond my mental and physical capacity? I remembered Chris's words to me when I told him the choices that had gone through my mind underwater and that I assumed I would surface, go to the chamber, and everything would be all right. Chris had replied, "I'd rather take my chances in the chamber than drown." The words came ringing back to me. I was overwhelmed, and wanted to know why I should have lived when they did not. It seemed to me that my survival was entirely arbitrary, and there was no reason that they also should not have survived. One man lives, then two men die. It was a painful example of the world's unfairness.

The parking lot of the Shelly Funeral Home was full, and cars were parked all along the rural road in Warrington, Pennsylvania. As Kevin O'Brien parked his car, he turned to me and asked, "Are you ready? You have any notes or anything?"

"Ready? How can you ever be ready for something like this?" I retorted. "You read about people dying during a dive, or you hear about it, but it's never anyone you know real well, is it? It's always somebody else, somebody you vaguely knew, or dove with a few times but aren't real good friends with. Your friends aren't supposed to die," I said, and the emotion thickening in my throat made me wonder how I was going to be able to eulogize them at all.

"You need more time?"

"Naw. That'll only make it worse. I know what I'm going to say. Let's get this over with."

As Kevin, Diana, and I walked into the funeral chapel, I felt as if I were in a dream, entering some wreck I'd stumbled upon entirely by accident. Were those really the remains of my friends in the two urns that stood on the table next to their pictures? Some of their shipwreck artifacts were displayed on the table, alongside their diving certificates and logbooks, which all now looked curiously like artifacts in a museum. The home was filled to overflowing, and those who did not get there early enough had to stand squeezed next to one another.

Cathie Cush had helped Sue organize the service, and she had asked a number of people to give eulogies. Besides many of the local divers, Marc Eyring had driven up from Florida, and John Reekie had come down from Canada to pay their last respects. Steve Berman was conspicuously absent. I wondered why. I knew that Berman disliked large social gatherings, but surely he could pay his last respects to people he was such good friends with. Steve's no-show disappointed me; the reasons for his absence was something that I would not understand until many years later. His grief over the loss of Chris and Chrissy was so great that he could not bear to attend their memorial. That same day, in his home at Ginnie Springs in Florida, Berman could only numbly recollect the many times that the Rouses had visited and the antics that defined them. Between tears of sorrow at the loss of his friends, and laughter over the memory of their antics, Steve Berman grieved privately and profoundly.

Berman could still see the three Rouses barreling into the Ginnie Springs dive shop in the evening after a long late-afternoon dive. Chris was completely disheveled, unshaven after a week of camping at Ginnie and totally unconcerned with what he looked like above water. He wore only a pair of tattered sneakers and his unwashed drysuit underwear, which looked like a ski suit. He was as oblivious as always of the unique odor the suit took on after he had been in it almost continuously for a week. Chrissy looked uncannily similar to his father, unshaven and dressed in his drysuit underwear, the sidekick to the superhero, both men ragged in their superhero costumes. Chrissy paced around the dive shop like a caged young lion, urging his father to finish their business so that they could do another dive that day. It looked to Steve as though Sue was exhausted, ready to fall asleep on her feet, and the thought of another dive draining her completely.

Chris turned to his worn-out wife and said, "I'm taking you guys out to dinner tonight." Sue perked up, obviously delighted that she would eat some decent food. Whenever they stayed at Ginnie Springs, she did not cook. As she told Chris and Chrissy, it was her vacation, too. But the two eager divers did not mind, and they both loved the packaged, premade sandwiches on offer at Ginnie Springs. Chris continued, "My treat. I'll spare no expense." He walked over to the store's large cooler, slid open one of the glass doors, reached inside, and grabbed a sandwich that he tossed to Chrissy. "Here, Chrissy, catch. Have a ham and cheese sandwich. It's on me. Yes sir! No expense spared. Put it on my tab, Steve!"

Steve Berman and the other staff at Ginnie Springs laughed in amusement. It was clear that Chris and Chrissy wanted to eat as quickly as possible so that they could get into the water again for a dive that would probably end sometime after midnight. Sue could only groan at the thought of another dive.

Chris turned to his wife. "What are you having, Sue?"

"Veal parmigiana," she said.

It was her way to nudge Chris, to get back for the disappointment he had given her. The couple had met in high school when they were both working in a diner, she as a waitress, he as a short-order cook. Every day after school, Chris was entitled to eat a meal as part of his wages, but he was limited to choosing from a certain section of the menu. The only thing he liked in that section was veal parmigiana, and he ate it every day. Soon, he became bored with the meal and would never eat it again after he stopped working at the diner. Sue knew that she could always tell him that she would make veal parmigiana whenever he complained about her cooking—or if he didn't take her out to eat as he promised.

Inside the funeral home, Denny McLaughlin had a churning feeling in his stomach, and he dreaded having to talk to Sue. McLaughlin had been Chris and Chrissy's first diving instructor and now he felt responsible for their deaths, even though the Rouses had clearly—and very consciously—gone well beyond the recreational diving limits that McLaughlin taught all his students of 130 feet in depth, no decompression diving, and no penetrations into caves and shipwrecks. Denny McLaughlin knew that the Rouses had taken far greater risks than recreational divers take, and he knew from his many conversations with them over the past four years that they were well aware that their diving was beyond what the recreational training agencies advocated as safe. He also knew from seeing the Rouses in the quarry that their skills were outstanding; he prided himself that he had given Chris and Chrissy the solid initial training that enabled them to develop in the sport and far exceed his own skills and limitations. It was a classic example of students excelling their teacher. All that, however, did not make it any easier for him to talk to Sue.

McLaughlin constantly wondered if there was anything that he, as an instructor and good friend, could have done or said that would have helped the Rouses avoid their tragedy. He knew that it was not in his power to save the Rouses, yet he still somehow felt as if he had failed in his duty to his former students. He walked up to Sue with his head held low, looking at her feet, and offered his condolences. He could not look Sue in the eye.

Sue could see that her friend was distraught and she gently nudged his shoulder. "Buck up, Denny," she commanded.

Denny looked up into the eyes of the woman who had lost her husband and son. Instead of the angry or accusatory glare he expected to find, he saw a composed friend. Denny felt as if she were saying, "It's not your fault. Get over it." The weight of the guilt he felt was instantly lifted from his shoulders.

Word was passed that the services would begin and the crowd assembled in the main room. A priest said a prayer for the Rouses and then Cathie Cush got up to speak.

"A few years ago, people started coming up to me and saying, 'Have you met the Rouses? You have to meet the Rouses. They dive like you do. You'll love the Rouses.' Well, I met them," Cathy continued. "And they didn't dive like me. The truth is that all three of them could dive circles around me with both fins tied behind their backs. And when we think of the awful thing that happened Monday, we should be humbled—because most of us don't have the skill, the discipline, or the composure that Chris and Junior had.

"When people said I would love the Rouses, they were absolutely right. Not because of their diving abilities, but because the Rouses were some of the most loving, giving people I've ever known. Whether you needed a spare O-ring or a shoulder to cry on, they were always there. I know I leaned on them a lot, especially in the last few months. And now it's time to give some of that back to Sue, because she really needs all the support we can muster.

"The world is just a little too silent today," Cathy went on, "and that's a tragedy. But it would have been an even worse tragedy if we had never heard all those stories and theories, never shared the laughter, never been a part of that wonderful energy that Chris and Junior generated. I know I'll miss them both more than words can say, but my life is richer for having known them."

As Cathie walked away from the podium, Steve Gatto, who had been on the dive boat when the Rouses made their last dive, stood in the back of the room, thinking about the immense number of dives the Rouses had performed in their four years, and the level of experience they achieved in that short time. While many others—nondiver and diver alike—thought that the Rouses had gone too far, too fast, Gatto knew that they earned their spots on the top expeditions. He knew from his own experience that what counted was not how many years a diver had been diving, but what he did in the time that he did dive. And then he shuddered when he thought about what other people might have said if he himself had died in a freak accident—and that was how he classified the Rouses' deaths—when he had first dived the *Andrea Doria,* during his third season of diving. Wouldn't those people have smugly said that he had pushed it too hard, too fast, and that his death was destined to happen, just what so many people were now murmuring about the Rouses? Gatto tried to shake the thought, but it clung like lint.

John Reekie sat in the midst of the mourners, his face even more glum than usual, his self-protective scowl even more pronounced. Reekie wished that he and Chris could be at Ginnie Springs again, with Chris energetically cramming his van with dive gear, hurling good-natured insults at Reekie to prod him to move faster so that they could go diving together sooner rather than later. Sometimes, Chris's bristly bombast got on Reekie's nerves, just as brothers get on each other's nerves and yet still love each other. Reekie had always felt that Chris and Chrissy Rouse were his brothers. Already he missed their clowning around, joking, underwater bumper-scooter games, and their long dives together.

Now that Chris and Chrissy Rouse were gone, there were two fewer of the precious number of people in the world whom Reekie trusted with his life underwater—especially inside a cave.

John Chatterton stood not far from John Reekie and Steve Gatto in the back of the room. His face was grim and his feelings were mixed, his grief grappling with his frustration. Chatterton felt that the Rouses died because they were breathing air when they should have been using trimix. On all of their previous very deep dives that Chatterton had witnessed, Chris and Chrissy used trimix. Chatterton knew that they had been among the first sport divers to use mixed gases during wreck diving and then decompress using oxygen. And only two weeks before their fatal dive they were experimenting in the quarry with a breathing mixture of argon and oxygen to see if that might be an efficient gas to use at some stage of a dive. It was ironic, thought Chatterton, that the Rouses, who were on the sport's cutting edge, died because they chose to turn their back on cutting-edge technology, for one expedition. He knew it just showed that you couldn't let your guard down for one moment.

As Chatterton replayed the accident in his mind, he pictured Chris Rouse standing on the *Seeker*'s ladder after the dive. Even though the elder Rouse got to the ladder before his son—and in spite of the excruciating pain he must have been in—Chris had insisted that Chrissy be taken up first. Chatterton, a battle-hardened Vietnam War veteran, had been so impressed with Chris's unselfish, even noble, action that he would forever remember that moment whenever he thought about the Rouses.

Barb Lander, who worked as a nurse when she wasn't diving and had attended to Chrissy on the dive boat, stood among the mourners. When Chrissy had been evacuated from the dive boat, Lander thought that he was going to survive; she had been distraught ever since hearing that he died in the hyperbaric chamber. She was haunted by the question: Was there something else that she could have done to help save him? Lander spoke to as many experts as she could, searching for a different answer from the one everybody gave her, which was that she had done all she could. She would eventually take a course to become a hyperbaric technician qualified in operating a recompression chamber. By her estimation, it would take her three years to even remotely get over the trauma of losing a diving colleague who she thought would survive the ordeal of the bends.

I walked numbly to the podium to deliver my eulogy. None of the other divers I knew who had died in the sport had been close friends, and I had never delivered a eulogy before. How can you possibly do justice to two such people in a thousand words? I knew how great an impact the Rouses' deaths had had on the diving community, both locally in Pennsylvania and throughout the Northeast, and also in Florida cave country, especially at Ginnie Springs. If there was any doubt about that, all I had to do was look at the packed room.

I once came across something that the writer and political and social commentator Jack London wrote early in the century, which struck me so forcefully that I wrote it down and pinned it to my bulletin board at work. I told the audience that besides being good friends and very generous to everyone, the Rouses burned a bright picture on the skies of our lives. As London had said, "I would rather be a meteor than a sleepy and permanent planet. For man's true purpose in life is to live, not to waste time merely sustaining himself." Although the Rouses died young, they were doing what they loved to do, and that meant more to them than just trying to live out their lives.

Chris's flight instructor, Ken Reinhart, stood in the back of the room, listening to me. Reinhart was the one who had convinced Chris that diving was a fun, safe activity, and for Reinhart—as for millions of other divers—it was. But Chris had always wanted to push further. When Reinhart and Chris went down to Ginnie Springs for the first time, Chris was immediately captivated by cave diving, whereas Reinhart was apprehensive. The cautious flight instructor was deeply disturbed by the warning sign placed in the water near a cave entrance that depicted the Grim Reaper with skeletons in diving gear lying at his feet and the bold title PREVENT YOUR DEATH! Later on that same trip, Reinhart tried to warn Chris about the danger of cave diving, but the other man would not be deterred; he went ahead to become enchanted with diving into caves and into shipwrecks. Although shipwrecks did not have warning signs posted around them the way caves did, Reinhart knew they were just as challenging when you ventured inside, as the Rouses did, seeking trophies for their mantel—and Ken's—and doing what they loved to do.

As Reinhart looked around the room, he saw that the vast majority of people were divers, and he did not know them. Although Reinhart was a diver, he was primarily a pilot, and his social circle consisted mostly of flying friends. After I left the podium and diver after diver delivered his or her eulogy, Reinhart could not help but realize that he had known the Rouses far longer than most people in the room. Yet all that was spoken of about the Rouses was their diving activity. Reinhart knew that diving was something that the thirty-nine-year-old Chris had done for only four years; there was so much more to Chris's life than diving, thought Reinhart. He felt like a stranger at his friends' wake. Reinhart knew Chris to be curious about the world in a way that bordered on childlike fascination. That curiosity had propelled Chris to fly, and it had plunged him into diving. Chris's abundant energy and generosity allowed him to work hard not only building his own house, but helping Reinhart to build a house at the same time. How could others appreciate the true depth of Chris Rouse from only a few years of diving? he wondered.

Sue sat in the front row. If there was a God, she thought, why would He let such a terrible thing happen to her men? She did not believe that everything had a reason, or that divine justice determined human fate. To her, the devastation she felt only tipped the scales heavily in favor of her doubt that there was a God. She remembered when Chris had blown himself up while welding in his workshop, and how badly burned he had been. Chris told her later that he had overheard their priest declaring that the accident would not have happened if Chris had attended church regularly. For Chris, the priest's belief was such an insult he did not enter a church again except to attend weddings or funerals. From that moment on, in Chris's mind, there was no God. And now Sue agreed with him.

Marc Eyring stepped up to the podium. He had always seemed a bit uncomfortable out of the water, and now, at a wake for his friends, he seemed even more so. Eyring set his jaw and tried to place his lanky six-foot, four-inch frame in a comfortable position. But once he started talking, he moved with nervous energy, pacing behind the podium. "I taught Chris and Chrissy cave diving several years ago, and then also taught Sue," Eyring began. "Right from the beginning, they stood out. Father and son were both so eager to learn and they didn't have any of the attitude that a lot of wreck divers from the Northeast have: They changed their equipment for cave diving without making any fuss, and that was my first clue that they were different from most people. The other thing was, the family always did things together, at least they were always diving together, and that struck me because it's very rare to see a family where everyone goes cave diving.

"All of us at Ginnie Springs looked forward to the Rouses' coming down to visit, like it was family coming—the part of your family that you really like. And they had such a unique style that all anyone who knew them had to do to see if they were at Ginnie was look for the big, green oxygen bottles that they always roped between trees around the outside of their campsite. I remember one time—it was Christmas—and we were all looking forward to the Rouses' coming down so that we could have a big celebration dinner with them.

"Well, it was snowing in Florida and it was like a freak snowstorm and all the highways were closed. So, we were all depressed because you just don't expect to get snowed in when you live in Florida, and also because we didn't think the Rouses were going to get through. And then, out of the snowstorm comes Chris Rouse, driving his van, with Sue. They were towing their camper trailer and everything, and they just barreled right through the snow. Heck, I don't think they could have gotten off the highway if they wanted to, so I think Chris drove straight down from Pennsylvania. Chris's attitude was 'I'm not going to let a little snow on the side of the road stop me from seeing my friends at Ginnie, or from cave diving.' I think the Florida state cops were so surprised to see anyone on the road, they let 'em through, even though the highways were officially closed. And once they got to Ginnie, everybody was so happy, and we had a great dinner and party. The Rouses were like that: They'd make you happy just by being around. Boy, am I sure gonna miss 'em!"

Chris's and Chrissy's ashes were not scattered immediately. Sue decided to wait until after another memorial service could be held in December at an annual cave-diving workshop in Florida that the Rouses had attended for the past few years. And after that memorial, another service would be performed a week later at Ginnie Springs, and here the Rouses' ashes would be scattered underwater, in the Devil's Cave System. Marc Eyring had proposed that a restriction 3,200 feet into the Devil's Cave System named the Hinkel be renamed the Rouse. A plaque in the Rouses' honor would also be placed in the cave. The discoverer of the Hinkel graciously agreed, though the name has never been officially changed.

Three months went by after the Rouses died until their ashes were scattered. Although Sue does not say it, it would be understandable if she had not yet been ready to let go of her husband and son.

John Reekie would carry Chris Rouse's ashes underwater, while Marc Eyring would bear Chrissy's. Several other divers joined the somber ceremony, including Tim Stumpf and Evie Dudas, who had lost her husband underwater many years earlier. Two divers who had planned to participate were emotionally overwhelmed and could not conduct the dive. Denny Willis was an instructor and close friend who had been introduced to cave diving by the Rouses and who would eventually go on to become the training director of the NSS-CDS, one of the two Florida-based cave-diving organizations. He was completely suited up and standing in the water not far from the entrance to the Devil's Cave System when he became so uneasy with the dive that he aborted before descending.

It was undoubtedly a wise decision, because if you don't feel well, either physically or emotionally, you are far more likely to get into an accident. For example, years later, inside a deep cave system during the filming of a memorial documentary for another diver, the deceased diver's best friend died in a bizarre accident because his rubber fin straps gave way, and he overexerted himself trying to get out of the cave system, passed out, and drowned. Sue did not make plans to be on the dive, and decided to wait on the riverbank while the ashes were scattered below.

To get to the restriction, the procession used scooters, the diver-propulsion vehicles that Chris Rouse had repaired and upgraded so well that he made a name for himself and his Black Cloud Scuba business among the small, hard-core diving community scattered throughout North America. When the procession had all squeezed through the restriction, Reekie opened the Tupperware container that held Chris's ashes, and let his friend's remains billow in the timeless flow of water throughout the cave.

When Marc Eyring uncapped Chrissy's container, he discovered that there had been a leak. Chrissy's ashes were a paste that clung to the inside of the plastic container. Even after death, the Rouses' black cloud followed them. Eyring was taken aback. No one close to him had ever been cremated, so it had been a new experience for him not to be able to view the body at the wake; now, he had to deal with getting his friend's ashes out of the container. There was only one way to do that. Eyring reached into the container with his hand and scooped out the paste that had once been Chrissy Rouse. It clung to Eyring's fingers and hand, as if Chrissy did not want to leave his friends.

Gradually, Eyring was able to release all of the clay that had been Chrissy into the outflowing water of the Devil's Cave System. Some of Chris's and Chrissy's ashes would permeate different parts of the cave, likely clinging to crevices of the limestone rock. Father and son thus became part of the cave system they had loved to dive so much. Symbolically, at least, they would always be cave diving.

On the riverbank, Sue Rouse watched as the water from the Devil's Cave System spilled gin-clear into the Santa Fe River in a smooth, steady flow, just as it had for tens of thousands of years before and as it probably will for innumerable years to come.

12

Ever Deeper

T HE *ANDREA DORIA* appeared below me in the water's green haze as I dropped down the anchor line for my fourteenth dive to the famous ocean liner. My German buddy, Wolfgang Kanig, who swam just above me, was descending on his second dive to the wreck. I had met Wolfgang at Ginnie Springs ten years before, when he and his German contingent had come over and cave-dived with Steve Berman, Chrissy Rouse, and me. Over the past ten years, Wolfgang, who had been diving since 1966, and I had been on diving expeditions together in Mexico and Scotland.

The previous day we had encountered numerous problems with our equipment as we prepared our foray to the *Doria*. We had to peel ourselves out of our drysuits to prevent heatstroke while we switched Wolfgang's tanks, which had released the expensive helium-based mixed gas into the sea air as the result of a bad O-ring seal at the tank valve. Then, when we were both suiting up again, I saw that the oral-nasal pocket inside my full-face mask was not properly held in place. I

312

thought that might cause increased gas consumption because the entire mask would fill with gas on each inhalation, instead of just the oral-nasal pocket filling.

Even though I was fully rigged to dive and had only to put my mask on before jumping in the water, I knew that these gear problems were a bad sign. My nearly fatal dive in 1991, when I swaggered past my flu symptoms to dive, flashed back like a bad dream. So did the Rouses' ill-fated dive to the *U-Who* nearly seven years before, when father and son plunged into the belligerent sea and returned to the surface as dying men. Now, I had the nagging feeling that I should not be diving after all of the problems I had just encountered. Tomorrow would be another day, I had learned to tell myself, and I planned on living long enough to enjoy it. I had aborted the dive before I even got wet.

But Wolfgang had gone ahead and dived. He had come a long way to dive the *Doria,* and he was not going to let equipment problems thwart him. Because he was a cautious diver, I was surprised when he told me that he would dive without me. It was the other way around on one expedition in Scotland, when he encountered equipment problems on the dive boat and aborted a dive to H.M.S. *Hampshire,* off the Orkney Islands. It is an intriguing wreck that remains mired in political controversy because it took the British secretary of war, Lord Kitchener, to his grave at the height of World War I, amid rumors of assassination or sabotage. While Wolfgang stayed on the boat, I dived alone and went down a little over 200 feet to the *Hampshire,* which had then been visited by only ten or eleven sport divers before me.

When Wolfgang got back onto the boat after his solo dive to the *Doria,* he told me that he should have stayed on the boat the way I had elected to do. "I only had one problem after another." One of his regulators began leaking gas, then one of his pressure gauges gave false readings, and finally one of his hoses had gotten twisted between some of his equipment. Overall, the dive had made him feel uncomfortable. Fortunately, he was able to make it back onto the boat without getting bent.

Would the bad luck from my last dive to the wreck, only a year earlier, again prevail? Though I am not overly superstitious, maybe there was something to the fact that my previous foray to the *Doria* had been my thirteenth dive on the wreck. Mark Haas, my buddy on that dive, had found a nice silver serving tray at a depth of 240 feet. Mark and I were both clearheaded as a result of the helium in the trimix we breathed, and we worked easily as a team, relaying the tray into my goodie bag, along with silverware both of us found. After we followed our guideline and exited the wreck, we began our decompression. When we reached the 15-foot stop, other divers saw the goodie bag and peered at its contents with curiosity. I was proud. We'd retrieved some truly distinctive booty this time. After hours of decompression, Mark and I followed the thick white rope that ran underwater from the anchor line toward the dive boat's stern, where its in-water oxygen lines with attached regulators (for the 20- and 10-foot stages of decompression) dangled in the water. I swam over the rope and got jostled by the waves and current. The bag's clip caught on the rope and snapped open, but somehow Mark snatched the bag before it could plummet even a few feet down. He clipped the bag back onto my harness and we both checked to make sure that it was secure. Ten minutes later, while I finished my decompression next to the boat's in-water oxygen line, I looked down and noticed that the bag was gone; the clip had come undone yet again and our prized artifacts were now nestled in the sand 240 feet below us.

"Where's your goodie bag?" Steve Berman asked when we finished our two-hour decompression and climbed back onto the boat. Everyone groaned when they heard the story. As Mark and I packed our gear away and prepared for the long trip back to port, several fellow expedition members came over to us in turn and offered us one of the artifacts that they had recovered. After the third diver had given Mark an artifact, he looked at me and joked, "I feel like we're the boat orphans!"

"Yeah," I agreed. "But it's a nice gesture. We'll have something to remember the trip by—even if we didn't recover it." Artifact fever could still run rampant among some divers, but the hoarding instinct had diminished since the days when divers would recover a hundred dishes and not give even one to somebody who had either not gotten anything, or who had lost his stuff.

Now, a year later, on my fourteenth dive to the *Doria,* I entered the wreck with Wolfgang, and I was again encountering equipment problems. This time it was a bit more serious than losing artifacts or wrestling with Wolfgang's leaking tanks as we'd done on the dive boat the day before. I could not feel the gas-switching block that I needed to turn to access the other half of my gas supply. One of my stage bottles hung in the way of the switch: Just before this expedition, I had discovered a leak when I tested the integrity of the unit in a water bucket, so I made some last-minute changes to the block and put one of the switches in a different position. Even when I tried to visualize where the switch should be as I swept my hand across my equipment, I could not feel it through the thick rubber mittens that prevented my hands from turning numb in the cold water. After several attempts, I turned to Wolfgang, who looked at me quizzically, and in the gestural language of divers worldwide I signaled him that the dive was over with a thumbs-up. If we had been wearing underwater communications equipment, I could have told him exactly what I needed. But the better part of a decade after the Rouse deaths, sport divers still eschewed communications gear, which most of us considered an extravagant encumbrance that might malfunction, and had several other drawbacks, including increased gas consumption when the diver talked, a limited distance the signals could travel, and helium-induced distortion of speech that caused it to be high-pitched. Because my full-face mask and gas-switching block were in no way standard among divers, I did not attempt to signal Wolfgang to try to switch on the other half of my gas supply. If Wolfgang turned the wrong switch, my gas supply would be completely cut off. Better to play it safe and abort the dive. I chafed at the decision, but I was too well acquainted with the consequences to choose otherwise. Although I would have liked to go inside the wreck and help Wolfgang get some artifacts, I could not risk both of our lives by continuing the dive with access to only half of my gas supply.

As we ascended, I repeatedly tried to turn on the gas switch. No luck. I switched over from my trimix to my air tank and checked the tank's pressure gauge. Something was wrong. Later, other divers would tell me that they had seen large volumes of gas being expelled from my full-face mask when I descended: I had some sort of a leak in my system. Now, I was very low on air. I would not have enough to complete my decompression stops, which started at 110 feet.

The thought of not completing my decompression brought back to mind Dr. Mendagurin's words after my nearly fatal encounter with the bends in 1991: "If you ever take another hit like this again, you'll never walk again. You've used up your extra neural pathways. You won't get another chance."

I switched back to my trimix, which under normal circumstances I would have breathed only on the wreck. Breathing trimix, with less than half my supply of gas accessible, I would have to extend my decompression time because my body was still absorbing lighter helium gas when it should have been eliminating helium with the aid of regular compressed air as my breathing gas. I watched my timer carefully and gradually made my way up to 70 feet, where I switched back to the air tank. When I started feeling more and more breathing resistance, I knew that I was getting to the end of my air supply. I had no choice but to go to another backup system, though I dreaded it.

To do that I would have to take off my full-face mask, which had two regulators built into it—one a lifesaving spare—and grab my extra free-hose regulator, a third unit that was attached to one of my back-mounted tanks. I would breathe from that unit while I reached into my goodie bag, took out my spare half-mask, which covered only the eyes and nose, and put that one on. When I took off the full-face mask, water would enter my specially made hood and work itself toward my ears. For most divers, that would not be a problem. But only a few years earlier I had suffered several concurrent ear infections that had eaten away 40 percent of my right eardrum; my elaborate equipment configuration, including an earplug, a special hood, and a full-face mask, was designed to prevent water from getting into that ear. Cold water entering my ear canal would give me vertigo, a spinning, disorienting sensation that might make me vomit. Still, I had no choice. I had to go to my second backup option.

I took my full-face mask off, consciously bracing for the cold water that would hit my face and repressing the reflex to breathe in through my nose. I grabbed regulator number three and put it in my mouth, breathing from it. But this regulator was attached to the almost-empty trimix tank. I hung on to the anchor line at 70 feet, bracing for the vertigo I knew was sure to hit me when the water entered my ear. What should I do next?

If I surfaced to get help, I could be crippled for the rest of my life, thanks to my 1991 bout with the bends. Surfacing was not an option. If I stayed on the anchor line, I would drown. I didn't like that option, either. Was Wolfgang above or below me? I couldn't see anything, now that I wore no mask. I could ascend, hope to run into Wolfgang or another diver, and see if he had gas to spare. If not, I could keep ascending and then go over to the boat's oxygen decompression line at 20 feet. That would mean omitting my decompression stops from 70 to 20 feet, but at least I would still be in the water, decompressing at 20 feet on pure oxygen. That wasn't optimal, but it probably wouldn't leave me crippled. I knew I had to do something quickly, before the cold water worked its way past my tight hood and then past the earplug. It became harder and harder to breathe from the regulator, which spurred me to start my ascent up the anchor line.

I saw the fuzzy outline of a diver above me. When I swam up to him, I saw that it was Wolfgang. I spit out my regulator and made a slashing motion with my hand across my throat: the diver's "I'm out of gas" sign. Everything was blurry without my mask on. I saw Wolfgang groping for a spare regulator at his chest, but I noticed a regulator at his shoulder, its pink protector hose beckoning me. Several men wore pink equipment; they would counter jokes about their color choice with the sharp retort that when somebody needed to see their equipment, the pink would stand out like a highway flare. I was now grateful that Wolfgang was undeterred by what others would think about his wearing pink, and that he had opted for safety rather than vanity.

I gently traced the regulator hose and discovered that it led to Wolfgang's back-mounted tanks. That meant the regulator was attached to a tank containing trimix, which was meant for use on the bottom, not for decompression. Although it was not the best choice, Wolfgang's trimix would keep me alive, and it would give me time to take the mask out of my goodie bag and put it on my face. Then I could see.

I urgently needed to breathe, so I grabbed Wolfgang's regulator with the pink hose protector and breathed from it. Then I got my spare mask out of my bag and put it on, clearing the water from it with exhalations from my nose. I checked my combination dive timer and depth gauge. We were at 50 feet. Wolfgang signaled that he wanted to ascend to the next decompression stop. I agreed. When we got to the 40-foot stop, everything started spinning. I held on to Wolfgang's shoulder strap so that I would not float away from him and his life-giving gas. The world around me was spinning faster and faster, and all I could do was hope that my body would quickly warm the water in my inner ear so that the spinning would stop. Gradually, the spinning slowed down, as if I were at the end of a carnival ride. Then the spinning stopped completely, and I was 40 feet below the surface, breathing, alive.

Wolfgang clipped his small oxygen decompression tank onto my harness. I gratefully accepted the oxygen and breathed from it, hoping that it would speed up my decompression enough so that the excess helium in my body did not form bubbles and bend me when I surfaced. I signaled that I was not going to continue my 40-foot decompression stop: Breathing more of Wolfgang's bottom mix, which I knew contained only 17 percent oxygen and about 35 percent helium, would not help my body decompress. I did not want to remain on oxygen at 40 feet and risk drowning from an oxygen-induced seizure. Into my head swam the dead face of the Rouses' friend Ed Sollner, who, shunning the U.S. Navy recommendations, had breathed a high-oxygen-content gas at too great a depth, had had a seizure, and had died. Breathing from Wolfgang's oxygen tank, I swam to the dive boat's in-water oxygen station and switched to the boat's oxygen. I would save the oxygen in Wolfgang's tank to breathe while swimming back to the boat's ladder. For now, breathing from the dive boat's plentiful oxygen supply, I would stay here and decompress as long as I could.

When Wolfgang finished his decompression, he swam over to me and asked in gestures if I felt okay. He put his hand to his chest and then pointed toward the glinting light above us. Was I willing to let him ascend? I signaled "OK." Wolfgang swam away and disappeared into the clouds of sunlight above. Soon a set of double tanks filled with air dropped down to me on a rope and hit my back-mounted tanks. Apparently, the guys above wanted to make sure that I got the message that they wanted me to breathe from the tanks they lowered. I breathed from the tanks periodically because air breaks were necessary to prevent the oxygen from building to a toxic level in my body.

My planned decompression schedule had long since been invalidated by my use of unplanned gas mixtures, including bottom mix at all of my stops from 70 feet to 40 feet: I'd also broken my 40- and 30-foot stops when I went straight to the pure oxygen at 20 feet. Other divers sometimes ran into problems requiring unplanned and unorthodox gas switches. When that happened the diver had to resort to what Steve Berman and John Reekie jokingly referred to as the "modified Yugoslavian method," which meant basically that you assembled your own order out of chaos. You did what you intuitively felt was the right amount of decompression at a particular stop, then ascended to the next stop; if you felt any pain develop, you went down one or two stops and spent more time decompressing there before moving up again. As I inventoried my body, I did not feel the pain I had felt so many years ago when I had gotten horrifically bent. After several hours of decompression, I ascended and climbed into the dive boat. My friends' worried faces broke into tentative smiles. I was relieved when bends symptoms did not appear.

When I returned home and crawled into bed at three in the morning, my wife sleepily told me that she'd heard that evening that Tony Smith, a friend of mine, had died diving while I was away on the *Doria*. He was diving in the warm, clear water of North Carolina, his intended destination a wreck at 130 feet. It was an easy dive for the experienced diver and New York dive-boat crew member, who had just returned from the Truk Island lagoon in the Pacific, the Mecca of wreck diving. His self-confidence combined forces with his urge to get into the water and start exploring for artifacts, and he forgot to turn on any of the three tanks he carried. He also neglected to make any of several pre-dive checks that would have alerted him to his imminent danger, and he failed to reconfigure his belt to carry less weight than he had to use in cold New York waters. When he jumped in, he plummeted to the bottom, was unable to breathe from his regulators, and drowned.

As exhausted and drained as I was, I didn't sleep much that night—or the next night either, for that matter. I kept imagining my friend's fatal accident and reliving my own uncertain breaths during my *Doria* ascent. My problems had been the direct result of changing my equipment configuration and not testing it in a shallow, safer environment like a quarry before venturing into deep water. I realized that work commitments now distracted me from fully preparing for dives like the *Doria*. What if I had died instead of being able to manage the situation as I had? Where would my family have been then? Gil was almost eleven now and entering a period in his life when having a father around was more important than ever. My death would be a blow to him that he would perceive on some level as abandonment. My own plans for my career and my family's security were entering a period of great promise and challenge. With so many obligations to people I loved, did I have the right to risk my life and livelihood by diving? As the sun came up that morning, I said goodbye to the *Doria* and to any kind of diving. I resolved I would not venture into the deep until I'd safeguarded my family's well-being.

The Rouses had been extremely active during a time of tremendous change and controversy in sport diving. In spite of their deaths, sport diving continued on its path toward what some considered radical, even dangerous, change. The use of mixed gases, penetrations into shipwrecks and caves, and the general employment of technology as a tool for sport divers to overcome the limitations and dangers of the deep now had a new name, technical diving, a term generally credited to Michael Menduno in 1991. Even though his magazine, *AquaCorps*, appeared only sporadically for a few years after the Rouses' deaths, it remained an important voice for divers who engaged in what recreational divers—those who stayed shallower than 130 feet and did not conduct decompression dives or penetrate into wrecks or caves—considered lunatic diving.

Recreational divers cited the deaths of the Rouses and of their friend Ed Sollner as examples of just how fatally foolhardy technical diving was. Despite protests from divers and diving organizations and even the soul-searching of technical divers themselves, the new techniques grew into the standard for an established sport, its risks matched by its rewards. A combination of *AquaCorps*'s macho "You're not a real diver unless you're diving deep and on mixed gas" attitude and divers' craving for more adventure has led to revolutionary changes. "Technical diving is being driven by the consumer, not the big training agencies who want to dictate what type of diving you can do and how that diving is done," Menduno has said. "It's the same as the personal computer revolution, which was fueled on a grassroots level."

The diver-inspired movement toward technical diving was helped along by both *AquaCorps* and two new organizations created to certify divers in the use of mixed gases. But at the time of the Rouses' deaths in late 1992, these organizations were still minuscule compared to the established diving-training agencies that had branches worldwide; many people in the diving business world did not recognize the new, small organizations, nor their certifications. They argued that sport divers could not successfully use mixed gases because the process was too complex: Special equipment was required to mix the gases safely and had to be specially cleaned periodically to prevent a fire or explosion, and the gases had to be analyzed after they were mixed. All this demanded too much planning and precision of execution for the average diver, or so the argument went. But the naysayers underestimated the kind of single-minded commitment that the heirs of Chris and Chrissy Rouse would bring to the urge to go ever deeper.

Ultimately, economics would play the driving role in altering the dynamics of the endeavor as it had throughout diving history, when men risked life itself—ignoring those who said that the underwater environment was a forbidden realm—in order to salvage treasure lost beneath the waves. In its winter 1991 issue *AquaCorps* published simple but persuasive pie charts showing the results of its own study on the huge amount of money technical divers spent on training, equipment, and travel compared to recreational divers. According to *Aqua-Corps*, the technical divers shelling out the cash required to get trained, go diving, and keep diving were the economic mainstay of the diving industry: Although technical divers made up only 8 to 10 percent of all the active amateur divers, their annual spending accounted for a third of the market, and their equipment investment accounted for over 40 percent of the money divers spent on gear.

In spite of the admonishments of large training organizations against sport divers' using mixed gases, many dive-shop owners and instructors did not want to be left out of the boom; they invested in training in mixed-gas diving to get themselves educated in mixing gases, and bought the very expensive equipment needed to safely concoct and analyze the gas. All this helped further fuel the expansion of technical diving. It was now possible to go into many dive shops, show proof of mixed-gas training, drop off your empty scuba tanks, and announce what percentages of gases you wanted in your refills. Trusting your dive shop to do the job was far easier than having to mix your own gases from large supply cylinders that you rented from a commercial gas supply company and stored in your garage, workshop, or apartment living room, the way Chris and Chrissy had done when they had the money.

Dive boats now started catering to technical divers, though some boats, like the *Seeker* and the *Wahoo,* had welcomed them even before the new practices became popular. Now, if you walked onto the average dive boat with a decompression tank clearly labeled OXYGEN, you would not be thrown off the boat, and old-timers would not mutter that you were an accident waiting to happen. At the same time that adventure travelers were lining up to climb Mount Everest, legions of divers were plunging into the water, their exotic gases opening up underwater expanses for more and more explorers. All it took was money, motivation, and a sense of mission.

As more and more divers turned to mixed-gas diving, the traditional training organizations grew alarmed at the loss in potential revenue. In 1995, the world's largest recreational diving training organization, the California-based Professional Association of Diving Instructors (PADI), and also Great Britain's largest certifying organization, the British Sub-Aqua Club, known as BS-AC, announced that they would be offering courses in the use of the oxygen-enriched-air mixes called nitrox, which limited divers to a depth of 130 feet. In ensuing years, every recreational diving training agency in the world did likewise. Smaller organizations that trained divers in the use of trimix gases containing helium for diving well beyond 130 feet gained the credibility and respectability previously denied them.

Divers went deeper and deeper. Sites once thought inaccessible were now viewed as realistic conquests. When the *Andrea Doria* came to rest at 240 feet below the sea's surface in 1956, it represented the very extent of where sport divers could safely venture. Over nearly forty years, some divers like Sheck Exley would dive much deeper than 240 feet, but only to test how far a diver could go and make it back in one piece. Bill Stone's 1987 Wakulla Springs cave-diving expedition proved that sport divers could use mixed gases to accomplish things underwater, as they mapped extensive tunnels at 360 feet. To organizations like BS-AC and PADI, however, this expedition was an aberration, because the average diver had nowhere near the level of skill and experience of Stone and his crew. In 1991, Team Doria showed how cave-diving techniques and equipment could be applied to the wildly changing conditions of open-ocean wreck diving. Over the next several years, cave-diving equipment configuration became de rigueur for technical divers. Divers exploring deep wrecks would clip extra tanks to their harnesses just as the cave-diving pioneers had a decade before.

In 1994, John Chatterton, John Yurga, Barb Lander, and Gary Gentile made up the American contingent of divers invited on the British diver Polly Tapson's expedition to the *Lusitania,* the Cunard liner that had fallen victim to an infamous World War I U-boat attack and was resting in 325 feet of water off southern Ireland. It was the first sport-diving expedition to the wreck—an expedition made possible by the use of mixed-gas diving and its availability to sport divers. It was a controversial and pioneering trip that Chris Rouse and his son would have second-mortgaged their house to go on—they would even have sprung for the trimix required.

Amid legal controversy over who owned the *Lusitania,* and whether diving on it could be restricted, Tapson went ahead with her expedition, ignoring a lawsuit threatened by Greg Bemis, an American who claimed ownership of the wreck. The expedition was a success as the team probed the deep wreck and established that a large team of sport divers could safely dive to over 300 feet in the open ocean. None of the divers were injured in spite of often-challenging sea conditions. The achievement was all the more remarkable because Tapson herself had been badly bent only one week beforehand. Doctors warned her against diving, especially so soon after her accident, but she dived to the wreck anyway. When Menduno interviewed Tapson for *AquaCorps,* she didn't want to discuss her decision. "I don't want to . . . be an example of someone who acted irresponsibly and got away with it. And then have someone else do the same thing who subsequently ends up in a wheelchair for life." Psychotherapists like Dr. Jennifer Hunt, who has written a psychological and sociological study of bent divers and who has interviewed me extensively, called Tapson's behavior an example of risk denial: Tapson was so focused on diving during the historic sport-diving expedition she had worked so hard to organize that she denied the very real possibility that she could be permanently crippled by another bout of the bends. Tapson herself felt good enough to dive and did so without incident. Her problem-free plunge into the cold North Atlantic indicates how little we really know about the bends and the effects of water pressure on the human body.

The long-term effects of deep diving remain mysterious. Divers like me, who can hear through at least one ear and have blazed new neural pathways, continue to be informal test subjects in the study of adventure physiology. People like Emmerman and Huggins—the seasick researchers who participated in the Team Doria '91 expedition to try to measure the degree of decompression stress on divers' bodies—still lack conclusive data about what deep diving does to us across the decades. But some of the divers who had been at the sport for a long time found themselves suffering strange, unexplained maladies that might or might not be related to diving. A commercial diver like Glenn Butler, who had been exposed in a hyperbaric chamber to experimental dives down to 1,000 feet and who had worked for long time periods in the ocean at depths down to 700 feet, could be expected to exhibit some sort of long-term physical effects. Butler did develop brain lesions from deep diving, and one of them may have contributed to his aneurysm in 1992. His later neurological problems were unanticipated when he was engaged in the deep-diving experiments and in his work. Ocean Systems' Dr. Bill Hamilton, the man Butler worked for in the beginning of his diving career, says an aneurysm completely explains Butler's condition. Hamilton maintains that making any connection between that condition and diving is unfair to both Butler and diving. Although commercial divers could reasonably be expected to have some sort of residual effects from diving, it was not expected that sport divers could also exhibit severe impairment. Chris Rouse conducted 771 dives and Chrissy 636 in four years, but compared to pros like Butler, sport divers like them were landlubbers.

Evie Dudas—who in 1967 was the first woman to dive the *Andrea Doria*, got severely bent in 1968, and participated in John Reekie's 1992 *Empress of Ireland* expedition with the Rouses—is one of those divers whose physical maladies baffle doctors. Problems with her inner ears and neurological damage cause her balance to be impaired for weeks at a time, a syndrome she experiences every three or four years, despite every precaution she takes, short of not diving at all. She suffers from "skin bends"—decompression sickness symptoms that affect the skin, such as rashes, itchiness, tingling, and numbness—if she does not use high-oxygen-content gases or pure oxygen to decompress after every dive, regardless of whether or not her dive schedules call for decompression stops. And even when she does take precautions, she still occasionally suffers skin bends. All of this has placed an almost continuous decompression stress on her body, which perhaps is the cause of her numerous bone problems, including severe ankle maladies that led doctors to recommend fusing her ankle to her leg bone. She refused that treatment because it would have hampered her ability to swim underwater. As a result of the bends, Evie has no feeling down the right side of her body. Her maladies are permanent, and doctors can offer no cure.

She continues to dive. Her West Chester, Pennsylvania, dive shop, Dudas' Diving Duds, and her diving-suit manufacturing business are both flourishing. The dive club she started in affiliation with her dive shop is also thriving as people are drawn to the underwater world by Evie's charisma and youthful enthusiasm for diving. All of her children, now grown to adulthood, not only dive but earn at least part of their family income through diving-related businesses, through their own or their spouses' work. Her life is diving. If you asked her, she would tell you she will dive until she can no longer swim or breathe.

Like Evie Dudas, I had also suffered severe neurological decompression sickness and also experienced strange physical syndromes. After my training-wheels return to diving in 1992, nine months after my accident, my recovery progressed as Dr. Mendagurin said it should, so that I could walk normally again. I even went back to deep decompression diving, venturing to depths greater than 300 feet. But over the next several years I experienced drastic mood swings and a decline in mental capacity: I had trouble remembering things. My concentration fragmented. Even forming sentences became difficult, as I grasped at words that were somehow unavailable. Talking to Gil, now starting elementary school, I would struggle to explain the answers to his questions about science and the world, even though I knew the answers. And physically, I became tired quickly. I remained in touch with Dr. Hunt, and during conversations I simply could not remember details about diving that I knew very well; at one point, she remarked sadly, "Bernie, you used to have an acute memory."

I felt that I had somehow become very, very old, very quickly. Would my mind continue to fray so that I would be left slurring, groping for words, like Glenn Butler? Or perhaps I would be left both mentally and physically impaired, my arms trembling, maybe unable to properly grasp things with my hands, like my childhood hero, Muhammad Ali? Had Evie Dudas, Glenn Butler, and I—like Ali—taken too many hits and been left permanently damaged?

Unwilling to give up the sport, I continued diving. Although Diana knew that my diving might lead to my being crippled or killed, she saw how much I loved the underwater world and the calming effect it had on me and she did not protest my continued involvement in the sport.

Just as diving had given me experiences that are precious and enlivening, so has my recovery from the major symptoms of decompression sickness given me a renewed commitment to my own aliveness. When Dr. Hunt and I celebrated over dinner our fiftieth and fortieth birthdays, respectively, we both assessed our lives at our milestones. When she lamented getting old, I told her that when you have faced the very real possibility of not getting old, you welcome aging. Each day I'm thankful for another chance to experience life, my family, and the occasional foray into deep water.

John Reekie, the Canadian diver who participated in Team Doria '91, also experiences continuing medical problems that may be related to diving. In 1993, Reekie dived with John Moyer's ambitious expedition to recover priceless art panels from the *Andrea Doria* and the ship's second bell. When the team brought up intact two 1,000-pound art panels by Guido Gambone, their success drew international media attention. The *Doria*'s second bell remained elusive.

During Moyer's expedition, Reekie had been assigned to look for the bell in an old paint locker. He conducted several dives where he worked inside the paint locker with an underwater vacuum cleaner called an airlift that sucks up mud and silt to dig around and find the bell. Reekie repeatedly swam through the opening at 220 feet and then into the locker at 210 feet and buried himself headfirst and waist-deep in the paint locker's silt as he groped for the bell. Almost immediately, he was struck with anguishing headaches, which he thought would go away once he withdrew from the compartment. Instead, they only got worse when he ascended. Reekie theorized that his body had absorbed the highly toxic lead-based paint residue and paint thinner buried in the silt. He continues to suffer various medical problems, including lung and skin maladies, that he attributes to this particular expedition.

Moyer disputes the idea that the *Doria* dives in the paint locker caused Reekie's woes. Some divers say that Reekie's problems are the result of being an overweight chain-smoker. His health issues are probably precipitated by some combination of his weight problem, his smoking habits, and his diving experiences: Not only was Reekie immersed in toxic chemicals during Moyer's *Doria* expedition, but during his diving career he also repeatedly exposed his body to extreme stress during dives that required many hours of decompression.

Of course, the physical problems that Evie Dudas, Glenn Butler, John Reekie, and I face might have been caused solely by some other medical problem, or they might be a combination of other medical problems and damage from the bends. In spite of myriad medical advances, doctors can never know for certain, which frustrates them.

Divers had complex perceptions of the medical doctors who treated them when they got bent, as Dr. Hunt noted in her psychological and sociological study of bent divers. According to Dr. Hunt, divers, doctors, paramedics, and nurses categorized people into those whose hits were "deserved"—for example, a diver who had done something stupid like omitting two hours of decompression—and those whose hits were "undeserved"—such as a diver who dived by the book but still got bent. Just as I had detected something like contempt from the doctor who first treated me in the recompression chamber, other divers had experienced medical personnel's disdain for someone whose symptoms meant that fate had done justice. Dr. Hunt theorized that the categorizing of divers into those with deserved and undeserved hits allowed medical personnel a clear conscience if they could not successfully treat a bent diver or if the diver suffered residual damage.

To complicate matters, however, not all medical personnel exhibited disdain when bent divers were brought in for treatment. Personnel who treated the Rouses grasped the tragedy of the situation immediately when they were confronted with a dead man and his son who was still trying to beat the odds and live. Had they not been compassionate, they would have likely told Chrissy that his father was dead when Chrissy seemed to be recovering during his treatment and asked about his father. Someone like Glenn Butler, who treated Chrissy in the chamber, could empathize with Chrissy because Glenn had been a diver and had been bent. To this day, Glenn is clearly bothered at not having been able to save Chrissy, even though the veteran diver and hyperbaric specialist knows that it was virtually impossible to save the young man's life under the circumstances. Doctors and other medical personnel are subject to the same range of human emotions as the rest of us; sometimes they can be overwhelmed with a bad bends case, and at other times the potential tragedy of the situation grips them as they strive to wear an unemotional mask and go about their job "professionally."

Other divers placed distance between themselves and someone who suffered a "deserved" hit. If the diver had done something stupid that you felt you would never do, then you could separate yourself from his foolhardy mistakes—and so believe that you'd never get the bends yourself. Dr. Hunt found much more empathy for a diver who had suffered an "undeserved" hit because others knew that they too could do everything correctly and still fall victim to a cruel cave or a capricious sea.

Dr. Hunt's 1993 *AquaCorps* article, "Straightening Out the Bends: Ongoing Research on the Social Reaction and Stigma Surrounding Decompression Illness," was met with disbelief and even anger by the diving medical community. It appeared just pages from the report of my bout with the bends and a detailed account of the Rouses' fatal dive. Soon, however, the Divers Alert Network (DAN), a large, prestigious nonprofit organization dedicated to diving research and the medical treatment of bent amateur divers, based at Duke University in North Carolina, went on to publish in its journal, *Alert Diver,* another article by Dr. Hunt about the bends and the stigma surrounding it. Other magazines followed suit. Therapists, sociologists, psychologists, diving researchers, and others started giving presentations at diving conferences about various aspects of psychology as it related to diving. Menduno, *AquaCorps,* and Dr. Hunt had initiated a vital dialogue meant to encourage divers to pursue their underwater quests safely and *consciously.* With a greater awareness of what it was in their psyches and histories that spurred them to dive, they could assess risk wisely and better correlate their challenges and their skills and avoid unnecessary risks. For example, reenacting unresolved relationship conflicts with a dive buddy might lead to taking unnecessary risks that in turn resulted in a diver's getting bent. Being aware, divers could make more conscious decisions. And they would have the insight to refrain from stigmatizing someone who had been bent.

By the mid-1990s Dr. Hunt was receiving letters of thanks from divers around the world. Her articles had helped them come to terms with their own case of the bends, or avoid getting bent in the first place by leading them to examine their own psychic conflicts and motivations. Dr. Peter Bennett, the head of DAN, sent Dr. Hunt a glowing letter heralding the importance of her work to both the diving and the medical communities. Though Dr. Hunt's study has concluded and she has moved on to other interests, her work has had a great impact on many divers, who have reexamined their diving habits, and on medical personnel, who are now more sensitive to the issues a bent diver faces. Every diver benefits when all of us know not just how we dive but why.

The advances in technical diving now could be matched by progress in understanding the psychosocial motives of men and women who employ those technical advances and risk their lives to plunge deeper and deeper. Chris and Chrissy Rouse did not survive long enough to take advantage of the science and psychology that might have kept them alive. Yet both men were headstrong, and so possibly neither would ever have stopped to examine the reasons he sacrificed so much to explore caves, the sea, and shipwrecks. And certainly today, many divers are so consumed with lust for adventure that they do not heed reason. Yet Dr. Hunt and her colleagues have saved lives.

If Chris and Chrissy Rouse were today to break the ocean surface bent, it is possible that they could be treated instantly with recompression. But it is not certain. Today's technical dive teams have available to them portable recompression chambers, which did not exist in 1992. Yet sport-diving boats, including those that cater to technical divers, do not usually carry these devices. The reason is economic: The portable chambers are expensive, costing roughly thirty thousand to fifty thousand dollars, depending on the features and the pressure capability. Weighed against this expense is their ability to recompress a bent diver immediately, usually to a depth equivalent of 33 feet or 66 feet, one or two additional atmospheres of pressure, and keep the diver under pressure while he or she is transported to a bigger recompression facility, which can put the victim under greater pressure, and further reduce the bubbles of inert gas that devastate the diver's body. With the increased use of helium mixes, which are much lighter than the nitrogen in compressed air, a diver experiencing the bends from omitted deep stops will start to bubble very quickly, leaving precious little time to begin treatment that could save the diver's life, or reduce the long-term damage to the body.

Thus far, most sport-diving operations have shunned tools like portable recompression chambers, claiming that they are too expensive. Even equipment that is less expensive than a portable chamber, but still capable of providing added safety, underwater communications equipment, is seen by the majority of sport divers as imposing too great an expense burden while adding another item of gear that could malfunction. There is some merit to this argument. Yet underwater communications equipment would allow a problem to be reported while divers are still underwater, where they can be assisted by other divers before matters get to the point where they have to rely on luck to survive. The technical issues involved with using underwater communications equipment while breathing helium gases, which distorts the voice, do pose a problem for sport divers who wish to use as their medium radio signals, instead of cables connected to each other. These issues, like any other in the history of diving, are not beyond resolution, however.

Like many people who engage in high-risk activities, divers like to deny or downplay the risks they face. Most divers say that they do not need expensive equipment like underwater communications gear and portable recompression chambers because they will not make mistakes, and nothing will happen to them. But diving is a sport where people rely on life-support equipment to go into an alien environment. Things can and do go wrong. As Dr. Bill Hamilton says, "The best way to treat an accident is to be prepared for it, to have the training, the equipment, and the personnel on hand to deal with it." Hamilton likes to remind divers that the bends itself is not an accident—it is a statistically predictable event, one that will occur in a certain percentage of dives, regardless of how good a diver is or what precautions are taken. His philosophy is summed up by the words on the button he wears at diving conferences: SHIT HAPPENS.

Technical divers know and accept the risks of diving without a chamber on site, but they usually do so while denying they can have an accident in the first place. I denied the possibility and I'm sure Chris and Chrissy did, even after we had discussed my accident so many times. Ironically, the more experience a diver has, the greater he thinks his immunity to an accident—because it happened to someone else, not him: Complacency leads divers to take ever greater risks. Without a recompression chamber at the dive site, divers like Chris and Chrissy Rouse will keep dying, while some divers like me and Evie Dudas will get lucky and survive to dive another day. And without underwater communications gear, divers will continue to die every year because they cannot communicate with each other or, like the Rouses, cannot ask for help from the surface. In spite of all the human-engineered gear required to go more than 10 feet under and stay there for any appreciable time, divers implicitly view voice communications as unsporting, as if by talking they would somehow cheat the silence of the deep. Without these tools, divers are lone wolves; if they run into trouble underwater, there are many things that will readily claim them, and then only luck will be able to rescue them. It seems that people who pride themselves on their technological prowess and physical skills should not have to rely on chance. Divers can greatly increase the odds of surviving an accident by using all of the available technology, not just some of it.

Diving does not occur in a cultural vacuum. Risk taking in itself has become a hallmark of our society: Many of us take extreme risks in our sports, in our financial endeavors, our sex lives. It is as if we cannot get enough of the thrill of living, and must enhance the thrill by the risks we experience like an elixir. And in spite of the dangers of diving and the means to avert its perils, many divers seek extreme risks underwater, and some even do so on the surface as well.

Bill Nagel, the owner of the *Seeker,* the dive boat from which the Rouses conducted their last dive, was by all accounts an excellent deep-wreck diver and a valuable teacher of other accomplished divers, like John Chatterton. Nagel dived deep and often, exhibiting what some would call a passion for the sport but others would call compulsive behavior. He also exhibited extreme compulsion on land, where he frequently consumed alcohol in great quantity. In 1994, after repeatedly being hospitalized for alcohol-related illness and ultimately being warned that he would die if he ever drank again, Nagel literally drowned in his own blood after drinking hard liquor, which caused a blood vessel in his throat to split open. "Bill Nagel helped discover the *U-Who* and he never got to dive it because of his alcohol-related health problems," John Chatterton says now. "Bill was my mentor in diving—almost like a father to me—and I hoped that the discovery of the U-boat would motivate him to overcome his personal demons and get better. But the alcohol was too powerful a force for Bill, and in the end, I think he was frustrated that he could not overcome it."

Sheck Exley—the Michael Jordan of cave diving, the diver whom Chrissy Rouse admired so much—persisted in his attempt to dive to a depth of 1,000 feet using standard scuba equipment and also numerous breathing-gas mixtures. In 1994, at a depth of 906 feet in Mante, a Mexican cave where he had previously set the world record for deep scuba diving at 867 feet, he died. Exley's body was recovered only because he had wrapped himself in the heavy plumb line that served as his guide to the bottom. Presumably to make sure his body could be retrieved, Exley bound the line around his body after he realized he had miscalculated the dive and did not have enough gas to ascend.

The Briton Rob Palmer was another diver whose work enthralled and motivated many divers, including the Rouses and me. His *Deep into Blue Holes* described his explorations of Bahamian caves, including the discovery of life forms scientists thought to be extinct. He dived in the Red Sea repeatedly to over 400 feet in depth while breathing compressed air, a practice he had publicly recommended against. He knew he was playing Russian roulette. Palmer was last seen descending past 400 feet in the Red Sea. His body was never recovered.

Palmer's death shocked many people. The British diver exhibited a gentleman's grace and charm and was extremely well liked in addition to being widely respected for the many television documentaries, books, and articles he produced. Yet his wife, the diver and macrobiologist Dr. Stephanie Schwabe, was not surprised he died diving. "I fell in love with Rob and married him even though I knew I would never spend the rest of my life with him," she told me. "I knew that he took too many risks and that he would die underwater. The odd thing was that because so many things had happened to Rob underwater and he had survived them all, he thought he was immune to death in the water." Dr. Schwabe readily admits she was smitten by Palmer's boyish charm. "I decided I was going to enjoy whatever time we would have together," she said simply, fatalistically.

Perhaps the most startling behavior was exhibited by Marc Eyring, the tall, rugged, and extremely intelligent former Green Beret who had been Steve Berman's cave-diving coach, as well as the diving instructor of Chris Rouse, Chrissy, Sue, and me. Like Nagel, Eyring often dived deep between bouts of hard drinking. After the Rouses' deaths Eyring had gotten married and moved to the North and seemed to have dropped completely out of touch with the diving community. After some years of mysterious silence, Berman received a letter from Eyring, who explained that he had gotten divorced, had a sex-change operation, and now went by the name Karen.

For years Berman could not talk to anyone about Eyring's revelation. As he recently explained to me, "He had been my mentor, the guy I looked up to like a cave-diving god. I mean, he was *perfect* in the water, and such a *dedicated* instructor. I wanted to be just like him." He chuckled grimly. "At first, I wished that Marc had died instead of doing what he did. Gradually, I realized that my thinking was selfish. If changing into a woman fulfills Marc, then that's his choice. It's just hard for me to accept, and I hope that . . . she . . . finally feels happiness."

I contacted Karen to interview her for this book. Over the phone, I could hear the same intense person I had always known, the voice more sinuous maybe, but the urgency as evident as ever. She came to visit me at my home. Although I had braced myself, I was still a bit shocked to see my friend in blue jeans, a woman's blouse—which her operation and hormonal supplements allowed her to fill out generously—and hair that now flowed past her shoulders. Her subtle makeup softened but did not disguise the masculine face I remembered from almost a decade earlier. Karen had achieved success in the commercial banking world, and made money with her personal investments. She finished her Ph.D. and then went on to start her own company designing and building a new type of magnetic resonance imaging machine incorporating technology that she herself had pioneered. As we strolled on my property, Karen remarked, "Bernie, I don't know if I'll ever be happy. I just pour myself into my work. I think that my intellectual ability and knowledge are just starting to come together. There's so much I want to do in the world of technology and so many exciting possibilities. I've accepted that I'm brilliant and I'm different. Maybe that's the best I can hope for." But why would Marc change into Karen? "I realized that all of my extreme behavior was just a way to overcome my feelings and desires to be a woman," she explained.

Do these examples of divers' extreme, life-changing, and sometimes life-taking behaviors mean that all risk takers are compensating for something, perhaps some loss, or some unfulfilled desire? For those divers who are dead, we cannot know for sure. In my own case, the journey of examining my motivations that I had begun with Dr. Hunt after my 1991 accident led me to conclude that my extreme diving was all the more enjoyable because it led to both recognition and a sense of belonging to a community, both of which I lacked as a child. My father's constant criticisms, like Chris's behavior toward Chrissy, spurred me to seek positive reinforcement from my activities. The tightly knit community of technical divers gave me something that I had never had as a youth moving from one country to another. Identifying with a particular diving community—whether recreational or technical—and internalizing that community's standard of behavior is a phenomenon that Dr. Hunt found strongest in the divers who dived most frequently and who were most active with things like diving clubs and organizations; their identities as people were closely connected to their status among their fellow adventurers.

For all the camaraderie they created and all the risks they took, Chris and Chrissy Rouse were among those intrepid divers whose explorations met with mixed success. They did not discover new forms of life, as they had hoped they might in Pennsylvania's Lahaska Cave, or elsewhere. They did not set remarkable records the way Sheck Exley did in cave diving. Nor did they uncover the mystery of the *U-Who*, although they died trying. They did, however, successfully recover artifacts and lobsters and also experimented with new ways of conducting sport dives and participated in a dramatic change in sport diving. Their gruesome deaths have ironically brought them the fame they sought through their triumphs.

Although the Rouses' deaths saddened him, Steve Berman has continued to dive. He still regularly leads diving expeditions to Mexico's spectacular warm-water caves and teaches cave diving and mixed-gas diving to the legions of enthusiasts drawn to his vigor, smarts, and experience. He has now accumulated over forty dives on the *Andrea Doria* and has recovered hundreds if not thousands of artifacts from the luxury liner. Yet amid his trophy collecting he too encountered trauma.

On one dive, Berman recovered the body of a diver untrained in mixed-gas diving who had used his 50 percent helium mix not only to breathe from but also to inflate his drysuit, which may have made him hypothermic in the 42-degree water. Or he may have been unaware that he was breathing the lightweight gas far more rapidly than he would have used up heavier compressed air. Berman found him lifeless in the bottom of a cargo hold, his tanks empty, yet another victim of an ocean liner that after nearly half a century still claims the careless and unwary.

On another dive inside the *Doria*, Berman was diving alone when he saw massive clouds of silt billowing from a hole leading into a notoriously obstructed area. Berman could hear a diver screaming through the silt, and he heard banging on the walls. He had to make a choice about whether to plunge into the silt to try to save the diver. As in the dive where Chrissy Rouse had saved the diver who was low on air and confused at 170 feet outside of the shipwreck, Berman was not personally acquainted with the other diver. But he knew from the banging and screaming that the other man was already in the throes of panic.

Trying to save the diver was simply too risky, he realized. Had

Berman gone inside, blinded by the silt, he was sure to be entangled in the flailing arms and gear of a diver too panicked to let himself be rescued, and there would most likely have been two fatalities instead of just one. Steve's friends and loved ones console him as best they can; he made a wise and inevitable choice, they tell him. The man could not be helped. Berman is still haunted by the man's screams. He still wonders if he made the right choice in not risking his own life to try to save the other man. His recriminations bring to mind the Frenchman who watched unmoving as a man committed suicide by throwing himself into the Seine. Years later, haunted by the image of the drowning man, the Frenchman said, "Oh, God, please let that man throw himself into the water again so that I may save myself!" Ultimately, Berman knows that realistically there was nothing he could have done, though that does not appreciably lessen his anguish.

Berman had another force pulling him away from the silted-out *Doria* chamber that day: his family. Unlike many other divers, whose allegiance leans more to the deep than the domestic, Steve Berman has a close relationship with his wife, Anita, and the two children from her previous marriage who live with them. If he takes unnecessary risk and dies, his wife and family are left without their husband and stepfather; that is a consideration he did not have to take into account during the many years of his diving career when he was single, when it was mostly only his colleagues who cared whether he survived to reach the surface.

Berman nonetheless dived deep to the ocean liner *Britannic,* one of the *Titanic*'s two sister ships. During World War II, the *Britannic* had been converted by the British for use as a hospital. It was painted white and had a red cross painted on it signifying that it was a nonmilitary vessel. When the *Britannic* sank off the Greek island of Kea in 1942, with the loss of twenty-one lives, many thought the Germans had torpedoed it, and others now think that it might have hit a mine. The British diver Kevin Gurr organized the first sport-diving expedition to the *Britannic* in 1997 and set out to find out what caused the sinking. Although the *Britannic* rests in clear, warm water, the 380-foot depth of the wreck both makes it challenging and gives precious little time for divers to solve the mystery.

Berman participated in the third expedition to the wreck, an expedition that was also unable to locate the wounds in the ship that would determine what sent it to the bottom. Fortunately he survived that challenge of the deep.

When he's not diving or parenting his stepchildren, Berman still actively teaches sport diving at its highest level, both full-cave and mixed-gas classes. He's been at it for twelve years now, and he's seen a lot of changes in his students. "We're now seeing a much better, more dedicated, better-trained diver who comes to us for full cave training than we saw ten years ago," he tells me. "Before, you had a lot of people coming to Ginnie Springs and they'd maybe take the cavern-diving course out of curiosity. Most of those people never went anywhere near the cave course, which is probably good anyway, because they just didn't have the right mind-set for cave diving. Now, when somebody comes down here, most of the time they already know what cave diving is about from the information that's out there. They know that they want to become full cave divers and that it's going to take training, practice, and dedication to get the skills and experience they need to survive, and to have fun in the sport." Berman is quick to point out that he avoids teaching anything but the most advanced sport-diving classes. For that reason, Steve's clientele are mostly referred by others he has trained.

Many of Berman's students today remind him of the dedication of his friends Chris and Chrissy Rouse, divers who understood that they needed to dive a lot to be good and who were willing to take their time in developing their skills. At least once a month, however, Berman sees other divers who stand in stark contrast to the Rouses. These other divers are overeager to move quickly through the ranks; they buy all the best gear immediately, and then they attempt to do dives that are beyond their skills and experience. "People who are in too much of a rush and who push it too far, too soon, run into trouble," Berman observes. "The lucky ones see the flowing robes of Jesus down there, survive a very close call, and then when they get out of the water, the first thing they do is sell all of their gear and give up diving."

Close calls can happen in any environment. As the *Wahoo*'s owner, Steve Bielenda, often says to divers on his boat, to his students, and to his audiences at presentations during diving conferences, "Experience is something you accumulate over time. You've got to pay your dues and do lots of dives. Then, when you're doing something under-water and you run into trouble, you have some insurance to fall back on to get yourself out of a situation. If you're doing anything at all underwater, something *will* happen and you *will* need that experience to get out of a close call."

What Berman and Bielenda do not say publicly is that even if he builds experience slowly, a succession of things can still happen to over-whelm the diver, and tragedy can still occur. The acumen the Rouses gained through their hundreds of dives over four years did not prevent them from dying. But it did get them out of a shipwreck under circum-stances that would probably have killed most other divers.

At thirty-eight, Berman reflects on his choice of career and says, "Heck, I've got the best job in the world. I thought about going to work in some sort of office environment. But I see how stressed out the guys who come down to dive with me are about their office jobs. Those guys—only after they've been down here almost a week do they start to relax. And just when they're relaxed, their vacation time is over and then they have to go back to the grind again. Me? I get to go diving all the time, I get to take off for weeks at a time when I want to, and go and do neat stuff like dive the caves in Mexico, the *Doria*, the *Britannic*, and even weenie stuff like shallow diving for lobsters in the Florida Keys. Man, I can't imagine any job other than teaching diving!" Unlike Chris and Chrissy Rouse, whose light burned bright and then flared out, Berman has become what the wisest divers aspire to be: a survivor.

John Chatterton, John Yurga, and Richie Kohler, all of whom were on the *Seeker* during the Rouses' last dive, took on a quest that they acknowledge became obsessive: solving the mystery of the *U-Who*. "No matter where I would go in the world," recalls Chatterton, "no matter if I was diving on the *Lusitania*, or the *Britannic*, or the *Doria*, people would always ask me, 'Hey, did you ever find out the identity of that U-boat?' And I realized that no matter what I did in diving, that was going to define me." After the Rouses died, all three divers wondered whether the risk was worth it. "The U-boat was a cruel wreck, an incredibly difficult wreck to dive," says Chatterton. "We had already lost Steve Feldman and then we lose Chris and Chrissy Rouse. We wondered how many more divers are gonna die before this thing gives up its secret." But for this trio, identifying the wreck would be not only a technical-diving achievement but a memorial to their lost comrades.

After Chatterton recovered from the wreck a dinner knife bearing the inscription HORENBURG on its wooden handle, Chatterton, Yurga, and Kohler examined the archives in Great Britain and in Germany to try and find out more about Horenburg, who they assumed was one of the U-boat's crewmen. They visited the U-boat archive in Cuxhaven, Germany, where the U-boat veteran Horst Bredow had compiled an impressive amount of material related to U-boats, including wartime diaries and war patrol records. The archive also has a memorial wall that lists the name of every U-boat man, including those who died, by U-boat number. Chatterton and his teammates found only one Horenburg registered, a man who had been the radio operator on the *U-869*. Logically, then, the *U-Who* should be the *U-869*. But the *U-869* was recorded as having been sunk on February 28, 1945, off the coast of Casablanca, the victim of depth charge attacks from the U.S.S. *Fowler* and F.R. *L'Indiscret*.

Part of the problem with the *U-Who*'s location was the result of the Allies' technological breakthroughs. In May 1941, the Allies were able to break the top-secret German naval code after they captured the *U-110* intact, thus obtaining its vital codebooks, cipher documents, and code machine. Breaking the German's code enabled the Allies to read the messages sent from the high command to U-boat captains; often the Allies knew the U-boats' orders before the captains themselves knew what their superiors were ordering.

A British technological achievement—radio direction finding, nicknamed Huff-Duff—would help in smashing the U-boat threat but would also add to the dive team's difficulties in solving the *U-Who* mystery. Huff-Duff enabled the British to pinpoint a U-boat's location quickly and accurately from the radio messages that the submarine sent to U-boat headquarters. Radio traffic was the key to coordinating a U-boat "wolfpack" attack: When a patrolling U-boat spotted a merchant vessel convoy, it first had to surface and send a radio message to its headquarters indicating the location, number of ships, direction, and speed of the convoy, and then await orders while maintaining visual contact with the enemy. Other U-boats would be directed to the

area via radio signals from headquarters, all coordinated by a numbered, lettered grid over the map of the world's oceans. The radio communications provided a vulnerability for the British to exploit. Unfortunately for U-boat crews, the German high command refused to
accept the possibility of radio direction finding, or the possibility that
their military codes could be deciphered.

The *U-869* was reported sunk off Casablanca because the Allies
had intercepted an encoded message ordering the U-boat from its
position in the mid-Atlantic to the African coast. When the U.S.S.
Fowler and F.R. *L'Indiscret* engaged a German U-boat off the coast of
Casablanca and attacked it, the Allies assumed that the presumably
destroyed U-boat was the *U-869*. As a result, Chatterton, Yurga, and
Kohler concluded that even if Horenburg was on the *U-869* when it
sank off Casablanca, his knife must somehow have found its way
onto the U-boat they discovered off the New Jersey coast. Maybe
Horenburg had left his knife behind when he was transferred from
another U-boat to the *U-869*, and the war records for the first vessel
had been destroyed. Or Horenburg might have lost the knife while he
was onshore, and someone else might have picked it up and taken it
onto the *U-Who*. In any case, the dive team concluded that the only
real way to solve the mystery and positively identify the *U-Who* was by
retrieving from inside the U-boat something that bore the warship's
identifying number.

But when they got inside the *U-Who*, Chatterton, Yurga, and Kohler
were all disappointed: Every place that should have borne an identifying tag had only screws where the tag had been held in place. The salt
water had literally eaten the tags away. This meant that they had not
been made of brass or other sturdy material, but tin or another soft
metal that quickly deteriorates underwater. The dive team had already
recovered a schematic drawing from inside the *U-Who* that identified it
as a Type IX-C boat, constructed at the Deschimag facility in Bremen.
They had also recovered a crockery bowl with the eagle and swastika
emblem of Germany's Second World War navy, with the date 1942
stamped onto it. The fact of the absent soft-metal tags was evidence
that during the war the air assault against Germany had combined
with military defeats on the ground to cause a shortage of war materials such as brass.

Chatterton was frustrated. Five years had passed since he discovered the U-boat, three divers had died diving it, and each member of Chatterton's team had invested a considerable amount of time and money in their expeditions to the wreck, and on their trips to archives in the United States, Great Britain, and Germany, yet the identity of the wreck remained a mystery. Surely, there had to be something inside the *U-Who* that would clearly identify it. As the three divers went over the puzzle like detectives solving a gruesome crime, they realized there was only one possibility left to find that elusive numbered tag and that lay inside parts boxes in the electric motor room, the one compartment that they had not been able to enter.

The electric motor room was the second-to-last compartment as one headed aft. Before the divers could attain that area, they had to go through the diesel motor room, which in most U-boat wrecks would usually offer a narrow but swimmable passage between the two massive diesel motors that had propelled the U-boat on the surface. But the *U-Who* was so badly damaged and the salt water had so extensively deteriorated the warship that massive pieces of metal blocked the entrance to that compartment. Richie Kohler had already hefted away some debris that obstructed the diesel motor room, only to encounter two more obstacles: a steel beam that had collapsed and now lay at an angle, dividing the already tight compartment into two partitions of roughly equal size, and also a huge metal container that had collapsed from the steel bracework near the compartment's ceiling. A diver wearing tanks on his back could not pass between the two obstructions. But now, desperate to solve the mystery, Chatterton came up with what was either an inspired solution, or an elaborate way to commit suicide.

A television production company contacted Chatterton, asking if he had discovered the identity of the *U-Who*. "I haven't solved the mystery, but I'm about to," said Chatterton. "How would you like to film it?" If the television company would pay for getting Chatterton and his fellow divers to the *U-Who* site, they would have a compelling story. Chatterton had just upped the ante for himself.

"We'll get you out there, but we've got to know your plan," said the voice on the far end of the telephone line. Chatterton described what he planned to do, and the executive agreed. After the call ended, the television company did some research, consulting with other divers. Three days later, the producer called Chatterton back. "You're not crazy, are you, John?" Chatterton was asked. Other divers had thought Chatterton's plan insane, and the television company's executives were alarmed that they might be getting involved with a daredevil.

"No, I'm not crazy," said Chatterton calmly. "I'm a professional diver, I work underwater for a living and have for years, which actually might mean I'm crazy. But as far as my plan goes, yes, it's dangerous. If it were easy, everyone would be able to do it and we'd have solved this thing long ago." He had thought out the dive meticulously, he told the producer. He would proceed one step at a time, with backup divers he trusted. "It'll take several attempts to complete this thing. You still interested?" he asked.

Reassured by Chatterton's reasoned explanation, the television outfit put up the funds to get the dive team to the U-Who again, with no guarantee of success. As Chatterton has always said, "A legitimate adventure has no predetermined outcome. It's not like going to Disney World." Chatterton's experience on the U-Who was anything but Disneyesque.

Descending to the U-Who to test his plan, Chatterton wore only a single tank on his back, with a second tank clipped at his side in the cave-diving style that by now all technical divers had adopted. Richie Kohler accompanied Chatterton and would act as the safety diver, just as Chris Rouse had been for his son. Since Chatterton and Kohler would be heading aft, they went inside the wreck at the opposite end of the same opening that Chrissy Rouse had entered on his last dive.

When they got to the hatchway, Chatterton took off his side-mounted tank and laid it on the floor. Then, he took off the jacket-style harness that held his other tank in place on his back. He pushed the jacket harness and tank first through the hatchway, and then over the beam, tethered by his breathing hose to his life-giving gas bottle and swimming behind it. Once he was on the other side of the beam, Chatterton put the jacket harness and tank back on, and swam into the electric motor room. He assessed the area briefly, then repeated the procedure as he exited the compartment. Kohler, who was waiting outside the diesel motor room, was relieved when Chatterton's light flickered into view. The two exited the wreck and swam up the anchor line toward the surface. When they got back on the boat a few hours later, everyone was excited that Chatterton was able to safely get in and get out of the compartment using his radical approach. Kohler and Chatterton made plans to go back and shoot some video footage inside the electric motor room before they disturbed anything looking for the precious tag that would identify this boat.

Their next dive went well—at first. Chatterton got inside the diesel motor room and put his single tank back on. But when Kohler pushed the bulky video unit over the beam, Chatterton could not reach it. His body was wedged against the debris inside the compartment and his tank was jammed against the ceiling. Then, disaster struck. A steel beam collapsed on top of Chatterton, spinning him around so that his tank was pinned to the floor.

The beam came to rest on Chatterton's chest. He was 230 feet underwater, pinned just as Chrissy Rouse had been. Fortunately, unlike Chrissy Rouse, he was faceup, and clearer-headed than Chrissy had been because of the trimix gas Chatterton breathed.

Chatterton looked at his bottom timer. He knew that Richie Kohler, wearing back-mounted double tanks, would not be able to come in and get him out of the wreck the way Chris Rouse was able to do with his son. With only a single tank of breathing gas, he would have to act quickly to save himself. He tried pushing the beam up with his hands. It moved, but it was so long that its far end got snared among other debris. Chatterton was still trapped. He tried wiggling the beam to one side, but that did not work either. His exertions caused him to breathe the lightweight helium gas faster.

In all of his diving experience, John Chatterton had never before been in such dire circumstances. His only hope was to wriggle out of the jacket harness that held his tank in place, then squeeze his body from under the beam, and finally pull his tank free. If he could not pull his tank free, he would have to hold his breath and swim the thirty feet without it toward Kohler, who would provide him with breathing gas from his tanks.

Had he pushed beyond reasonable limits? In his obsessive desire to positively identify the U-boat, was he tempting fate? Had the persistent curiosity and encouragement he encountered from others, including the TV producers, clouded his judgment about what he could accomplish underwater? So close to finding that identifying tag, and so close to death, Chatterton faced either a crossroads or an abyss.

Chatterton unhooked the jacket-style harness that held his scuba tank in place. He contorted his body like Houdini escaping from the bonds of chains that held him confined in a water-filled box. Chatterton's struggles eliminated all visibility and he worked by feel alone, squeezing his body out from under the steel beam above him and his jacket harness and tank below him. When his body was out from under the beam he could feel himself being pulled upward by the gas in his drysuit, which now was not counteracted by the weight of his scuba tank. Chatterton had to hold on to the beam so that he did not shoot toward the U-boat compartment's ceiling and lose his tenuous mouth grip on his regulator. Chatterton pulled himself down so that his body was next to the steel beam and then he yanked at the harness and tank, liberating them both from underneath the wreckage. He grabbed the tank, pushed it in front of him, and squirmed over the debris that had made it so difficult to enter this area in the first place. Shaken from his ordeal, he exited the wreck with Kohler. During his two-hour decompression, Chatterton wondered whether the *U-Who* would ever give up its secret.

On their next dive, Chatterton and Kohler would be assisted by Pat Rooney, a highly skilled, experienced wreck diver with—like Kohler—a reputation for near fearlessness. Chatterton shot some video after manhandling the bulky camera unit past the obstructions. Back on the surface, he reviewed the video to make sure he knew exactly where to go to retrieve the parts boxes. Then, he descended again, moving determinedly through the wreck, sliding past the now-familiar obstructions until he got inside the electric motor room and proceeded to the parts boxes. Incredibly, he faced yet another obstacle: A steel pipe had fallen on the stack of boxes, and when he tried to move the pipe, the encrustation held it tightly in place. He could not move the pipe, or get to the parts boxes that would, he hoped, contain a tag with the U-boat's identifying number. He cursed into his regulator, bitterly frustrated. He knew he would have to bring tools down with him on yet another dive.

The next time Chatterton entered the electric motor room, he carried a heavy hammer, which divers call either a mallet or a lump hammer, depending on whether you are from America or another country. He swung the tool like Thor, his boyish frustration removing any caution left within the professional diver. The hammer blow was very nearly Chatterton's last act in this world: As the silt fell away, Chatterton saw he was hammering not at a pipe but at a pressurized aluminum oxygen container from an escape lung designed to let sailors swim out of a sunken submarine. Chatterton froze.

He knew well what he was looking at and how lethal it could be. He had recovered one of these containers from the *U-Who* on a previous expedition because he knew it should have a sailor's name engraved on it. But when he took it to the surface and cleaned it off, he was disappointed to find that it bore no name. He put the bottle on a shelf in his garage. When he came back to it several days later, he found only twisted metal and mangled shelving—the oxygen bottle had exploded.

Chatterton now hovered carefully next to the stack of boxes pinned down by the oxygen cylinder. With the mallet in his hand he considered what he should do. Another blow could cause the oxygen cylinder to explode. If that happened, Chatterton would probably be killed outright from either the percussion waves that would burst his stomach, lungs, and intestines or from the debris that was sure to rain down on him. Yet he had come too far and risked his life too often in this quest not to take another chance.

With faith that the German-engineered cylinder would maintain its integrity, Chatterton whacked away a second time.

He was lucky. The encrustation holding the oxygen bottle affixed to the boxes fell away, and Chatterton brushed the time-bomb aside. Grabbing the top box, Chatterton muscled it toward Kohler and Rooney, who waited on the other side of the steel beam, just inside the diesel engine room. Rooney grabbed the box and forced it out of the wreck, where he attached a lift bag to it and then sent it to the surface. In the meantime, Chatterton went back for a second box, which he removed and shoved toward Kohler, who took the prize out of the vessel. With no visibility inside the electric motor room, and little time left, Chatterton exited the U-boat for what he hoped was the last time. He gave a quick respectful nod to the maw of wreckage that marked the destination of Chris and Chrissy Rouse's last dive.

On the surface, the dive team opened the parts boxes and found what they were looking for: a tag bearing the U-boat's identifying number: U-869. It was August 31, 1997. They had solved the mystery one day short of six years after the wreck's discovery, four years and ten months after Chris and Chrissy Rouse had been entrapped only two rusted compartment walls from the grail they sought. The television camera dutifully recorded the relief and elation each man felt.

The big question now was: Why was the *U-869* recorded as having been sunk on the other side of the Atlantic Ocean? Chatterton has given the explanation so many times during interviews for the media and at diving club meetings and conferences that he speaks as if he were reading from a script:

"During the war, the Allies picked up and decoded the radio message from U-boat headquarters ordering *U-869* to change its original patrol station from the U.S. East Coast to the African coast. The Allies knew from their radio direction finding and previous messages from the U-boat that *U-869* was in the mid-Atlantic. But records show that *U-869* never acknowledged the order to change its patrol area. They continued to the U.S. coast as originally ordered. When U-boat headquarters received no more radio transmissions from *U-869*, it was written off as missing, with its final location probably anywhere from the mid-Atlantic to the African coast. At war's end, the Allies assigned a British officer to make a final determination of each U-boat's fate so that the Allies could be sure there were none in hiding. That officer determined from the battle reports of U.S.S. *Fowler* and F.R. *L'Indiscret* that their probable kill of a U-boat must have been from their encounter with *U-869*; the status was upgraded from probable kill to confirmed kill, and entered into the archives and history books as such."

If the *U-869* was not destroyed by the U.S.S. *Fowler* and F.R. *L'Indiscret,* how was it sunk? The answer lies in the torpedo head found next to the *U-869*'s mutilated control room, close to the area where Chrissy was nearly crushed. The serial number on the torpedo head revealed it to be a German T-5 acoustical torpedo, designed to home in on the noise of the target vessel's engine room. According to German naval records, at least 30 percent of German torpedoes early in the war were either duds or detonated at the wrong time and place, which made U-boat attacks a dicey business for commanders and crew. The German U-boat command knew in late 1943 that a T-5 torpedo could malfunction when fired, and come back to destroy its own U-boat. J. P. Mallmann Showell, the author of *U-boats Under the Swastika*, speculates that the *U-377* and the *U-972* were destroyed by their own T-5 torpedoes. Probably the *U-869* fired one of its T-5 torpedoes but it homed in on the noise from the U-boat's own control room, made a circular run, and destroyed the vessel, killing its entire crew instantly.

Solving the mystery of the *U-869* had claimed three divers' lives, including our friends Chris and Chrissy Rouse, and had nearly claimed Chatterton's life. He knew on his last dive to the U-boat that he had pushed his luck and skills to the very edge; if one other thing had gone wrong, he would most likely have died. A thin line divided the outcome of his effort from that of the Rouses' fatal dive. Some people would view that line as the filament of pure chance. Others would distinguish Chatterton's survival and success from the fatal failure of father and son by declaring the Rouses' deaths to be a result of their choice not to dive on mixed gas. They could not afford the clarity of mind that had saved Chatterton, but they could not afford to be without it, either.

The U-boat changed Chatterton's life. He had known from his combat experience in Vietnam that an individual's façade is stripped away by the razor's edge of imminent death; how the person deals with that edge reveals who he really is. Chatterton decided he could not turn away from the potentially deadly challenge of solving the *U-Who* mystery. "The greatest risk I took in diving the U-boat was the risk of failure," he says. "I did not have to dive the U-boat, or spend about forty thousand dollars of my own money trying to solve the mystery. I could have just walked away from it. Other people kept saying, 'Probably somebody who is just diving the wreck for the first time will pick up something in the sand that will identify it.' I was amazed—it was as if they expected me to do nothing to try and identify it, and wait until somebody happened along and solved the mystery out of pure chance. It just showed me how good people can be at putting up barriers, making excuses not to do something instead of expending their energy on solving the problem in front of them. I made a very conscious choice that I was going to do everything I could to identify the wreck."

■   ■   ■

After he had solved the *U-Who* mystery, Chatterton knew he had reached the pinnacle of his wreck-diving career. He had to stop. "The circumstances, the intensity of effort and how long it took to solve—that sort of opportunity will never come along again for me. And I don't want it to. I've learned what I could from it, and now I've turned more introspective, and I hope to apply the lessons learned on the U-boat quest to other areas of my life." Although he still works as a commercial diver and is now a supervisor, coordinating pier and harbor repair and dredging and salvage projects from the surface, he has given up technical diving and life at sport diving's edge. He still enjoys introducing others to the thrill and wonder of the underwater world and still teaches recreational diving, but says he has no further desire to engage in the level of diving intensity that he experienced during his years diving the mystery U-boat. But I wonder how long Chatterton can resist the call of the deep.

Chatterton's diving expeditions and his research forays led to frequent absences from his wife, who spent her time involved in the equestrian world. The two were divorced. Chatterton has found a new love in his life, an adventurous woman who is a nondiver, and who knows little about Chatterton's diving past—"She doesn't know and I don't dwell on it," says Chatterton. "I've moved on."

Chris and Chrissy's deaths focused Sue. Their deaths had shown her how short life could be and how necessary it is to make the most of it. She hated her job as an insurance saleswoman, and she decided to quit. At first she contemplated going back to college full-time. Although she had taken college courses at night, she had never completed her degree, even though she felt that graduation from college would be a notable achievement. Yet there was another, more immediate plan she could follow. Ever since they all became involved in cave diving, she, Chris, and Chrissy had always aimed to move to Florida together and make diving their livelihood. Their intention was to make the move to the Ginnie Springs area in 1993. Not only was it convenient to the cave diving they all loved so much, but the land and house prices were low compared to those in Pennsylvania.

Chrissy had felt that it was far more realistic for him to eventually be able to buy a house near Ginnie Springs than in the northeastern United States. Sue resolved to continue to work toward the family dream, even if Chris and Chrissy were not standing next to her to share it.

Rather than returning to college, Sue became a diving instructor. She had always enjoyed assisting with classes and helping students who were having the greatest difficulty learning to dive. She felt that her own training had been inadequate, and she wanted to help others avoid the discomfort she had felt so that they could truly enjoy the sport. In partnership with another diving instructor she had known for many years, Sue opened the Blue Abyss dive shop in northern New Jersey. Although she wasn't in Florida with Chris and Chrissy as they had planned, she was making a go of a diving livelihood.

Yet even as she began to build a new life, Sue remained haunted by questions as to why Chrissy had died in the hyperbaric chamber. She spoke to Dr. Bill Hamilton about her son's treatment, and then tried to contact Glenn Butler, who had operated the chamber. She was not successful in getting through to Butler, and he did not return her calls, which struck her as odd. (Butler says he was not aware that Sue was trying to contact him.) Equally peculiar, she received no medical bill at all for the treatment given to Chris and Chrissy; although her husband had medical insurance, Chrissy did not. Six months after their deaths, Sue requested the hospital records of the incident. When she had no success obtaining the files, she contacted a lawyer. But the lawyer she spoke to was interested in making money by bringing a lawsuit against everyone involved in the accident. "I just want to know what happened," Sue told the lawyer. "I don't want to sue anybody." With no big money in it for him, the lawyer lost interest. She contacted other lawyers, who also didn't want to represent her if she didn't plan to litigate. Although she was able to get the Coast Guard reports and the autopsy reports, the hospital records of her son's treatment were elusive. Apparently, they had disappeared, along with the clothing that her husband wore when he was admitted to the emergency room. She never brought a lawsuit against anyone involved.

Although it was painful for her to think about another intimate relationship, she eventually grew closer to a man who had worked at

Underwater World, where Chris and Chrissy had been certified and where Chrissy had eventually been employed. Sue had known Scott Kee for years, and their friendship blossomed into a romance. In 1997, Scott moved into the house Sue had built with Chris and Chrissy. A year later, Sue sold the house, and she moved to Florida with Scott to begin a new life. They have a beautiful waterfront house, which Scott uses as the home base for his electronic engineering consulting business, specializing in satellite navigation.

Friends of the couple's have noticed how much Scott differs from Chris Rouse in physical type, interests, and temperament. Where Chris was excellent with anything mechanical, and with the use of his hands to fix things, Scott is not a handyman at all: He relies on his intellect to solve problems with satellites that are literally out of this world. When Sue was married to Chris, she hadn't thought about things like changing the oil in her car. That was something that Chris handled automatically.

While she may not have deliberately sought a partner unlike her husband, Scott is well liked by Chris's diving colleagues and the Rouses' other acquaintances who perceive a harmony in the relationship that was not evident in Sue's life with Chris and Chrissy. She remembers the constant contentiousness between Chris and Chrissy and says, "I always had to act as the mediator between the two of them." She pauses, somewhat sadly, then smiles and laughs. "You know what, Bernie? I started bickering with Scott, and all he said to me—in a really gentle tone—was 'You're bickering with me. Hmmm, there seems to be a common element here!' Who knows? Maybe he's right. Maybe Chris and Chrissy bickering all the time was something I caused. I don't know, I always thought it was just interacting, not fighting or arguing." She trails off, lost in thought, the peacemaker who no longer has combatants she must adjudicate or separate.

Some of Sue Rouse's friends contend that her relationship with Chris was emotionally stuck in the high school years, when they met. The teenage Sue and Chris, like all couples, probably developed a pattern of interaction early on, where Chris constantly nitpicked at Sue so as to maintain the upper hand, and Sue retorted by firing back salvos, as if the two were a TV sitcom couple entertaining each other and their audience. Sue's friends see her new relationship with Scott as a much more mature bond, one between two grown-ups who do not have to use each other to prove themselves because they already know who they are.

The marketing and development consulting I had conducted with Inabata and its client Seiko in 1991 for the creation of new diver-carried computers resulted in new consumer products. At first, these computers calculated only air dives, and as such joined the many similar diving computers that were already on the market. Then, in 1992, after my consulting contract expired, the project resulted in the Bridge computer, the first mass-market diving computer that calculated the use of various oxygen-nitrox mixtures, including pure oxygen. I was happy with the results. I had also forecast that these production methods would serve to create a computer that could calculate mixes of helium gases, at a time when the interest in and market for mixed-gas diving were increasing. The British diver Kevin Gurr successfully brought a mixed-gas computer to market in January 2000, and Inabata and Seiko will soon release their product.

The skills I built in diving and the risks I took all encouraged me to become a diving entrepreneur not only underwater, but on land. The sense of adventure I had while diving—and even the experience of getting bent—taught me that my life was too short not to act on my aspirations. I wanted more freedom than I could ever have working on Wall Street. I wanted to do something I loved. Like Chatterton, I made some big changes in my life in the wake of my accident and then the Rouses' deaths. But unlike Chatterton, I became more involved with diving, just as Sue Rouse had. I took inspiration from Chris and Chrissy Rouse. They had the courage to follow their dreams, and though they met a terrible fate, they lived the life they wanted, and they were fulfilled, if only for a very brief time. I knew that in order to be truly happy, I had to do the same. Just like Chris Rouse when he started Black Cloud Scuba, I cashed in my assets and took a big financial risk. With a group of other divers and investors I started *immersed: the international technical diving magazine. immersed* is now well into its fifth year of publication and it has become a resource I am proud of, and one that advanced, technical, military, and commercial divers, as well as government agencies and scientific institutes, look to for information, advances in the sport, advice, and adventure.

Though I continue to have my physical challenges, I have done what I can to use technology to overcome them. After my accident I organized an expedition to Iceland, during which Steve Berman and the Canadian diver Kim Martin surveyed and mapped the island nation's most geologically significant cave. I participated in a British Army expedition to find the H.M.S. *Pheasant,* a World War I destroyer lost off the Orkney Islands in Scotland. We located the wreck and dived it at 280 feet. I also conducted my deepest dive, a little over 300 feet, on the German World War II wreck *Blücher,* in Oslo Fjord.

Though I left active diving for a while to make sure I had grounded myself on land, the tide of my blood pulls me back toward the water. I know that with my family secure and my livelihood stabilized, I will soon heed the siren that calls me to dive again and return to the realm where I belong.

As I continue my fascination with diving, I also look upward. I have become a certified hang-glider pilot, and I am working toward my ultralight aircraft pilot's certification. The connections between diving, flying, and even space exploration are far more numerous than people realize: The first pressurized altitude flying suits were based on dive-suit designs from the 1800s; space-suit development has also been heavily influenced by deep-diving suit development, especially the hard one-atmosphere suits that have allowed manned dives exceeding 2,000 feet in depth. The suits that astronauts wear in space in the twenty-first century may well be hard suits modified from those deep-diving suits, and workers of the future who construct space stations may well be first trained as commercial divers because of the similarity of the deep sea's and outer space's inherently alien environments.

Space, water, land—we humans now belong everywhere. We are drawn to explore ever more distant horizons. The knowledge that we gain from our explorations on earth will undoubtedly be applied in some form to successful space exploration. As we learn to overcome the limitations of our bodies, wherever that journey leads us, we will venture ever deeper into ourselves.

Author's Note

WHEN I THINK of so many of my friends, like Chris and Chrissy Rouse, and other fellow divers who died while diving, I wish this were a book that never had to be written. It was in 1998, almost six years after the Rouses' deaths, that I started writing the proposal for this book. I thought the passage of time would make it far easier, from an emotional standpoint, to write about their experiences as well as my own. I was wrong. Through the many interviews and review of various documents related to Chris's and Chrissy's deaths, I have relived their accident and the trauma to all of those who knew them countless times.

Although this has been a difficult book to write, I still feel as I did so many years ago when I was new to diving that divers and their world are fascinating; I am privileged to know many divers around the world, including many who are or have been on the cutting edge of the sport. My sole regret is that I have been able to include only some of these many outstanding divers and parts of their stories in this book.

As I liked to tell my students when I was teaching, diving is a sport offering so many possibilities that you can grow with it over the years to whatever level of complexity you want to achieve. For those divers who wish to stay in relatively shallow water and enjoy the colorful warm-water reef environment, diving is a relaxing and reasonably safe sport, just as hiking through the mountains is reasonably safe. The edge of sports like diving—going into wrecks and caves—and mountain climbing—ascending Mount Everest or K2—will always act as a beacon for a small group of people who have the motivation to develop the skills and get the experience and equipment that are needed even to be considered for expeditions. It is at that edge that the stakes are highest and that we learn the most about ourselves, our world, and our limits, as well as how to extend those limits. There are numerous lessons to be learned at the edge by those willing to look.

I wish to thank the many people who gave so generously of their time and let me interview them, or who answered questions by correspondence. Listed alphabetically, those people are Steve Berman, Steve Bielenda, Janet Bieser, Julia Bissinger, Jim Bowden, Bob Burns, Glenn Butler, Pete Butt, John Chatterton, Sue Crane, Paul Curtin, Cathie Cush, Billy Deans, Evie Dudas, Steve Foreman, Hank Garvin, Steve Gatto, Gary Gentile, Terry German, John Griffith, Mike Gucken, Kevin Gurr, Janet Hall, M.D., Peter Hess, Karen Jensen, Ph.D., Richie Kohler, Ann Kristovich, D.D.S., Barb Lander, Leslie Leanie, Don McDevitt, Steve McDougall, Denny McLaughlin, Michael Menduno, John Moyer, Kevin O'Brien, John Reekie, Ken Reinhart, Stephanie Schwabe, Ph.D., Tim Stumpf, Lisa Teklits, John Thornton, and Denny Willis.

In addition, I would like to thank several people who spoke with me casually about incidents related to the book and whose recollections helped fill in gaps in either the story or my technical knowledge. They are Dennis Anacker, Jim Baden, John Harding, Howard Klein, Wings Stocks, and Joe "Zero" Terzuoli. Several people also reviewed parts of the manuscript related to themselves and their areas of expertise, and I would like to give them a special thanks for their time and their valuable suggestions. They are Mike Emmerman, Bill Hamilton, Ph.D., and Karl Huggins. Jennifer Hunt, Ph.D., read most of the manuscript, including several revisions, and I am grateful for her suggestions, support over the years, and behavioral and psychological insights. I would also like to thank Graciella Ramos for her insights.

I would especially like to thank Sue Rouse, without whose support this book would not have been possible.

I have learned a great deal about the craft of writing and publishing, for which I would like to thank Jenny McPhee, my favorite instructor at the Gotham Writers' Workshop in Manhattan, and Bob Sterner, my copublisher of *immersed* magazine. Besides Bob, I also thank my other business partners in *immersed* magazine, Tom Easop, Mark Haas, Kevin O'Brien, and Harry White, for their support of the vision I approached them with many years ago, and for the insights into business and publishing that they have shared with me.

Elaine Goodman did a fast and excellent job transcribing the many interview tapes I burdened her with, and I would like to thank her for her efforts.

I would like to thank my neighbor Lloyd "Butch" Ward, who read my work in progress and gave me valuable feedback.

Many thanks to editor David Groff, for helping me adjust to a new writing style, as well as for his enthusiasm, excellent edits, and suggestions for improving the manuscript.

To my editor at HarperCollins, Trena Keating, my heartfelt thanks for believing in this story and in my ability to present it, as well as for all of her support, edits, and invaluable suggestions for improving this book.

This volume might not have happened without the efforts of my devoted agent, Andrew Stuart of Literary Group International, who went above and beyond the call of duty to make it a reality. His sharp editorial eye, enthusiasm, and support were essential to this project.

Special thanks to my parents, Benoy Chowdhury, Ph.D., and Lilli Chowdhury, for giving me so many unique and valuable life experiences, and for the curiosity about the world that those experiences ignited. I would especially like to thank my mother for teaching me German and giving me the gift of entrée into another culture that a language provides. I thank my departed grandmother Lizzi Krüger for her unconditional love and the many memorable times we shared, as well as for her gift of snorkeling equipment when I was a child.

I remain indebted to the dedicated professionals of the U.S. Coast Guard, and in particular those who took part in the helicopter evacuation after my accident in 1991, for their efforts. I would also like to thank

Dennis Anacker, Dan Crowell, Dave Dannenburg, John Harding, Dr. Ignaccio Mendagurin, the late Captain Bill Nagel, Kevin O'Brien, Peter Thompson, and the doctor who treated me in the recompression chamber for their efforts on my behalf.

Finally, I would like to thank my wife, Diana, and our son, Gil, for their patience, support, and love.

I regret that all those who have had a hand in creating this book do not have their names on the cover. Of course, any errors are solely my responsibility.

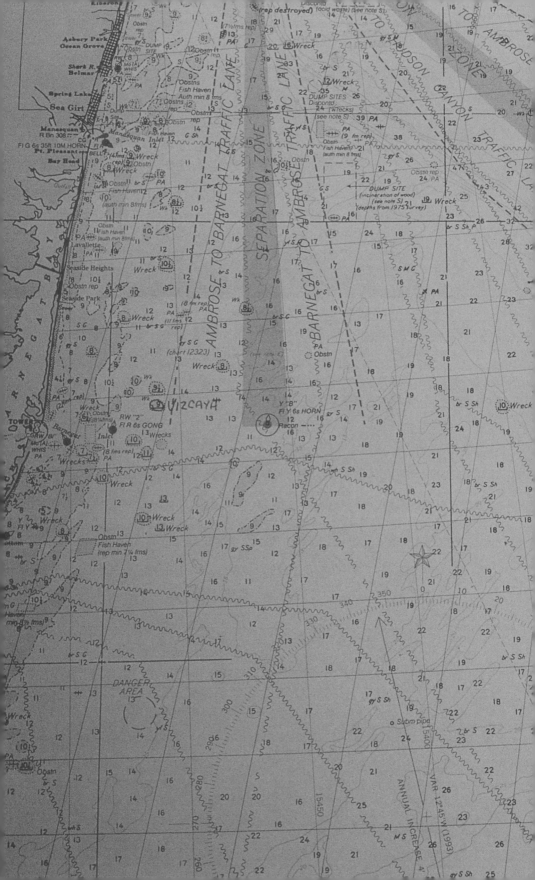